A Fragile Capital

A Fragile Capital

Identity and the Early Years of Columbus, Ohio

Charles C. Cole Jr.

Ohio State University Press

Columbus

Library of Congress Cataloging-in-Publication Data

Cole, Charles Chester.
   A fragile capital : identity and the early years of Columbus, Ohio /
Charles C. Cole, Jr.
      p.   cm.
Includes bibliographical references (p.   ) and index.
   ISBN 0-8142-0853-3 (alk. paper)
1. Columbus (Ohio)—History—19th century.   2. Ohio—Capital and
capitol.   I. Title.
   F499.C757 C57 2001
   977.1'5703—dc21

                                                                00-008894

Text design by Ron Starbuck.
Jacket design by Gore Studio, Inc.
Type set in Adobe Sabon by G & S Typesetters, Inc.
Printed by Sheridan Books.

9 8 7 6 5 4 3 2 1

CONTENTS

ILLUSTRATIONS

PREFACE

I first discovered Columbus as a city meriting further study when I wrote my biography of James B. Finley, chaplain in the Ohio Penitentiary from 1846 to 1849. If Finley had not been active in so many reform movements, I might not have discovered the complex and conflicting images of the city's early growth that these movements reflected.

One must depend on written sources to assist in finding foundations that lead to interpretations. Discoveries make research more productive than expected, modify one's original assumptions, and add human dimensions to the writing. I recall my surprise the day I learned that young apprentices in Columbus started their own library in 1821. When I read the journal of Maria Kelley Bates and learned that at her wedding in 1837 she asked the minister, "[D]on't make me promise to obey," I saw a spark of feminism at a time when women had few rights.

Especially important are the librarians who assist in delivering books and documents and answering questions. I am grateful to the many helpful, capable, conscientious librarians at the Ohio Historical Society Library/Archives, The Ohio State University Libraries, the State Library of Ohio, the Ohioana Library, the Bexley Public Library, and the New York Public Library. They make research such a joy.

A book such as this one goes through several drafts. I am especially grateful to George W. Knepper, Cathy Manus-Gray, and David Kyvig for making helpful comments and suggestions while the manuscript was being written. I am indebted to Robert W. McCormick and to two other readers who made useful recommendations for improving the final draft of the manuscript. I also thank Barbara Hanrahan, former director of the Ohio State University Press, freelance editors Barbara Lyons and Lynne Bonenberger, and other members of the press staff for their interest and assistance. I am also indebted to Mrs. Fred Fisher of Bexley, Ohio, for telling me about her ancestors, and to Edward Lentz and Jay Hoster for sharing their knowledge of Columbus's past. My thanks goes to the seven members of Trinity Episcopal Church in Columbus who transcribed the Joel Buttles diary. Patricia Williamsen provided valuable help in taking and developing most of the illustrations, some of which were photographed from books in the Ohioana Library.

Portions of an earlier draft of part of chapter 13 appeared under the title "When the Arts Took Hold" in *Columbus Monthly* (May 1995: 123–25).

A more detailed account of the public double hanging mentioned in chapter 15 appeared under the title "The Last Public Hanging" in *Columbus Monthly* (December 1993: 91–94). I thank the magazine's senior editor, Emily Foster, for her expert editing.

If there are errors of fact or interpretation, only I am responsible.

INTRODUCTION

The few histories of Columbus were written in the nineteenth and early twentieth centuries without the benefit of modern historical methods, and they lack the perspectives of the current decade. The first, William T. Martin's *History of Franklin County,* was published in 1858. It contains useful information about the pioneer period written by a long-term resident. Alfred E. Lee's two-volume *History of the City of Columbus,* published in 1892, is available in library reference rooms for those who want more details regarding particular events. The other histories of the city cover a longer period of time and emphasize biographies of community leaders.

This book examines Columbus's first forty years, and focuses on the area selected by the General Assembly for the third state capital. The volume is based primarily on original sources such as letters, diaries, documents, and newspapers. The specialized secondary sources I read are listed in the bibliography.

The book's perspective encompasses all the city's economic classes and ethnic and racial groups, in contrast to earlier accounts that addressed mainly the roles of white male leaders and inadequately recognized the contributions of women and other minorities. Earlier histories also failed to show, as this volume endeavors to do, how events and decisions of the first forty years influenced the city's development. Furthermore, this study shows how Columbus residents reacted to and reflected major political, economic, and social trends in the United States at that time. The narrative also examines the founding of and early directions taken by the city.

Except for the first and last chapters, the work is developed by topics rather than by chronology. For example, transportation improvements are examined in a separate chapter rather than by when they occurred in the four decades. Forty-year accounts of the arts, education, religion, and the Ohio Penitentiary, for instance, serve to sharpen the focus on their relation to Columbus's development. The subject of politics deserves two chapters. One addresses the emergence of the two-party system in the 1820s and '30s, the significance of the Harrison campaign to Columbus, and local politics in the 1840s. The other focuses on how efforts to abolish slavery influenced political events and on the subsequent intensification of sectionalism that eventually led to the Civil War. Although women are mentioned throughout the work, they deserve a separate chapter because their status was so much lower than in modern times and because their contributions to the life and the economy of the city have not been sufficiently recognized.

The major theme in my account is the tension created by the conflicting aims of the settlers who moved west to seek more freedom and find security and stability. Individual preferences competed with collective requirements for order. Unrestrained self-interest had to be balanced by the cooperation needed to survive in a risky environment. The first residents had to gird unwanted trees and remove their stumps, for example, and they had to work together to accomplish the task.

I also explore how a state capital, created before there was even a town, went about becoming a community, and what challenges occurred to that sense of community as more strangers arrived from other states and from Europe. I examine the contributions made by business, government, education, religion, and the press to the shaping of the community.

A related question is to what extent the inhabitants were aware of Columbus's identity and whether that image agreed with or contradicted the one held by the rest of the nation. To what extent did the city's relative inaccessibility in its early years contribute to a sense of its inferiority in the eyes of its residents? During Columbus's first forty years, when attempts were still being made to move the capital elsewhere, it is not surprising that the city's image seemed ambiguous. Residents could be assertive because of their city's status as state capital; on the other hand, they could be defensive and apologetic because of its size and vulnerability.

Among my discoveries and interpretations, I provide a new view of the contest to select a permanent state capital, indicate that more women were in the labor force than has been estimated, give information on the population's mobility and turnover, illustrate the changes that occurred in the arts in those decades, add to the evidence of the role of blacks in the city's economy, comment on the extent of racism in this period, and examine the reform movements that involved some of Columbus's citizens.

There are advantages in historical accounts that focus on a few decades in one community, especially when that community has been ignored by eastern historians. What occurred in Columbus's first four decades tells much about the attitudes, convictions, and prejudices that prevailed in nineteenth-century American thought and culture.

Even in a period as short as forty years, the presence of change may be seen on every page of this work. Columbus started with a handful of settlers and approached a population of twenty thousand by midcentury. There were transformations and innovations in business and the arts, in politics and religion, in the reform movements and the diversification of culture.

Columbus is now the largest city in Ohio, and the fifteenth largest in the nation. Its thousands of new residents understandably have little or no awareness of the city's past. Indeed, as we approach the bicentennial of Ohio's statehood in the year 2003, we all could benefit from a better grasp of the capital city's beginnings and earliest decades.

1

Contested

Creation

Unlike other towns in Ohio that were formed by the people living there, Columbus was created in 1812 by the General Assembly. The third state capital was located on the high eastern bank of the Scioto River. "It was a forest all around,"[1] recalled the enterprising Joel Buttles, who moved from Worthington to Columbus in 1813 at the age of twenty-six.

Chillicothe was the first capital when statehood was approved in 1803. By that time, most political leaders considered themselves Jeffersonian Republicans. A minority, approximately one-quarter of the white male voters, were Federalists handicapped by the popularity of Jeffersonian ideas and by the policies of Arthur St. Clair, former governor of the Northwest Territory, who had opposed statehood for Ohio.

The Republicans, however, were not united on all issues. Many believed that the legislature should be the dominant division of government. The 1806 legislature passed a law authorizing justices of the peace to try cases involving fifty dollars or less, contrary to what the Ohio Constitution required. Judges in two decisions ruled the law unconstitutional because the first constitution required a jury trial in cases involving more than twenty dollars. The General Assembly tried to impeach Chief Justice Samuel Huntington and Associate Judge George Tod but failed to get a two-thirds vote in the Senate. The legislature also passed a "sweeping resolution" removing many state-appointed officers. Conservatives and some Republicans supported the judiciary and opposed the Chillicothe group led by Gov. Edward Tiffin and U.S. senator Thomas Worthington. This factional dispute over the relative powers of the legislative and judicial branches of government created a division in the General Assembly. Some members of the majority party were incensed at the efforts of the Chillicothe members of Tammany, a secret society, to dictate Republican policies and rebelled against their elite leaders. They were so irritated that they decided to deprive Chillicothe of its status as the capital. A combination of Federalists and rebelling Republicans finally repealed the "sweeping resolution" in January 1812.[2]

When the votes of Zanesville representatives were needed in the fight against the Chillicothe leaders, the seat of government was moved there for the legislative session beginning in December 1809. Zanesville also offered a new brick structure for the capitol building. Legislators had no sooner unpacked, however, when the House of Representatives resolved that "a committee to bring in a bill for the establishment of a permanent seat of government be instructed to receive proposals, as a donation to the state toward the erection of the public buildings, and that they may make a report to the house, the amount offered at the different places."[3]

Residents of Worthington, which had been settled in 1803, had offered their town as early as 1808.[4] Some men in the small town of Franklinton on the west bank of the Scioto River, including Lucas Sullivant, who had surveyed and founded it in 1797, thought that their area would make a better site for the capital than Chillicothe or Zanesville. Several of them, including Sullivant's brother-in-law, Lyne Starling, who had moved to Franklinton in 1806, had already bought land in the wilderness across the river. Starling wrote his sister, "I have lately purchased an elegant seat and tract of land opposite town on the other side of the river, which I have an idea of improving."[5] He was referring to the half section he bought July 11, 1809, in the forest on the high bank. John Kerr frequently wrote letters to Joseph Vance, who had surveyed lands in the area, to check on whether the ones in which he was interested were unencumbered. In 1808 Kerr and Alexander McLaughlin had bought a half section there. Kerr wrote a confidential letter to Vance in 1810 to say that the move of the capital to Zanesville was "an immense injury to us all."[6]

By that date a number of Ohio residents held large quantities of land. They had been able to accumulate property over a decade. Back in 1783, the Continental Congress had promised to compensate "for their virtuous sufferings in the cause of liberty" those residents of Canada and Nova Scotia who supported the revolution but who were forced to lose their homes and move south to the United States. In 1798, the Congress honored this obligation and set aside lands later known as the Refugee Tract to compensate those who had been residents of Canada prior to July 4, 1776, and who left their homes. The secretary of war and the secretary of the treasury had to examine all the claims and decide how many acres to award in each case. In 1810, the law's provisions were extended to widows and heirs. Much of the original part of Columbus was in the Refugee Tract.[7]

When the Congress in June 1796 provided, in place of pay, 2.5 million acres of land in the Northwest Territory for those who had fought in the War for Independence, speculators bought many of the military warrants from veterans who needed cash or who were not interested in moving west. In 1804, the act was reenacted for another two-year period. Investors hungry for land were delighted. The warrants were not equal. Major generals received eleven hundred acres, captains received three hundred acres, lieutenants received two hundred acres, and regular soldiers received one hundred acres.

John Kerr. From Lee, *History of the City of Columbus,* vol. 1.

In 1802, the lands on the plateau across the river from Franklinton were patented to Revolutionary War refugees John Halstead, Martha Walker, Benjamin Thompson, Seth Harding, and James Price. Walker and Harding received 2,240 acres, and the others received 640 acres. The Franklinton residents had bought the land from the original patentees. By 1810, fewer than one-half of all men living in Ohio owned land, and land ownership was inequitably distributed. Ten percent of the largest property owners possessed one-third of all properties and one-half of all acreage.[8]

In the early weeks of 1810, legislators realized that if they wanted their state house built by others, they had to plan for both a temporary and a permanent capital. Otherwise, they would be stuck in Zanesville longer than they wanted. The two legislative houses disagreed on the future temporary site. A majority of senators favored Franklinton, while the House of Representatives favored Zanesville. By February 20, a joint session elected James Findlay, Joseph Darlington, William McFarland, William Silliman, and Reazin Beall as commissioners to select a permanent site near the geographical center of the state. When commissioners met the following September in Franklinton, they rejected that town because the Scioto River had flooded in 1798, requiring Lucas Sullivant to move some of his town westward. The commissioners had no desire to select a place likely to be flooded and instead favored nearby Dublin.

Franklinton residents were shocked into action by the commissioners' decision. Lyne Starling, James Johnston, John Kerr, and Alexander McLaughlin, with financial encouragement from Lucas Sullivant, decided to persuade the legislature to make a change. Sullivant was the largest landholder in the state and owned more than forty-one thousand acres by 1810. The men offered one thousand acres of land, one-half of which would belong to the state, plus four thousand dollars for four lots from the state's half if the so-called high bank were designated as the site of the capital. Sullivant offered additional proposals of donations on January 16, 1811.[9]

Seven proposals were received by the legislature, and a bidding battle occurred. James Kilbourne, the founder of Worthington, offered more land and increased donations totaling $25,334 from 136 persons. In early February the two houses still disagreed on their choice of a temporary capital. The Senate favored Lancaster; the House insisted on Chillicothe. A majority in the House preferred Dublin as the permanent site. The Senate was more divided. After motions for Dublin and Delaware were defeated, a motion to postpone a decision until the following December passed 12 to 11 on January 20, 1811.[10]

The political leaders were hopelessly divided. They seemed to agree only that the location be near the geographical center of the state and close to a navigable river. Beyond those considerations, regional preferences prevailed. The bidding battle intensified as stakes were raised. When the legislature met in December 1811, a complicated lobbying effort developed as proponents of the various sites maneuvered for support. In order to attract votes, attempts were made to link the selection of the permanent site with the choice of a temporary one until a permanent state house was built. Joseph Foos, a Franklinton resident and senator representing Franklin, Delaware, and Madison Counties, tried on December 16 to get the Senate to consider the question of the permanent seat. He failed when the vote was tied 11 to 11.[11] Foos was hoping to gain financially if the land across the Scioto from Franklinton were selected; he operated a ferry across the river and ran Franklinton's first hotel. He could count on only seven colleagues completely committed to his choice. The seven, who consistently voted with him on substantive matters, were John Bigger (Warren County), Samuel Evans (Highland County), Othniel Looker (Hamilton County), Alexander McBeth (Champaign County), David Purviance (Montgomery, Miami, and Preble Counties), Jacob Smith (Greene County), and the Speaker and acting governor in 1807–8, Thomas Kirker (Adams County).

The lobbying continued into January 1812. The Delaware proposition included a state house, an office for the auditor, secretary, and treasurer, and more than four thousand acres. In Dublin, John and Peter Sells offered more than three hundred acres, including the houses on the land, one of which was a distillery. John had built the Black Horse Tavern but he lacked the cash others could offer. Thomas Backus, partway between Dublin and Franklinton, offered one thousand acres. George Stevenson was willing to give five hundred acres or $2,000 if either Franklinton or the high bank were picked. The Pickaway Plain supporters in Circleville offered land they thought could sell for $35,000; if it didn't, they offered to make up the difference. Worthington was still in the running, but its residents were not able or willing to raise the ante. Later, forty-one persons favoring Circleville could come up with only $5,095. On January 20, 1812, Starling, Johnston, Kerr, and McLaughlin were permitted to withdraw their proposal in order to revise it.[12]

The four men had gone to Zanesville early in January to lobby for their proposal. When they heard that the Delaware offer was being favorably considered, they realized that they had to do better. Lyne Starling wrote Lucas Sullivant that Moses Byxbe and Henry Baldwin from Delaware had offered to construct a state house, prison, and public offices, and he and his colleagues had to make a similar offer. They also needed more land to offer and asked Sullivant to persuade James Hoge, a Presbyterian minister, to donate or sell his tract east of the river. Starling urged Sullivant to join the men in Zanesville, saying that he considered it "indispensably necessary that you should be here to lay in our proposals on Monday next."[13]

Kerr also enlisted Lucas Sullivant's extended help. He wrote Sullivant, "The probability is that we may succeed in obtaining the permanent seat east of the River if we can agree to make the public buildings, you will therefore have the private subscriptions extended to as great an extent without delay as possible to assist us in this work."[14] Sullivant and others enthusiastically participated in the effort. Hoge contributed eighty acres, and another Franklinton resident, Thomas Allen, gave twenty. The legislature received the revised high bank proposal on February 10, 1812.

The four men offered to lay out the town, convey ten acres of land to the state for a public square and state house and ten acres for a penitentiary, and erect buildings to the legislature's specifications: "state house, offices and penitentiary and such other buildings as the legislature will appoint." They promised to complete the penitentiary by January 1, 1815, and the state house and offices by the first Monday of December 1817. The structures, they promised, would be worth some $50,000, or they would make up the difference if they were not valued that high. They offered a bond of $100,000, which they would forfeit unless they "shall truly and faithfully

Lyne Starling. From Lee, *History of the City of Columbus,* vol. 1.

comply with the proposals." They offered to let the legislature determine the width of streets and alleys. None of the other contenders could match the $50,000 offer.[15]

The politicking was intense for the next two days. Sullivant had joined the effort in Zanesville, bringing subscription pledges from other Franklinton residents. Efforts in the Senate to postpone the decision until December were defeated twice. Foos was so discouraged he even voted to postpone a final decision. However, on February 11 and 12, efforts to select Delaware were defeated. Some legislators were reluctant to make a commitment forever, so the four men from Franklinton revised their proposal to designate their site the state capital effective only until 1840. The Senate amended its motion accepting the high bank offer, but not until after rejecting an amendment to limit its commitment to 1825. The final vote was 13 to 11. Foos and his supporters had lobbied persistently and had been able to get additional support from John Bureau (Gallia and Scioto Counties), James Dunlap and Duncan McArthur (Ross and part of Pickaway and Fayette Counties), Thomas Irwin (Butler County), and Levi Rogers (Clermont County). The opposition represented the northeast, east, and southeast counties of the state, a regional and political split that was continuing. Opponents in the House of Representatives on February 13 tried to replace both Chillicothe and the high bank designations and lost. They then tried to postpone a decision until December but were defeated. The final vote in the House that day for the high bank was 27 to 19, but many representatives were unhappy with the Senate's pressure. The next day, Lucas Sullivant offered to guarantee payment of the individual pledges from other Franklinton residents in an effort to mollify those legislators who were still unhappy.[16]

On February 19, the legislature passed a joint resolution mandating the dimensions of the capitol building and penitentiary. It included the requirement that the capitol be "on a stone foundation according to the most approved models of modern architecture, so as to combine, as far as possible, elegance, convenience, strength and durability."[17]

On February 21, Sen. Samuel Evans from Highland County moved that the new town be called Columbus. However, Joseph Foos apparently was the first to suggest the name. (One of Foos's favorite books when he was learning to read was a biography of the explorer.)[18] When the Senate asked members of the House to concur, they rejected the name 22 to 19. The Senate asked a second time, and the House finally agreed, 24 to 10.

The House opponents had the last word, however, before the legislature adjourned. Thomas G. Jones from Trumbull County persuaded eleven of his colleagues to sign a long, spirited protest against the decision. The protest declared that "due regard should have been paid to the geographical centre and to the probable future centre of population." The protest indicated that Delaware was closer to the center and was situated "in a dry, elevated and healthy" place. The document pointed out that the original commissioners were against the Columbus site and that the public had been deprived of a voice in the matter. The protesters claimed that there had been no real majority for Columbus and that a fictional majority had been created by including a single vote for Chillicothe as the temporary seat of government. They concluded by disavowing the right to bind their constituents or a future legislature to the contract. All of those who signed the petition were from the eastern and northeastern counties. Despite their unhappiness, many of the legislators recognized that they had accepted the most attractive financial proposal.[19]

The *Western Intelligencer* in Worthington broke the news to its subscribers on the same day that the House finally approved. The paper ran the long protest statement signed by the twelve representatives on its first page on March 13. Residents of Worthington and Delaware were especially disappointed. Those of Franklinton, except for the ones who had invested in the eastern bank of the Scioto, were dejected. Some were envious and jealous. Others nurtured their dislike of Columbus for many years. Still others started considering a move across the river. The population of Franklinton thus was doomed to remain small for many years, and Columbus annexed it in 1864.

The fifty-thousand-dollar offer was not only the most attractive one; it was also a safer one in that the legislature avoided having to show favoritism to an established town. Delaware was closest to the center of the state, but the Byxbe and Baldwin offer of buildings and four thousand acres was considered inadequate. The growing town of Worthington had many advantages. It was only eighteen miles south of the geographical center, on high ground near a navigable river, and just south of falls on the Whetstone River (now called the Olentangy) that provided power for mills. However, it had distinct disadvantages. The town center was a distance from the Whetstone River. Supporters offered less money. The town's settlers were from New England, and the legislative majority traced their roots to Kentucky, Virginia, and the Middle Atlantic states. There may also have been some hesitation to give James Kilbourne, Worthington's founder, an opportunity to benefit financially.[20]

In the end, despite the fragility of the coalition pushing for the high bank, regional, political, and economic considerations prevailed. Those who led the campaign gained financially and politically. Lyne Starling became one of the foremost landowners. He had contracts to supply the army during the War of 1812 and served as clerk of the circuit and district courts of Franklin County. Initially, Alexander McLaughlin was one of the wealthiest men in town, but he failed in the first depression and his lands were sold at auction. John Johnston also overextended his land purchases and met the same business failure.[21] John Kerr became company agent for the four property owners to handle financial matters relating to their contract. He had a land office on Broad Street, served in 1818 and 1819 as Columbus's second mayor, and was a councilman until 1823, the year he died.[22] Joseph Foos also profited. A general in the War of 1812, he gained income from his hotel and ferry service and from quarrying stone and buying and selling land. He even received $225 in 1817 for delivering firewood to the capitol building. He was an associate judge of the Franklin County Court of Common Pleas from 1803 to 1808 and served four terms in the Ohio Senate between 1808 and 1828.[23]

People in Chillicothe were pleased with the legislative decision. The editor of the local paper, the *Supporter,* wrote, "We believe a more eligible site for a town is not to be found and it must afford considerable gratification that this long contested subject has at last been settled." John Sells, however, never gave up trying to praise Dublin. In 1818 he announced in a long advertisement, "A New Town For Sale. The subscriber will offer for sale . . . about 200 town lots . . . 12 miles above Columbus, and on the very place that the commissioners of the state made choice for the seat of government, and at the expiration of the time specified by contract, it is probable that the legislature will turn their whole attention to said town, for as much as the convenience for building is equal to any part in the Union." Sells praised the quality of the local building stone and large springs and mentioned the excellent sawmills nearby. He added, "This town stands on a high bank and known to be remarkably healthy." [24]

Thus Columbus was made the permanent state capital before it was a town. Its very existence was the result of a major lobbying effort. Despite the grumbling of a few, the four men in Franklinton started immediately to breathe life into their creation by beginning the construction of the public buildings. First, however, there were trees to remove.

2

Creating a
New Community

Columbus, along with many other western frontier communities, did not grow randomly but was started through a partial planning process.[1] The first streets in the city were laid out at right angles in the spring of 1812, and it was incorporated as a borough on February 10, 1816. Some historians have interpreted the choice of a right-angle grid as reflecting a democratic and accessible openness in the start of community building. It may have simply been copied from certain eastern cities such as Philadelphia. In any event, the town planners undertook to assure an orderly expansion.[2]

The legislature had authorized Joel Wright to plat the area and named him director of the town. Apparently it was he, with assistance from surveyor Joseph Vance, who selected the areas for the square where the public buildings would be located and for the first penitentiary. The original plat, which has long since disappeared, left open space between Fourth and Seventh Streets. Lots were laid out east of Seventh (now Grant) for future sale.[3]

The Ohio legislature expressed satisfaction with Wright's work as surveyor. Meeting again in Chillicothe in December 1812, legislators did not ignore what was happening in Columbus. A Senate committee reported that John Kerr's deeds had been defective because they lacked the usual subscribing witnesses but were now in order. However, while legislators had been shown the floor plan for the public office building, they did not know its intended height and thought its windows were too small. Wright resigned as director after a year, and on February 10, 1814, William Ludlow replaced him. Most of the construction was done under Ludlow's supervision. He resigned October 9, 1815.[4]

Only a few persons lived in the area east of the Scioto River prior to 1812. John McGowen had a house in a small, cleared field south of an Indian mound. The Deardurf family squatted in a log cabin near what is now a corner of Front and State Streets. John Brickell lived in a cabin in a clearing near where Wyandot Indians had formerly grown corn and where the final Ohio Penitentiary in town was later built, near what is now Neil Avenue north of Spring Street. Brickell, who had been a captive of an Indian tribe earlier in his life, had bought ten acres from Lyne Starling. The location of the new capital was east of the Appalachian plateau in what geologists called the Central Low Plains. The high ground on which High

Street was laid out was called Wolf Ridge. Several streams cut across the land toward the Scioto River. The area was covered with tall beech, maple, oak, and hickory trees.[5]

The sale of lots began on June 18, 1812, the day that war was declared against Great Britain. Most of the first sales, ranging from $200 to $1,000, were for lots on Broad and High Streets. The terms were standard at that time: one-fifth of the purchase price required immediately and the remainder required in four equal annual payments. Interest was charged if payments were late. There was an 8 percent discount on additional cash paid on the day of the purchase.[6] James Galloway bought the first plot for $200 and Lucas Sullivant the second for $302. Two of the first buyers, Jacob Hare and Peter Putnam, still lived in Columbus in the 1850s. Two German immigrants were among the eighteen buyers at the first offering. William Altman, who worked on the large wooden columns of the State House, was another of the first property owners. Volney Payne had a tavern at High and State Streets as early as 1813. It later was called Russell's Tavern. The Ohio Tavern and Columbus Inn were hotels that opened in the first few years.[7]

Other 1812 property owners who became active in the town's early history were William McElvain, who was county commissioner in 1815 and associate judge in 1829 and 1837; Jarvis Pike, who owned the Yankee Tavern and was mayor from 1816 to 1818; and John M. Edmiston, the town's first physician. A majority of the first settlers played key roles in the town's development. George B. Harvey was in the first Methodist class (the smallest group of church members before a meeting house was built), became marshal and clerk of market in 1833 and 1836–43, was a director of the poorhouse, and served on the board of health twice. Michael Patton was justice of the peace in 1814 and on the first council in 1816. John Shields had a colorful career as justice of the peace from 1813 to 1816. He built the first sawmill on the Scioto River in 1813, surveyed and platted John McGowen's addition in 1814, and did masonry work on the second prison. In 1817, he built the second market house, where he rented two rooms, one for a printing office and one for preaching.[8]

Three hundred residents lived in Columbus by the end of 1813. Some of them contributed two hundred dollars to remove the tree stumps from High Street, the first example in the community of private contributions for the common good. The public square given to Ohio for the capitol building also was covered with trees. Gov. Thomas Worthington arranged with Jarvis Pike to cut them down.

The harshness of the environment meant that those who survived were resourceful and independent persons who showed great initiative in economic and political activity. Whether Ohioans really were more rugged

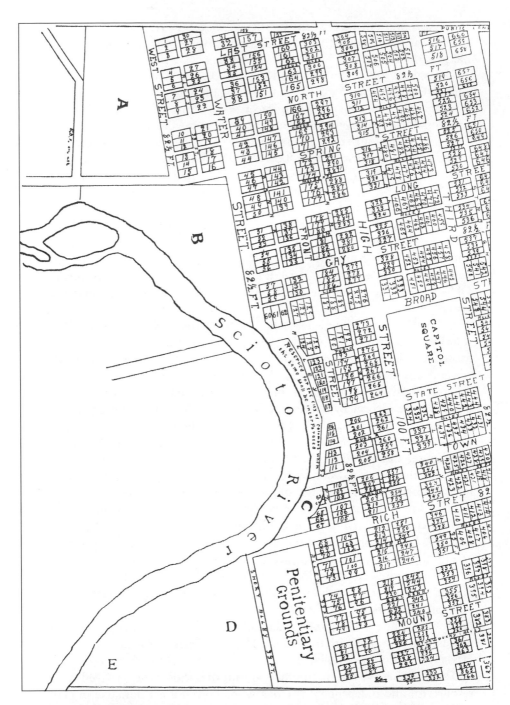

Original plat of Columbus, west section. From Lee, *History of the City of Columbus*, vol. 1.

Original plat of Columbus, east section. From Lee, *History of the City of Columbus*, vol. 1.

than people in the East is debatable, but they perceived themselves that way. John Otstot certainly overcame adversity in walking five hundred miles from Lancaster County, Pennsylvania, to Columbus. He was a wagon maker and lived on the same Front Street lot the rest of his life. William T. Martin was another example of a resourceful survivor who contributed to the community in a variety of ways. He first taught school in the Methodist log church in 1816. He was a justice of the peace, a councilman, mayor, clerk of the penitentiary, county recorder, and associate judge. In 1858, he wrote the first history of Franklin County.[9]

One of the earliest appraisals of his neighbors was written by Robert W. McCoy, who moved from Pennsylvania to Franklinton and then to Columbus. He wrote his father, "I did not like this country when I came to it . . . but have now become so accustomed to the habbits [sic] and manners of the people that I believe I could spend my life here." He added that the area was a good place to acquire property and live well despite the initial privations. About his neighbors, he wrote, "[T]he country being settled by people from all the other States—each bringing their own particular customs along with them—Some being strictly Religious and some very wild."[10]

Before long, two distilleries owned by John Notre and John McCoy were in operation. When Joel Buttles arrived in 1813, he had the impression that the town was considered by many people "with little regard and slight expectation." Buttles continued his association with the *Western Intelligencer,* which was first printed in Columbus on March 16, 1814, but he was more interested in his general store, and he finally gave up the editorship. He managed the post office from 1814 to 1829 but later became more influential as a successful businessman.[11]

The War of 1812 added to the concern and uncertainty associated with a new undertaking. Some three thousand Indians remained in Ohio, and residents feared attacks by them and perhaps incursions by their British military allies from Canada. Gen. William Henry Harrison had his headquarters in Franklinton for a time, but after the army moved north residents felt especially vulnerable. American military defeats resulting in Gen. William Hull's surrender in August 1812 and the defeat of James Winchester's Kentucky militia in January 1813 made those clearing trees on the high bank more aware of the seriousness of the conflict. John Johnston, the agent for Indian affairs, tried to calm the uneasiness. When the Delawares moved near the border of Miami County, he issued a notice to reassure settlers that the Indians had been encouraged to move there to prevent their control by the British. Newspaper accounts of frontier attacks, however, fanned some persons' fears. The *Western Intelligencer* of August 13, 1814, reported on the trial and acquittal of an Indian party that "butcher[ed]" members of three families in the Wood River settlement in the Illinois Territory. The same newspaper issue confirmed that five hundred more militia men were called in Ohio.[17]

The few hundred residents of Columbus had two main concerns: a love of liberty and a yearning for security and stability. People had moved west searching for both political and economic freedom and safety. Tension occurred when the conflicting goals clashed. Stability in a new town was translated into a need for social control. The settlers' liberty had been won in the War of Independence, and they wished to enjoy it in relatively un-populated, fertile lands where they could raise their families in a safe envi-ronment. They lived close together near Broad and High with a minimum of conveniences and cooperated with their neighbors in improving their living conditions. Their daylight hours were devoted to laboring, building, clearing the forest, leveling roads, digging wells, planting, going to the mar-ket, and learning the news of the town, the nation, and the world. By 1815, Columbus had one printing office, four lawyers, and six stores.

During the summer of 1814, something occurred that created con-fusion and division. On or around July 4, some residents planted a tree of liberty and a flag near the site of the capitol building construction. Accord-ing to a long, detailed account in the *Western Intelligencer,* on the night of July 16th the tree was cut down and the flag "feloniously taken off." The residents replanted the tree and raised another flag. On the night of Au-gust 1, the tree was again cut down and the flag destroyed. Some citizens met, created a "Vigilant Corresponding Committee," and advertised "100 Dollars Reward" for the "clear discovery of the perpetrator."

In the account of the incident, the committee members indicated that they assumed the perpetrator must be unpatriotic, sympathetic to England, and "lost to all sense of decency." (With children and teenagers making up about one-half the population, they might have come to a different conclu-sion.) They decided, however, to express their vigilance beyond offering a reward and seeking the guilty person. In their statement, signed by ten men led by Jarvis Pike, they indicated that their object was also "to use due means to consolidate the republican interest, and to obtain a knowledge of the character of men, as to their motives and capacity, that the best possible judgment may be formed enabling us when the time comes, to give our expression in favor of those who are qualified by disposition and informa-tion to serve the people by promoting their interest and happiness." They wished no injury to innocent people, but they intended to "discover those internal enemies whose prepared poison is designed for the death of repub-licanism."[13] The town survived its loss of a tree and flag and went on to other pursuits. Jarvis Pike, however, managed to become the first mayor.

Lyne Starling, James Johnston, John Kerr, and Alexander McLaughlin, the four men from Franklinton who had won the contest for the permanent

First state buildings at Columbus. From Studer, *Columbus, Ohio: Its History, Resources, and Progress.*

capital site, had two main concerns. One was to sell plots of land to new arrivals. Kerr opened a land office on Broad Street. The other objective was to construct the public buildings before the deadline. The building for state offices was erected on High Street next to the State House in 1815. The first State House, two stories high and built of stone and brick with a bell steeple, was constructed at the southwest corner of the public square and was completed in 1814, ahead of schedule. It was fifty by seventy-five feet with a balcony and square roof, and the top of the steeple was one hundred six feet high. The bricks in it were made partly from bones— apparently human skeletons—dug up from a handsome, high mound that was removed from the corner of High and Mound Streets. Governor Worthington asked some women in Columbus to make a carpet for the State House in the autumn of 1816, a year so cold that there was little summer warmth. Mrs. George B. Harvey, Mrs. George McCormick, and Mrs. William T. Martin led the sewing circle. One early visitor called the first capitol building "handsome" and thought it gave to the public square "an air of magnificence." Others were more critical. Cyrus Bradley, who visited in 1835, thought the building too small and noted that it lacked a lobby, which made the representatives' hall "very unsuitable for silence, deliberation or convenience." However, he did like the carpet.[14]

One of the first visitors to Columbus in 1815 was John Cotton, a Massachusetts physician. He counted two hundred houses and learned that there were seven hundred residents. He wrote in his diary, "The streets are filled with stumps of trees and environed with woods, which give the town the appearance of having emerged from the forest. . . . The people have been collected from every quarter, and having great diversity of habits and manners, of course, do not make the most agreeable company."[15]

On February 10, 1816, the General Assembly, still in Chillicothe, created the borough of Columbus and authorized a meeting of those electors who were qualified by at least six months' residence to elect nine citizens to serve as mayor, recorder, and common councilmen. The mayor and council were given power to pass laws and ordinances, levy taxes, and erect public buildings. The first tax passed by the council was a fifty-cent levy on dogs.

The legislature moved into its new quarters for its first meeting on December 2, 1816. Some of the representatives arrived on horseback, others in small boats. One of the legislature's first crises was the discovery that the prison was too small. Built in 1813 under the supervision of William Ludlow, it was a three-story structure, thirty by sixty feet. The first floor was half below ground and contained basement cells, a kitchen, and a dining room for the prisoners. The keeper, as the warden was called, lived on the second floor, and the third contained thirteen cells. The building was primitive by even the most generous standards. A stockade near the Scioto River not far from the foot of Mound Street surrounded a log structure with whipping posts. The General Assembly passed a statute that year in 1815 that provided for the punishment in prison for certain crimes that formerly had resulted in whippings or stays in county jails.[16]

Governor Worthington spoke before the legislature on December 9, 1816, and observed that there was too much latitude given in the punishment of crimes. He reported that the board of inspectors had recommended "the absolute necessity of enlarging the penitentiary in the course of the ensuing year." The current building accommodated sixty persons. The board estimated that there would be 110 convicts in three years and recommended adding twenty more cells and enlarging the prison yard. The committee reviewing the report agreed that the building and prison yard needed expanding, but at a cost of $21,490.[17]

At the time, there were only thirty-three prisoners in the building. Their ages ranged from seventeen to fifty-three, but most of them were in their twenties. One of them was a young woman, a servant named Polly Miflin, who had been sentenced to a three-year, four-month term for stealing bank notes. She was described as a "smart, active woman, not very industrious." Fifteen men were in for larceny, four for horse stealing, and three for forgery. The first inmates were brothers John and David Evans, given five years for assault and battery with intent to murder and robbery. Only one prisoner had lived in Franklin County.[18]

The legislators reluctantly appropriated $15,000 for a second building. It was constructed in 1818 at a cost of $33,391. The original structure was modified into a residence for the keeper, whose first assignment every morning was to wake the inmates at 4 A.M. The prison yard was expanded to 160 by 400 feet and was surrounded by a stone wall eighteen feet high and three feet thick. The building contained sixty-four cells.[19]

The legislature also had to deal with a memorial from the four proprietors who had constructed the public buildings. They had spent more then they had expected. Their costs on the three buildings totaled $90,006.56, instead of the $50,000 they had anticipated. The price of some materials had increased during the war. It was the first cost overrun in the town's history. On the same day that the House learned that the prison was too small, that body passed a resolution creating a joint committee to review the request for more funds from the four proprietors. The committee made a report on January 8, 1817, stating that the bills from joiners working on the building were too high. The legislature passed an act requiring the governor to appoint one or more skillful mechanics to evaluate the joiners' work and revise their bills. The appropriation to the four proprietors at the end of the session was for only $24,000. The legislature also appropriated $2,000 to Fanny Thompson, the widow of a man who had contracted to lay bricks at a low price for the public buildings, but who had had to pay so much for them that he was left penniless.[20]

The legislature addressed a variety of issues that winter, including the authorization of new roads, new towns, and new taxes; incorporation of new businesses; and a request from the governor of New York for financial assistance toward the construction of the Erie Canal. The legislature was not interested in sending funds to New York. An annual concern of the legislature was the allocation of the 3 percent from the sale of public lands for the construction of roads. In 1816 Governor Worthington recommended that the funds be allocated only to the leading roads in the state to make them more permanent.[21]

One legislative action of interest to Columbus residents resulted from the submission of a petition from some German residents who asked that the laws of the state be printed in their native language. After the joint committee of propositions and grievances deliberated, the legislature passed a resolution approving the request and appropriated $1,300 for translating and printing the Ohio Constitution and part of the laws in German. In 1826, the legislature passed an act providing for the printing of important laws in German. This practice became an issue for debate in subsequent decades.[22]

The first U.S. Court House was erected in 1820. It was a two-story brick building with a stone foundation fifty feet square. A courtroom and jury room were on the second floor. Some of its construction costs were paid for through contributions by Columbus residents. The Franklin County Court House was moved from Franklinton to Columbus in 1824.[23]

Columbus residents were kept informed of the legislature's actions through newspapers. The legislators, who stayed in hotels or with friends, added a new, temporary dimension to the growing population and helped spur economic activity along High Street. When the legislature adjourned at the end of January, the editor of the *Western Intelligencer* observed, "With some partial acceptions [*sic*], the utmost harmony and order pervaded the intercourse of the members with the citizens and of both with each other." He regretted their departure. The interactions between town residents and legislators sometimes helped and sometimes hindered the development of a sense of common purpose.[24]

Most of the early settlers initially were strangers to each other, but they were intent on forming a community. One of the newest German arrivals in 1813 was Christian Heyl. He rented a small cabin, built an oven for a bakery, and opened a temperance "house of entertainment," later called the Commodore Perry. In the spring of 1841 the building became the Franklin House. Heyl became a member of the city council, county treasurer, and associate judge. While the word "community" has many definitions, the most common one suggests that people develop mutual interests and connections in the place they live. They bring their customs and heritage to a new locale and learn about the habits and ideas of others. It may be easier for a small population living relatively close together to create the semblance of community than for masses of people to do so. The earliest settlers in Columbus appeared to build what Martin Buber called "a common relation to the centre overriding all other relations." Mobility, diversity of background, language, religion, and economic class differences deterred development of a strong community identity. Those in leadership positions tended to expect others to follow their social and moral examples. Continuous change also eroded community cohesiveness almost as fast as it developed.[25]

One way for residents to build a sense of community was through experiencing public events together. By the start of the nineteenth century, the most popular public celebration was the observance of the Fourth of July. By 1818, Columbus residents accepted a custom of coming together in a festive mood. That year they gathered in Jarvis Pike's Yankee Tavern in the morning and paraded to the State House, led by Maj. John McElvain, who was marshal for the day. The celebrants stood in the sun to hear Ralph Osborn read the Declaration of Independence and give a short speech, then returned to the tavern for dinner. Afterward, they enjoyed many toasts and tributes to the forty-second anniversary of independence and to

George Washington, Revolutionary War heroes, heroes of the War of 1812, President James Monroe, Vice President Daniel Tompkins, John Quincy Adams, John Calhoun, Henry Clay, and others. The Fourth of July parade became a Columbus fixture for many years.[26]

January 8, the anniversary of Andrew Jackson's victory at New Orleans, became another day for community festivities. That date was on a banner in large type in the journal of the House of Representatives on January 8, 1817, and it became a Democratic holiday for many years, especially after Jackson was elected president.

Parades always drew residents together. The Columbus Artillery and the Columbus Light Infantry frequently marched in front of the State House to admiring observers. One group paraded on August 23, 1819, and the other the following morning. The military organizations enabled strangers to get better acquainted with an activity that reflected how close the country was to the threat of war. They also encouraged the development of a patriotic spirit. Reflecting the democratic spirit of the time, the first Ohio Constitution required that captains in the militia be elected by those in their company. Majors, colonels, and brigadier generals were elected by other officers. Military parades occurred frequently throughout the 1820s. The Columbus Guards were active in 1827, and the Franklin Rifle Company in 1830. After Germans arrived in large numbers, they also formed military units.[27]

It did not take long for the town to attract an animal act, which became a popular recreational magnet for the community. On Friday and Saturday, July 30 and 31, 1819, people could pay twenty-five cents to see a male elephant, supposedly the first in the country, perform a variety of tricks. Children twelve and under were admitted at half price. J. B. Gardiner's show also had two camels and a jaguar on display, but it cost an extra twenty-five cents to see them. Animal acts visited the town for many summers.[28]

Because of the new settlement's vulnerability, the city leaders realized that community ties would be fostered by creating a greater sense of stability and order. By 1818, the city council had passed and publicized several ordinances. One fixed the width of sidewalks on all streets and alleys. Another prevented "hogs and pigs from running at large." Fines of twenty-five cents were authorized for catching and impounding each one, plus twelve and a half cents for each advertisement and for each day an animal was kept. Later the council passed an ordinance "to regulate stage players and public exhibitions." It required those performing or exhibiting to apply for the mayor's permission and to pay a license fee of five dollars for two days and ten dollars for longer periods of time. Fines were twenty dollars for failure to apply.

The city council ruled that "if any person or persons shall become infected with the small pox, or any other contagious disease [they] shall be removed to a convenient and safe distance from the inhabited part of the Borough." That body also appointed a town surveyor and passed an ordinance "to prevent persons from discharging firearms within the Borough." The fine for doing so ranged from twenty-five cents to five dollars at the discretion of the mayor.

The council also required that carcasses of dead animals be removed "as soon as possible" and authorized the marshal to remove them at the owner's expense after three hours of giving notice. The fine could not exceed three dollars. The council further required that streets "shall not be obstructed by manure from stables, lumber from workshops, materials for building" and prohibited slaughtering on in-lots or reserves west of Fourth Street. The fine for the offense could be as high as seventy dollars. Any "necessary" (privy) at the front of a lot had to be removed, and any new ones had to be dug at least six feet deep. Fines for failing to comply were up to twenty dollars. In 1819, the council increased the tax for owning a dog to one dollar each. Another ordinance provided that when anyone complained of a nuisance on a street, lane, or alley, the mayor had to remove it at the owner's expense. By 1821, the city council required property owners on High Street to have their front sidewalks paved "with good sound brick." Later that year an ordinance "to prevent running or galloping horses" was passed. The fine was a steep three dollars. Only stage horses could race down High Street.[29]

State laws were designed to preserve order and punish unwanted or criminal activity. By the 1820s, justices of the peace had jurisdiction over a long list of criminal offenses. They included "Sabbath breaking," with fines from one to five dollars; "interrupting public worship," up to twenty dollars; and "tavern keepers selling liquors on Sunday," "profane swearing," "exciting disturbance at elections and other public meetings," and "bullet playing and horse racing in streets of towns," among many others.[30] These restrictions regulating personal and economic conduct were designed to enhance the general welfare.

The town's political leaders continued to be concerned with the preservation of order. Grocers who sold liquor in small quantities had to secure a license, and "rioting, revelling, gambling, or drunkenness" were prohibited. In 1830 an ordinance was passed "to protect the citizens against mad dogs." Dogs were prohibited from running at large, and it was lawful for anyone to kill an unleashed dog. Several ordinances were enacted requiring property owners in the heart of town to pave their sidewalks with brick. Persons arrested at night were held in a small "calaboose" behind the State House. When George Harvey was marshal, he patrolled at night with a strong cane and lantern. Regulations were enacted affecting various businesses, and in 1830 an act was passed levying an annual tax on the income of practicing lawyers and physicians.[31]

City leaders also wrestled with the problem of gambling. In 1827, the city council was still trying to impose order and decorum on the town. An ordinance was passed prohibiting gambling not only in gambling houses but in nine-pin alleys and ball alleys. A section of the ordinance forbade serenading or making unnecessary noise or disturbance. The penalty for disturbing sleepers with drums, bells, or horns was a fine of up to ten dollars or prison for up to twenty-four hours, or both. Ordinances were ignored by some people and poorly enforced. Three years later the city council passed another ordinance adding gaming tables and machinery devices to the prohibited practices and stipulating that anyone found "guarding the door" to a gaming room who obstructed the marshal "shall be deemed as owners and partners" and fined upon conviction for up to seventy dollars.[32]

The most sweeping ordinance was one in 1837 "to suppress immoral practices." It provided that if anyone was "found strolling about the streets or alleys, apparently with an improper or evil design, after ten o'clock at night, without giving satisfactory evidence of the honesty of their intentions, or their being necessarily out on business," they would be fined up to twenty dollars or imprisoned up to ten days, "or both at the discretion of the mayor." Householders were authorized to apprehend those who violated the ordinance. Apparently, no one asked for a definition of an "improper or evil design."

Two years later, perhaps in reaction to an increase in noisy nightlife that troubled light sleepers, the ordinance to suppress immoral practices was amended. It began, "Whereas, it is represented that idle, lewd and dissolute persons, of both sexes, are in the habit of getting up and attending dances and carousals, to the great annoyance of neighborhoods and corruption to the manners of youth, who are seduced with these receptacles of vice and wretchedness, to remedy these evils, Be it ordained . . . That all such dances and carousals shall be deemed unlawful."

Those attending these "dances and carousals" were subject to fines of from five to twenty dollars plus the cost of prosecution, and marshals were authorized "to enter such houses at any time, and bring the inmates forthwith before the mayor for trial."[33] This sweeping ordinance with its high fines and threat of prosecution reveals the anxiety of those responsible for the safety and stability of the town. It also suggests that those in power sought to regulate the conduct of the entire population and make citizens conform to middle- and upper-class customs and standards. It was only the dances of the "idle, lewd and dissolute persons" that were prohibited, and the marshal was expected to know whom to arrest.

Community building was enhanced by the creation of a variety of clubs and organizations. Residents were able to devote at least some time to things other than cutting down trees and building houses. A library called the Columbus Literary Society was founded in 1816 at the Columbus Inn. Participants in 1819 paid five dollars a share, and the "annual tax" was one dollar. However, the library soon ran out of money and closed. The Juvenile Debating Society and the Columbus Mechanical Society were meeting as early as 1818. Officers were installed in a Masonic lodge on December 31, 1817, and the Grand Royal Arch Chapter of Ohio convened in December of the following year. Other groups that were organized included an Ohio Law Society and a Handel Society, whose members sang at the July 4, 1822, celebration. The busy Joel Buttles was the Handel Society's president.[34]

By 1819, the young town contained three hundred houses, fourteen hundred residents, a post office, a market house, distilleries, taverns, two printing offices, ten stores, and five private schools, one of which was described as "a respectable seminary for young ladies."[35] The population was already diverse and became more so with new arrivals in subsequent decades.

Before taste and culture could be improved, Columbus residents faced many challenges. Even when the populace was not burdened by disease and floods, work was long and hard. Much time had to be devoted to getting and preparing food, making clothes, improving houses. Most people were busy scraping out a bare existence. The population had increased to fifteen hundred people by 1820, but more than half of them were under sixteen years of age.

Because the city was so new, some townspeople believed it compared poorly in terms of economic and social activity with larger cities in the East. Richard Bushman has suggested that westerners accepted the East as their primary gauge of civilization and were uneasy in dealing with their own cultural inferiority.[36] Columbus residents also were defensive when they heard or read about disparaging comments by easterners. In 1826 one resident wrote, "Many of the Eastern Editors have such a prejudice against western writers, that they will scarcely believe that a well written essay can appear in a western journal."[37] There was a coarseness to life at Broad and High, but both old-timers and new arrivals seemed bent upon improving taste and culture.

Columbus was surrounded by farms and other towns. Some Franklinton residents moved across the river, and that town remained small. Other townships were increasing in population: Perry and Washington to the northwest, Clinton and Sharon to the north, Mifflin to the northeast, Truro to the east, Madison to the southeast, Montgomery and Hamilton to the south, and Jackson to the southwest.

Roads had to be cut through the thick forests nearby. The land had to be cleared; nature had to succumb to civilization. People assumed that animals existed for mankind's benefit, and when they got in the way, they had to be removed. The August 29, 1822, issue of the *Columbus Gazette* notified its readers of what became known as the grand squirrel hunt: "The squirrels are becoming so numerous in this country, as to threaten serious injury if not destruction to the hopes of the farmer during the ensuing fall. Much good might be done by a grand turnout of all citizens." People were asked to meet "in a hunting caucus" at the house of Christian Heyl on August 31 at 2 P.M. People came from other townships to participate, and thousands of squirrels were killed throughout the city and state.[38]

Frequent sicknesses and deaths were constant reminders of the fragility of human life. Dr. J. H. Harris opened an office in his home on the east side of High near State Street and promised to "attend to all calls." In 1822 Elizabeth Deshler wrote to her parents in Pennsylvania: "[N]one feel safe. There has been much more sickness this season than has ever been known since the settlement of Franklin County. Our burying ground has averaged ten new graves per week, for a number of weeks." The following year Joseph Dunlop Jr. wrote his uncle in Pennsylvania, "[T]here has been a gret many deths about Columbus." A typical obituary would report in a few lines: "Died yesterday morning, Mrs. Rachel Barr, wife of Samuel Barr. 34 years. Her illness long and painful. . . . She has left several small children."[39] Philo H. Olmsted, editor of the *Columbus Gazette,* was almost poetic in conveying the mood he sensed the summer of 1824. He wrote, "Life is a fountain fed by a thousand streams that perishes if one be dried. It is a silver cord twisted with a thousand strings that parts asunder if one is broken. Frail and thoughtless mortals are surrounded by innumerable changes. . . . We are encompassed with accidents ever ready to crush the mouldering tenements that we inhabit. The seeds of disease are planted in our constitution by the hand of nature. . . . We see our friends and neighbors perishing around us."[40]

Disease continued to be a problem throughout Columbus's first four decades. In 1832 a cholera epidemic spread from Asia and Europe to the U.S. It raged in Columbus that year and the next. The first case was discovered July 14, 1833, and the last victim died on September 29. Unsanitary conditions and polluted water spread the disease, which brought on muscle cramps, diarrhea, vomiting, and dehydration. The speed with which cholera victims died was fearful. No remedies seemed to work. One treatment was a tablespoon of salt and one of red pepper in a pint of hot water. Panic spread through the streets and alleys. One quarter of the population, those who could afford to do so, left Columbus. The city council took delayed action in September by passing an ordinance prohibiting the sale of "apples, peaches, pears, plums, grapes, cabbages, cucumbers, water and musk melons." The board of health's final report was not published until November 1833. Ninety-two people died that year, eleven of whom were in the penitentiary. The board blamed the epidemic on "imprudent exposure, improper living" and warned people against overuse of medicine, consumption of fruit, and excessive eating and drinking.[41]

A smallpox scare raced through Columbus in 1843 and 1844. The first resident to succumb was an officer of the Clinton Bank. It was rumored that he must have handled currency coming from Cincinnati. By January 1844 several cases alarmed the population. Panicking legislators sought physicians to get vaccinated "for the Cow Pox."[42] They were not the only residents with sore arms. Almost every letter written that decade to family members and friends mentioned a sickness or a death.

Another serious cholera epidemic hit the city from June to September 1849. The first person to die, on May 27, was a traveler from Cincinnati. A family of four died suddenly on June 21, and panic gripped the populace. Most people had ignored the filth, manure, and discarded garbage scattered in the streets, alleys, outhouses, and stables. The ineffective board of health, which had been reestablished in 1848, was replaced by a new one in late July. The board reported 162 deaths of Columbus citizens and 116 in the penitentiary. The names of those who died were listed daily in the papers. Among the dead were Gen. E. Gale, quartermaster general of Ohio, and brewer Bernhard Burck. The wife of D. B. Cheney, the pastor of the First Baptist Church, who stayed in the city to comfort victims, also died. A meeting of Columbus citizens was held on July 13 to consider what might be done for the convicts. Five resolutions were passed. A committee was appointed to cooperate with prison officials to "alleviate the miseries" of the inmates. Another committee was asked to confer with city council, and a recommendation was sent to the governor to exercise his pardoning power in meritorious cases. A day of fasting was held on Friday, August 3. Most businesses were closed, and the churches held services. It was not until September 17 that the *Ohio Statesman* could report that business was normal again, the market house well supplied, and hotels full.[43]

There were 225 deaths the following summer when cholera returned once more. One-quarter of the population deserted the streets of Columbus that July. Eliza Sullivant, wife of William Sullivant, was one of those who left, but she died of cholera in August. Uriah Heath visited the city twice. On July 26 he wrote, "I found the cholera to be very bad and a deep gloom over the place. I felt as if the atmosphere was loaded with death." He recorded on August 1, "Passing through Columbus I saw the people under deeper gloom than before. The epidemic was fearfully fatal and the road north was lined with carriages and waggons leaving the place." Asa Lord, superintendent and principal of the high school, favored postponing the reopening of school that summer. Later that August, Thomas Mooder, a bank cashier, reported that cholera was still severe, although some people recovered if they received medical treatment promptly. Samuel Medary was effective in getting city officials to improve standards for sanitation. There were one thousand deaths from cholera in two years in central Ohio and more than thirty-seven thousand deaths in the country.[44]

Hazardous weather also caused crises. The Scioto River flooded in 1832, 1834, and 1847. In 1847 people woke on Friday, January 1, to see the river over its banks and higher than it had been for twenty years. Some of the National Road in Franklinton was submerged. The pork houses along the banks of the Scioto were inundated, and there was much damage. John McElvain's pork house was carried downstream. Joel Buttles and others involved in the slaughtering business worked constantly over the weekend to save their meat and buildings, but Buttles's building was washed away on Sunday. A part of the railroad bridge over the Scioto was destroyed, and the embankment was washed away. The canal dam was threatened and saved only with great efforts. Farms in the valley lost soil, crops, and fences. The *Ohio State Journal* called the damage "unprecedented." Buttles wrote that the water was nineteen inches higher than the crest in the 1832 flood.[45]

Families, which were large by modern standards, were often reminded that life was short and uncertain. Infant mortality was high. The first persons to marry in Columbus, Jane Armstrong and Philo H. Olmsted, newspaper editor, hotel owner, and mayor in 1833 and 1838–39, had twelve children. Joel Buttles and his wife had twelve children, but seven died as infants or children, three of them in 1829. Muriel Broderick, who married cabinetmaker John M. Walcutt, had sixteen children; eleven lived to adulthood. Mary and Alfred Kelley had eleven children, only six of whom lived beyond childhood. The merchant John Brooks and his wife had thirteen children. Christian and Johanna Jaeger, who arrived in 1834, had eleven children. Birthrates declined toward the end of the period. Men at the age of forty considered themselves old.

Because Columbus was young, and because of turnover and mobility, a sense of newness was one of the city's characteristics. Although to some the past seemed irrelevant, there appeared to be a conscious effort on the part of community leaders to create a tradition. The newspapers contributed to the effort by recording bits of the area's history and by providing readers with accounts of national and international events as well as debates and actions in the state legislature. Festivals and parades continued to strengthen the ties people felt with their town.

In 1834 the General Assembly passed an act incorporating the city of Columbus. Boundaries were clarified, elections were authorized, and the powers and duties of mayor and council were defined. The city had authority to levy taxes and to build a prison. The city council increased its production of ordinances. Bathing in the river was prohibited. Taverns and groceries were regulated; more streets were repaired and sidewalks paved; combustible materials could no longer be burned on streets and alleys. The council allowed itself to borrow $11,000 at 7.5 percent interest. Gustavus Swan, a successful lawyer, was repaid the $6,500 he had loaned the city. By 1835 only 41 log cabins remained out of 977 buildings.[46]

3

Economic

Development

Individuals and families moved west from the eastern states in the early 1800s. Some moved for adventure, some for independence, some because they found it too crowded at home. The majority, however, saw an opportunity to better themselves economically and, caught up in the land hunger of the day, packed their belongings and set off for an unknown future. The price of public land in Ohio was only a fraction of the price of land in the populated eastern states. People may have been pious or poetic, well educated or ignorant, aristocratic or common, but they had to make a living and they had to work.

Merchants played a key role in the economic development of the new town of Columbus. They led in applying their energies to fostering capitalism, seeking profits, and taking risks. Lyne Starling, for instance, was the first businessman to risk shipping a cargo of produce down the Scioto River to New Orleans.[1] Joel Buttles was particularly successful as a merchant. In 1814 he was selling a variety of merchandise including maple sugar, cloth, furs, flour, and whiskey. In 1817–18 he partnered with Lincoln Goodale to sell medicines and drugs. He also was postmaster for fourteen years, from 1814 to 1829, until he was removed by President Andrew Jackson for political reasons. Buttles later became president of the City Bank. In 1831 he went into partnership with Buckley Comstock, a commission merchant, in the pork-packing business. The Buttles & Runyon hardware store was a profitable operation. Buttles also invested in commodities and land. He married Lauretta Barnes, James Kilbourne's stepdaughter, in 1814. Their extended family of twenty lived in a large house on South Third Street built by Joel's brother, Arora.[2] Two of their sons helped Joel build the United States Hotel.

Another newcomer was David W. Deshler, who arrived with his wife, Elizabeth, from Easton, Pennsylvania, in August 1817. He bought a lot on Broad Street for a thousand dollars with a down payment of two hundred dollars and a gold watch worth an equal amount. Afterward he built a one-story, two-room house, doing most of the construction himself. By April 1, 1820, he had paid the remaining balance of six hundred dollars. David Deshler became successful and an active advocate of city advancement. He bought and sold many lots in town. He was a cabinetmaker and later a merchant. In 1834, he was cashier of the Clinton Bank, and in 1854 he became a bank president. His wife wrote her parents on August 11, 1817, to report, "Columbus is a flourishing town."[3] Their first child born in Columbus died in early 1819 at the age of nine months. Their son William was born later that same year.

Merchants needed a place to sell their goods; buyers needed a secure site where they could inspect what they intended to purchase. One of the first public structures in town was a market erected in the middle of High Street south of Rich Street in 1814. The market was built through voluntary contributions from property owners. This action was significant as an early example of cooperative effort by citizens and a commitment to a market economy. City council regulated the market's hours and operations. An ordinance required that a market should be held every Wednesday and Saturday from fifteen minutes before sunrise to 10 A.M. Buying or selling marketing articles elsewhere was prohibited. It was unlawful "to monopolize by purchase or barter, for the purpose of retailing again, any such article or articles as may be offered in the market house." The position of clerk was created to announce the opening and closing, to weigh items on complaint, to prohibit the sale of unfit items, and to lease stalls and settle disputes.

In 1818 the city council authorized construction of another market house, a two-story building on State Street west of High. Because of the lack of meeting houses, some sermons were preached there on Sundays, and other special events were held there. It was replaced in 1830 by a much larger shed-like building with a center aisle at the southwest corner of State and Front Streets. Market days then were held three times a week. In 1830, the city council authorized fines for causing any filth or nuisance and required wagons to be kept out of the street near the market. Prime beef was sold by butchers at two and a half cents per pound. By November 1841 some 140 wagons were bringing produce to the market house on the days it was open for business. The market became a magnet for economic activity and a social center where people exchanged news. Residents had to shop frequently because food could not be preserved easily.[4] On January 25 and 26, 1828, Frederick J. Lehman, a German artist, gave an amusing one-man show at the market house. Occasionally lectures also were given there.[5]

Stores were opened to supplement the market house. Enterprising businessmen as early as 1815 included Henry Brown, who sold dry goods, groceries, hardware, glass, books, and stationery, and I. and R. W. McCoy, who specialized in dry goods, groceries, liquor, hats, shoes, cotton, tobacco, powder, and lead. The McCoys built their store at the northwest corner of High and State Streets, and initially it was one of the most prosperous. The energetic Robert W. McCoy became one of the wealthiest merchants and served on the city council for thirty-seven years.

John McIntire sold whiskey out of his home by the barrel or in smaller quantities. John Warner and William Platt competed as jewelers, watchmakers, and silversmiths. Some businessmen took advantage of convict labor and contracted with the penitentiary to make and sell badly needed merchandise. As early as 1816, for instance, James Kooken was selling "coarse shoes, wash tubs, barrels, and meat tubs." Merchants who sold goods other than those made in the United States had to get a license. Peddlers and traveling merchants were also required to have a license costing eighteen dollars for the year.[6]

Merchants and laborers were attracted to Columbus in several ways. Some received letters from residents; others read gazetteers. Some enterprising persons in town advertised for a tailor in 1817 and were rewarded by the arrival of Daniel Smith from New York the following year. Silas Williams arrived in 1818 to open his store selling crockery, glass, cotton, and woolen goods. Because of the shortage of cash, some merchants were willing to barter. Williams was willing to take in payment "wheat, rye, corn and oats." Hiram Platt announced in his advertisement, "Most kinds of domestic products will be taken in exchange for books and stationery." Isaac Taylor, who ran a distillery, sold whiskey in return for corn and rye.[7]

Some customers bought the goods they needed at public auctions. John Martin held a successful auction February 4, 1817, selling broadcloth, silks, cotton shirting, shawls, buttons, and thread. The following year Michael Patton auctioned lots in town.[8]

A number of residents found more profit in land speculation than in selling goods. Land was considered extremely important as a measure of status, a commodity, and a source of wealth. Inequality in land ownership was inevitable because veterans received land on the basis of their rank, and because of the practice in the late 1790s of buying up military warrants by those who wanted to invest in land. Some veterans were happy to sell for cash, even at a discount, to persons eager to grab many acres. Speculators bought up large quantities of warrants and had an advantage in selecting choice lands. Jonathan Dayton acquired more than fifty thousand acres in Ohio. He was a New Jersey legislator in the House of Representatives from 1793 to 1797 and was elected to the Senate in 1799. Dayton corresponded frequently with Joseph Vance and other surveyors in central Ohio and owned land that later became part of Columbus north of Fifth Avenue.[9]

In newly established towns and in places when towns might be established in the near future, the practice of "town-jobbing" occurred. Persons with knowledge of the area could select choice locations for investing in land at low cost, hold the land while the population increased, and then sell it at much higher prices. The possibilities for favoritism, bribery, and corruption were tempting. Some scholars have concluded that speculators impeded the original intent of encouraging widespread land ownership.[10] An early traveler to the old Northwest observed, "Gain! Gain! Gain! is the beginning, the middle, and the end, the *alpha* and *omega* of the founders of American towns."[11] Two decades later, when Alexis de Tocqueville interviewed residents, he recorded, "In Ohio everyone has come to make money."[12]

Real estate transactions occurred early in the town's history. In 1814, Edward D. Long advertised the sale of his one-story house and lot on High Street. The house was sixteen by thirty-four, with a "convenient porch the whole length of the house." He boasted, "A good bargain may be had, if prompt pay." In 1818 Uriah Case advertised five in-lots with buildings on them. Because of the shortage of cash in town, he wrote, "An elegant horse would be received in payment."[13]

The city council, like individual residents, was short of cash. In 1816, the council printed $555.75 in small bills in denominations from six and one-quarter cents to seventy-five cents to pay its expenses. Cash flow problems bothered a number of residents. In 1817, some sixty owners of lots were delinquent in paying taxes and had to be warned that failure to pay by April 11 would result in the sale of their lots.[14]

Banks were crucial to the expansion of business, but their role in the economy was not well understood and sufficiently regulated. The legislature passed an act in 1815 to gain revenue from bank operations and placed a 4 percent tax on dividends. Twenty banks were chartered in that decade, and the amount of paper money in circulation increased greatly. Inflation resulted from 1815 to 1817. The legislature prohibited unincorporated banks from issuing paper. Some paper that was issued became worthless; other paper was heavily discounted. Counterfeiters profited despite newspaper warnings about them. Because of speculative fervor and easy credit, more persons plunged heavily in debt. A crisis was soon to occur.[15]

The Franklin Bank of Columbus was incorporated in 1816 with $100,000 in capital stock. Its first president was Lucas Sullivant, succeeded by John Kerr in 1819. The bank's president in 1823 was Gustavus Swan, who moved from Franklinton in 1815. A skilled lawyer, Swan was elected to the legislature. In 1821 he bought 115 acres of land from Lucas Sullivant. He compiled the state's land laws and later became president of the State Bank of Ohio.[16] Swan was on the committee of citizens who met President James Monroe, escorted by the Franklin Dragoons, at a huge reception in the State House in 1817. The next day, the merchant James McCoy wrote his brother to report that Monroe, who had stayed at his house, said his treatment in Columbus was the most elegant he had received on his trip.[17]

The Scioto River, called Scionto by the Wyandot Indians, marked the western boundary of the town. The shipping trade was important to the town's growth at that time, and docks and warehouses lined the riverbanks. Although there were few buildings east of Fourth Street, additions were approved to the boundaries of the town as the population increased. They usually carried the name of the principal landowner, such as John McGowen, whose addition expanded the town in 1814.[18]

Some of the early settlers who contributed to the economic advancement of the city were Lincoln Goodale, John Kerr, William Merion, Isaac and Jeremiah Miner, and Samuel Parsons, who moved to Columbus from Franklinton in 1816. John Kilbourn, nephew of James Kilbourne, who founded Worthington, sold books, initially in the Columbus post office. He also was the author of the first book published in Columbus, the *Ohio Gazetteer: or Topographical Dictionary, containing a Description of the Several Counties, Towns, Villages and Settlements in the State of Ohio.* The book, published in 1816, went through many editions, became a bestseller, and served to attract settlers to Ohio. Many immigrants, however, were attracted through private correspondence.

Early efforts at manufacturing were not successful. The growth of industry was slow for several reasons. The earliest settlers came from agricultural backgrounds in Pennsylvania, New York, and Virginia and were more interested in investing in land than in factories. Raw materials were not abundant, there were few skilled laborers, wages were low, markets were limited, and initially the town was relatively inaccessible. Despite early failures, some factories did thrive. Joseph Ridgway's company began manufacturing plows in 1822 and converted to steam power in 1830, a move that increased productivity. There also was a small copper, tin, and sheet ironware factory.[19]

In its early days manufacturing in Columbus was primarily associated with agriculture. Even the editor of the 1843 business directory had to admit, "Of mills and manufactories, further than the common branches of mechanism, we have nothing to boast."[20]

Attracting laborers was one key to getting businesses going. The town needed carpenters, masons, tanners, and other skilled workers. Ads and articles in newspapers and gazettes attracted not only those who could afford to migrate west but also those looking for jobs or those wanting to improve their economic situation. Although most of the migrants went west with their families, some single persons migrated in search of jobs. The arrival of German immigrants, especially after 1840, brought more skilled workers. Some new arrivals discovered apprentice opportunities in occupations where demand was greater than supply. Eli Stone conducted a school on bookkeeping in 1834 and offered a series of twenty four lessons for young men interested in entering that occupation.[21]

In response to the increased traffic on the Scioto, the city council authorized the construction of a wharf in 1830. Three of the most successful business leaders—Buttles, Goodale, and McCoy—were appointed commissioners to manage the Wharfing Fund, which borrowed money and sold stock in the enterprise.[22]

Business was temporarily threatened in the early 1820s when other towns lobbied the legislature to move the capital. Arguments against Columbus included the poor roads, the high prices, the shortage of hotel rooms, and the unexpected costs for the penitentiary. The high postage rate of six cents a single sheet was a burden for those whose income relied on mail. Fortunately, the legislature had more pressing concerns at that time than moving the seat of government.[23]

A severe economic depression hit in 1819. The crash resulted mainly from overexpansion of debts incurred from land ownership by persons who took advantage of easy credit provisions in federal laws to buy more acreage than they could afford. Many local banks loaned excessively and were squeezed by the Second United States Bank, chartered in 1816, when it refused to redeem their shaky paper currency with specie. Commodity and real estate prices fell in 1818 and precipitated bankruptcies. One-third of the population suffered as a result of the panic. Bank notes were discounted drastically when they were sent east. Joseph Dunlop wrote his brother-in-law, "[T]here is no trade here for money."[24] Some Columbus residents supported the legislature's decision to tax the United States Bank and the forced removal of money from the Chillicothe branch, even though the U.S. Supreme Court ruled the act unconstitutional. Despite the decision in *McCullough* v. *Maryland,* many Ohioans resented the United States Bank as an intruder profiting by foreclosing property.[25]

Although the depression was nationwide, Ohio and other western areas suffered heavily. The state's surplus agricultural production lacked a sufficient market because of access problems and transportation costs. Columbus residents were most affected when they failed to pay land taxes and lost their property. The *Columbus Gazette* regularly listed details of sheriff's sales. The July 8, 1819, issue contained a list of twenty lots to be sold. Sheriff's sales in Columbus continued for the next several years. The sale by Sheriff John McElvain on August 1, 1822, disposed of sixty properties. The local paper ran lists of auditor's sales in every county during 1822. The table of lands delinquent for 1820 and 1821 for Franklin County contained the names of 42 residents, 58 nonresidents, and 103 nonresident landowners in the Virginia Military District. More than one hundred lots

Alfred Kelley. From Bates, *Alfred Kelley, His Life and Work*.

were sold at the sheriff's sale in 1823. The list of delinquencies in 1823 was even larger and included leading figures such as Jonathan Dayton, Alexander McLaughlin, Joseph Vance, John Kerr, and Duncan McArthur. Successful businessmen and speculators bought the lots sold by the sheriff, some of which went for as low as eight dollars.[26]

Some merchants tried to help their customers by extending credit. Others resorted to extra efforts to keep their customers. William Platt, who sold shoes, looking glasses, books, scissors, steel chains, penknives, and shooting irons, advertised, "To relieve those who have been bitten by depreciated paper, the following bills will be taken," followed by a list of banks in Cincinnati, Zanesville, Hamilton, Urbana, and Lebanon. James Culbertson, who had an inn on Front Street, announced, "[W]ill receive in payment of old debts due him whiskey, sugar and linen."[27]

The legislature was under pressure to give more help to those who were financially squeezed. The tax on one hundred acres of first-rate land had been $2 in 1818. The following year it was reduced to $1.50, and in 1821 to $1. In 1822, however, it was increased by fifty cents. In 1819 Alfred Kelley submitted a bill in the House of Representatives to abolish imprisonment for debt, but the Senate was still debating the bill's merit in 1823, and it wasn't passed until 1838. The next year the legislature passed a law for partial relief of insolvent debtors, and the following year it made the methods for levying taxes more "equitable." Two years later, however, merchants were taxed on the basis of their assets.[28]

In 1820, Congress sought to relieve economic pressure by passing the Public Land Act, which reduced the minimum price of public lands from $2 to $1.25 per acre and the minimum size from 160 to 80 acres. The Ohio Legislature responded to additional pleas for relief. An act was passed in 1822 "to provide for the remission of penalties, and for the sale of land for taxes." The law exempted delinquents from all penalties that had been levied prior to 1820. However, it also authorized the sale of land on which taxes were unpaid by December 10, 1822.[29]

Financial problems were accompanied by concerns over monetary losses from fire. In 1818, the editor of the *Columbus Gazette* observed, "All ready has there been considerable damage done by fire in this place. We would most earnestly recommend to the citizens of this town to take this subject into serious consideration, and adopt some measures which will tend to secure our property against that devouring element." It took city council four years to pass an ordinance "to prevent destruction by fire." It formed "one hook and axe company" consisting of fifteen men and one ladder company of twelve men. It authorized twelve men as guards to property. The remaining citizens between fifteen and fifty years of age were required to serve as "bucket men." The town marshal was required to ring the bell upon alarm of fire and patrol the streets, keep the peace, and "confine disorderly or suspicious people." There were fines for those refusing to perform their duties. The mayor was authorized to purchase two long ladders, four short ladders, four axes, and two hooks. Every property owner had to furnish as many water buckets as a committee required.[30]

The procedure apparently did not work. After a fire in 1822 in which several buildings were destroyed, city council passed an ordinance establishing a fire company and selected twenty-five residents who were governed by a captain elected by the members. They were required to meet on the last Saturday of each month to train themselves in their duties. The council members sought to buy a building but initially were unsuccessful. The following year they failed to persuade the legislature to let them build a firehouse on the public square. One urgent problem was in getting rapid response to fires. James White's coach factory, along with a blacksmith shop, burned in 1830. An agent of the Protective Insurance Company increased his sales. In 1831 the city council offered a bonus of five dollars to the first member of the fire company to arrive at a burning building. The second to arrive received a four-dollar bonus, and the third was given three dollars. The council also directed the safety committee to inspect stovepipes and chimneys, and if a danger of fire was found, the owner was fined five dollars a day until the condition was corrected. Despite the bonuses, fires continued to be one of the city's worst hazards. One of the biggest fires occurred in John Young's Eagle Coffee House in 1839 and resulted in $1,200 damage. Later that year a burning stable and warehouse lit up the sky.[31]

A series of suspicious stable fires occurred in 1843 and 1844. Neil's stable at Broad and Front Streets was partially burned on February 13, 1843. Three others were burned within a short time. Some of the fires interrupted lectures, parties, and church services. A warehouse at the junction of the river and the canal completely burned at the end of May. Samuel Medary's stable was torched on February 11, 1844, and everything was lost except one horse. Ten days later James Aston's cabinet shop, which was attached to his dwelling, burned down at night, but he and his family were saved. The *Ohio Statesman* editorialized, "It is not any wonder that our city is in a state of fear and excitement." The firemen found it difficult to cover the town. One company had its engines housed on State Street and the other on Mound Street east of the new courthouse. So great was the fear in town that the city council advertised a three-hundred-dollar reward for the arrest and conviction of anyone setting a fire. In an effort to calm the people, the two fire brigades held a torchlight procession around town on March 11, 1844.[32]

Many residents decided to carry fire insurance. The Columbus Insurance Company instructed its agents to "acertain from actual view . . . the peculiar hazards of the building or property on which insurance is requested." It supplied sample forms covering the information owners had to supply and warned agents, "[I]t is well to have some regard to the character of the individual" seeking coverage. Annual premiums ranged from twenty cents to seventy-five cents on the property's value for brick or stone, 1 percent for wood, 2–3 percent for factories, and more for distilleries and soap and candle factories. There were additional premiums when hazardous goods were stored. Agents received a 10 percent commission.[33]

Despite the depression, more merchants were attracted to the growing town. In 1823, a new saddler's shop opened. John Kilbourn moved his bookstore south of the bank on High Street. Nearby, O. & S. Crosby sold drugs and medicines along with hardware, whips, and shoes. In 1824, J. & B. Cunning sold leather either at their tanyard near the bridge or at their saddle shop south of the market house. J. W. Smith and E. Thomas opened a woolen factory and M. Jewett a new cotton factory. That December, residents were pleased to learn that Young & Brodrick were selling "twenty kegs of superior oysters."[34]

Other professions followed as the population increased and business improved. Dr. J. W. Burrell advertised his availability for professional services and offered to operate on indigent patients gratis. Doctors Cooper and Seever announced that they were prepared to treat diseases of the eye. In December 1827 a medical convention met in town to implement the law requiring medical societies to incorporate to regulate the practice of medicine and surgery.[35]

The mood in Columbus by the end of the 1820s was brighter with the addition of more newcomers and improved business prospects. In addition, sectional disputes were resolved when Congress agreed to the Missouri Compromise, which admitted Maine as a free state and Missouri as a slave state and prohibited slavery in the Louisiana Territory north of the 36°30″ parallel. An upbeat editorial in one of the newspapers reflected residents' spirits: "We of this generation are but pioneers; we have done much but nothing in comparison with what the next generation will do . . . ours is emphatically the age of bile—theirs will be the golden. For everything around us—improvement in building—the bustle of business in villages— the emigration of intelligent and enterprising men—the successful prosecution of the canals—the improvement in roads—the increased travel and facilities afforded to travellers—the increased attention to education [will lead to] . . . a higher tone or moral feeling pervading the community . . . Ohio is rapidly progressing in all that renders a people happy and respectable."[36]

There were many improvements in the 1830s. Business was expanding, and the price of real estate increased considerably. In 1832, Thomas K. Wharton recorded in his journal that the "sidewalks are broad, paved with brick, and present quite a busy scene." He was impressed by the "endless train of wagons, horses and horsemen." John Young opened a public bathhouse at his Eagle Coffee House in May 1832 with warm, cold, and medicated baths. A separate "ladies apartment" was carpeted and "handsomely fitted up."[37]

By the time Columbus had been in existence for twenty-five years, merchants had much more variety in the goods they sold. Construction of houses continued at a brisk pace. The Mechanics Beneficial Society and the Columbus Typographical Society held monthly meetings. The market house continued to offer better prices than the stores. Customers could pay seven and a half cents per pound for bacon and butter, and cheese was available for eight cents a pound. A bushel of corn was priced at forty cents and a bushel of wheat at seventy-five cents.[38]

By 1837, R. and S. Cutler started their Coach and Fancy Carriage Manufacturing Company. The Franklin Foundry, on the corner of Scioto and Town Streets, began manufacturing stoves and plows in 1838. There was also a saddle, harness, and trunk factory at 37 High Street, a paper mill a few miles northwest on the Scioto River, a cotton yarn mill, a plow factory, and a steam sawmill.[39]

Demand for land in the city and elsewhere led to more speculative risks, which led to more bank loans and an increase in bank notes. Ten more banks, including the Clinton Bank in Columbus, were chartered in 1834. However, a depression began in 1837 and continued into the 1840s. The hopeful prosperity of the 1830s came to a sudden halt. The Panic of 1837 occurred when banks in New York stopped making specie payments in reaction to President Jackson's 1836 antibank policies and his Specie Circular requiring gold or silver to buy federal land. Some banks in Ohio followed suit. Those in Dayton, Wooster, Urbana, Xenia, and even some in Cincinnati suspended payments. A large public meeting was held at the courthouse on May 16, 1837, to consider measures to respond to what was called at the time "the deranged state of the currency." Resolutions were passed and quickly forgotten. Wages declined sharply in 1839, and unemployment increased for the next five years. Money was scarce but food was cheap because of abundant crops. All residents except the very rich struggled to buy the bare necessities. The feelings of inferiority some people held were understandable.[40]

By 1840, because of the prolonged depression, the city government's debt had reached $22,000, which was being carried at a 7.5 percent interest rate. By that time even the credit of the state of Ohio was in jeopardy. The state's debt reached $17 million by 1841. Some legislators were talking about repudiation.[41] Alfred Kelley, who had devoted most of a decade to supervising the planning and construction of the Ohio and Erie Canal, had to go to New York to pledge his fortune as security so Ohio would not be bankrupted by the cost of the canal's construction. A December 10, 1841, letter to Kelley from Noah H. Swayne, one of his fellow canal commissioners, reveals how dire the state's financial situation was. Swayne wrote, "I am greatly alarmed by what you say in regard to the prospect of raising means to pay our interest. Stocks dull at 75! The London agents forbidden to make advances! The banks pressing for the payment of their temporary loans! Money tight beyond example, panic and paralysis universally present, every thing covered with gloom and despondency, and tending downward to the lowest point. It is a crisis calculated to quail the stoutest heart."[42]

Financial conditions continued to be bleak throughout the winter. Gustavus Swan wrote Kelley on January 13, 1842, to report, "The course of our Legislature and the public prints, with the fearful condition of affairs every-where, is producing a universal panic in the mind of the community, the end of which can not be forseen." Swan had good reason to be concerned. In 1838 he had invested $10,000 in Ohio bonds, and the next year he, Simon Perkins, and others purchased another $85,000 worth.[43] Kelley was able to get a loan in New York of a quarter million dollars to preserve Ohio's financial standing. He went to Europe to sell stock. Swan, who was full of praise for his friend Kelley, wrote in his biography of him, "No citizen of this state . . . ever performed a more praiseworthy, a nobler action."[44]

The city's business and financial leaders probably profited most by Kelley's audacious venture. One would not get that impression, however, from the special report issued by Swayne, Kelley, and Swan, the board of canal commissioners, on July 28, 1842. The report, which addressed Ohio's dire financial situation and the Kelley loan, was probably written by Kelley himself. The document stated that it was highly important "to maintain the character of the state, hitherto unsullied, for integrity in her dealings with those who . . . intrusted her with their money." The report asserted that a failure to pay interest on the state's debt would "produce mischief and suffering, far-reaching in their ramifications." The writer added, "Another immediate effect would consequently be in many instances to deprive the aged and infirm, the widow and the orphan, of the means of bread and raiment."[45]

Few of the widows and orphans in Columbus held stocks, but those who did were relieved that repudiation had been avoided. Nevertheless, a depression continued in the nation. Several more local banks in Ohio collapsed. Some of the wealthier lawyers in town made loans to their business associates. The depression seemed to deepen in early 1843 partly because of the lack of hard currency. The small property owners and laborers suffered the most. There were many foreclosures and sheriff's sales. Political bickering and financial instability continued until the middle of the decade.

Business progress was hurt when petty crimes plagued the community. In December 1840 thieves who may have had anti-Catholic motives broke into the Catholic church, destroyed a crucifix, and stole some valuable objects. They were not recovered for two years. A series of thefts and burglaries occurred during the summer of 1841. By December the police had apprehended some of the criminals. They raided a house near Alum Creek, six miles east of the city, where they found large quantities of stolen goods and arrested three men. One, a lawyer who had stolen some copies of the Revised Laws, made his escape.[46]

In June 1842 some "rogues" were caught after they cleverly removed a trunk from a stage as it was crossing the bridge over the Scioto. They turned out to be former prisoners from the penitentiary. On December 13, 1842, M. J. Gilbert offered a twenty-dollar reward for information leading to the conviction of a thief who stole "8 silver tea spoons, 6 table spoons,

one dessert spoon, 2 pair of sugar tongs, 1 silver bladed, agate handle, butter knife, a mahogany portable desk, family rings and a small box filled
with splendid quartz crystals." That same month someone tried to break
into the home of Gustavus Swan, and a thermometer was stolen from Samuel Medary's home.[47]

Although the depression continued, the 1843 Columbus business directory listed 1,018 names of white persons who were working at that time.
The city's population had reached 7,184 by that year, which meant that
there were about 1,100 white families and 100 black families in town. The
1843 business directory was incomplete because blacks and residents in
what was called south Columbus were excluded. Although there were a
few very rich individuals, most of the citizens had modest incomes. Most
of the power and influence was in the hands of the business and political
leaders who had lived in Columbus the longest. A closely knit inner circle
decided many issues. It took a long time for most of the new arrivals to
establish themselves. There also were members of what John C. Burnham
has called the "underworld" or "lower order," mainly single males who
were "idlers" more interested in drinking, fighting, and sex than in more
socially acceptable careers. These men were the ones society expected to
become failures or "fizzle out," a favorite expression in Ohio at that time.[48]

The business directory, which did not necessarily include all who were
employed, listed fourteen farmers living in town in 1843. There were,
of course, many others in the vicinity. According to the directory, there
were eighty-nine carpenters, eighty-eight laborers, twenty-five shoemakers,
twenty-four blacksmiths, and twenty-three seamstresses. The directory did
not distinguish between skilled and unskilled laborers. Some of the laborers
probably worked on farms. There were thirty-nine merchants, twenty-one
lawyers and the same number of physicians, but only four dentists. The
directory listed one architect, eight saddle and harness makers, six peddlers, fourteen wagon makers, and six washerwomen. There even was an
umbrella maker, who lived on High Street. The penitentiary employed a
warden and ten guards. Thanks to the canal, there were three boat captains
and two boatmen in town, as well as a canal commissioner. The police
force included a U.S. marshal, a sheriff, a city marshal, a deputy marshal,
and two constables. There were more than thirty grocery stores, twenty-
five dry goods stores, three drugstores, two shoe stores, two bookstores,
and seventeen licensed taverns. There was at least one brothel, called at the
time an "assignation house," located near Mound and Front Streets.[49]

In addition to the adults listed in the business directory, many children
in poor families had to work. Those who were fortunate were apprenticed
to learn a skill or trade. Hours were long, and not all masters were consid-
erate of youth. Boys who were indentured sometimes managed to escape.

Ezekiel Brown in Sunbury offered "six cents reward" for Thomas Burger, who ran away on May 20, 1818. William Joun probably had to pay more for the advertisements he took in the *Columbus Gazette*. When Elijah Brethard, an indentured apprentice making wagons, ran away in 1819, his master posted a five-dollar reward, a remarkably high sum at the time.[50]

Although the 1843 directory did not list blacks, they were part of the labor force. As early as 1838, there were at least five shoemakers, three blacksmiths, two painters, one stonemason, and one house joiner in the black labor force.[51] Black women also worked, but no one thought to record their numbers.

Workers' wages were low. Even as late as 1850 day wages for laborers were fifty-six cents with board and seventy-eight cents without board. Day wages for carpenters were $1.45. One dollar in 1840 was comparable to twenty dollars at the end of the twentieth century.[52]

Trade with eastern markets was lively. While Alfred Kelley was in New York, he wrote his wife on August 14, 1841, to report that he understood there were a dozen Columbus merchants in the metropolis. He was wealthy enough to do his own shopping and shipped home tablecloths, dress patterns, and large quantities of madeira, malaga, and port. By May 28, 1844, John Teesdale, the editor of the *Ohio State Journal*, could boast, "The assortment of staple and fancy Dry Goods is as complete, as the most fastidious could desire, and in Groceries the quantity and variety, is not less desirable . . . every variety of merchandise, whether of foreign or domestic production, can be had for less than it has ever before been offered in Ohio."[53]

James M. Westwater was one of the more successful and civic-minded merchants in this decade. He was sixteen when his family arrived in New York from Scotland in 1832. The family traveled first to Wheeling, then arrived in Columbus in 1840. Westwater became a glass cutter, and with his father and his brother, William, he created the firm of John Westwater and Sons. They sold china and glassware at 105 High St.

Westwater became a member of several benevolent societies. He joined the Columbus Horticultural Society, became a patron of the arts, and volunteered as a nurse in the cholera epidemics of 1849 and 1850. He was a charter member of the Columbus Gas Light and Coke Company and a director of the Green Lawn Cemetery Board. He was a Democrat in the 1840s and became an active abolitionist. One of his volunteer positions was as treasurer of the Franklin Fire Engine Company.[54]

Despite the city population's interest in commerce, agriculture continued to play a dominant role in the local and state economy. Approximately four-fifths of Ohio's labor force was engaged in agriculture in the 1840s. Farmers were sometimes as effective in lobbying as were lawyers, bankers, and merchants. They used the occasion of a two-day state agricultural convention in Columbus in July 1845 to draw attention to the needs of agriculture and to push for state support. In 1846, the General Assembly responded to pressures from agricultural interests and passed an act "for the encouragement of Agriculture." The law stipulated that whenever thirty or more residents of a county or district (consisting of two counties) organized for the improvement of agriculture and raised at least fifty dollars, they could apply to the state for an equal amount of money, provided that the amount did not exceed one-half cent for every resident. The society had to offer and award premiums for the improvement of the soil, crops, and farming and publish its list of awards. Public funds thus matched private monies to support ways to increase farm production. The act also created a board of agriculture. Michael Sullivant, Lucas's second son, a highly successful farmer who introduced new methods and machinery, helped to get the new board organized. He also was one of the founders of the Ohio Stock Importing Company, which sought to import the best breeds of cattle.[55]

The uncertainties of weather were a constant concern to farmers. The summer of 1849 was disastrous. The wheat crop was extensively destroyed. Jonathan C. Noe wrote to a friend in New Jersey, Aaron M. Condit, to report that many farmers in northern Ohio had neither grain nor hay and were driving their stock south for the winter. The *Ohio Statesman* reported, "[T]housands of acres are not worth cutting."[56]

Regardless of the economy's fluctuations, sudden unemployment, business failures, and serious sickness were continuous hazards in Columbus as well as in the rest of the country. Only a very few families enjoyed long-term economic security. Public and private efforts to provide financial relief to those in need were inadequate. Some individuals and a number of churches provided what charity they could. The Columbus Female Benevolent Society gave some aid to the poor. The Mechanics Beneficial Society, organized in 1830, had as its objective advancing the best interests of mechanics, artisans, and manufacturers "by a more general diffusion of knowledge" and by supplying financial relief to its more unfortunate members. The first part of its objective resulted in the 1841 construction of Mechanics Hall at the corner of High and Rich Streets, where meetings were held for the society's one hundred members. The second part of the goal was achieved by providing benefits from members' dues to those so sick that they could not work or attend to their business. Death benefits were also given to members' widows. This assistance to members was minimal. The majority of laborers and other workers had no such help.[57]

Business improved by the mid-1840s, especially because the banking crisis was addressed by political action. Nevertheless, some factories improved the business climate. Coaches and carriages were built on the southeast corner of High Street and Lynn Alley beginning in 1837. Saddles and harnesses were made on High Street, and after 1839 John C. Deming manufactured agricultural machines. John Funston started the manufacture of soap and candles in 1840. The city also had a paper mill, flour mill, and starch factory. Meat packing became important in the 1840s when there were hog-slaughtering sheds near the canal. Joel Buttles slaughtered fifteen hundred hogs a week in November 1841. His company killed ten thousand by the end of the season in January 1843, primarily for the purpose of making lard. By 1844, a rope and cordage factory was being managed by a woman, Mrs. E. J. Middletown. O. P. and A. H. Pinney were making agricultural implements. Columbus also had its share of breweries.[58]

Agriculture remained the main activity in Franklin County as it was throughout the state. Corn production in the county exceeded 1 million bushels as the decade began and reached more than 2.5 million bushels by 1849. Wheat was another important product. Cattle, swine, and sheep were abundant in the surrounding areas. In his *History of Agriculture in Ohio,* Robert L. Jones recorded that six thousand sheep were slaughtered in Columbus in 1845 when the price of wool fell. Market gardening was also important.[59]

Columbus residents became more aware of the contributions made by free blacks to the economy when the 1845 business directory was published. This directory was the first in the city to list "colored" workers in the alphabetical listing. Ninety-eight persons were included with their occupations and residences. It was a partial listing, but it nevertheless included thirty-three laborers, fifteen barbers, six cooks, two carpenters, one cartman, one drayman, one dyer and scourer, one farmer, one grocer, one stable groom (known then as an ostler), four painters, three porters, one ropemaker, four shoemakers, one stonemason, one teamster, two waiters (one of whom was the headwaiter at the Neil House), four whitewashers, one woodsawyer, one chambermaid, and twelve washerwomen. Most of the adult black women and many children no doubt were working. Only one minister was listed, even though there were two black churches by that time. Other hotels employed black waiters who were not included in the directory. Although many of their jobs paid poorly, blacks were an important part of the Columbus labor force. Most of the black population lived in poverty. Prior to 1840, only twenty-three black Columbus residents owned real estate.[60]

Despite the availability of labor, and although more manufacturing establishments were started after 1845, industry was still not very successful in the city. The business directory for 1843 gave one of the major reasons in terms of investors' apparent preferences: "Although Columbus possesses a liberal amount of wealth, and of money-making talent, the attention of our capitalists has never been much turned towards manufacturing; but more directed toward speculating upon the productions of others, by buying, selling, etc., than to creating new or additional wealth."[61]

Some corporations started new ventures. In 1846 Hubbell, Martin & Company opened a paper mill in a three-story building. Charles Ambos and James Lennox established the Eagle Foundry in 1849, and in the same year the two Ridgways and Pease Kimball started manufacturing railroad cars even before the railroad reached the city. Some two hundred workers were employed making boots and shoes, sixty of them in A. C. Brown's factory. Peter Hayden's "Birmingham Works" near the east bank of the Scioto was a four-story limestone building that made saddling hardware. Nearby, the Hall, Case & Company factory manufactured carpenter's planes. Engle's candle factory stood at the west end of Friend Street, while Pinney & Lampson's tub and bucket works was at Front and Spring Streets.[62]

The most visible new venture was the first experiment with gaslights in Ohio, which occurred in December 1842 in a store in the Buckeye Building. The General Assembly approved the incorporation of the Columbus Gas Light and Coke Company in 1846. Joel Buttles and Samuel Medary were among the original directors. The corporation was given full power to manufacture and sell gas in order to light the streets and buildings. It was not until September 1, 1848, however, that an *Ohio State Journal* editorial favored introduction of gaslights on High Street. The first street lighting by gas was in 1850.[63]

Other physical improvements also resulted in economic progress. The first telegraph went into operation on August 11, 1847. The *Ohio Statesman* editor was ecstatic: "The wonders of science have brought us within the means of momentary communication with all parts of this continent." The first sewer was on Broad Street in 1849; a tunnel carried it twelve feet under High Street. In 1847 the city council decided to replace the old market house with a larger one with more parking room. The two-story building was erected on the west side of Fourth Street near Town Street, and the second floor became the city hall. Until the new building was completed, the old market continued to attract farmers, merchants, and customers. Someone counted 234 wagons on the east side of High Street on November 14, 1849.[64]

The expanded city directory in 1848 was dramatic evidence of the city's growth. The population by that date totaled 12,804, 1,007 of whom were blacks. A total of 1,848 white males (out of 3,718 then in the city) were listed in the directory with their occupations and addresses. One hundred fifty businesses advertised in the directory. New occupations listed for the first time included telegraph superintendent, army general, oil manufacturer, silversmith, railroad engineer, sausage maker, power pressman, daguerreotypist, tobacconist, and undertaker. The directory didn't use the word "mechanic" in its listings, although it did use "machinist." The word was used more loosely than it is today to denote a workman skilled in using tools. Although Joseph Ridgway became a successful factory owner and a legislator, he often called himself an old mechanic.[65]

A comparison of the names in the 1843 and 1848 directories reveals that fully one-half of those white males listed in the 1843 directory were no longer listed in the 1848 directory. Not all of them could have died. Of those who are listed in both directories, 14 percent had new occupations and 37 percent had moved to new addresses. Some of the new occupations represented lateral moves and a few persons slipped on the economic ladder, but most of those who changed occupations had somewhat more income. These statistics suggest the level of upward mobility in the labor force. The fact that 14 percent of the labor force in Columbus changed jobs in five years suggests that the economy was more conducive to occupational movement than one might expect. Stuart M. Blumin, who has studied occupational mobility in Philadelphia in the 1840s, estimated that city's upward mobility at 13.4 percent and downward mobility at almost 25 percent. For Philadelphia, downward mobility was usually a move to a poorer neighborhood, but for Columbus, those who couldn't find jobs usually moved westward.[66]

The statistics also reveal a considerable migration out of Columbus during this five-year period. Sixty-one laborers, presumably the least skilled segment of the labor force, left. Thirty-nine carpenters were no longer listed, representing about one-half of that occupational group. One-half of the clerks, printers, shoemakers, tailors, and teamsters were no longer in Columbus. Most of the farmers listed in the directory were gone. They probably had made a profit on their farms and found cheaper land elsewhere. An attitude described as "settle and sell" characterized many of the migrants moving west.[67]

Few attorneys or merchants, who constituted the wealthy and socially prominent people, had left. Those who couldn't make a living probably left the city when they could. According to one estimate, one-fifth of all Americans living before the Civil War went broke at some time in their lives. Physicians were one group that did not fit the pattern. Seven of the seventeen physicians in 1843 had left Columbus by 1848, probably motivated by more attractive offers elsewhere. The words L. D. Marty wrote to Aaron M. Condit in 1846 probably were typical of many people's attitude: "I can I presume stay as long as I please. But I think I shall not stay long. As soon as I think I can do better I shall leave."[68]

These figures on movement out of Columbus fit the generalization made by Stephan Thernstrom and Peter Knights that there were very high rates of population turnover and mobility in nineteenth-century cities. Men in the lower classes who were "less rooted" tended to be the ones to leave. Stuart M. Blumin found that for the same period of time, only 55 percent of Philadelphia males continued to be listed in a directory ten years later. He called the attrition rate high.[69]

When the working man lost his job, entire families sometime had to move. Oren Wiley wrote at length about the mistakes some easterners made in going west too quickly. Based on his firsthand experience, he concluded that married men did not realize how hard they would have to labor to "gain a scant subsistence" and predicted that many of them would face disappointment, fatigue, and suffering. He wrote, "It is not a light thing to travel with a family and goods."[70]

For every word of warning, however, there were several books of encouragement. John M. Peck's *A New Guide for Emigrants to the West* was a popular volume in the late 1830s and 1840s. After his travels Peck praised the Scioto valley and other parts of central Ohio. He may have misled some readers with his optimistic accounts. He wrote, "The common mechanic is on a social equality with the merchant, the lawyer, the physician, and the minister. . . . Any sober, industrious mechanic can place himself in affluent circumstances, and place his children on an equality with the children of the commercial and professional community, by migrating to any of our new and rising western towns."[71] The reality was a more rigid condition of inequality and a higher rate of movement out of towns than people realized. While some children of mechanics and unskilled laborers could climb the economic ladder, most of them remained in the lower classes.

The experience of the Cephas Buttles family was a typical chapter in Columbus history. Cephas was a cousin of Joel Buttles. He and his wife, Nancy, had five sons and one daughter. Cephas had a tavern in Clear Spring, Maryland, but was unsuccessful and lost most of his property. The family decided to move to Columbus partly because Cephas had met Joel in New York. They left Maryland in mid-May 1843 and boarded boats in Pittsburgh to travel down the Ohio River. The children arrived in Columbus on Friday, May 31, and stayed at Mrs. Anderson's boardinghouse. Their parents arrived with their trunks on June 5. The family met Joel that very day. Anson, the oldest son, found him to be "a very fine man." Joel undoubtedly tried to help the family but they had a difficult summer finding work. They then decided to try their hand at farming and left September 21, 1844, for Milwaukee by way of the canal to Cleveland. Joel loaned his cousin one hundred dollars because the family was destitute. He visited them the next year, learned that they had failed again at running a tavern, and gave them forty acres of land he owned near Milwaukee. The family succeeded at farming and on July 31, 1850, two weeks before he died, Joel gave his cousin another eighty acres of land adjoining his farm. Cephas was so overcome he wept.[72]

Although successes and failures in the Buttles family were well documented, other experiences, especially in minority families, were not sufficiently recorded. One hundred fifteen names of blacks were included in the 1848 city directory. The listing was incomplete because that year in Columbus there were 293 black males over the age of twenty-one and 244 black females over the age of eighteen, and many of them must have been working. Turnover among black males was about as high as it was among white males. Almost one-half of those listed in the 1845 directory were listed in the one in 1848. Most of those included were laborers, barbers, waiters, or cooks. Charles Dew had a restaurant in the basement of City House. William Jenkins was a tobacconist whose store and residence were on the north side of Friend Street west of High Street. J. Mansferd was an auction crier, and Thomas Watson was a fireman at the paper mill. Only eleven women were listed, but more women must have worked.

Of the forty seven black males listed in both the 1845 and 1848 directories, six had new occupations and fourteen had moved to new addresses. Although a few continued to live on High Street and the center of town, the majority had moved out of the area southwest of the courthouse and into the less expensive rental houses in the streets and alleys north of Gay Street.[73]

This high turnover in both races affected the progress and stability of many organizations and institutions in Columbus as it did elsewhere. The constant arrival and departure of those called "movers" brought extra income to realtors, lawyers, stage and canal workers, hotel and boarding house owners. Churches experienced considerable fluctuation in their congregations. The First Baptist Church, for instance, had a membership slightly over 200 through the 1840s. During that decade the congregation welcomed 139 arrivals from Baptist churches in Ohio and other states and dropped from membership 107, who left mostly for the west.[74]

4

Transportation
Improvements

Improving transportation was crucial to the future of Columbus. Only by increasing access could the capital survive, grow, and prosper. The first settlers realized that contact with Franklinton other than by ferry was an urgent necessity. Fortunately, by November 1816 Lucas Sullivant's bridge across the Scioto was completed. He encouraged people to buy yearly permits at reasonable terms to cross the bridge.

The first roads built out of Columbus linked the town with Worthington, Newark, Lancaster, and Springfield. Others were carved out of the forests. Still, initially a mood of isolation remained pervasive. The few streets and houses seemed insignificant, especially to those who migrated from cities. The population needed goods. Merchants needed markets. At a time when most settlers were moving westward down the Ohio River, Columbus was poorly positioned. More and better connections were badly needed, not only to nearby counties but also to the East Coast.

Good roads were needed also to bring in freight. Stagecoaches were coming into wide use, but faster ones were sought. The stagecoach business was one economic activity that did become highly successful in Columbus. William Neil was most responsible for seeing the value of developing stage routes to other urban centers, and in time he became known as the "Stagecoach king." Neil arrived in Columbus in 1818 as a stonemason and first lived at the northeast corner of Gay and Front Streets with his wife, Hannah Schwing Neil. He went into partnership to sell flour. After constructing a keelboat, he went to New Orleans, where he failed as a merchant. Returning to Columbus with a heavy debt, he became a cashier at the Franklin Bank in 1818. Later he bought his first stage line, from Columbus to Granville, with Peter Zinn. Zinn had been operating a mail stage line between Columbus and Circleville since 1819. Neil then expanded to other lines. He bought land heavily in the area, most notably three hundred acres from Joseph Vance that later became part of the campus of The Ohio State University. He was best known for constructing the Neil House in 1839.[1]

Columbus residents in the 1820s still wanted better land connections to the East Coast. A bill providing funds for the construction of roads and canals was vetoed by President James Madison in 1817. The Maysville

Road Bill was a more hopeful sign. It would have provided federal support to construct a sixty mile road in Kentucky and established a precedent for future western road construction. President Andrew Jackson vetoed the bill in 1830. However, he later signed the Cumberland Bill, which was a major federally supported construction project.

The first significant improvement in land transportation for the city of Columbus was construction of the National Road, an idea begun even before the town was created. The 1802 Ohio Enabling Act, which Sen. Thomas Worthington had participated in drafting, provided that some of the money from the sale of federal lands should be applied to construct a road from Cumberland, Maryland, to Wheeling on the Ohio River. The road reached Wheeling in 1817. In 1825, construction resumed westward through Ohio. Construction in Ohio brought business to many contractors and jobs to thousands of laborers. Initially, the National Road was expected to benefit the Chillicothe and Cincinnati areas, but by the time the road reached the state's eastern border, it made sense to direct it due west through the capital cities because of the larger population in the center of the state.[2]

The eighty-foot-wide National Road reached Columbus in 1833. As it approached the city, those living north of Broad Street and those in the southern section competed with each other to bring the road to their part of town. A compromise brought it along what at the time was called Friend Street (now Main Street). The road turned north on High Street for four blocks, then went west on Broad Street and down the hill and across a bridge over the Scioto River. Residents contributed eight thousand dollars to Joseph Sullivant to relinquish the bridge rights he inherited from his father so that the bridge could be free. They looked upon the National Road as providing an impetus for a major economic boon for the area. Merchants received more goods and helped supply travelers passing through as well as residents. Tavern and hotel keepers gained more business. Although the National Road was a toll road, schoolchildren, soldiers, and ministers were not charged, and passage was free for people going to church, funerals, markets, mills, or voting places.[3]

Tolls were charged at tollhouses every ten miles to pay for repairs. Rates were set by how much the road was likely to be worn. Cattle were charged more than sheep or hogs. Each horse and rider was charged three cents, persons in a mail stage four cents. Chariots and coaches cost eighteen and three-quarters cents.[4] Initially, tollgate keepers were appointed by the governor, and they received a salary taken from their collections. While completion of the National Road was a boon to travelers and residents of Columbus, it was much more important to the economy because it meant more frequent delivery of freight.

Stages eventually arrived in Columbus and departed daily to most parts of the state. There were direct connections to Baltimore, Washington, Philadelphia, and Detroit. A stage trip to Chillicothe lasted only nine hours. One to Wheeling took twenty hours. William Neil finally owned all the stage lines from Cumberland, Maryland, to St. Louis, and the city became the hub for stage transportation. Neil's brother, Robert, became his associate in the Ohio Stage Company. Robert Neil married Martha Mitchell Hoge, daughter of the Rev. James Hoge. He was elected to the Ohio legislature in 1838 and was treasurer of the Whig state committee in 1844. The Ohio Stage Company hired Darius Tallmadge to supervise the southern routes. Good stagecoach drivers could earn as much as five dollars a month.[5]

When Charles Dickens rode from Cincinnati to Columbus in 1842, the road was macadamized with a solid bed of broken stones and he sped at the rate of six miles an hour. When the stages delivering mail arrived in town, their approach was announced by a long blast on a tin horn, and people would stand at their doors to watch the horses rush by. Stage traffic in the winter, however, was uncertain. The line from Columbus to Sandusky replaced its stage in winter with canvas-covered wagons whose wheels often sank in the mud. Most roads in the vicinity were extremely poor, and many became impassable in rainy weather. Accidents were frequent. One passenger boasted of having survived thirteen overturnings in the state in three years. Andrew Reed, who took the stagecoach from Sandusky to Columbus, found the road "intolerable": "I was literally thrown about like a ball." The floor of the coach was caked with mud that splashed up through holes, and there were broken windowpanes and torn and dirty curtains. Most of the stagecoaches leaked badly in the rain. Even the Great Western, which carried twelve passengers on four benches and five more on top, was not well protected against the weather.[6]

Improvements in road construction continued through the decade. The Columbus-Portsmouth turnpike was built in 1847. The following year a turnpike was built between Columbus and Harrisburg, Ohio.

Even with more and better roads, Columbus residents felt isolated in contrast to Cincinnati and Cleveland, which benefited from water traffic. The Scioto River was the only connection to the Ohio River for commerce and travel. If the interior of the state were to compete with river and lake towns and attract more settlers, improvements in water transportation had to occur. Fortunately, the success of the Erie Canal in New York, completed in 1825, inspired Ohio leaders to explore a similar approach. Under the leadership of Gov. Ethan Allen Brown, the General Assembly created a state canal commission to explore possible routes to connect Lake Erie with the Ohio River. The act to create the canal system for the purpose of internal improvement was passed in 1825.

Intense political lobbying influenced the route to some extent, but the commissioners, led by Alfred Kelley, had to use the state's geographical configuration to achieve their goals. Because the southern part of the canal ran up the Scioto valley and turned east 11.7 miles south of Columbus, there had to be a feeder canal linking the capital with the main Ohio and Erie Canal at Lockbourne.[7]

On April 30, 1827, work began on what was called the Columbus side cut, the eleven-mile feeder from Lockbourne to Columbus. That day Gustavus Swan gave a speech at a ceremony that recognized the significance of the occasion. The first mile of the canal from the Scioto River was dug by prisoners, forty-five of whom were pardoned for their work. The first canal boat, carrying leading citizens from Circleville, arrived with much fanfare on September 23, 1831. Canal workers often enjoyed setting up a band on deck after work, and in Columbus young people frequently gathered near the warehouse to square dance. Although the canal was used mainly for commerce, some Columbus residents rode a packet boat, the *Sea Serpent,* to Circleville and back for recreation. The Ohio and Erie Canal was opened for its entire length on April 15, 1832. Canals continued to be a preferred way to travel for many people until the railroad reached Columbus in 1850.[8]

The canal's utility, however, did not last long. As midcentury approached, some people found canal travel slow and costly. Columbus residents were relatively late in receiving the benefits of rail traffic. One major event that marked the end of one era and the beginning of a new one was the arrival of the first passenger train in 1850. It was a long time in coming. Back in 1825, James Kilbourne had written a pamphlet proposing railroads in the state instead of a system of canals. He gave cogent economic reasons why railroads were superior to canals, especially in their cost and speed. In October 1824 he had criticized the canal route, favoring a northern one through Sandusky, where he owned some land.[9] He found few followers at the time.

As the decades passed, interest in railroads increased in Columbus as it did throughout the country. Several companies were formed in the 1830s to seek charters for the construction of railroads. The Columbus, Marion, and Sandusky Railroad gained one in 1832. The Cleveland, Columbus, and Cincinnati Railroad was incorporated in 1836, and the Columbus, Piqua, and Indiana Railroad received a charter in 1849.[10]

Rail-and-stage service between Columbus and Cincinnati became reality in August 1845. People left Cincinnati by rail at seven in the morning and arrived in Xenia around noon. After lunch there, they boarded one of William Neil's stages and arrived in Columbus around eight in the evening. A similar schedule was followed for the trip in the opposite direction. On August 13, the first day ride took place between Columbus and Cincinnati. Passengers rode the stagecoach to Xenia then took railroad cars to Cincinnati.[11]

Alfred Kelley became as active in railroad development as he had been in canal construction. In 1848 he was busy seeking to sell a million dollars' worth of stock in the Cleveland, Columbus, and Cincinnati Railroad Company. He thought Columbus's share should be $150,000, $50,000 of which should be the city's contribution, with the remainder bought by individuals. Sixty thousand dollars had been subscribed by the middle of August. Kelley wrote a ringing appeal that reflected much of the entrepreneur's philosophy at the time: "We live in an age of improvements. Every thing around us is advancing. We cannot contain our present relative position, unless we advance also. If we remain idle, we shall soon be left behind— out of sight. . . . Columbus has long been reproached for its lack of enterprise and public spirit . . . it is high time to open our eye to our true interests."[12]

The first railroad line built into Columbus was the Columbus and Xenia, incorporated in 1844. Sale of stock totaling $500,000 was authorized, but later amendments to the charter restricted routes, freight rates, and passenger fares. Even the railroad's future profits were regulated by the legislature. One provision of its incorporation dictated, "Whenever the dividends of said company shall exceed the rate of six percent, the legislature may impose such reasonable taxes, on the amount of such dividends, as may be received from other railroad companies." Only $100,000 had been raised the first year. Those who profited from canal and stagecoach traffic were unenthusiastic about competition from railroads. The directors who formed the company intended the line to connect with the Cincinnati and Springfield line. Columbus citizens finally voted in 1847 by a large majority in all the wards to authorize the sale of stock. Alfred Kelley became president of the Columbus and Xenia Company at a salary of five hundred dollars a year. He was able to sell its bonds in New York. The *Ohio State Journal* observed, "The subject of Rail Roads seems now to occupy a large share of attention of this community."[13]

The laying of track began west of the Scioto River in November 1849. Columbus residents were aware of more young Irishmen in the area working on the construction. (Because of the potato famine, 1.5 million Irish eventually migrated to the United States.) The men were paid low wages and were housed and given board in camps by the company. People argued over the station's location in Columbus. A temporary one was placed in

Franklinton. On February 20, 1850, a locomotive with one car, a "low-side gondola," left Xenia with Alfred Kelley, Samuel Medary, and railroad officials including the chief engineer. They arrived in Franklinton in mid-afternoon, having reached a top speed of fifteen miles per hour. The next day the train made a round trip from Columbus carrying a number of city officials. Regular passenger service began on February 27 when about a hundred passengers left town shortly after midnight. Soon there were two round trips daily between Columbus and Cincinnati. Construction of a bridge over the Scioto began in March. The Columbus station was put at the north end of High Street where it met what was later named Naghten Street. The first train to cross the bridge and enter the station arrived on December 14, 1850.[14]

Other railroad lines soon followed. The charter for the Cleveland, Columbus, and Cincinnati Railroad was reactivated, and construction was started from the Cleveland end through Galion and Delaware. The line entered Columbus from the north, ran along the east side of Fourth Street, and turned southwest into the station. The energetic Alfred Kelley was involved in its completion. The tracks had easy grades and long stretches of straight lines that allowed fast travel.

On Friday, February 21, 1851, a train filled with 425 passengers, including the governor, legislators, city officials, press people, and residents left Columbus for Cleveland at 8:30 in the morning in heavy rain. A shouting crowd waved them off with cannon roars. They stopped for dinner in Shelby and arrived in Cleveland at 5:30. The hillside there was covered with people who fired more cannon. There were public ceremonies Saturday morning, followed by a twenty-four-mile trip on the Cleveland and Pittsburgh line to Hudson. The return trip to Cleveland was delayed when the locomotive ran off the track because of the rain-soaked ground. There were church services on Sunday, and the party left Cleveland Monday morning. After the Monday meal at Shelby, the crowd enjoyed singing a new song, the first lines of which were:

> We hail from the city—the Capital city—
> We left in the storm and the rain;
> The cannon did thunder, the people did wonder
> To see pious folks on a train!

The only casualty on the ride back to Columbus was a cow hit by the locomotive. Regular traffic began in April of that year.[15]

Officials of the Central Ohio Railroad, which received its charter in February 1847, promised a rail link to the east, but construction problems delayed scheduling the work from Zanesville until January 1852. The line reached Columbus in 1853.[16] The arrival of the railroad marked Columbus's transition from a small political/mercantile city to a larger urban metropolis. Railroad service was a dramatic novelty that brought rapid economic and social change. With railroads running in several directions, the residents' sense of isolation finally disappeared.

5

Politics

Politics understandably played a dominant role for many people in Columbus. Legislator John Armstrong Smith wrote to his wife that politics "is all a grand scheme of intrigue, where honesty of heart and rectitude of conduct cannot flourish."[1] The capital city housed many legislators and lobbyists. In the early years, many elected officials stayed in private homes while the General Assembly was in session. Columbus also had its share of lawyers because of the number of courts.

A marked change occurred in politics during the city's first forty years. In the first party system, dominated by the Jeffersonian Republicans, loyalty and deference to the individual were important, and local groups formed fragile confederacies. Political leadership came from the upper classes, especially from the large landowners and those who had been instrumental in the War of Independence. Candidates for offices were traditionally selected in closed caucuses. The Federalist minority placed priority on the federal system of government embodied in the U.S. Constitution. When the War of 1812 started, New England Federalists opposed the war for economic reasons, and after the war the party withered. President James Monroe was easily elected in 1816.

There was significant political change in the 1820s. Columbus residents were attracted to the ideas of Henry Clay, who favored internal improvements and protective tariffs to encourage American industry. Political rivalries became more intense as four candidates competed for the presidency in 1824. Franklin County voters favored Henry Clay over John Quincy Adams and Andrew Jackson, and the state's electoral votes went for Clay. No candidate received a majority of electoral votes, although Jackson received more popular votes than Adams, William H. Crawford, or Clay. Jackson supporters were indignant when the House of Representatives selected Adams.

Jackson was furious when Adams appointed Clay secretary of state, and the campaign for the 1828 election soon began. Martin Van Buren, who favored a stronger party system, joined with Vice President John Calhoun to support Jackson. Northern and Southern Democrats formed a coalition and chose to ignore the issue of slavery. In 1828, Ohio's total vote helped elect Jackson in a bitterly fought campaign, although Franklin County voters favored Adams by 57 percent because a majority of voters were conservatives who were not attracted by Jackson's ideas.

Jackson's election solidified the new Democratic Party and marked a major change in American politics, even though the party claimed Jeffersonian heritage. Jackson was the first American president lacking in wealth or aristocratic background. His fame was primarily as a military man. His administration ushered in more of a middle-class approach to governing and a strengthening of party politics with public selection of candidates in party conventions. Jackson increased public participation in politics. His policies were antagonistic to the upper classes, especially leaders of corporations, and his decisions led to deep divisions of opinion at the federal, state, and local levels. He followed a "spoils system" approach in replacing Adams's appointed governmental employees because he wanted to remove inefficient workers. His first administration was marked by bitter factional disputes, and he had to forcefully oppose Calhoun's nullification arguments against the tariff. Jackson's removal of Native Americans to the West was greeted favorably by those Columbus residents interested in buying additional land. His attack on the Second National Bank divided Columbus citizens. When he withdrew federal deposits from the National Bank, political divisions solidified. Jackson opposed special corporate charters and disliked paper money. His Specie Circular action in July 1836 to require that only gold and silver be used to buy government lands spurred additional opposition to Jacksonianism. He was especially popular with those in business who wished to be free of governmental restraints.

Opposition to Jackson had already solidified with the creation in 1834 of the Whig Party by those upset by the president's veto of the Maysville Road Bill. The Whig Party was a coalition of some of the old National Republicans, Antimasons, and unhappy Democrats. Its national leaders were Henry Clay and Daniel Webster. In Columbus, the Whig Party attracted bankers, businessmen, large landowners, farmers, and the socially conservative. The Whigs considered themselves engaged in a moral renewal effort, and they favored a more liberal interpretation of the Constitution, especially federal support for internal improvements.

Cyrus P. Bradley may not have realized that the second party system was emerging when he visited Columbus in 1835. He was a young man of seventeen from New Hampshire when he recorded his political impressions: "I visited the legislature. They had a short session and did nothing. . . . Many of the members were smoking, and a great portion rested their legs and part of their bodies on the desks before them. . . . In the evening, I visited the State Library, which tho' small, is far superior in numbers and selections to ours. Many of the best periodicals and newspapers are here regularly received. Everything goes by anticipation in the west—the spirit of speculation is the heart's blood of the country."[2]

In 1835 the state of Ohio was engaged in a boundary dispute with Michigan. A special session of the General Assembly was held, and the newspapers were filled with articles on the controversy. Columbus residents, however, were more concerned with local issues.

The depression that followed Andrew Jackson's Specie Circular intensified the disagreements between the two political parties. The Whigs continued their criticism of Jackson's economic policies when Martin Van Buren succeeded him as president. May and June 1837 were desperate times for business. The Whigs decided to hold their state convention in Columbus on the Fourth of July. As a result, there were two celebrations that day. About a thousand enthusiasts poured into the city at 9 A.M., led by the Fairfield delegation and two bands. The politicians met for an hour in the theater and adjourned in time for a huge dinner on the public square attended, some claimed, by more than fifteen hundred celebrants. Meanwhile, about three hundred Democrats gathered in a grove south of the city for their dinner, speeches, and toasts. Thus fortified, they marched up High Street looking for the Whigs, who by then had disappeared. It was one day when the Declaration of Independence was publicly read twice.[3]

There was a great sense of excitement in Columbus at the beginning of 1840. Activity seemed frenetic at times. Political interest rose as the campaigning for the presidential election approached. Some Columbus residents expressed increased criticism of the Van Buren administration because they were struggling through the depression brought on by the Panic of 1837. The States Rights Association met in Columbus on January 29, 1840, to work for the election of William Henry Harrison. The leaders were David W. Deshler, Isaac Taylor, George Jeffries, and John G. Miller, editor of the *Ohio Confederate and Old School Republican*. The group was disenchanted with Van Buren and represented potential additions to the Whig cause.[4]

This intensified partisan spirit was no more evident than when the Whig state convention was held. Four years earlier, in 1836, the Ohio Whig convention, meeting in Columbus, had nominated Harrison for the presidency at a meeting of more than fifteen hundred persons. Those who were opposed to Andrew Jackson's policies for enhancing presidential powers and removing government funds from the Bank of the United States took the name of Whig to associate themselves with those in the Revolutionary War who fought against the king and the Tories. Thus these new Whigs opposed what they called the tyranny of the power-hungry "King" Andrew. Harrison lost in 1836 but continued to be politically active.[5] He spent the summer of 1838 speaking in Ohio and Indiana, claiming to be the candidate of the people and reminding audiences of his military career. Harrison had been nominated again for president at the Whig national convention in Harrisburg, Pennsylvania, in December 1839, but the campaign commenced in earnest on February 21, 1840, when a noisy, excited crowd of his supporters met at the corner of Broad and High in the pouring rain.[6]

The Ohio Whig leaders followed the custom of holding their annual convention on Washington's birthday, but winter weather frequently kept the attendance small. Alfred Kelley decided that special efforts were needed to draw a crowd. As chairman of the State Central Committee, he sent out a ringing call to the faithful party members. He wrote, "To the true friends of their country, to the descendants of those patriots of the revolution who, unclad and unshod, braved the winter storms of 1780, marking the line of the march with the blood of their lacerated feet, for whom the canopy of heaven formed a tent, the frozen earth a bed, and the fleecy snow their only covering—to the children of such fathers, we say, 'Come up once more to the rescue of your country . . . to rescue the ark of the Constitution, and save your beloved country.'"[7]

A platform was erected on the public square for the convention so that the delegates could see the speakers. It was the kickoff to a successful political campaign that became a model for others ever since. Most of the delegates arrived in the city with wet clothes splashed with mud. The ones from the east charged into town on the National Road. Those from the west formed a mile-long procession past Franklinton. Twenty-seven canal boats brought delegates from the south. Enthusiasm for their candidate and their confidence in victory were high.[8]

A Democratic newspaper reporter had criticized Harrison, a former general and military hero. He wrote, "Give him a barrel of hard cider, and settle a pension of two thousand a year on him, and my word for it, he will sit the remainder of his days in his log cabin by the side of a 'sea coal' fire, and study moral philosophy."[9] Whig leaders used this comment to transform the image of their candidate from someone who had been born on a Virginia plantation into that of a rustic frontiersman.

The Ohio Whig convention was chaired by the seventy-one-year-old Reazin Beall. He had served with Maj. Gen. Anthony Wayne in 1793, been a brigadier general in the War of 1812, and been a member of Congress. The crowd heard enthusiastic speakers; passed resolutions, many of which had been written by Alfred Kelley; and cheered their approval of nominees for other offices selected by a committee. The meeting passed many resolutions that constituted an informal political platform. The first two were the foundation on which the Whigs expected to inspire support from a disenchanted populace:

> Resolved, That the permanency of our republican institutions depends upon preserving, unimpaired, to the several states, and to each branch of the General Government, the full and free exercise of their respective constitutional rights.

Resolved, That the practical tendency of our Government, as at present admin-
istered, is to concentrate all political power and influence in the National Government, and to throw the power, thus concentrated, into the hands of the
President.[10]

Several leading Columbus residents were named to the State Central
Committee to oversee the campaign. They included Alfred Kelley, Joseph
Ridgway Sr., Robert Neil, and Lyne Starling.

That night, according to John M. Woodbridge, a delegate from Washington County, the city was "brilliantly illuminated." On Saturday morning, February 22, people woke to hear bells ringing and cannons roaring.
A mile-long parade wound through the city streets, which by this time contained mud "knee deep." Thousands cheered the twenty marching bands
and colorful floats that made up the procession. One band played the
"Marseillaise." Some marchers carried banners. The delegation from Cuyahoga County had a ship on wheels with Harrison's picture on the masthead. The float from the Mad River area was a large log cabin with a cider
barrel at the door. Another contained canoes filled with women. Some of
the houses on the route displayed flags and streamers. Women waved hand-
kerchiefs and cheered from open windows. The parade lasted for hours.[11]
Songs written for the occasion and for the campaign were sung lustily. One
popular with the crowd was called "The Buckeye Cabin":

> Oh where, tell me where, was your buckeye cabin made?
> Oh where, tell me where, was your buckeye cabin made?
> It was built among the merry boys, that wield the plough & spade
> Where the log cabin stands in the bonnie buckeye shade.

Sixty of the revelers from Cleveland slept that night on the floor of the
library in Alfred Kelley's mansion, with a feather bed as a pillow. John M.
Woodbridge wrote his uncle, the governor of Michigan, to report, "Never
since the days of '76 was there so much rejoicing. Every heart beats with
high anticipation of the Success of our Cause."[12]

It was the biggest, loudest celebration in the town's history, and according to Whig editors, news of it electrified the nation. The highest estimate
of the number of people participating was twenty-five thousand.[13] Some
people in the country learned about Columbus for the first time. The
Boston Atlas reported, "There was probably never before so great a turn
out, such unanimity of thought, such universal enthusiasm at any political
meeting in the United States."[14] Throughout Saturday and into the night
crowds listened to stump speakers, sang songs, and drank more than cider.

The *Ohio State Journal* claimed that twenty thousand people had participated in the event. Only the Democrats in town failed to be caught up in the celebration. Samuel Medary, the editor of the *Ohio Statesman,* criticized the "drunkenness, low and filthy songs, the yells of the savage, and acts degrading to the beasts of the field." He was not alone in deploring the destructive torchlight parade that night.[15]

By April Harrison supporters had built a log cabin sixty feet long on State Street between High and Third for political meetings. A visitor to the city wrote that it was "looking rather on the ludickarous [sic] order for its situation which is in the center of the city." But every little village had to have its log cabin. On April 9 John G. Miller, who was about to be elected mayor, spoke at a meeting in the Eagle Coffee House at the creation of the Franklin County Straightout Tippecanoe Club. Campaigning continued throughout the year. It was the first presidential campaign to use so extensively songs, slogans, speeches, parades, banners, posters, and other devices to get attention. It was the first in which the candidate so openly sought his election. It was the first in which the candidate was portrayed as one of the common herd. John Quincy Adams called the campaign "the Harrison Whirlwind." Others called it "a triumph of demagogy."[16]

Oren Wiley, a traveler from Vermont, recorded caustic sentiments about the campaign in his journal for June 24, 1840. He had seen "vast assemblies collected together at great labor and cost, not to respond to any principles, or listen to any argument but to drown the voice of reason in shouts of revelry, and lead captive the feelings of the people in a senseless excitement." He was disgusted at the claims of Harrison's poverty and at all the log cabins and cider barrels rolled through the streets. He called the mummery and mockery "disgraceful to the country." He concluded, "It is saying to the people, you are too ignorant for self government, and is a down right insult to the good understanding of the American freeman."[17] The *Ohio Statesman* continued to campaign against Harrison at every opportunity. A July 3, 1840, headline read: "Gen. Harrison Proves A Downright Prevaricating, Double-dealing Imposter." Another article in that issue called Whig supporters "drunken, song-singing cider-suckers." An article in the May 15 issue referred to the Whig state convention as "the Baboon Convention."[18] Others, however, were excited at Harrison's popularity. Writing from Washington, Garratt Davis notified Thomas Moseley: "Old Tip is rising like a volcano and striking back like a thunderbolt. His strength has amazed every body here & is carrying consternation to the white house & throughout the whole host of office holders."[19]

Harrison's candidacy also served to intensify military spirit. Columbus residents rushed out early on Saturday, May 30, 1840, to watch a parade by army troops and a cavalry brigade. James S. Buckingham, an English visitor, was struck by the conversations favoring a war with England and the increased popularity of irregular militias. He was amused that many of the participants were boys fifteen and younger who wore uniforms, carried "wooden lances," marched in the streets with a band, "and [went] through their evolutions very much to their own delight and satisfaction."[20]

On June 6 Harrison came to Columbus and gave an impromptu, hour-long speech to a crowd of people in front of the Neil House. He made some favorable comments about Columbus and Franklinton, where he had had his headquarters for a while during the War of 1812. He said that he disliked his opponents, claiming that he was kept in an "iron cage" by a "committee of conscience keepers." He was mortified at the abuse and slander against him. He assured his listeners that he and Gen. Eli W. Gynne answered all the letters he received. He criticized the *Richmond Enquirer* for calling him a "Black Cockade Federalist." He answered other "gross misrepresentations." He talked about the Battle of Tippecanoe and refuted criticisms against his military conduct. He said if Van Buren were a better man than he, he would support him. He condemned what he called "political warfare which seeks success by foul detraction, and strives for ascendancy by the ruin of personal character." He admitted that part of his residence was a log cabin, but what he said about hard cider was drowned by the raucous laughter of the crowd.[21] His remarks can be considered the first real campaign speech given by an American presidential candidate. Earlier on his visit to Columbus Harrison went to Whig headquarters, where he shook so many hands that his hand was bruised and he had to wear a glove.

As Harrison headed up High Street he was enthusiastically cheered and escorted by many people, including the mayor, who spoke briefly. A band played "Hail Columbia" as he rode north. He was met south of Worthington by residents on horseback with sprigs of buckeye leaves in their saddles. For people in Columbus and elsewhere whose families had lived in the Ohio River valley during the late eighteenth century or at the time of the War of 1812, Harrison was a revered hero whose popularity was based more on his military reputation than on his political ideas. Partisan feeling was especially high in Columbus.

Whigs in Columbus organized a parade out of town on Saturday, June 20. Floats, wagons, and other vehicles filled with celebrating men and women wound their way to a grove, where they were joined by other revelers to hear speeches all afternoon long. According to one observer, the most popular float was one containing several attractive young women, each carrying a large buckeye tree branch serving as an umbrella. Again that year Whigs and Democrats in the city held separate celebrations on July 4.

The Whigs made special efforts to convert Democrats who were disenchanted with President Van Buren. In Columbus, John McElvain, who had been a Jackson supporter, became chairman of the Jackson Reform True American Association. John Tyler, Harrison's vice presidential candidate, came to Columbus on September 24 and gave an eloquent speech to several thousand disenchanted Democrats, much to the pleasure of the local Whigs, who were encouraged to anticipate defections of voters. A special Original Jackson's Men's convention was held on September 25. Seven thousand former Van Buren supporters marched in the city singing, "Van's a used-up man." This group published a long statement critical of Van Buren. Sen. Daniel Webster, the famous orator who was to become Harrison's secretary of state, was in Columbus September 26 and stayed at the American House. He not only campaigned for Harrison but also advanced his own political career.[22]

By fall Harrison had visited some twenty towns in Ohio. One of his campaign promises was that he would serve only one term. The Whigs capitalized on some of Van Buren's mistakes and found considerable support for their call for a national bank, protective tariffs, and government support of internal improvements. But the emotional portrayal of a former general who had fought Indians and the British attracted the support of many men whose knowledge of politics was marginal.

Columbus residents learned many new songs during the campaign. One titled "Dying Groans of the Tin-Pan" contained twelve verses, the first of which went:

> We have had a hard time on account of the road,
> But we looked not behind, for we knew our cause was good.
> The object of our journey was plain to discover,
> 'Tis to row Mat Van Buren way up Salt River,
> Ching ring a ching, O ching ring a ching.

One of the more popular songs was sung to the tune of "Auld Lang Syne":

> Should good old cider be despised,
> And ne'er regarded more?
> Should plain log cabins be despised,
> Our fathers built of yore?
> For the true old style, my boys!
> For the true old style!
> Let's take a mug of cider, now,
> For the true old style.[23]

The Democrats countered with their songs written for the occasion:

> In sorrow ye Whigs of Ohio
> And the rest of the Whig party too,
> Must bid a final good bye, O!
> To the prospects of Tippecanoe.[24]

Harrison won easily, gathering 234 electoral votes from nineteen states to Van Buren's 60 electoral votes from seven states. He received more than 52 percent of the popular vote. Eighty percent of the eligible male voters went to the polls. Harrison became the first Ohioan to be elected president. Ohioans elected a Whig candidate, Thomas Corwin, governor and sent twelve Whigs and only seven Democrats to Congress. The Whigs won through more effective use of campaign tactics and by avoiding potentially controversial issues that might have lost votes.[25] Samuel Medary wrote to Van Buren that the campaign was "as though every man, woman, and child preferred politics to anything else."[26] The young Rutherford Hayes was so impressed with Harrison's victory that he wrote his own "History of the Presidential Campaign of 1840." He ended his account with the words, "I never was more elated by anything in my life."[27]

Some of the methods used so effectively in the Harrison campaign seem copied from the techniques employed by preachers in the Protestant revivals of the early nineteenth century: the emotional oratory, the fervent singing, the persistent call for a life-changing commitment, the pitching of tents, and the parades and the protracted meetings. As scholars have pointed out, the idea of the holding of a national convention can be traced to the practice of the religiously oriented benevolent organizations.[28]

The Whig state convention in Columbus in February 1840 dramatized what historians and political scientists later characterized as a significant turning point in American politics. Although political parties were active earlier, their organization was more informal and less efficient. They were transformed into impersonal parties, more national in scope, that regularized the political process and required more dedication and support from their members. This transition led to increased power for the party, a more extensive use of rhetoric in appealing to voters, and a stronger partisan flavor. Partisanship led to an almost continual adversarial relationship between the major parties. Joel Buttles observed, "Everything . . . is done with a view to party influence."[29]

The 1840 campaign was noted for the many catchy slogans that were used to fuel political fervor. In addition to shouting "Tippecanoe and Tyler too!" the Whigs used slogans on their election posters: "Farmer of North Bend," "He leaves the plough to save his country," and "Van is a used-up man." The Democrats retaliated with "Another gourd for General Mum" to criticize Harrison's evasion of issues, and "Old Tip-ler" to attack him for his heavy drinking. To most men, the Whig slogans seemed more attractive.

The 1840 campaign was also the first in which so many women participated actively, even though they could not vote. They sang the songs and waved at the parades. Lucy Kenney wrote a pamphlet for Harrison and became, according to Harry L. Watson, the first American woman to write political campaign literature. A Columbus paper boasted, "[I]f the ladies only were entitled to vote, Old Tip would be unanimously elected." Whig leaders took advantage of women's support by getting them to prepare the food for their many special events. Democratic women undoubtedly baked bread and prepared meals too, but there weren't as many of them in Columbus.[30]

One of the reasons for Harrison's popularity among women was his reputation as a protector of women and children from Indian attacks in previous decades. The "Harrison Ladies" of Roseville expressed their adulation at a Fourth of July party where they put up a "liberty pole" and drank tea to the following toasts to Harrison: "We love him because he first loved us," "He saved us from the savage tomahawk," "The Hero who defended us in war, shall in peace be defended by us," and "He who protected the Widow and Orphan in 1813, will not be by them forsaken in 1840."[31]

The reference to 1813 reminded people that during the War of 1812, those living in central Ohio initially were fearful that the Native American tribes in the area might side with the British and attack their homes. However, on June 21, 1813, at a time when the war was not going well for the Americans, General Harrison met in a great council with fifty representatives of the Wyandot, Delaware, Shawnee, and Seneca nations to ask them either to move into settlements or agree to join him in his campaign if he needed them. When they agreed to support him, the threat of Indian attacks was lifted and the area became more attractive for settlement.[32]

But most women were simply passive audiences admiring their men, who exploited their availability as cheerleaders to their campaigning. The Whigs were smart to take advantage of the increased participation of women in religious services and temperance organizations. However, men did not expect women to do anything more than adorn the political scenery.

Columbus residents were proud that Harrison's triumphal campaign began at the corner of Broad and High. They believed that their little town had made an important contribution to national politics. City leaders were filled with a new sense of civic pride. The name of the city even was heard in one of the campaign songs people sang:

'Twas on Washington's birthday, the Whigs of the State,
In Columbus assembled—their number was great;
From the North, from the South, from the East and the West,
By ten thousands they came, at their country's behest.

They were freemen assembled their rights to maintain
And to rescue their land from corruption's foul stain,
To consult on the means their lov'd country to save
And to drive from high places base traitors and knaves.[33]

The Whig elation at victory was soon dampened when Harrison died of pneumonia on April 4, 1841. Columbus residents learned the sad news three days later. The *Ohio State Journal* issued a special one-column paper at 10 A.M. and copied a *Baltimore Sun* printing of the announcement by the cabinet members, who released the news in the absence from Washington of the vice president. They reported that "his death was calm and resigned." They added a somewhat partisan observation: "The last utterance of his lips expressed a fervent desire for the perpetuity of the Constitution, and the preservation of its true principles. In death, as in life, the happiness of his country was uppermost in his thoughts."[34]

Whether Harrison would have been an effective political leader had he lived is problematic. Edwin M. Stanton was with him on a boat in Steubenville before his inauguration and wrote Benjamin Tappan on March 7 to confide that even Harrison's close supporters' conduct made it clear that they considered him "an imbecile."[35] Before Harrison died, the English visitor James Buckingham summarized his evaluation of the newly elected president by observing, "It is therefore to the absence of all prominent objections, rather than to the presence of any great qualities, that the General will owe his success; his virtues will be negative, not positive . . . a political nonentity."[36]

Harrison's successor, Vice President John Tyler, failed to carry out the Whig Party's policies. He vetoed the Fiscal Bank Bill, which would have established a new government bank. Rutherford Hayes was no longer elated. In Columbus on August 25, at the start of his senior year in college, Hayes confided to his diary, "The grogshop politicians of this goodly city have been in constant ferment for a few weeks past because of the veto of the Bank Bill by President Tyler. The Van Buren men who opposed him so strenuously last fall, now laud him to the skies for his integrity and firmness in disregarding his party relations for the sake of the Constitution."[37]

Not all Whigs were disenchanted with Tyler. A meeting of his followers was held in Columbus on September 5, 1841.[38] There were government jobs to be had, and even as early as February 1841 John Reeves observed to John McLean, associate justice of the Supreme Court, that the parade of office-seekers passing through Columbus to Washington was worse than when Jackson was elected. But most traditional Whigs felt left out when John G. Miller was named Columbus postmaster and given control of federal patronage in the state.[39]

By this time, Columbus residents were focusing on local politics. Construction of the new capitol building was in jeopardy in 1840. The city faced the loss of its status as the state capital. Ill feeling developed between some legislators and Columbus residents who were accused of meddling too much in legislative affairs. The climax came on February 13, 1840, when sixty-three residents, described in the 1843 business directory as "principally young men," signed a statement supporting William B. Lloyd, a representative from Cuyahoga County who was under investigation for altering dollar figures in his loans. Lloyd was found guilty, but a motion for his expulsion from the House of Representatives failed to get the required two-thirds vote. The young men's petition complimented Lloyd, stated that it was "impossible [he] should be guilty," and assured him of their "undiminished confidence in the integrity of [his] character."[40] When their names were published in the *Ohio State Journal*, many politicians who were not Columbus residents took offense.

One of the stories that circulated blamed the anti-Columbus feelings on the wife of George H. Flood, a Licking County legislator. She was a beautiful Southerner who charmed lawmakers at parties and receptions and had the reputation of being persuasive. One night after the Floods attended a play at the theater, Mrs. Flood gave birth in their carriage on the way home. The couple tried to keep the matter quiet, but because of the attending physician's conversations, Columbus women heard about it and ostracized her. When she learned about the 1840 deadline and the Lloyd case, Mrs. Flood instructed her husband to introduce the measure to repeal the bill permitting construction of the capitol building.[41]

Whether or not the story is true, some legislators agitated to get the capital transferred. Many in the city were worried. As early as 1837, the editor of the *Ohio State Journal and Columbus Gazette* expressed concern about talk of moving the capital: "The matter is of high importance to our city."[42] Politicians and others outside Columbus were critical of residents for their "metropolitan airs." They also thought that the city was too unhealthy and too far from the geographical center of the state. Newark, Delaware, and Mount Vernon were mentioned as possible new sites.[43]

Lobbyists filled the floor and gallery of the State House when the issue was being discussed. Seabury Ford, who was to become Ohio's last Whig governor, sat at his desk and wrote to Peter Hitchcock on February 20, 1840, while the debate swirled around him. Ford was appalled at what he considered the absurdities and corruption displayed by the majority.[44]

Rep. Flood, chair of a joint select committee, presented arguments on March 13 for a resolution instructing the governor to issue a proclamation allowing all portions of the state to have the opportunity "of offering such inducements as they may deem proper for [the capital's] permanent location." He asserted that removal would not hurt Columbus's prosperity. A March 1840 law repealed the act authorizing construction of the capitol building.[45]

Columbus residents were dismayed. The stability of their growing town was threatened. If the legislature moved away, the economy would be shattered. Merchants, lawyers, and hotel keepers saw their profits disappearing. City political leaders worried about their future influence. The state printer feared that his contract would end. Those who were adept at lobbying would certainly leave. Others saw the city doomed to become as small as Zanesville. An atmosphere of uncertainty hung over Broad and High. Some people thought Columbus would be looked upon as inferior if it lost its status as the state capital. And what would become of the public square? The controversy continued into 1843, when the issue was referred to a committee. A majority report was opposed to removal of the capital, while a minority report favored it. The Senate voted to ask the governor to call for proposals to move the government elsewhere, but the House of Representatives defeated the measure. Some Columbus residents were relieved and thought that their struggle to keep the seat of state government was won, but the question continued to be unsettled until 1846.[46]

Although the issue of the permanent capital simmered after 1843, sentiment throughout the state increased in favor of completing the construction of a new capitol building. Some legislators, however, thought that residents of Columbus and Franklin County should pay for part of its construction. Others in the House of Representatives used the debate to propose that the capitol building be constructed in Pickaway County. Still others opposed the plan because of its cost and because convict labor was to be used to construct the building. Andrew Barkin voiced his objection to his representative, Ezekiel Brown: "I have no doubt there will be an effort made by the Whigs of Columbus to have their friends in the legislature to pass a law to build a new State House. I think it would be bad policy to tase [tax] the people say three million of dollars to gratify the Nabobs of Columbus for I think the present house will answer for several years."[47]

Both houses debated the question during January and February. The bill finally passed the Senate February 17, 1846, by a vote of 17 to 16. When the legislature agreed on February 21 to make Columbus the permanent capital and authorized resumption of construction of the new capitol building, the city's citizens were delighted that the issue was finally resolved. Columbus's status and economy were salvaged. In 1851, the delegates to the Constitutional Convention added a section to Article XV that stipulated, "Columbus shall be the seat of government until otherwise directed by law."[48]

Little work on the building was done for two years. A railroad track was laid from the stone quarries to the public square. The walls of the building were fourteen feet high by 1849, and thirty feet high by the end of the next year. But the building wasn't completed until 1859. Many persons were critical of the "rickety" wooden fence that enclosed the public square to prevent the convicts working on the project from escaping.[49]

Because politics was of major interest, political clubs had frequent meetings and many parades were associated with political themes. Electoral campaigns served to focus on issues of concern in the city and resulted in a stronger bonding among residents, even though only white males were eligible to vote. Independence Day continued to be a popular holiday. Its celebration reminded old and young of their country's revolutionary founding. Two companies of light artillery, filled with recent German immigrants, usually held a parade as part of the Fourth of July festivities.[50]

The main disagreement between the two political parties at this time centered on banking issues and on the question of how much government regulation should be allowed. The Democrats wanted to reform the banks, while the Whigs defended them. Thomas Ewing, who had been elected a U.S. senator in 1830 and was appointed secretary of the treasury by President Harrison, was a tireless advocate of a national bank in order to improve the economy.[51] Clark Guernsey, who was visiting Columbus, attended a session of the legislature. He wrote in his journal, "There were several profound legislators upon the floor and their exertions proved the anxiety which they felt for the prosperity of their constituents." James Buckingham, the English visitor, recorded a more negative impression in 1840. He wrote, "The members are described as coarse in their manners, and violent in their tempers." He thought that the legislature's reputation was marred by its "many disorderly scenes" and heard that its nickname in town was "The Beer Garden."[52]

The Democrats gained majorities in both houses of the General Assembly in the October 1841 elections. Several banks applied for new charters that year, but little was accomplished in solving the economic problems. In 1842, the focus shifted to redistricting congressional districts because of the 1840 census and a requirement passed by Congress. In a special session that summer the Democrats proposed a redistricting that the Whigs called a gerrymander. In order to prevent its passage, Whigs in both houses resigned to prevent a quorum. That action led to more political bickering.[53]

Visits by national elected officials also served to remind residents of the importance of politics. Former president Martin Van Buren arrived for a visit on June 6, 1842. He was met fourteen miles west of town by citizens on horseback and in carriages. He attended a reception in Franklinton, then a military escort accompanied him to Broad Street, which was filled with "a dense mass of human beings." Someone estimated the crowd at ten thousand people. The procession moved down High Street to the State House, where Van Buren gave a speech. After meetings with political leaders he went to a reception for ladies at the Medary residence attended, it was claimed, by some five hundred women. A band of recent German immigrants played; there were fireworks and a bonfire.[54]

Most of the population was caught up in political campaigning again in the fall of 1842. Edwin Stanton reported to Benjamin Tappan on July 17, 1842: "The prospects for Ohio for the next election are very cheering so far as my own observation has extended. . . . The democrats are full of hope and confidence. The whigs are divided and dismayed."[55] Whigs and Democrats were equally divided in Ohio, although in Columbus the Whigs had a slight majority. The focus of the election was on economic issues. Because the Whigs were in disarray during the Tyler administration, and because the abolitionists in the newly created Liberty Party were able to garner some 4,500 votes, the Democrat candidate, Wilson Shannon, defeated Gov. Thomas Corwin by a slim margin. Both sides accused the other of electoral fraud. The Democrats accused the Whigs of "pipe-laying," that is, bringing illegal voters to the polls.[56]

Political and economic issues continued to be hotly debated in the General Assembly when it convened in December 1842. Edwin Stanton kept his friend Benjamin Tappan well informed. On December 27 Stanton described what he called "a most glorious battle" over the bill to extend the charters of existing banks. He wrote, "Although the paper money men have a large majority in the house, and the lobbys have been thronged with bankers urging them on, yet by various means our men were able to keep off the bill, until yesterday."[57]

Of the seventeen contests between the two parties between 1832 and 1853, the Democrats won nine and the Whigs eight. Except for the race for governor in 1838, the Democrats always received less than 50 percent of the votes. The Whigs' largest majority was in 1840. In subsequent years they lost votes to the Liberty and Free Soil Parties, thus enabling the Democrats sometimes to win close elections. The Liberty Party benefited from the participation of Salmon P. Chase, who was involved in its organization. Chase, a Cincinnati lawyer with strong antislavery views, wrote the call for a state convention in Columbus to begin December 29, 1841. The convention was well attended and laid the groundwork for Chase's later political victories. The *Ohio State Journal* on December 31, 1841, reported that seventy delegates attended the two-day meeting and that "members were divided upon the question of a political organization" but "the political abolitionists carried the point." The article ended with the statement, "Medary chuckles over the measures with much satisfaction, under the impression, doubtless, that Loco Focoism [referring to the Democratic Party] is to be advanced by a separate political organization on the part of the abolitionists. The expectation is natural enough, but we trust will prove delusive."[58]

The solution to the banking crisis that had bitterly divided the two political parties probably was the most important boon to the economy after 1845. Democrats were suspicious of banks and their reputation for profitability, so when they controlled the legislature they rejected requests from banks for rechartering. They knew that the majority of bank directors were affluent Federalists, not Democrats. One exception was the Clinton Bank in Columbus, with seven Democrats and six Whigs as directors.[59]

In 1843 Democrat Bela Latham, who also was a director of the Clinton Bank, submitted a bill placing more restrictions on banks. The Whigs were able to profit from the general discontent that resulted from the failure of the Democrats to solve the currency problem. They made "banks or no banks" the main issue in the 1844 election campaign, and they were returned to power in Ohio.[60] Their campaigning was almost as vigorous as it was in 1840. Their broadsides called on Whigs "once more to buckle on your armor, and go into the thick of the fight. The battle is now for the great national measures and principles of your Fathers—and if decided against you will bring ruin to our beloved country."[61] Joel Buttles tried to be objective, but he was always a loyal Whig. On September 23, 1844, he recorded in his diary, "There was a great Locofoco [Democrat] meeting here. Gov. Cass and others to make addresses. A great procession of wagons and banners—a torch light procession in the evening and a great noise during the whole day & evening. But it all seemed forced. There was not that apparent alacrity that was exhibited at the Whig meeting nor was there that respectable appearance in the crowd that there was then."[62]

Alfred Kelley was one of the Whigs elected in 1844 to the Ohio Senate. He proposed a sweeping banking bill that the Democrats attacked and tried to weaken. Levi Cox, a Whig, wrote to his associate, John Sloane, on January 25, 1845: "The locos have offered all their amendments and we have some of Governor Bartley's best licks. He is very able on banking. . . . If we can pass the bill as it is I think it will do pretty well and can be put in operation. Kelley is more pliable and compromising on nearly all questions than I could have expected and our trouble and delay has not been occasioned by him." Kelley's banking bill was passed that month. It established a state bank with branches and with provision for independent banks. The Whigs were able to claim a victory for economic progress. The bank law resulted in an increase in capital at a time when it was needed for an expanding economy. According to James R. Sharp, it "provided the foundation for Ohio banking throughout the next twenty years." At the time, however, many of the Democrats in Columbus were opposed to Kelley's plan. Vigorous protests were lodged in the legislature. An *Ohio Statesman* editorial warned, "The wit and ingenuity of man, has been drawn upon, to cover up, in the most clandestine manner, provisions for selfish and villainous purposes."[63]

Columbus had two branches of the newly established State Bank of Ohio: the City Bank and the Franklin Bank. The City Bank was established in Columbus in 1845 with Joel Buttles as president. It was housed in the same rooms as the Columbus Insurance Company, a convenient arrangement because both shared the same stockholders and directors. Columbus Insurance had $200,000 of its capital in Ohio bonds. The City Bank took over the business of the Mechanics Saving Institute, which had been a bank of deposit. Samuel Parsons was president of the Franklin Bank, in which Gustavus Swan had an interest.[64]

Prosperity returned to Columbus in 1846, and the economy continued to improve throughout the rest of the decade. Farming became especially profitable, and speculation increased. Columbus became more attractive as a place in which to succeed. The conservative leaders in the city attributed the prosperity partly to the well-managed banks. The enterprising Gustavus Swan was examiner of state banks in William Bebb's administration.

Because of the increased population, the city council in 1846 divided Columbus into five wards with three councilmen from each ward. The First Ward comprised the area north of Gay Street. The second, the most affluent area, covered the blocks between Gay and State. The third was between State and Rich. The Fourth Ward included the people between Rich and Mound, while the fifth covered all the area south of Mound. Most of the German-speaking migrants were in the Fifth Ward. Blacks lived in all five wards, although about one-third of them were in the First Ward.[65]

The Whigs revised the state's tax system in 1846. Alfred Kelley, who favored taxing property in order to increase state income, led his party in proposing reforms. He proposed a resolution "to adopt a system of taxation that will impose upon all the property of the State, both real and personal, except as shall be expressly exempted by law, according to its true value, an equal per centum of taxation." A bill passed both houses by March 2, 1846. Its main provision was "that all property, whether real or personal, within the State, and the moneys and credits of persons residing therein, except such as is hereinafter expressly exempted, shall be subject to taxation." The exemptions were "public property, burial places, property used for public worship, State stocks, household and kitchen furniture to the amount of two hundred dollars, wearing apparel excluding watches, food provided for the family, and farming and mechanical implements and tools in actual use." [66]

The tax assessor sent residents a one-page form on which they were to list the amount of their personal property, currency, and credits. The form contained spaces for the number and value of horses and cattle over two years old on the first of June 1846, sheep and hogs over six months old, pleasure carriages, gold or silver watches, pianofortes, personal property, and property pertaining to mercantile business and manufacturing.

The most vocal citizens expressed considerable resentment. Throughout the spring, the columns of the *Ohio Statesman* were filled with articles and editorials objecting to the tax and castigating Kelley for creating a plan to hurt the poor and help the rich. Angry articles contained complaints that farmers' pigs were taxed but not bank stock. An editorial on March 2 predicted that the legislative session would be long remembered "for the ultra character of its proceedings, and the strong aristocratic tendency of its acts." The tax law was condemned for not allowing the poorest "to escape imposition" and for exempting "the artificial property of a privileged class from bearing its fair proportion of the public burthens." The *Ohio Eagle* complained, "The coon legislature . . . passed one of the most unjust and unequal laws for the regulation of taxes, that was ever passed in any country." Although many criticized the taxes there was little effective concerted effort to repeal them. [67]

Although in 1844 the Whigs won control of the legislature in Ohio and elected Mordecai Bartley governor, Democrat candidate James K. Polk defeated Henry Clay and James G. Birney for the U.S. presidency, much to the disappointment of many in Columbus. Joseph Sullivant, an important community leader and the youngest son of Lucas Sullivant, was probably the most disappointed. In October he had published a pamphlet, *To The Liberty Party in Ohio,* pleading with the party's members not to throw away their votes on Birney because that would help elect Polk, who was in favor of immediate annexation of Texas. Sullivant began his plea by boasting that he was probably the first person in Columbus openly to advocate antislavery. He wrote that even though he supported the American Anti-Slavery Society and was related to Birney through marriage, he believed that the election of Polk would strengthen slavery's political power. Confusing the Constitution with the Northwest Ordinance, he wrote that he was convinced that the founders of the Constitution intended slavery to be confined to where it then existed; otherwise, they would not have approved its prohibition north of the Ohio River. Sullivant concluded by asking his readers to be practical. If they voted for Birney, he assured them,

Samuel Galloway. From Lee, *History of the City of Columbus,* vol. 1.

they would be aiding in sustaining principles and measures "repugnant to all your feelings."[68]

Because many Whigs were concerned about the political implications of migration, efforts were made to deny the vote to transients. A law was passed in 1845 requiring voter registration at least one month prior to elections. People in Columbus criticized the legislature for enacting it. The Whigs were accused of trying to restrict voting by transients and recent immigrants who were unfamiliar with electoral details. The *Ohio Statesman* printed an article condemning the "registry abuse." Calling it a British scheme to restrict the right of suffrage, the article complained that many busy workers, most of whom were Democrats, would forget to register and that the registry law would lend itself to fraud.[69] The Whigs continued to hold the governorship in the 1846 election. That year, William Bebb was elected in a close race over David Tod, the Democratic candidate, and Samuel Lewis, the Liberty Party candidate. The Whigs had a majority of eight in the House of Representatives, and both parties were tied in the Senate.

Samuel Galloway was one of the active members of the Whig Party at that time, having come to Columbus in 1844 as secretary of state. He was born in Gettysburg, Pennsylvania, in 1811, but his family moved to Ohio after his father died. After studying law, Galloway was admitted to the bar in 1842 and elected to the legislature in 1843. He was opposed to slavery and frequently gave temperance speeches. In addition to serving as secretary of state he was superintendent of schools and contributed to the improvement of education.[70]

The two parties were so evenly divided that a third party, particularly one organized on the emotional issue of slavery, could threaten to upset the balance. Several of the races for governor were decided by fewer than two thousand votes. There were also rivalries and disputes within the Whig and Democratic Parties. Some Democrats were more opposed to banks than others, for instance. Ohio Whigs became disenchanted with the expansionism of their southern party members. Columbus residents could easily follow the shifting political winds thanks to their newspapers. In 1844 the Democratic state convention criticized its opponents for pushing power into the control of the upper class. One member wrote, "The Whigs have changed the entire policy of the state from one based upon the equal rights of the people, to one based upon property and money." Samuel Medary was especially critical of Whiggery. Articles in the *Ohio Statesman* in 1845 claimed that another Whig victory would increase social and economic inequalities and intensify the differences between classes. Democrats saw the political struggle as a fight between monopoly and equality.[71]

Although economic issues were the main ones dividing the political parties, there were other reasons why some men supported the Democrats and others became Whigs. Stephen C. Fox has studied voting records in Ohio and has concluded that most of those who had migrated from New England supported the Whigs, while those from the Middle Atlantic and Southern states voted for Democrats. In addition, many independent farmers and those from evangelical churches were Whig supporters. German and Irish immigrants flocked to the Democratic Party, much to the irritation of Columbus businessmen.[72] Joel Buttles, who preferred Whig policies, often condemned the Germans for their political views. On October 14, 1842, after that year's election day, he wrote in his diary that naturalized foreigners had an unfortunate influence on elections because almost all of them voted Democratic: "In doing this [they] indulge the exercise of that prejudice against royalty and nobility which they imbibed in Europe with this only difference. Here they have no nobility, and, therefore, finding the better class of people all on one side, they oppose them and that party. The association may be a natural one for them to make but it certainly is not just, for the clan to which they attach themselves is the party which if ever a despotic form of government is established here will be the party that will support such government."[73]

Buttles did not attend the inaugural ball, which was held in Wilson Shannon's honor on December 14, 1842, following elaborate suppers served at the Franklin House and the City House. The next night, the Whigs held a supper and dance at the Neil House in Thomas Corwin's honor. Corwin was famous for his oratory and great learning, as well as for his large forehead, thick eyebrows, and expressive eyes. On this evening he delivered an hour-and-a-half-long speech that may have made the occasion even more solemn.[74]

The Democrats celebrated on January 8 every year to mark the anniversary of the Battle of New Orleans, Andrew Jackson's victory at the end of the War of 1812. Because the date fell on a Sunday in 1843, the occasion was celebrated on Monday instead. The morning was marked with the roar of artillery. There were drills and parades, especially by the German military companies in town. Since it was a mild and sunny day, large crowds turned out to watch the festivities. That night there was a Democratic dinner at the American Hotel chaired by Samuel Medary. Many resolutions were offered; many toasts were drunk.[75]

Planning for the next Democratic anniversary began early. Characteristic of the intensity of the partisan feelings at the time was Medary's editorial on December 27, 1843, praising the annual Democratic political event. Medary ended by asserting, "Federalism must be beaten anyhow—the monstrous doctrines of that monarchical party must be met and overcome." Medary's notion that anyone still favored a monarchy almost seventy years after the revolution revealed how partisan he was. The Whigs resented being tied to the discredited Federalists. On December 16, 1843, Joseph Vance wrote to a friend expressing his desire that the Whigs not postpone their traditional February meeting until May: "I hope then our friends will stick to the good old birthday of Washington as their political Sabath [sic]."[76] These patriotic celebrations and other public events served to remind residents who attended them that there was more to their history than the founding of their town.

6

Beginnings of
Culture

Economic and political issues were primary concerns for many Columbus residents, but they also directed attention to other subjects. Social customs were established, organizations were formed, and special events became part of the changing city's collective memory. The State Library was created by a legislative resolution in 1817, and in 1824 the legislature set the state librarian's salary at $200 a year and appropriated $350 for books. It incorporated a Historical Society of Ohio in 1822, and the shareholders met in December and in January 1823 to elect officers.

In May 1821, the apprentices in Columbus, mostly boys and young men, formed a society in order to establish a library for their benefit. They contributed all of their own books and sought gifts of books from others in town. In their appeal they wrote, "It is hoped that the public spirited citizens of Columbus, will not let this opportunity, to confer a lasting benefit on an important class of the rising generation, pass unheeded." The editor of the *Columbus Gazette* described the apprentices as "ardently engaged in the pursuit of knowledge."[1]

This library was an early example of some young people's desire to improve their economic status through self-education. The first American library for apprentices was founded by a Boston merchant, William Wood, in 1820. Its Columbus counterpart was one of the first to follow it and was different in that it was controlled by the apprentices from the start. Those in Boston didn't win the right to operate the library themselves until 1828. Boys in working families frequently learned skills or crafts by becoming apprentices. By their early twenties they were skilled enough to become journeymen or day laborers. The Capital Library Society, another subscription library, was incorporated in 1831 and met quarterly.[2]

Part of the heritage Americans shared in the early nineteenth century was an interest in efforts by European nationalists to gain their own liberty. Columbus residents were aware of the struggle of Greeks for independence. A meeting was held on January 9, 1824, to express sympathy and adopt measures to aid them. At a meeting on January 27, "crowded with the ladies and gentlemen of the town," speeches were given on Greek history and the population's current miseries. Five hundred dollars had already been collected. Later that summer, a local newspaper carried news about the death of Byron and details about the provincial government of Greece.[3]

The Franklin County seat was moved from Franklinton to Columbus in 1824. Gov. De Witt Clinton of New York was one of the growing number of political leaders who visited Columbus in the 1820s. On his tour to inspect sites for the planned canal in Ohio, he attended ceremonies in the town on July 6, 1825, at which both he and Gov. Jeremiah Morrow spoke to a large audience of men and women.[4] Henry Clay arrived July 22, 1830, for a public dinner attended by four hundred residents. He spoke without notes for two hours, and many toasts followed. Daniel Webster visited June 15, 1833, for three days but declined Lyne Starling's invitation to a dinner.[5]

Other famous visitors included Charles Dickens and John Quincy Adams. The thirty-year-old Dickens described New York as "by no means so clean a city as Boston. . . . Take care of the pigs. . . . They are the city scavengers."[6] He was not much kinder in his remarks after he visited Columbus in 1842. Dickens, his wife, Catherine, her maid, and his secretary, George Washington Putnam, arrived at seven in the morning on April 21, after a twenty-three-hour ride from Cincinnati. They slept until dinner and held a half-hour "levee" that night, where Dickens was greeted by many eager admirers, the men "with a lady on each arm." The next morning he hired a stagecoach for his party and left for Upper Sandusky with a hotel basket of food for the trip. He later criticized Columbus residents' conduct and dress in his letters, but at least he didn't call them "boring," as he did Cincinnatians. He described Columbus as "clean and pretty" and praised the Neil House, where he stayed. He was impressed with "the polished wood of the black walnut" and the spacious hotel's "handsome portico and stone verandah." The hotel was built at a cost of $100,000. One of the hotel customs was the ringing of a bell at mealtimes, which were 6 A.M. for breakfast, noon for dinner, and 6 P.M. for supper. Few residents of the city could afford to stay there, of course.[7]

Former president John Quincy Adams visited Columbus on his tour through Ohio on Saturday, November 4, 1843. He traveled on the canal and in a stagecoach from Akron in a snowstorm. He arrived at four o'clock in the afternoon and stayed at Neil's Hotel. Crowds had already gathered to greet him. There was a public reception at the First Presbyterian Church at eight that evening. The mayor welcomed Adams, who gave his usual response and shook hands with most of the audience. People were told he was hoarse and had a sore throat, but he attended two church services on Sunday and received visitors until late at night.[8]

Early on Monday morning, "just after daylight," according to Adams's diary, David Jenkins, a black community leader, visited him. Since 1836, as a congressman in the House of Representatives, Adams had fought the gag rule prohibiting the reception of petitions about slavery. Efforts to censure him failed in February 1842, but the gag rule remained in force until 1844. Adams recorded that the meeting was "the only time, he said, when he [Jenkins] could expect to obtain access to me, to return the thanks of the colored people of this city for my exertions in defence of their rights." Adams remembered having had correspondence with Jenkins. Adams expected to leave for Cincinnati at eight A.M. but couldn't reject the offer of the two German military companies to escort him across the river. In the hour's delay, many more residents, including Gov. Wilson Shannon, filled the hotel lobby to see him. William Neil accompanied him across the river behind "the German companies, with a band of martial music."[9] Adams's brief visit dramatized how knowledgeable both races in Columbus were about the bitterly fought petition issue in the halls of Congress. The issue served to draw attention to the evils of slavery and probably was more influential than abolitionists in changing people's attitudes in places such as Columbus at that time.

Migration continued despite economic problems, and the population of Columbus increased to more than 2,400 people by 1830, 216 of whom were black. Two years later, the mayor took a census and counted 2,721 whites and 252 blacks.[10] Two of the recent German immigrants improved the town's reputation for fine beer. Louis Hoster began the City Brewery in 1836. Hoster had intended to settle elsewhere but was so impressed by the Fourth of July celebration in 1833 that he returned permanently the following year. Hoster became active in civic affairs and served on the city council for eight years beginning in 1846. Conrad Born arrived from Bavaria in 1835. He operated a meat stall at the market house for sixteen years and later became a brewer. Dr. Otto Zirckle started treating patients in the 1830s. Philip Schoedinger arrived in 1829. He was a cabinetmaker who later made caskets and became an undertaker in 1855.[11]

On July 4, 1839, the cornerstone was laid for the new capitol by former governor Jeremiah Morrow, who also spoke to a vast assembly. Postmaster John G. Miller gave an eloquent oration, and a procession of five thousand, including three military companies from Lancaster, marched into the square to witness the event while the bands played "Hail, Columbia." William Davis Gallagher wrote a poem for the occasion. The cornerstone contained historical documents and records and 150 newspapers from American cities. The design for the classical building was a combination by Henry Walters of the proposals submitted in a competition.[12]

Patriotic toasts were made at many parties that night. James Kilbourne preserved a copy of all the toasts at the celebration he attended. No. 11 was a toast to the cornerstone of the capitol: "Emblematic of the great State of whose civic temple it is destined to be the support and ornament;— Gigantic in its magnitude, impregnable in its strength, and enduring in its integrity." [13]

Other social organizations in town provided the beginnings of culture for the area and gave new arrivals some awareness and understanding of the past. Columbus residents appeared to be as eager as their eastern neighbors to form clubs and associations. A botanic society formed as early as 1830. The Historical and Philosophical Society of Ohio was chartered in 1831 and Benjamin Tappan elected the first president. The charter members from Columbus were Gustavus Swan, John M. Edmiston, Alfred Kelley, Dr. Benjamin Platt, and Joseph Sullivant, who was the society's corresponding secretary for many years. Timothy Walker, who spoke at the society's 1837 meeting, described its primary purpose: "to collect and preserve the scattered and decaying materials of our history." He gave an optimistic picture of the city's economy: "We see some very rich, and some very poor, but all commanding the necessaries of life, and looking forward to its luxuries—the levelling disposition will work upward, instead of downward." [14]

The society issued its first pamphlet, a 131-page journal, in 1838. A second volume was published the next year. Salmon P. Chase gave the society's annual lecture in December 1839. The society was transferred to Cincinnati, where a larger population could support it, in February 1849. Other Columbus residents joined the Logan Historical Society, which sponsored the publication of the *American Pioneer* in 1842. The society's purpose was "to collect and preserve for the use of posterity, all that can be collected of early or incidental history, of the early settlement and successive improvements of the Western country." [15]

Not all cultural organizations were for white residents. In 1843, a literary society for black residents had twenty-five members. The Columbus Typographical Society was founded in 1831 "to advance the interests of journeyman printers" and "to afford relief to deserving indigent members, their widows and orphans, and to preserve the honor of the profession, by the adoption of such measures as shall to them appear necessary for the encouragement of industry, sobriety, good order and morality among its members." It was one of the first organized efforts by a society to provide financial support to its poorer members. After twenty-five years the typographical society became a union. A lodge of the Independent Order of Odd Fellows was in existence as early as 1840, and two more were created in 1843. Four masonic lodges met in the city. St. Mark's, the masonic lodge for blacks, was especially active when it was organized in 1851. There also were Bible and tract societies in town. [16]

The most publicized scientific accomplishment in this period was the construction of a large planetarium by James Russell, a Worthington resident. Russell had migrated in 1808 from New England, where he worked as a carpenter and cabinetmaker. He exhibited the planetarium in the Columbus council chambers on State Street for a week in 1836. It had taken him twenty years to make, and according to the *Ohio Statesman,* it gave "a splendid view of the solar system." At the time it was called an "Orrery" after an English earl who first sponsored a mechanical solar system model. The planets were opaque glass globes. The machine contained five hundred cogwheels and weighed one and a half tons. Russell took it east, where it was displayed at the American Institute in New York. Nathaniel M. Miller, editor of the *Old School Republican and Ohio State Gazette,* probably was exaggerating when he claimed that the planetarium was "the most astonishing achievement of mechanical art and astronomical science the world ever beheld." Hyperbole was characteristic of many nineteenth-century writers.[17]

Many of Russell's neighbors petitioned Congress in 1845 for funds to permit him to build a planetarium in Washington. On February 12, 1847, the General Assembly passed a resolution urging the Smithsonian Institution in Washington, D.C., to employ Russell to build a planetarium. When Russell ran for mayor in 1845 the *Ohio Statesman* declared, "Mr. Russell stands by the side of a Franklin and a Rittenhouse in mechanical skill, and he is one whose private worth is equal to his reputation as a man of science."[18]

Scientific lectures were given on Monday evenings in Mechanics Hall, which had been built by the Mechanics Beneficial Society at the southeast corner of Rich and High Streets in 1841. The building also held a small scientific library. The society gave aid to sick members, and some members practiced debating every two weeks. Other lectures in science were given in August 1843 and January 1844. Interest in astronomy increased when a bright comet appeared in the sky on March 8, 1843. It was visible during the day later that month, and its appearance created nationwide controversy. Joel Buttles watched it on the night of March 22. He wrote, "The comet . . . excites as much curiosity as ever. It appears most brilliant about an hour after sunset." On February 24, 1844, the Ohio Senate approved a resolution permitting Samuel Medary, William Chapin, Dr. Ichabod G. Jones, and their associates to erect a large reflecting telescope on the north side of the public square. Subscribers and their families had another reason to stroll to the center of town at night.[19]

There was strong public interest in self-improvement, partly because of changes occurring in the workplace. Clerks, for instance, were not as important on the economic ladder as they had been, thanks to changes in commercial activities. Fewer of the young men starting out in shops and stores lived with their employers. They were off by themselves in boarding-houses or hotels. These young men were concerned with improving their skills, getting ahead, and becoming more influential in the city. They felt the need to join more organizations and learn more than they knew. Columbus residents reflected the general trend to form voluntary associations for mutual benefit. The Mechanics Beneficial Society of Columbus was incorporated in 1831. It was formed not only to serve the interests of artisans and manufacturers but also to improve knowledge and to give financial aid to members. The Columbus Lyceum, a branch of the American Lyceum, was active as early as 1832. It was a discussion group that encouraged attendance by both men and women and met in the basement of the Presbyterian Church. One of its subjects that year was whether imprisonment for debt was "consistent with moral principles." A Columbus Literary and Scientific Institute was established in 1837 and planned a series of weekly lectures.[20]

Lectures were held regularly on a wide variety of topics. They were well attended by diverse audiences and provided people with the opportunity not only to gain information but also to meet and become better acquainted with their neighbors. In 1840 the Englishman James S. Buckingham gave three lectures on Egypt in the hall of the House of Representatives and was impressed that the crowds included many women, who attended despite the rain. Popular subjects included geography, religion, history, and science.[21]

The Western Lyceum sponsored a series of lectures during the 1840s. Its reading room over Brunson and McLane's dry goods store was open to visitors daily in December 1843. Newspapers from around the country were available, and there was a circulating library "at very low terms." The lyceum's series of sixteen public lectures that winter cost two dollars, and single lectures were twenty-five cents. Although the lyceum movement began in New England in 1826 to provide practical information for workers, it became very popular in Ohio. More than sixty lyceum organizations received charters in Ohio from 1831 to 1845. In terms of its interest in lyceums, Ohio enjoyed more cultural vitality than any other state. Sufficient numbers of Columbus residents had what Oliver Larkin called a thirst for self-improvement to support the lyceum events.[22]

The Franklin Lyceum was formed in December 1846 after a speech by Alfred Kelley. A long statement describing its purpose was printed in the *Ohio Statesman* on January 9, 1847: "Looking round us, we see that the whole world is putting on new aspects." The prospectus mentioned new philosophies and religions, changes in governments, and westward expansion as challenging subjects for consideration. "What ingenious and noble mind, knowing these things . . . can fail to desire . . . to mingle in social harmony with other minds, giving and receiving new light, new thoughts, new hopes, new courage?" the statement asked. Plans were announced for public lectures and a library. A committee solicited donations of money and books. Membership cost two dollars a year.[23]

One of the arguments advanced to justify more lectures in town was that they helped the many young men who were recent arrivals to avoid becoming "corrupt, immoral, licentious, and wicked" citizens. In this way, the Franklin Lyceum was similar to Benjamin Franklin's "club of mutual improvement," which he called a Junto.[24] Monthly meetings of the lyceum were held beginning in February 1847. At the first meeting Joseph Sullivant spoke on geology. In March Alfred Kelley spoke on "Heat and its practical uses." The Franklin Lyceum's most popular public discussion in 1848 was on March 4, when the topic was, "Resolved, That the punishment of crime by death should be abolished." Although some support for the abolition of capital punishment existed in the city, it was insufficient to effect change. The following winter the Franklin Lyceum held free weekly lectures on Mondays that were open to the public because of the increased interest.

Public debates on political and economic subjects drew relatively large audiences. Even on Christmas Eve in 1841 there was a lecture on the currency and balance of trade at the Mechanics Beneficial Society building. According to William H. Venable, "talking politics" became an "exercise of the democratic art." People also were interested in economic issues such as banking and government debts. In 1844, Alfred Kelley and John Brough held a debate at the market house on the state's finances. Lectures by visiting speakers continued to be popular. Large audiences came out to hear talks on mesmerism and *Hamlet*. William H. McGuffey, the educator known for his *Eclectic Readers* for children, called the most widely read books in the United States, spoke several times on education. Lectures on geology were given in January 1845, and in the same month, Charles Whittlesey spoke on an agricultural survey and the formation of the State Board of Agriculture. There were programs on the magnetic telegraph and a display of its apparatus.[25]

Change and expansion, however, brought rifts in the community fabric. Neighbors moved away and were replaced by new strangers. Transient communities lacked close ties. Gaps between classes were widening. Despite city ordinances, rowdiness and lawlessness increased. In 1833, a perceptive visitor shared his criticisms with the town: "The better class of people appear to be much more attentive to business than to the cultivation of the social virtues. They are cautious of strangers, even those who come recommended, and seem too much engrossed with their private concerns." Although the visitor was impressed with the churches filled with well-dressed congregations, he found no decent schoolhouse. He wondered where the police were when "degraded," drunken customers poured out of the many taverns and grogshops. He was especially critical of the many boys who "scream and fire guns" late at night to the annoyance of sober citizens.[26] Other visitors made different criticisms. In 1835 Cyrus P. Bradley recorded, "This would be a cleanly place, were it not for the pigs."[27]

Despite its progress, Columbus was still considered by some to be "a crude, unshapely western town, with very little style about it."[28] However, some residents celebrated New Year's Eve in 1839 with a ball at the American Hotel at the northwest corner of High and State Streets. Evan Edmiston, a student at the college in Granville (which later became Denison University) who escorted Eli W. Gwynne's daughter, found the weather very cold. Others marked New Year's Day by attending the theater on High Street between Broad and Gay Streets, where Mr. Kent and Company, consisting of seven men and seven women, performed *Romeo and Juliet*. Residents marked the beginning of each year by visiting each others' homes. Young men collected candy given to them by their girlfriends.[29]

Migration increased dramatically in the 1840s. Ohio was in the middle of the westward movement in the years before the Civil War. As James S. Buckingham traveled from Zanesville to Columbus on Saturday, April 25, 1840, he passed some fifty wagons containing families with their furniture and provisions, the women and children perched on top and the men and boys walking alongside. He saw several houses advertising "Movers' Accommodations" and counted one hundred log cabins on the route. Kenneth Winkle has pointed out that westward migration brought many social and political problems, but it also supplied manpower—and woman power—to help solve those problems. Passenger arrivals in Columbus in the 1840s totaled more than 23,000; the population increased by more than 11,000. Most of the arrivals who didn't remain moved on to seek more promising prospects elsewhere. Even so, the city's population grew during the decade by an average of more than three persons a day.[30]

Some visitors who criticized Columbus commented especially about its muddy streets, but eastern cities had their mudholes, too. The capital of Ohio in 1840 was a restless, bustling, expanding city of more than 6,000 persons. That year the city contained 3,024 white men, 2,441 white women, 317 black men, and 256 black women. Blacks were 9.5 percent of the population. There were 667 white boys and 660 white girls under ten years old, and 66 black boys and 76 black girls under the same age. Some 944 families were living in the three wards of the city. The median family size was five, but 186 families consisted of eight or more members. Children and youth of both sexes made up 43 percent of the population. Almost one-quarter of the black population was ten years old or younger.

Forty-five percent of the whites in town were twenty years of age or younger. Twenty-six women, either widowed or divorced, were heads of single-parent families. Blacks lived in all three wards, but almost one-half of them were in the First Ward in the northern part of town. Forty-seven of them lived with white families as servants.[31]

Much of the population had arrived from the Middle Atlantic states. By 1850, 14 percent (2,918) had been born in Pennsylvania, New York, and New Jersey. Some 1,251 came from Pennsylvania alone. Those born in New England numbered 831, and 1,160 had been born in the South, 901 of them in Virginia. They arrived by canal, on the National Road, or overland after a trip down the Ohio River. Others came north from Kentucky and Virginia. By 1850, 9 percent had been born in Southern states, a smaller proportion than in the city's first decade. Five percent reported their origin as New England. German migrants had arrived from the beginning, but a big influx occurred in the 1840s. By 1850, approximately 20 percent of the population had been born in Germany. The blacks in Columbus, those who had not been born free in the North, had moved from the Southern states as freed or escaped slaves.[32]

One of the newcomers in 1840 was twenty-year-old Theodore Leonard, who was born in Canada and who had only fifty cents when he arrived. He worked in a brickyard, learned the skill, supervised the construction of many houses, and became one of the largest landowners in the area.[33] Others who settled that year were not as fortunate. "Rags to riches" was a popular dream for many enterprising persons who moved west in the years before the Civil War. Nationwide, only about 3 percent of those who became major leaders in business were born poor. The proportion in Columbus was probably similar.[34] Nevertheless, the new arrivals as well as earlier settlers reflected the spirit of the age in their interest in acquiring wealth, especially in commerce and in holding land. Speculation was a popular and profitable activity. Harriet Martineau commented on this attitude when she wrote, "The pride and delight of Americans is in their quantity of land."[35]

Although Columbus still displayed some characteristics of a frontier town, it was rapidly becoming an important political and economic force in the center of the state. It remained in the shadow of Cincinnati, which was favored by its location on the Ohio River and, with its forty-six thousand residents, was far more significant in the economy of the Midwest. Inasmuch as the entire population of the United States in 1840 was 17 million, the community of Columbus made little impression beyond its borders. Nevertheless, its earliest settlers actively sought to make it a livable place. Those who had lived in the city for some time had more influence economically and politically than the recent arrivals. There was an informal inner circle of leaders adept at influencing decisions and able to lobby the legislators who lived temporarily in their midst.

By 1840 the village of Franklinton, which was on land formerly occupied by Wyandot Indians, had a population of 394. Worthington, nine miles north of Columbus, had 440 residents and was the site of the Ohio Reformed Medical College, founded in 1830. The Worthington Female Seminary, the first school for girls west of the Alleghenies supported by the Methodist Church, was established in 1837 through the efforts of ministers Jacob Young, William Herr, and Uriah Heath.[36]

Although the first residents of Columbus had to fell many trees to build their community, by the mid-1840s it was fashionable to bring trees back to town as ornaments. Joel Buttles observed, "People are transplanting forest trees, mostly sugar maple, into streets in front of their houses to a considerable extent in town."[37] By 1845 a new generation was exercising leadership, the population was increasing more rapidly, and the city's limits were expanding in several directions.

Columbus residents enjoyed a number of taverns and coffeehouses. The Eagle Coffee House, on the west side of High opposite the State House, was a two-story brick building with an eagle painted over the entrance. It was considered the Whig headquarters and was frequented by Lyne Starling. It was popular with lawyers, served the choicest game, and had the finest wines and liquors, including old bourbon and Kentucky rye. The proprietor, John Young, was famous for his mint juleps. Eating, drinking, and gambling were popular pastimes there despite the city's ordinances against them. Faro and roulette were preferred by the gamblers, some of whom were senators and representatives who enjoyed "stag wine parties." Lida Rose McCabe recalled "prominent men and ablest statesmen, with white fixed faces bent over the green cloth." When Evan Edmiston visited he found "lots of gambling in town." The legislature finally responded to pressure from pious residents and passed a law in 1846 prohibiting persons from keeping a room or area for gambling. The penalty was a fine from fifty to five hundred dollars. The law was poorly enforced. Ten years later there still were plenty of gaming tables in town.[38]

The Tontine was a popular two-story building with a coffeehouse on the market square that was frequented by Democrats. Its name was later changed to the Tin Pan because it was the only place in town that served oysters in chafing dishes. Russell's Tavern at the northeast corner of High and Rich Streets was a favorite of many legislators. It had been the scene of frequent fights between canal workers and city residents, but by the 1840s such violence seemed to have decreased. Andrew Reed, who stopped there, praised his breakfast of "good coffee and eggs, and delightful bread." Other popular taverns were the Globe and the Franklin House, formerly called the City House. The first German Lutheran congregation was organized in one of the public rooms in Christian Heyl's Perry Inn in 1818.[39]

In addition to the usual beers, wines, and liquors, other popular drinks at that time included blackstrap, which consisted of gin and molasses, and calibogus, which was a combination of rum and spruce beer. Late in the evening some people preferred a nightcap, which was a glass of hot toddy or a gin sling. Those who could manage a second nightcap called it "a string to tie it with."[40]

By 1840 Columbus had nine hotels to accommodate legislators and travelers. There also were several boardinghouses. The Eagle Hotel, a favorite of Whig politicians, was on the east side of High between Town and Rich Streets, and the Red Lion Hotel was across the street from it. The Eagle for many years had the only public baths in town. According to one account, water was pumped by a black bear chained to a treadmill. Nearby were the American House and the original Neil House, which was constructed in 1839. The Buckeye House was on Broad Street near the Episcopal church. It was enlarged in 1840. The pious Methodist circuit rider Uriah Heath, who preached in Worthington in 1838–39 and in Columbus 1852–54, once stayed there. According to his journal, "Here we saw sin all around us though the land lord treated us with kindness." Guests could not always count on being given single rooms. Even Salmon P. Chase had to share a room with a stranger when he registered at the American Hotel in February 1848.[41]

People knew that life in Columbus was improving when the city council on July 12, 1841, approved the digging of eight public cisterns at corners in the heart of town. The engineer and inventor Thomas W. H. Moseley, who had earlier patented an improved hydrostatic pump, devised a window sash lock in Columbus in 1841, allowing residents to sleep more peacefully.[42]

One person whose arrival in Columbus attracted little notice was Rutherford B. Hayes, a recent graduate of Kenyon College. He came on October 17, 1842, and spent the next ten months reading law in the office of Sparrow and Matthews before entering Harvard Law School the following August. During his time in Columbus Hayes rose at seven and spent six hours a day reading Blackstone, two hours reading Chillingworth, and two hours studying German. He retired by ten, read no newspapers, and took little interest in the life of the city. On November 26, however, he neglected Chillingworth "for the ladies."[43] Hayes had been in the city before when he spent summer holidays with his sister, Fanny, who had married William A. Platt in 1839. Platt's father had been a silversmith and opened the first jewelry store in 1815. He worked at the Ohio Tool Company and was president of the Green Lawn Association and the Columbus Gas Company. He died in 1882.[11]

An exciting event occurred on the Fourth of July in 1842 when the first balloon ascension in Columbus took place. In Europe, the first balloon flight was in 1783 in France. The first in this country was in Philadelphia on January 9, 1793, almost fifty years before this type of technological development arrived in the heart of Ohio and eight years after the first balloon flight from Cincinnati. Sleepers were awakened in Columbus at 3 A.M. by twenty-six rounds of cannon fire. People from the countryside flocked in, and by early morning the streets were crowded. Various volunteer military groups played fife and drum music. At midafternoon people rushed through the gates around the public square to gape at the inflating balloon. Others looked on from windows and the tops of buildings. As the crowd roared, the balloon rose gracefully and floated eastward. People were able to watch it for half an hour until it disappeared. It landed five miles east of Newark.[45]

In 1843 an ordinance was passed providing for the paving of Gay Street between Front and Third. A new street was opened from the intersection of Broad and Water to the front of the penitentiary. A bathing establishment opened in the summer of 1843 on Rich Street. It admitted women in the morning and men in the afternoon and offered warm, cold, shower, or medicated vapor baths.[46] It was thought at the time that bathing was a good remedy for influenza, which was prevalent. Increased interest in bathing was a reflection of a greater concern for cleanliness among the middle class. Those who couldn't afford the public baths could always visit the Scioto River. The day after he arrived in Columbus in 1843, Anson W. Buttles recorded in his diary, "Went down to the river and washed myself."[47]

A parade by the fire engine companies, the two German companies of artillery, and the Odd Fellows Society marked the Independence Day celebration in 1843. The German bands played lustily, and there was "a multiplicity of banners, badges, and elegant decorations" on that sunny summer day. People who could afford it went afterward to Jacob Oyler's City House for a twenty-five-cent dinner "precisely at half past 1 o'clock." The following year, the German artillery fired its cannon all morning long; people flocked to the market to hear patriotic songs. After the usual parades by Sunday school children and temperance societies followed by feasting, the recent arrivals from Germany returned to the State House for more singing. The parades and other special events encouraged a public expression of national loyalty that also intensified awareness of the local community. The *Ohio Statesman* complimented immigrants for their "promptings of patriotism and love for their adopted country."[48] (Because of a failed attempt at a revolution, many more Germans immigrated to the United States after 1840.) The celebrations also probably defused any developing sense of alienation that poor residents might have felt when regarding their wealthier neighbors. In this respect, special events and social life among the poorer classes might have served as a safety valve that made violence and disorder in town less likely.

On July 18, 1843, three of the principal chiefs of the Wyandot nation came through Columbus to bid goodbye to Gov. Wilson Shannon. The Wyandots were the last Native American nation to be forced out of Ohio. In a treaty signed in 1842 they agreed to exchange their lands in Upper Sandusky for an area west of Missouri. Henry Jacques, the principal chief, delivered what was called "a beautiful address." The governor replied and "wished them happiness and prosperity in their new home."[49] Most of the Wyandots marched through Urbana and Springfield on their way to Cincinnati, where they boarded two boats for the west.

Indicative of the interest Columbus residents had in this event was the fact that the August 1, 1843, issue of the *Ohio Statesman* contained the text of the two speeches. A later issue reported on the chiefs' departure from Cincinnati and recorded an anecdote about how one of the chiefs had once given a war whoop in the Columbus theater for a poor actor. Three other issues of the newspaper that fall contained letters from a Wyandot chief giving details of the tribe's journey and its new home at the confluence of the Missouri and Kansas Rivers. However, there was greater interest in town in learning when the new lands in Upper Sandusky would be put on the market. When the General Land Office finally announced that the lands would be offered for sale on September 22, 1845, the *Ohio Statesman* reported, "This Reserve embraces some of the best land in the State, and presents great inducements to those who wish to purchase for actual cultivation." There was no evidence that anyone lamented the treatment suffered by the displaced Wyandots, who never received all the money promised them for their lands.[50]

Thursday, December 14, 1843, was Thanksgiving Day, a state holiday by action of the legislature and the governor. Stores were closed, and services were held in most of the churches. The holiday gave residents one more opportunity to pause and reflect on their past. The editor of the *Ohio State Journal* observed, "We rejoice that the time honored custom of the descendants of the Pilgrims, is gaining favor throughout the land; amidst all our difficulties and embarrassments, we have still to acknowledge that we are a favored people."[51]

One of the characteristics that influenced most aspects of everyday life in Columbus was, of course, its small size. Practically everything was in walking distance of Broad and High. Most people had to walk to work. Residences were near shops. Private and public buildings were on the same street. The residence of William Middletown, a ropemaker, was on the northwest corner of Front and Broad Streets where the city hall now stands. William Neil's stable was nearby. A baker by the name of E. Gavin lived across the street on Broad. The houses of two grocers were on the other two corners of the intersection. David Perry, a clerk, lived near the Columbus Foundry, which was on the east side of Water Street near the Scioto bridge. The bridge at that time was a wooden covered structure with open side passages for pedestrians.[52]

Although community spirit existed among long-term residents, it was difficult for newcomers to develop an affection for a place that was only a wilderness before 1812. In addition, individualism and materialism were pronounced characteristics of most settlers. Many of the children of the first families, however, settled nearby. Some of the leaders were related through marriages. William Neil's son, Robert E., for instance, married William Sullivant's daughter. Some of those who arrived were welcomed by the earliest families; others were not. It was sometimes difficult for strangers to be accepted by those who had been in town a few years. Some enterprising persons came with letters of introduction. Two years after the inventor Thomas W. H. Moseley arrived, he asked Gustavus Swan to write Col. Edward Livingston on his behalf. Swan wrote that Moseley had "much perseverance and industry" and contributed to benevolence. The fact that Moseley felt he needed a letter from a prominent resident suggests that the upper-class, long-term residents probably expressed some hostility toward newcomers and poor immigrants. Whether people remained or not depended on whether they could succeed financially. Columbus and other nineteenth-century towns in Ohio contained two groups, those who were economically successful and shaped community values and policy and those who were unsuccessful and sometimes moved away.[53]

Despite the outward image of equality, noticeable differences were emerging between the homes of the most affluent and those of the poorer classes. Many black families were crowded into small, inadequate houses on streets and alleys. Alfred Kelley's mansion, constructed in 1838 on Broad Street east of Fifth, was a stark contrast to the shacks and stables in another part of town. Kelley, Dr. Lincoln Goodale, and Lyne Starling, the handsome, six-foot-six merchant and court clerk, were the wealthiest residents. Kelley, an attorney who had worked intensively on planning the Ohio canal, was a successful leader in politics, banking, public finance, and internal improvements. By the time Lyne Starling died he owned land in practically every Ohio county and in Illinois, Iowa, and Missouri. William Neil and his brother, Robert Neil, and Michael and William S. Sullivant also owned extensive acreage.[54]

By 1843 there were enough German-speaking residents to support three German schools and two German military companies. The German artillery company started drilling in 1840, and soon a second company, the German Washington Artillery, was created. The German migrants may have been continuing their military traditions, but their military units were welcomed at parades and other events. During the War of 1812, Columbus men formed a troop of dragoons who continued together until the group was disbanded in 1832. The southern part of town was called "Little Germany." Other breweries were erected south of the courthouse, and German singing societies enriched the musical life of the city. Two German Beneficial Societies were founded in 1846 to assist sick members. Louis Lindeman reached Columbus from Bavaria in 1837 when he was eighteen. He met his second cousin, Peter Ambos, and became an apprentice in his confectionery shop. Nathan Gundersheimer was the first of his family to arrive before 1840 and later opened a clothing store at his residence at 170 High Street. Judah Nusbaum reached Columbus shortly after 1840. Simon Lazarus and three brothers arrived in 1851, attracted to Columbus by letters from friends. Lazarus was forty-four at the time and had been born in Bavaria. He had studied to be a rabbi and continued to do so, but also opened a clothing store that over the years contributed much to the Columbus economy. He brought his wife, Amelia, a son from her first marriage, and a year-old son, Fred.[55]

The German-speaking residents also added to the slang of the area. According to Joel Buttles, the Germans called people west of the Scioto who traced their ancestry to Virginia "Pinchguts" because they were so stingy. They called persons who arrived from New England "Cold Dumplings." Buttles was accurate in perceiving the attraction of German immigrants to the Democratic Party, but many more native-born were Democrats than Buttles realized. By the end of the decade, 43 percent of the residents of Columbus's Fifth Ward were foreign-born and the Democratic vote in that ward was running about 70 percent.[56]

One of the continuing debates in the legislature was over the issue of whether to print official documents in both English and German. Those who favored only English argued that to become Americanized, recent immigrants should quickly learn the language. They expected newcomers to conform and accept American ways of speech and custom. Some of those who favored printing in both languages thought that recent arrivals from Germany would develop closer ties to their community if they quickly learned in German papers about local laws and political events. Settlers from Wales also were unhappy when the governor's message was printed only in English and German. They were not as numerous as those who spoke German, however, and the legislature failed to add a Welsh version. While foreign-speaking immigrants brought their own cultures and sought to preserve something of their heritage, they contributed to the enrichment of life in the city, and as they experienced American customs, they made cultural adjustments to their new environment.

The expectation that foreign settlers would quickly assimilate and learn English was a majority view and was reflected in the legislative debates over printing laws. The "melting pot" theory that was based on the assumption that all immigrants would become Americanized prevailed for many years. In recent times, the "salad" or "symphony" metaphors have been more popular. However, the metaphor articulated by Kathleen Neils Conzen seems more appropriate to apply to the Columbus experience. Conzen uses the image of "the braided river valley" to describe the "localization of immigrant cultures." [57] The contribution of German and other European immigrants to the economic, social, and cultural life of Columbus gave a particular stamp or influence to the community. German customs, foods, music, and culture infused the life of the city at the same time that the new arrivals learned about Ohio customs and culture.

Although native-born and immigrant families had active social events, they were not as well publicized as those of the upper classes. Large parties among the wealthier families became fashionable in the late 1840s. Joel Buttles's diary entry for January 11, 1846, noted, "Columbus during the winter is always remarkable for its gaiety and parties of pleasure." He counted three hundred guests who came to his house on Friday, January 22, 1847. The last guests left at 1:30 A.M. Toward the end of the evening he regretted that the young people danced a few reels because of the religious attitudes against it. Despite that prejudice held by pious residents, James E. Bailey's Dancing Academy gave instruction in "redowa, polka, quadrilles, mazurka, and waltzing" in 1848. Twenty-four lessons cost six dollars. The old 1839 city ordinance prohibiting "dances and carousels" by "idle, lewd and dissolute persons" was probably the least enforced law ever passed. An event called "the Widower's Ball" in the winter of 1849 was the biggest party of the decade.[58]

As the gap widened between the richest and poorest residents, an inevitable tension developed as thoughtful Americans sought to reconcile their dedication to social equality with the increased materialism that drove some enterprising persons to amass great wealth. By 1850 the real estate ownership rate among men was only 20 percent. By midcentury in Columbus those who were economically prosperous were becoming more influential than those who had only social status or were primarily in politics.

Joel Buttles's views were probably representative of his class. He wrote in his diary in reviewing his career, "I resolved on being something in the world—I resolved on being rich." [59]

Fortunately, some Columbus residents combined benevolence and community service with their materialism. The city's leaders were interested in improving the quality of life in town and identified ways through which to apply their philanthropy. Dr. Lincoln Goodale was one example. He was born in Brookfield, Massachusetts, in 1782 but moved to Marietta, Ohio, in 1788. He arrived in Franklinton in 1806 and practiced as a physician for many years. He volunteered as a surgeon's mate during the War of 1812. After the war he moved to Columbus, gave up medical practice, and became a merchant, selling medicines and drugs. He also gained wealth through trade in leather and land investments. By 1837 he had built Goodale's Row, a series of shops on High Street south of State Street. In 1845 he participated with others in planning to build the Franklin and Ohio River Railroad.

Goodale enjoyed sharing his large fortune and gained a reputation for generosity. He gave gifts and made loans to many individuals. One young man wrote, "I never have before appreciated enough Dr. Goodale's kindness." Goodale joined the board of trustees of the Starling Medical College in 1849. In 1851, when he donated land for the park that bears his name, news of his gift was reported even in the *Boston Transcript*. He later gave land for the first campus of Capital University at Goodale and High Streets. When he died in 1868 his estate amounted to $1.5 million.[60]

In their social and cultural activities, as well as in their politics, Ohioans from the start sought to preserve individualism and to curtail aristocratic tendencies in their government. But there was also great interest in having government assist in internal improvements, which would accelerate economic development and reward those who had made shrewd investments. While political equality was defended as a right for all white men, there could not be economic equality where some appeared more industrious and more fortunate than others. The wealthiest persons in Columbus were the established merchants, lawyers, doctors, and large landowners. At the lowest economic rung were the white laborers, coachmen, boatmen, and most of the black residents. As economic inequality intensified, crime seemed to increase and there was more concern for the preservation of the fragile fabric of society.[61]

7

Women

On and Off the Pedestal

Women in Columbus in the 1800s, as well as in the rest of the country, were far from equal to men. Men praised them and seemed to honor them but deprived them of the right to vote. Their main role in life was to serve as wives and mothers. Laws and social customs restricted women's activities and their economic advancement. Those who were poor were expected to fill menial jobs or become sex objects. The male-dominated society in Columbus and elsewhere dictated to girls and young women what was expected of them in their conduct and personality. In 1824 the local newspaper gave "Advice to Young Ladies" that included the following: "It is always in your power to make a friend by smiles—what folly then to make enemies by frowns. When you have an opportunity to praise, do it with all your heart. When you are forced to blame, do it with reluctance. If you would preserve beauty, rise early. If you would preserve esteem, be gentle. If you would obtain power, be condescending. If you would be happy, endeavor to promote the happiness of others."[1]

In 1825, the paper ran a long extract from Dr. Spring's *Discourse on Female Character* on its first page: "Neatness and Taste are peculiarly ornamental to the female character . . . they will be modest, pleasing, and dignified. . . . A Christian woman ought to be distinguished by her simplicity, her neatness, her economy, her healthful becoming attire, but never by her stiffness and precision. . . . A woman without respectability is without influence; and without influence she is without the power of doing good. . . . Of all others, Personal Piety forms the distinguished excellence of the female character."[2]

Ten years later the newspaper was still pontificating on female behavior: "One of the chief beauties in a female character is that modest reserve, that retiring delicacy, which avoids the public eye." Indelicacy in conversation was criticized: "Wit is a most dangerous talent which a female can possess."[3]

While women may have had great influence in the home and in family life, they exerted such power through persuasion and strength of character. In marriage, the husband gained what property his bride owned. In common law, the husband and wife were considered one—and that one was the husband. Single women seemed to have more independence and status than married women. Only single women were employed as teachers in most schools. Married women could not sue or make contracts. They had no custody rights over their children and no full-scale property rights until the Married Women's Property Act was passed in Ohio in 1861. Arthur W. Calhoun, writing in 1918, used the word "medievalism" to describe women's status in this period.[4]

Some relief had been granted on a piecemeal basis. In 1822 and 1824, the Ohio General Assembly allowed the wife to recover some portion of her property in a divorce. In 1824 the Supreme Court of Ohio ruled that a married woman could make a will "devising real estate in her own right." The legislature in 1845 passed a law protecting a wife's furniture and household goods from being taken to pay her husband's debts. But these steps were relatively insignificant. Edward D. Mansfield's book *The Legal Rights, Liabilities and Duties of Women,* published in Cincinnati in 1845, provided details on women's rights and limitations from biblical times to the present and reminded readers that women acquired "protection" and "maintenance" through marriage. Mansfield's main theme was, "The first great principle of Scripture, the unity of husband and wife, is repeated by the law. They are in law, one person."[5]

As early as 1809 Connecticut permitted married women to will property they owned, and in 1839 Mississippi allowed married women to control their own property. Some form of a married women's property act was passed in eight states in the 1840s. When New York and Pennsylvania passed such laws in 1848, Ohio women were impatient to see action on the subject in Columbus. (However, in New York support for reform was primarily because of men's economic problems, and judges weakened the law in favor of common-law precedents.) Reform was slow on this issue. According to Peggy A. Rabkin, the effort to reform the law of property was the first effective women's rights movement and led in turn to the fight for female suffrage.[6]

Most nineteenth-century men believed that women belonged in the home. In 1837, the editor of the *Ohio Observer* declared, "Females fill a peculiar station in society. They move in a sphere of their own which they, and they alone, were designed to occupy. It would be singular, if we did not find in woman, powers as different from those of man as the station which she is required to fill is different from his."[7]

That same year William A. Alcott published the second edition of his book *The Young Wife, or Duties of Woman in the Marriage Relation,* which was widely read at the time. Alcott put into words the general feeling held by men at that time. A woman was supposed to be "a help-meet to her husband." Alcott asserted, "Woman is made to supply, in some measure, the defects in her husband's character—thus making him a more perfect man than otherwise he would be." Women, however, had to be submissive to their husbands. Alcott believed that women's best virtues were their purity of conduct, neatness, order, punctuality, cheerfulness, sobriety, modesty, and frugality. Toward the end of his book, he repeated his notion that "Every wife has it in her power to make her husband either better or worse." She could not do this solely through advice and instruction, but "it is by the general tone and spirit of her conversation, as manifesting the temper and disposition of the heart, that she makes the most abiding impressions."[8]

According to several reports, Columbus had many beautiful, talented women who were active in the life of the community. Jane Hoge, wife of the Presbyterian minister, had eleven children, entertained frequently, and helped her husband start the first Sunday school in Columbus in their home. She also was president of the Female Benevolent Society and an advocate of free education. Amelia Aldrich Swan, wife of Gustavus Swan, was a popular hostess who was known for reading the entire Bible every year. Hannah Schwing Neil, whose husband was one of the wealthiest men in town, gave generously to the poor. Mrs. Margaret Mitchell ran a successful boardinghouse on Town Street. The men, however, were probably better acquainted with Mary Miner, the tall, slender, golden-haired woman known for her "exceptional cultivation." She married Henry Wharton, an Englishman. After he died, she was a friend of Clay's and Webster's and for a while traveled to and from Philadelphia to teach in the Friends Seminary. According to Lida Rose McCabe, "There was no belle more quoted in her day."[9]

Women, however, were far from equal in any aspect of life. The assumption that women were inherently inferior to men was one of the attitudes carried down from generation to generation. Nancy Tuana, in her book *The Less Noble Sex,* convincingly documents the deeply rooted prejudice that she calls "part of the fabric of Western culture."[10] Wages for working women were much lower than for men in Columbus and elsewhere.[11] Members of the white middle and upper classes didn't expect women to work unless they were forced to financially. Joel Buttles wrote his sister: "I have undertaken as much business as I can get along with. I have use for a great deal of money, but I would sooner earn the money while others sleep than that you should by necessity be required to work at any time in your situation." Although married women were not considered part of the work force, there was plenty of labor inside the home. Most women in the city's early history made clothing and other household items and contributed to the economy in ways that were not recorded. Because housework didn't produce value in the marketplace, men devalued it. Women's economic dependence upon men's earnings became even greater when factory-produced goods replaced those made by housewives.[12]

Matthew Sorin, whose book *The Domestic Circle; or, Moral and Social Duties Explained and Enforced* was published in 1840, also reflected male popular opinion when he wrote, "According to the order and constitution of the divine government, man is appointed to rule in the affairs of this life. It is his prerogative to hold the reins of domestic government, and to direct the family interest, so as to bring them to a happy and honorable termination." Thomas Palmer's *The Moral Instructor,* which was written to be used as a text in school and was first published in 1842, contained idealistic descriptions of model boys and girls. Typical was the author's praise of "Mary," who was "gentle, kind, and affectionate. . . . Mary was so mild and passive, that she was always ready to yield to the wishes of her brother." The popular McGuffey readers presented a similar picture of boy/girl relationships.[13]

When in February 1840 Benjamin Tappan spoke in the U.S. Senate against women signing petitions, his views were representative of most men's. He declared, among other things, that "Nature seems to have given the male sex exclusive power of government. . . . To the female a more delicate physical organization is given. . . . Hers is the domestic altar; there she ministers and commands, . . . let her not seek madly to descend from the eminence to mix with the strife and ambition of the cares of government; the field of politics is not her appropriate arena."[14]

That same year, state Senator David T. Disney made similar remarks in a speech to a men's lodge in Columbus. He declared that it was not woman's place to be "struggling in the heated and impure strife of ambition." He asserted that her competition was "in the mild contest of love and truth." He believed that "Man constructs the building, but woman renders it a home."[15]

Columbus resident Margaret Coxe contributed extensively to the literature on women. *The Young Lady's Companion* was published in 1839, and a second edition came out in 1846. Coxe described her book as "friendly hints" on the subject of female education and believed that "a work issued from a western press, might be more calculated for usefulness in this interesting portion of our Union, which as yet has been untried ground for authors of works prepared for young ladies." In her chapters giving advice on conduct and character, Coxe emphasized sobriety, meekness, and industriousness. She urged her readers to avoid passions and to be moderate in dress, and emphasized the development of a Christian moral intellect. She believed that "the appropriate and legitimate sphere of female action, lies within the bosom of the domestic circle."[16]

Coxe's next major work on women was a two-volume book titled *Claims of the Country on American Females,* published in 1842. Coxe covered a wide variety of topics in her work. She devoted chapters to the status of women in biblical times, antiquity, Greece, Rome, "Mohammedan culture," and primitive Christianity. The bulk of her attention, however, was on women in the United States. She was interested in the characteristics of American females, their responsibilities as wives, and their influence on society. She was critical of the contemporary reformers who pictured women as having been "subjected to a rigorous and oppressive vassalage" over time and condemned to "an inferior and degrading class of duties." She believed that women's most important characteristics were "meekness, humility, gentleness, love, purity, self-renunciation, and subjection of will." [17] In the second edition of *Claims of the Country,* published in 1851, Coxe added a six-page list of books recommended for young female readers.

Coxe's volumes were filled with optimistic advice for members of her sex who, she believed, had "a holy and honorable" destiny to be instrumental "in the moral regeneration of a fallen world." She declared that wives, even when they were being dutifully submissive to their husbands, could improve men through their conversation. She wrote, "It is a point of no little importance in securing the morals of society, that men, and especially young men, be accustomed to associate ideas of purity of sentiment and practice, with the female image." She also encouraged her readers to influence American society by becoming writers.[18]

Coxe was a prolific author. (Her other titles will be mentioned in chapter 10.) However, she never gained the recognition and influence that Catharine Beecher achieved through her publications, which were widely read not only in Columbus but throughout the nation. Catharine Beecher was the remarkable daughter of Lyman Beecher, Presbyterian minister and president of Lane Seminary in Cincinnati. She became probably the best-known woman in the United States in the 1840s.

Catharine Beecher first received national attention for writing *An Essay on Slavery and Abolitionism with Reference to the Duty of American Females* in 1837. She was critical at that time of abolitionists because she thought that their methods were not likely to end slavery, which she deplored. What was revealing about the work was her view of her sex, which was summarized in her statement: "But while woman holds a subordinate relation in society to the other sex, it is not because it was designed that her duties or her influence should be any less important, or all-pervading." Beecher credited Christianity with giving woman her true position in society. "Woman," she wrote, "is to win every thing by peace and love; by making herself so much respected, esteemed and loved, that to yield to her opinions and to gratify her wishes, will be the free-will offering of the heart." Woman's influence, however, was to be gained in "the domestic and social circle." She was supposed to become so cultivated, so intelligent, that men would respect her judgment. Beecher concluded that the way to end slavery was through "free discussion" and that in that regard women had an important role to play.[19]

Catharine Beecher's most influential work was *A Treatise on Domestic Economy for the Use of Young Ladies at Home and at School*. It was first published in 1841 and was reprinted every year for fifteen years. Although Beecher might be called conservative in accepting the picture of woman as a domestic figure in a special sphere, she was innovative in dealing with domesticity as a science. Her book was extremely influential. Its chapters dealt with such topics as ways to improve domestic economy, caring for health, making food and drinks more healthful, the care of infants and the management of children, and making the home safer. One of her messages was:

> In this Country, it is established, both by opinion and by practice, that woman has an equal interest in all social and civil concerns; and that no domestic, civil, or political, institution, is right, which sacrifices her interest to protect that of the other sex. But in order to secure her the more firmly in all these privileges, it is decided, in the domestic relation, she take a subordinate station, and that, in civil and political concerns, her interests be intrusted to the other sex, without her taking any part in voting, or in making and administering laws.[20]

However, Beecher insisted, women had a superior influence in their children's education, the selection and support of clergy, all benevolent activities, and all questions relating to morals and manners. To women had been given the most important responsibilities. She believed that educating a man improved one individual, but educating a woman secured the interests of an entire family. Furthermore, labor in the home was important and not degrading. "It is refined and ladylike to engage in domestic pursuits," she wrote. But Beecher claimed that women in her generation knew more about academic subjects than how to cook, make a bed, or sew a dress properly, and that was why she thought her book should help women in their domestic duties. She treated housekeeping as a science, and as Keith Melder and Kathryn Sklar have suggested, she applied industrial methods to running the home.[21]

Beecher's strongly held views ranged across a wide spectrum of concerns to members of her sex. She emphasized the importance of cleanliness and criticized tight dress, such as the wearing of corsets: "Any mode of dress, not suited to the employment, the age, the season, or the means of the wearer, is in bad taste." In respect to charity, her position was unbending: "The primary effort, in relieving the poor, should be, to furnish them the means of earning their own support, and to supply them with those moral influences, which are most effectual in securing virtue and industry." [22]

Beecher did not limit her attention to married women. In 1842 she contributed a thick book of advice and encouragement to those who were in domestic service. Writing in the form of letters, she called domestic jobs important and responsible. She gave reasons why the work was honorable and emphasized the need to raise its respectability. She made practical suggestions on ways to economize, on the care of children, and on other practical matters. Domestics were important, she believed, because they helped sustain "the family state." She thought domestics were superior to shop and factory girls. In addition to their management of household tasks, she asserted, their experience made "the duty of self-denying benevolence more easy to learn." [23]

Teaching, Catharine Beecher believed, was woman's singular calling. She developed her ideas in a speech and pamphlet titled *The Evils Suffered by American Women and American Children: The Causes and the Remedy*. She considered the educational system "deplorable" and claimed that 2 million children in the mid-1840s had no teachers. She blamed apathetic women and men who were "too lazy or stupid to follow the appropriate duties of their sex." She concluded, "The education of children, that is the true and noble profession of a woman." Many women took her advice. In the decades before the Civil War, about one-quarter of women born in the United States had done teaching of some kind. [24] However, many people probably preferred to hire women teachers because they could be paid less than men. Columbus women were allowed to become teachers after 1835. Wages for women teachers in Columbus in the 1840s were less than one-half those for men. Feminization of the profession also included the absence of women as principals.

While Beecher favored a more important role for women, she did not alienate men because in effect she accepted her sex's inferior role in society at large. Nevertheless, women gained support from her books for increasing their participation as writers, teachers, public speakers, and workers in various reform movements. In addition, more women were writing fiction, poetry, biographies, histories, plays, and religious works, many of which were sold in bookstores or reviewed in papers and magazines.

Despite the economic and political discrimination against them, women were highly respected, even revered, by most men. William Brown, an Englishman who lived in Cleveland for two years, wrote in 1849, "There is no country under the sun where women are paid so much deference to, or where they are more carefully nurtured." [25] By this time, at least in the middle and upper classes, the notion had been accepted that women lived in a separate "sphere" because of their delicate nature and domesticity. An article in the February 1843 issue of the *Ladies Repository and Gatherings of the West* claimed woman's "more delicate sensibility is the unseen power which is ever at work to purify and refine society."[26]

Most of what was written about women's special sphere was directed to white women. Black women, however, also were placed on a pedestal. The March 27, 1844, issue of the Columbus black newspaper, *Palladium of Liberty,* contained a long article praising them. It declared that black women exerted "a powerful influence; and it depends in a great degree on them to give that tone to the morals of the community, which is so desirable and necessary to the harmony and happiness of mankind." The article emphasized the value of education to women and asserted that domestic peace improved the character of men. Furthermore, the author wrote, "If we can make men exemplary at home, we shall do a great deal towards making them peaceful abroad." The writer concluded that the greatest role in life for a woman was as a mother.[27]

The fact that women were placed on a pedestal had interesting results. Many men resented as well as revered them. Their higher standards, values, and increased interest in religion caused some men to seek escape from their domination. According to William Brown, there were more divorces in Ohio in one year than there were in a decade in the United Kingdom. He asserted that in 1843 there were 447 bills of divorcement in Ohio, and the majority were begun by women whose husbands had run away, neglected them, or abused them. Obviously, for some men the pedestal was not high.[28]

It was the general expectation that women would get married. Columbus physician Thomas Hersey spoke with authority when he wrote in his 1834 manual, *The Midwife's Practical Directory:* "The marriage union is paramount to all the ties of natural consanguinity." Hersey told married women that their destiny was motherhood. His volume supplied practical suggestions for a variety of problems associated with pregnancy. The fact that one of the first authors to be published in Columbus wrote on such a subject suggests that he was meeting a popular need in society.[29]

Lydia H. Sigourney was one of the most prolific women writers before the Civil War. The opening lines in her *Letters to Mothers,* which was first published in 1838 and had a sixth edition in 1845, were, "My Friend, if in becoming a mother, you have reached the climax of your happiness, you have also taken a higher place in the scale of being. A most important part is allotted you, in the economy of the great human family." Sigourney encouraged women to realize that in parenting they had gained "an increase in power. The influence which is truly valuable, is that of mind over mind."[30] Columbus women probably were familiar with some of Sigourney's other books, such as her histories or her *Letters to Young Ladies,* which reached its sixteenth edition in 1849. In *Token of Friendship,* published in 1844, she stated, "Home is the empire, the throne of woman. Here she reigns in the legitimate power of all her united charms."[31]

Married women led rugged, challenging, and sometimes lonely lives. When Mary Seymour Welles married Alfred Kelley, she did not expect him to be absent so frequently. Kelley was a canal commissioner for nine years, a legislator, and a railroad company president, and was away from home for months at a time. Mary and Alfred wrote to each other regularly when Alfred was traveling. He was aware of her heavy duties. Once he wrote, "I am glad to hear you get along so well with the children, every night I think of you and of the task you have to perform."[32]

Before 1830, while she was in Cleveland and Alfred roamed the state, Mary frequently expressed her loneliness, pleading with her husband to move their family to Columbus. In 1830 she wrote him on September 20 to express her grief at the deaths of several of their children: "As one after one of our dear children are taken away from us my heart involuntarily clings closer to those that are left, and closer closer still to you." She concluded, "I should have some fear of my housekeeping talents and acquirements when put in competition with so much style as is found and expected at Columbus."[33]

Mary little realized in what style she would soon be living. In 1831 Alfred Kelley bought more than eighteen acres along Broad Street for $917. Beginning in 1836 he built a commanding residence of Ohio sandstone with stone columns in front. It was a popular place for entertaining large groups in the 1840s and lasted as a residence until 1906. Kelley kept open house and frequently entertained guests at meals.[34]

Even after their move to the capital, Mary continued to write about Alfred's absences. On July 28, 1841, she wrote, "I know it is wrong to feel impatient when you are progressing with your labor as fast as possible, but I do so much want to see you once more . . . have you any idea of the probable time of your coming home?" The next year, when he was in New York, she wrote, "The newspapers are so filled with accidents of travellers that I can not feel easy about you when away from me, until I hear you have reached your destination." In his absence in 1849, she wrote, "You would have smiled dear husband to see me this morning when I saw your letter. [I] take it and carry it round some time, fearing to open it lest I should learn you were indeed going further away." Alfred was frequently apologetic that business took him out of town. That year he wrote, "I have been trying in some degree to compensate for my long absence by procuring sundry articles which will contribute to your comfort and that of the family." Mary Kelley's most revealing letter reflecting on her condition was the one that began, "I did not write you last week because I was so much engaged with my domestic concerns that I felt harried and worried with hard work all the while. . . . I know as well as you dear husband that it is *you alone* who both set the example and give the precept. Tho I ought in many cases to be able to give good counsel to you if I did not set good example." If one of the most affluent wives in Columbus in the 1840s was "harried," imagine how less fortunate women felt.[35]

According to custom, single women had one disadvantage in terms of their social life. They were not supposed to attend public events such as concerts or church socials unaccompanied. Organizations adjusted to this restriction by modifying their ticket prices. If admission normally was fifty cents, they would charge one dollar "for one gentleman and two ladies."[36] The practice permitted single women to tag along with couples and enjoy social life without receiving disapproving comments.

Women in Columbus, as well as in the rest of the country, increased their participation in society's activities through the years as they gained self-confidence. Their active participation in religious services and revivals gave them more independence, plus experience and methods that they could apply in more secular pursuits. They played a crucial role in the benevolent and reform movements that became more important as their memberships grew.

Although women were expected to rule over moral and spiritual matters in the home, they nevertheless were expected to be subservient to their husbands. One who resisted this view was Maria Kelley Bates, daughter of Alfred and Mary Kelley. At her marriage on October 18, 1837, she asked the minister, "don't make me promise to obey." As she later wrote, "Mr. Preston actually complied with my wishes and made me promise the same as he did James."[37]

While there may not have been many feminists in Columbus at that time, the leading women were involved in a variety of charitable activities. Hannah Neil, wife of the "Stage-coach king," was not only generous with her own gifts but also encouraged others to contribute food to the poor. She created a center for children in 1858. At the first Ladies Fair in January 1834, women sold articles they had made as well as food and collected five hundred dollars.[38] The Columbus Female Benevolent Society was organized on January 5, 1835, with 107 original members. Jane Hoge was the president, and Maria Kelley, then a young student in school, was treasurer. Mrs. John Patterson wrote the constitution. The society's purpose was "to seek the poor and afflicted females in the city of Columbus, and provide them relief, aid, instruction or employment, as may be deemed best, and to afford moral, physical and intellectual instruction and improvement to orphans and other poor children, and also to aid and care for worthy women in the perils of childbirth, and for infants."[39]

The organization was incorporated in 1838. By that time Alfred and

Hannah Neil. From Lee, *History of the City of Columbus*, vol. 1.

Mary Kelley had given the society a small lot on the east side of Fourth Street between Oak Alley and State Street. A building was erected, and a free charity school opened in 1836 and served the community until the system of common schools was implemented. Public contributions were solicited. In 1847 the Female Benevolent Society was able to distribute eighty dollars to the poor. The organization held fund-raising concerts at the Neil House the following year. The society had a distinguished record of benevolence.[40]

Black women also became involved in this type of charity. There were two black female benevolent societies with forty active members in 1843. A social club in one of the churches collected money and distributed food to the poor.[41]

Women still remained a subservient sex not only in Columbus but throughout the country. Harriet Martineau probably gave the most cogent summary of their condition when she wrote: "The Americans have, in the treatment of women, fallen below, not only their own democratic principles, but the practice of some parts of the Old World."[42]

Despite their second-rate status and their isolation on the pedestal, women developed close, friendly ties with each other. As Carroll Smith-Rosenberg has documented, they expressed value to each other in visits and through letters and gained a kind of power "in the lives and worlds of other women." As a result, they probably gained strength and validation that helped them adapt to their subordination.[43]

As indicated earlier, women played a role in the 1840 presidential campaign even though they were not allowed to vote. Their participation must have resulted from men's recognition that they could be productive. Sexual equality or suffrage were not planks in political platforms. Women were included as recipients in the toasts that were drunk at political meetings and dinners. It was a tradition Columbus citizens honored beginning at the Fourth of July dinner in 1819 when men drank to "the Fair of America—May they ever wear their charms, as an attendant on their virtues; the satellites of their innocence, and the ornaments of their sex." One of the toasts in 1845 was, "The fair sex—We acknowledge the aristocracy of their virtues; we bow to the despotism of their beauty, and hope they may never forget that to the democracy of christianity, they owe the deference they receive." At the Eighth of January celebration at the American Hotel in 1846, one of the toasts was to "the Democratic Ladies of Ohio—Their smiles are the rainbow which gilds the storm clouds of political conflict." The following year the toast to the ladies was, "The only endurable aristocracy, they elect without votes, they govern without laws and are never wrong."[44] But in politics as well as in other facets of life, deference to the pedestal was a salute to women's charm and passivity, not to their intelligence and strength.

Columbus women became more active in the life of the community in the late 1840s. Hannah Neil continued her philanthropic activities even to the extreme of giving away her own clothing. Women participated in fund-raising efforts at their churches. On January 20, 1846, the Methodist women held a supper to raise money for their new church. They charged fifty cents per person and one dollar for "one gentleman and two ladies." Women of Trinity Episcopal Church held a tea party the same day with "splendid entertainment." Both events charged extra for ice cream and oysters.

Men did not always appreciate the leadership shown by women. Joel Buttles, whose wife was one of the more active fund raisers, was probably representative of his generation in belittling women's money-raising efforts. In his diary for January 11, 1846, he expressed his view that females raising money for churches were laudable and perhaps indispensable, but that the real donation was the husband's through his wife. If women found pleasure in collecting funds, he did not object. He concluded, "And if some are thereby induced to employ a fraction of that time, which would have otherwise been spent in idleness, to some useful employment, much good will thus be accomplished."

By 1850 women were seen at all political rallies, and feminine symbols in campaigning became more prevalent. Women also became more outspoken. Those who spoke in public drew considerable criticism. Their work on behalf of slaves in the South led some of them to be more concerned about their own treatment as slaves. The campaign for legal rights for women, led by Elizabeth Cady Stanton, Ernestine Rose, and Pauline Wright Davis, collected more followers. As women's rights laws were passed in other states, more women in Ohio wanted similar action closer to home.

In 1847, for instance, 142 women and men from Mount Pleasant in Jefferson County sent a petition to the General Assembly complaining about how women lost property when they married. The petitioners deprecated "all interference with individual freedom, as tyrannical and unjust." They described the loss and horror married women felt when their profligate husbands squandered their money and condemned the denial to widows of all the estates of their dead husbands. They wrote, "And though she may earn ever so much, after marriage it is not a mutual store but belongs to the husband, as the earnings of the southern slave to the master." They ended their petition with a protest against "this relic of barbarism."[45]

One of the best examples of women's increased activism occurred at the statewide convention of the "Colored Citizens of Ohio" in Columbus in January 1849. The women in attendance threatened to walk out in protest if they were not permitted to participate in the discussion. On the evening of the third day, Jane P. Merritt informed the leaders, "Whereas we the ladies have been invited to attend the Convention, and have been deprived of a voice, which we the ladies deem wrong and shameful. Therefore, Resolved, That we will attend no more to-night, unless the privilege is granted." After considerable debate, and because the women were persistent, the convention agreed that the women could participate as full members and were given the right to speak.[46]

Most of the literature on women's "separate sphere" and domesticity focused on the upper and middle classes. For many women there was little time to think of the finer things of life. Scratching out an existence and finding food for the next day consumed most of their energies. Even middle-class wives were productive in their homes, although people didn't think of them as being part of the labor force. Many of the 4,250 adult women in Columbus in 1850 had to work. The male census takers, however, failed to record all those women who were working. Apparently, census takers that year asked men their occupations but not women. If women volunteered information, then the census takers recorded it. Only thirty working women are so listed. Many middle- and upper-class families had a young woman or two with a different last name, and born in another state or in Europe, living with them. Presumably their job was to help take care of young children or do housework. Almost 350 young women worked in that way. Some merchants, grocers, and hotel keepers had employees living in their homes. Seventy-five women were listed with their occupations in the 1848 business directory. Thirty-five others were in the 1850 city directory, which, however, neglected to include blacks. Two years later the city directory, referring to 1850 mentioned 117 "female hands employed." Although the records are not complete, possibly 20 to 25 percent of the city's adult women worked at jobs or were self-employed because of economic necessity.

Women worked as laborers, clerks, grocers, milliners, "tailoresses," teachers, and washerwomen. They worked on canal boats, in foundries and rolling mills, and as attendants in asylums and servants elsewhere. There was at least one blacksmith, butcher, druggist, plasterer, printer, and cabinetmaker. They ran boardinghouses, and one, Mrs. S. Seibert, who was married to a bookbinder, was involved in manufacturing vinegar. These women were the shadow part of the labor force, and many were at the lowest rungs of the economic ladder.

Others who were not on the pedestal included thirty-nine adult women and sixteen females under the age of twenty who lived in the poorhouse. One hundred ninety-six white women were patients in the lunatic asylum. That figure constituted 5 percent of the adult white women in Columbus in 1850. Six women were convicts in the Ohio Penitentiary.

Sixty percent of the adult women in Columbus in 1850 were married. While the traditional two-parent family with many children was the unit most frequently seen and written about, the city had many single-parent families struggling to survive. In 1850, 153 white women and 16 black women were heads of their households. They were widowed or divorced, or their husbands had left them. Sixty-five of this group were foreign born. One hundred eight of them had children too young to work, did not own their homes, and had no visible source of income. They probably worked as dressmakers or washerwomen, took in transient boarders, or received charity from generous neighbors.

Eliza Davis, twenty-nine, had three children. The eight year old was born in Wales, the four year old and two year old in Ohio. Thirty-six-year-old Anna Leeds from England was blessed with eight children. Her oldest son was a laborer, so there was some income. Elizabeth Flood, a former slave from North Carolina, was struggling with six children. Mary Parks, living in the Fourth Ward, also had six hungry mouths to feed.

One of the nontraditional families in the Third Ward consisted of a thirty-nine-year-old woman from Kentucky, a twenty-one-year-old woman from Switzerland, a fourteen-year-old girl from Germany, and a thirty-six-year-old black man from Virginia. They owned no real estate and had no visible source of income. The census taker did not list their occupations.[47]

8

Asylums and

Poorhouses

Columbus's asylums and the penitentiary became popular tourist attractions. One visitor wrote, "No intelligent traveller, unless forbidden by the urgency of his circumstances, will pass the city without visiting the various Asylums."[1]

Concern for the disadvantaged, the mentally ill, and the handicapped—as well as for better treatment of prisoners—registered early in the city's history and continued to be expressed throughout the nineteenth century. The 1848 business directory boasted that "all are united in regard to charity and justice" and that Columbus "has been one in providing for the afflicted." Part of this sentiment was the result of the influence of churches in Columbus and the leadership of the Presbyterian minister, James Hoge. Some Americans assumed that the stress and temptations of the city handicapped persons accustomed to benign, rural surroundings and made them dependent upon society. Columbus leaders, reflecting the prevailing attitude toward those with limitations, decided to set them apart from the rest of the community. People were persuaded that the blind, the deaf, the insane were best treated in isolation. This attitude resulted in the building of institutions on the outskirts of the city, thus reducing their visibility to those living and working near Broad and High. They were places to visit on occasion, perhaps to attend programs presented by the deaf or blind, but otherwise to ignore.[2]

James Hoge urged Gov. Jeremiah Morrow to recommend the creation of a deaf and dumb asylum in his 1826 message to the General Assembly.[3] A survey the previous year had revealed that there were 420 mutes in Ohio, 279 of whom also were poor. Hoge also wrote the legislative body asking for immediate action and garnered many signatures of support. The institution, the fifth of its kind in the country, was incorporated in 1827. In 1829 Columbus was selected for the location of the Deaf and Dumb Asylum. The first trustees included Hoge, Gustavus Swan, and Thomas Ewing. The legislature appropriated five hundred dollars for three lots, one of which Hoge owned, but their total cost was only three hundred dollars. The first appropriation for a building came in 1832, and the first superintendent was Horatio N. Hubbell, a Presbyterian preacher. The original site was a rented building at High and State Streets. By 1834, when the institution had fifty-seven pupils, it had moved three times. Enrollment initially was low, partly because people were not aware of the school's instructional advantages and partly because many families could not afford the expenses.[4]

Ten years later the school's enrollment was one hundred, necessitating an extension to the building, now on Town Street. After 1844, admission was free for all applicants. Hubbell's 1845 report described his vacation tour with two students to thirteen towns and cities to hold exhibitions and distribute information about the asylum. Some two thousand visitors toured the institution annually in the 1840s.[5]

By 1850 enrollment was up to 135, 64 females and 71 males. Outside of school hours, teachers in the industrial department supervised the boys in their work around the grounds. This practice reduced the amount of hired help needed. The girls were kept busy outside of class by making beds, sweeping rooms, making and mending their clothing, and clearing the tables after meals. In 1852, the school's name was changed to the Institution for the Education of the Deaf and Dumb.[6]

That year, a woman from Hungary who visited the asylum discovered that some of the teachers also were deaf and dumb. She attended a religious service there and recorded in her diary that "one of the teachers read the prayers by signs, which all of them repeated, and the expression in the countenance of some of them, was that of the most exalted devotion."[7]

State support for educating the blind began in 1835 when *Western Monthly Magazine* asserted that they had a right to education and supported the idea of an institution "for the instruction in letters and the mechanic arts, of this unfortunate portion of our population. . . . We rejoice to know that the sympathies of the community for a neglected and afflicted class, are awakening." The state's medical society found that there were 250 blind persons in Ohio. The eminent Cincinnati physician Daniel Drake supported the idea in his *Report on the Subject of the Education of the Blind,* which was published in Columbus in 1835. In 1836 a committee consisting of James Hoge, Noah H. Swayne, and Dr. William M. Awl collected information on the need for such an institution. Their report described a number of schools for the blind in Europe and reviewed the establishment of institutions in Massachusetts, New York, and Pennsylvania. They reported on statistics collected from a questionnaire from fifty-nine Ohio counties that indicated there were almost three hundred blind people in the state. They estimated that between fifty and a hundred would attend a school for the blind. They emphasized that the main purpose of such a school was to help blind persons support themselves. They recommended immediate establishment of a school and an appropriation of $2,500 for a building and its operation. They concluded that it was "surely an object worthy of public attention."[8]

Dr. Howe the director of the New England Institution for the Blind, gave lectures in Columbus accompanied by his blind students, who made a favorable impression. The school created in 1837 was the fourth in the nation and the first established under the direction of the state. Most states followed that policy in subsequent years. Hopes were high for the school's prospects.

The Ohio Institution for the Instruction of the Blind opened July 4, 1837, in the Presbyterian church with one teacher and five pupils. The opening ceremonies were attended by nine hundred Sunday school students. Initially, tuition was one hundred dollars for a ten-month term. The instructor was A. W. Penniman, who also was blind. A boardinghouse for the school was run by Mr. and Mrs. Isaac Dalton. The school's 1839 report boasted that "the once dark minds are cheered by the light of science" and that "their souls are irradiated." Poor students were given free admission. In 1851, all were admitted free. Columbus citizens contributed to the purchase of a lot on the National Road for the school. N. B. Kelly was named superintendent. A five-story brick building was constructed. The building contained a chapel, which was used for public exhibitions, student examinations, and public meetings. There were thirty-six pupils in the school in 1840. By this time, there were four teachers, and William Chapin was superintendent.[9] In 1842 the name was changed to Ohio Institution for the Education of the Blind.

The students' schedule left little time for recreation. They rose at five-thirty, had prayers and sang a hymn at six, and attended school for an hour and a half before breakfast. Instruction resumed at nine, with singing at ten. School continued until dinner at one. The afternoon was devoted to work. According to the 1843 report, male students made brushes, willow baskets, doormats, and carpets, while the females made a variety of worsted articles.[10]

The institution's directors cleverly used the students to publicize the program and earn a little profit. On the morning of January 1, 1842, the pupils sang for the public and sold articles they had made. They performed at the start of every year and on several other occasions when the public was invited to visit. They also traveled to other towns in Ohio to publicize the school. They were taken to Kentucky and Indiana when those states were considering establishing similar institutions. The school became a popular place for travelers to visit. When the Methodist ministers in Ohio held their annual conference in Columbus in September 1847, they attended the school one afternoon. Uriah Heath was impressed with the students' "proficiency in study and their orderly behavior." The school had seventy students by the end of the decade.[11]

Agitation for an insane asylum gained momentum when a state medical convention meeting in Columbus on January 5, 1835, sent a recommendation to the legislature. It acted swiftly and concluded that the asylum should be located in the state capital. Other terms for the insane used at the time were "idiot," "feebleminded," "imbecile," and "lunatic." Some people considered the insane to be dangerous or a burden to society, so handicapped that they had to be isolated from others. Throughout the nation, the mentally ill who were poor were often lumped together with vagrants, beggars, the physically impaired, and criminals. The population schedules used in the 1850 census had a column to record those who were "Deaf, dumb, blind, insane, pauper, etc."[12]

Concern for the mentally ill and a feeling of responsibility for their care increased throughout the 1830s and 1840s. Furthermore, an optimistic expectation developed that they could be cured in institutions. What Albert Deutsch has called "the cult of curability" took hold on the minds and imaginations of some reformers. Having assumed that mental illness was caused by certain conditions of the times in which they lived, they sought to create buildings that would allow patients to recover from the urban ills that had assailed them. As described earlier, physicians and others thought that city life brought on stress that some people, accustomed to living close to nature in a rural environment, could not handle. Great care, therefore, was taken on the details of building design. As David J. Rothman has indicated, the lunatic asylum existed to give persons a chance to recover from those "public disorders" from which they suffered. In this sense it was a utopian effort to reform society, part of the idealistic attempt of those who assumed that humans could be perfected.[13]

There were few institutions available for the insane in the United States. The New York Hospital created the Bloomingdale asylum in 1821, but the leading institution in the East that became a model for others, the Worcester State Lunatic Hospital in Massachusetts, did not open until 1833. An asylum had been in operation in Kentucky since 1824, but it did not have a medical superintendent until 1844. In the 1840s Dorothea Dix worked to publicize the need for such asylums. Ohio was ahead of most other states in taking action. Although the institution in Columbus was among the first of its kind in the country, it was not the first authorized in Ohio. The state legislature authorized a "Commercial Hospital and Lunatic Asylum" in Cincinnati in 1821.[14]

The directors of the Ohio Lunatic Asylum from Columbus were Dr. William M. Awl and Dr. Samuel Parsons. N. B. Kelly was appointed architect in July 1835. He modeled it on the asylum in Worcester. The Ohio building, following the custom elsewhere, was built on the outskirts of the city, a half-mile east on Broad Street and well back from the thoroughfare. The plan was not only to isolate the patients but to place them in a therapeutic environment with lots of open space. The building was designed with a central portion accommodating 120 patients with future wings to be added. Money was appropriated in 1836, the cornerstone was laid in 1837, and the building was completed in November 1839, although patients were admitted beginning in 1838. It cost $37,280, about $7,000 of which was the charge for using convicts from the Ohio Penitentiary for much of the construction.[15]

Samuel Parsons, William M. Awl, and Samuel F. MacCracken, who were given the assignment of erecting the asylum, submitted a report at the end of 1838. Their publication revealed the depth of their concern for their patients but also reflected some of the prevailing attitudes toward the mentally ill. They decided to build two additional small buildings behind the main one. Their purpose was, they wrote, "for the reception of the violent and filthy classes who are entirely destitute of the power of self-control, and cannot with safety and propriety be confined with the cleanly and peaceful in the wings of the Asylum."[16]

They indicated that experience had shown that insane persons could be profitably employed in farming and recommended that one hundred acres be devoted to that purpose. They justified using prison convicts for the construction not only for economic reasons but also for the purpose of having something good result from something bad. As they put it, "A correct and liberal state policy may turn even the vices of community into a useful, economical, and benevolent account."[17]

When the institution opened in 1838, its first superintendent was the thirty-nine-year-old William Awl, who became one of the city's leading citizens. Awl had moved to Columbus in 1833 and advertised his services.[18] His excellent reputation was partially based on the fact that he was the first surgeon in the area to successfully tie the left carotid artery, which supplies blood to the brain. He may have been aware of William A. F. Browne's pioneering book published in Edinburgh in 1837, *What asylums were, are, and ought to be,* because many of his ideas sounded similar to Browne's. He soon became known throughout the country for his work, but Awl tended to be too optimistic about the institution's success in treating patients.

The first annual report, submitted in 1839, was mostly Awl's work. He indicated that 157 patients had been admitted during the first year and that there had been a 71 percent recovery rate in the first eight months. He called the number of people admitted "extraordinary" and said most of them were poor. He looked upon the asylum as "bare and defenceless" but added, "Experience has proved the Asylum buildings to be well adapted to the purpose for which they were designed." He stated, "The patients in general are reconciled to their condition and appear to be happy and contented." In his message in December 1839, Gov. Wilson Shannon indicated that the asylum was "in a flourishing and prosperous condition."[19]

Not everyone agreed. Criticism of the asylum and its superintendent occurred occasionally in the press. The brothers J. and T. McKibben condemned the management of the institution and complained that ragged and filthy paupers had been released prematurely. Awl denied the charges and explained that the paupers had been kept for forty-one weeks and discharged by a director in accordance with the law and only "after the house became crowded and we had tried our skills in vain."[20]

Each annual report contained a table giving basic information about the patients admitted. Although their names were not included, the table reported on their age, sex, marital status, means of support, apparent form of insanity, supposed cause, duration, condition, prospect, and result. The variety of supposed causes reflected the attitudes, prejudices, and misconceptions of that age. The leaders of the asylum movement were convinced that institutionalization was the answer. They discouraged patients' contact with family and friends. Awl even disliked their receiving letters from home. In his 1840 report he claimed that correspondence might destroy progress toward recovery.[21]

That year Awl modified his early optimism. He wrote, "The disposition of cures between old and recent cases, confirm the fact, that the earlier the care of insanity is treated, the greater the prospect of success." In 1843 he claimed a 100 percent recovery of recent cases. By 1846 he had seen 866 patients. Only 247 of them paid their way. The remainder were supported by the state. Awl and others had a strong economic justification for institutionalized medical care designed to cure the patient. In the long run, it was less expensive than permanent hospitalization because of the good recovery rate. Dorothea Dix used Awl's statistics on curing insanity in her memorial to the New Jersey legislature in 1845.[22]

By 1843, the editor of the *Ohio Statesman* was recommending that the asylum be enlarged "to meet the wants of the community." The west wing was started in 1845, the east addition in 1846, and the center wing in 1847. The care and treatment of the insane became more challenging in an urban environment, and most of the patients were poor. Columbus residents were proud of their institution, although they remained confused about what efforts were being made to help the patients. The building became a tourist attraction. The kindest words about the place were uttered by a visiting minister who thought it was "a benevolent retreat, a safe home, a grand hospital."[23] In 1846 Awl asked the General Assembly for funds for a chapel so that patients could attend religious services. The little chapel was dedicated September 16, 1847. The highlight of the program was the singing of two dedication hymns written by patients. By 1848 the Columbus institution had its own book, *Hymns for the Ohio Lunatic Asylum,* published in town. Some doctors thought that emotional religious revivals led to lunacy, and they favored a less rigorous religious type of service.

In his reports Awl, who became known nationwide for his work in curing mental patients, continued to be optimistic about his high recovery rates and the asylum's work. He claimed that almost one-half of his patients in the first five years had been cured. In 1846 the directors wrote, "The great object of the Institution is to effect cures."[24] Despite Awl's optimism, however, public skepticism continued. It was difficult for Columbus residents to be convinced that insanity was curable and that the way to cure it was through asylums. Partly because of some of the public's concerns, the legislature in 1846 appointed Awl, Joseph R. Swan, and Noah H. Swayne to "prepare a system of laws for the safe keeping and management of idiots and lunatic persons."[25] By the end of the decade the asylum had treated 1,365 patients and Awl was able to claim that 639 had been cured. The fact that initially some patients paid for their treatment and others did not created difficulties. The directors of the Columbus institution recognized the problem and abolished all charges in 1851. By the end of the 1840s, however, the main difficulty was a rapid increase in the number of patients treated, as much as 16 percent in one year. Apparently, some husbands incapable of coping with their wives authorized their admission as the solution to their marital problems. Almost 200 women were patients in 1850, compared to 180 men. This constituted between 4 and 5 percent of the white adults in Columbus that year. The proportion might seem high, but some of what was construed as lunacy then was probably what is called aberrant or antisocial behavior today.[26]

Because asylum superintendents were politically appointed, Awl lost his position in 1850 and was replaced by Dr. Samuel H. Smith. Awl was named physician at the Ohio Institution for the Education of the Blind.

Dorothea Dix, who traveled through the United States visiting asylums and prisons, reported in 1848 that there were approximately 22,000 persons with mental illness in the country, but only 3,700 spaces for them in asylums. Ohio added two state hospitals in 1855. The mentally ill sometimes ended up in prison. Dorothea Dix reported that there were two "decidedly insane" persons in the Ohio Penitentiary when she visited it.[27]

Probably the most famous person to pay a visit to the insane asylum was singer Jenny Lind, who had known Dr. Smith when he lived in Stockholm. After Lind's concerts in 1851, she walked to the institution and spent two hours visiting with the patients. Smith told another visitor that most of the patients were farmers because "they work too hard and have no holidays."[28]

The state legislature approved an act in 1831 authorizing the establishment of poorhouses, which some called infirmaries. In 1833 the city of Columbus built a poorhouse for sick paupers on a farm at the confluence of the Olentangy (originally called Whetstone) and Scioto Rivers. It was moved to twelve acres of land in the southern part of the city in 1839. Some of the land was used as a vegetable garden. A two-story building served as a home for the poor. Later, according to the 1848 city directory, another building was added "for the noisy and filthy." The directory may have inaccurately referred to the hospital erected by city council in 1844 to house sick travelers found to have infectious diseases. In 1848 the poorhouse contained thirty-eight people, some of whom were orphaned children. The figure jumped to forty-five the following year. One of the earliest and oldest occupants of the poorhouse was Mary Sours, who died in 1849 at the age of 105.[29]

The poorhouse, or almshouse as it was sometimes called, was not an effective governmental effort at economic relief. The stigma attached to poverty influenced attitudes. The destitute were isolated from what people considered the injurious and immoral surroundings that must have caused their poverty. They were preached to and encouraged to believe that hard work would help them solve their economic problems. But the investment in their situation was minimal, and most people looked down upon the poorhouse as a necessary evil, partly because they assumed that the poverty-stricken were themselves the cause of their condition. Michael B. Katz has maintained that many more of the poor received help from outside the poorhouse than from inside. Religious and dedicated residents in Columbus and elsewhere, concerned about poverty in their midst, found

ways to provide food, clothing, and shelter for their less fortunate neighbors in the absence of a federal or state welfare program.[30] Katz also
suggested that population turnover hid part of the problem. When some
people lost their jobs and faced poverty, they moved away and were never
seen locally again.

9

The Ohio Penitentiary

By 1834, the imposing new Ohio Penitentiary stood one-quarter mile northwest of Broad and High. The ominous building and its occupants were apart from the city and yet also were a part of the community. The penitentiary contributed to Columbus's economy but also served as a threat to free labor in some occupations. It was a constant reminder in a place that made the laws that there were always those who broke them. It symbolized the determination of society to preserve order and punish offenders. Its high stone walls were like a dike holding back potential threats of violence and loss of profits to the stability and progress of the town. People could ignore its existence, except on a few momentous days, or they could live in its shadow and be reminded that there were imperfections in their bustling world.

The move to lock criminals in prisons rather than physically punish them is generally described as enlightened progress. A civilized society looked down upon previous eras characterized by coarse brutality. Political leaders and others in the revolutionary era, influenced by the European Enlightenment writers and also possibly by early Puritan theology, rejected the corporal punishments associated with the colonial period: the whippings, the stocks, and the occasional mutilations. The next generation in the nineteenth century continued the trend toward replacing bodily punishment with incarceration in prisons. The barbarism of an earlier period gradually disappeared.[1]

Placing lawbreakers in buildings where their minds could be punished was looked upon as a way to enforce discipline at a time when order was so necessary in a potentially fragile society. David J. Rothman has carried this interpretation a step further in suggesting that the emergence of the penitentiary in the United States in the nineteenth century was a way for Americans in power to preserve stability in their effort to cope with the increased social disorder around them.[2]

Construction of the first and second prisons has been mentioned previously. A law was passed in 1821 authorizing state funds to supply each prisoner with a Bible and authorizing the directors to get a minister to preach to the convicts. In 1822 the prison's name was changed to the Ohio Penitentiary.[3]

From the outset some members of the legislature were unhappy with prison costs. A joint committee was appointed to review penitentiary finances. Its 1823 report was sweeping in its criticism. The document described a $5,130 loss to the state for prison operations. The committee recommended that the prison spend less money on expensive materials and that the convicts manufacture articles from cheaper raw materials. The committee also recommended more severe discipline. Legislators thought that all sentences should be "to solitary confinement in the dungeon or cells, to be fed on good and wholesome diet, and at hard labor."[4]

By 1826 there were 152 convicts, including 14 blacks and 2 women. They spent their days making barrels, shoes, wagons, or cloth. Discipline was lax, and the overcrowding was unbearable. Most of the prisoners had been convicted of horse stealing, burglary, or larceny. There were cells in the basement for solitary confinement. The keeper had the authority to put prisoners there for up to four days for a variety of infractions, including assault and battery, swearing, idleness, negligence in work, or just plain disobedience. Prisoners' food consisted mainly of cornbread, beans, bacon, and soup.[5]

Several governors over the years expressed concern about the overcrowded conditions and suggested that additional buildings be constructed. In 1827, for instance, Allen Trimble declared in his annual message, "The utter inability of the Penitentiary to meet the constantly accumulating charges upon it . . . has given rise to a prejudice against the system and to opinions favorable to a more summary, severe, and less expensive mode of punishment." He called the prison "a school for vice."[6] The women prisoners were confined to one room, which was partly underground. A chaplain, James Chute, was appointed in 1828 at a salary of thirty dollars a month, which was raised by Presbyterian ministers, but his results were meager. In 1830 a board of three directors was appointed to evaluate the prison and make a report. The board's conclusion was that housing was inadequate, equipment lacking, and food poor. Prisoners slept on the floor on beds of straw. In the winter they were crowded four to a cell because of the shortage of blankets.[7]

The General Assembly criticized the prison again in 1831 and stated that "a more perfect system for the dissemination of vice could not be devised." The cells were extremely cold in winter. The inept guards feared the prisoners, who frequently devised plans to escape. As early as 1832, Ebenezer Chamberlain, who toured Columbus and found it a "pleasant and flourishing village," was critical of the warden, whom he called "a tyrant the liberty of whose subjects is dependent upon his own despotic and capricious will." Cyrus Bradley, who visited the prison a few years later, described it as "a sink of corruption, a nuisance to the community, an expense to the state, a hotbed of villainy. Insurrections were frequent, no subordination, no obedience."[8]

A legislative committee also wrote a critical report, calling the organization of the prison "defective" and expressing doubt that hardened offenders would ever be reformed. The committee recommended solitary confinement for serious crimes. Nathaniel McLean, the keeper, had to advertise a twenty-dollar reward every time a prisoner escaped. One slipped away in September 1823, another the following month. Six escaped in February 1830 and, according to one observer, "paraded our streets, armed with knives and other weapons." The next year, when seven prisoners working on the canal eluded their guards, the keeper offered a reward of $350.[9]

In 1832 the General Assembly authorized the construction of a new building. One of the directors visited penitentiaries in the East and was impressed with the Auburn system of prison control, which required isolation, enforced silence, and hard labor. The new Ohio building was based on the prison in Wethersfield, Connecticut.[10]

The Auburn system was hailed at the time as an important improvement in penal reform. It was praised by Gustave de Beaumont and Alexis de Tocqueville, who were sent by the French government to study American prisons. Their book, *On the Penitentiary System in the United States and Its Application in France*, was published in 1833. They concluded that the Auburn approach had three advantages: "impossibility of mutual corruption of the prisoners; great probability of their contracting habits of obedience and industry, which render them useful citizens; possibility of a radical reformation." The French visitors, however, were not impressed with the Columbus prison. They wrote, "Ohio, which possesses a penal code remarkable for the mildness and humanity of its provisions, has barbarous prisons."[11]

Prisoner silence was the major characteristic of the Auburn system. People assumed that convicts who communicated with each other became more corrupt, thus reducing the possibility of reformation. The main duty of the assistant keepers in Columbus was to enforce silence: "The preservation and the effect of the whole system of discipline depends upon non-intercourse between convicts. They will, therefore, make use of every exertion to prevent any communication between them." In the long list of "Duties of the Prisoners," the first was, "They are not to exchange a word with each other, under any pretense, not to communicate any intelligence to each other in writing; they are not to exchange looks, winks, laugh with each other, nor make use of any signs, except such as are necessary to convey their wants to the waiters."[12]

Prisoners everywhere developed a sign language, however, to get around such rules. The foreign traveler Harriet Martineau documented the practice of convicts communicating both during the day and at night. Henry

Thomas, recalling his time in the Ohio Penitentiary, wrote, "I became conversant with my fellow prisoners. . . . They were not backward in instructing me in the mysteries of roguery." J. H. Matthews, in his 1884 book about the Ohio Penitentiary, confirmed that plenty of communication occurred among inmates despite the rule of enforced silence. "A look, a wink, or a certain movement of the head signifies more to the convict than an entire written page," he wrote.[13]

The Auburn system had its deleterious aspects. Orlando Lewis, a twentieth-century scholar, asserted that it turned persons into "automata." Another critic of the system was appalled at the "atmosphere of repression, humiliation, and gloomy silence" within the prison walls, where life was "hard, monotonous, and degrading."[14]

Another characteristic of the Auburn plan was the requirement of convict labor. Indeed, in terms of economics, contract labor was the most important part of the system. Included in the "Rules and Regulations" for the Ohio Penitentiary was the requirement that the warden "shall use proper means to furnish the prisoners with constant employment, the most beneficial to the public—having proper regard to their various capacities; and he shall employ such prisoners as are not engaged in the building of the Prison, in such manufacturing or mechanical business, as he may find to be most proper."[15]

Construction of the penitentiary, by prisoners under the supervision of Nathaniel Medberry, began in March 1833. It was interrupted by a cholera epidemic that summer and resumed later in the year; the building was completed in 1837. The site selected by the directors was on the east bank of the Scioto northwest of town. They made an agreement with four residents, Joseph Ridgway Jr., Otis Crosby, Samuel Crosby, and David W. Deshler, who were commissioned to purchase fifteen acres from landowners in Philadelphia. The area contained a good supply of sand and fine clay for brick making.[16]

Although the building was only partially finished in 1834, the convicts were transferred from the old building on October 28 and 29 of that year. The wall surrounding the prison was completed the following year. It ran for four hundred feet along the front. The warden's residence and guard room were in the center. It was designed for seven hundred cells in two wings of five stories. According to Clark Guernsey, a Pennsylvania printer who visited the penitentiary in 1837, the cells were eight feet long, three feet wide, and six feet high with arches overhead. Each cell had an iron door with holes to admit air. The cells had a hammock and blanket.[17]

Workshops extended along the eastern and northern sides of the yard. Visitors were not allowed inside, but for twenty-five cents they could look through small holes at the workers. There were shops for boot and shoemakers, one for woodworkers for saddle trees, a spinning and weaving room for coach and carriage trimmings, a blacksmith room, a carpenters' shop, a shop for coopers, and a large one for stonecutters.

A mess room was also on the first floor. It contained long tables and benches. On the day Guernsey visited, there were wooden plates containing pieces of cornbread plus knives and forks on the tables. A kitchen and bake room adjoined the mess hall. A shop for tailors was on the second floor.[18]

A separate building for women prisoners, initially with eleven cells, was constructed in 1837 east of the main building inside the prison yard. It also contained a work room. The total cost of the penitentiary was $93,370.50 plus 1,113,462 days of convict labor, which someone estimated was a savings of $78,428, or seven and one-half cents a day per convict. The materials and equipment that could be salvaged from the old building were transferred to the new one. Columbus residents were impressed with their new attraction. One newspaper editor boasted, "This admirable structure is truly deserving of public notice . . . visited by members of the General Assembly as well as strangers . . . highly gratified at what they see and hear . . . design possesses a rare combination of symmetry, grandeur, and utility." Cyrus Bradley, a visitor, was impressed. He called the new penitentiary "a noble structure, an ornament to the city and an honor to the state."[19]

The number of convicts increased even as the building was being constructed. There were 189 in 1834, 276 in 1835, 308 in 1837, and 489 in 1839. Two thirds of them were described by the directors as "grossly ignorant." About the same proportion were under thirty years of age. The prison population was 460 in 1843.[20]

The legislature elected three directors for three-year terms. One was elected each year, and they received salaries of one hundred dollars a month. The directors in 1844 were Robert Lee, John Greenwood, and Andrew McElvain. The directors hired and fired the warden, whose salary was set at one thousand dollars a year. He could appoint up to twenty guards. In 1835 a deputy warden was authorized at a salary of five hundred dollars a year.[21]

Another part of the warden's responsibilities was to "pay particular attention and constantly use his best endeavors for the moral reformation and culture" of the convicts. In 1835 Russell Bigelow, who had been a Methodist preacher in Columbus in 1821–22 and 1833–34, was appointed chaplain. He preached frequently, counseled the inmates, and was highly regarded, but the work weakened his health and he soon died. He was followed by Nathan Emery, who had been on the Worthington Methodist circuit in 1835. In 1836 the legislature eliminated the position of chaplain. The Young Men's Prison Society of Columbus sought to get volunteer preachers for a while. In 1838 the Reverend Charles Fitch served as "moral and religious instructor," and his compensation, according to the directors' report, was "paid out of the fund raised by the admission of visitors." The Reverend Samuel F. Mills contributed his time in 1841. However, the directors irritated the community by firing him. One editor commented, "It is a contemptible piece of meanness, but if a mean thing is to be done, it takes Whigs to do it." Although there were feeble efforts to restore the position, there was no resident chaplain until 1846.[22]

The arrival of each prisoner was dramatic. A sheriff usually escorted the prisoner by stagecoach and led him toward the gatehouse in front of the massive stone walls. If the prisoner looked up he could see the rows of iron bars across the windows. The building reminded some of a medieval castle, evoking terrifying tales of dungeons and death. An armed guard took the prisoner into the building, where he received his striped uniform and learned the rules that now restricted him. It was then that some of the criminals discovered that they could cry.[23]

The convicts had daily quotas to accomplish and worked long hours every day except Sunday. They moved from place to place in long lines, marching in lockstep in their blue-and-white-striped clothing. Silence was required at all times, including at work and at meals.[24]

Living conditions were appalling. The building was damp, and the stench must have been difficult to ignore. Fires were kept going in stoves to absorb some of the dampness. Convicts woke at dawn, carried their drinking-water cans and "night tubs," and marched in lockstep to wash. Disease was a constant problem.[25]

After working all morning, when the noon bell rang the convicts assembled in their companies to march again in lockstep to their meal. They marched in silence with their right hands on the shoulders of the men in front of them and their heads turned to the left so that the guards could observe any talking. They shuffled their feet as they marched, and their noise echoed from the stone walls. Their actions in the dining room were dictated by bells. Once they were all seated, a bell told them when to remove their caps and another when to begin eating. After the meal, they marched back to their work in the same fashion. When Henry Howe visited the penitentiary he reported that the convicts ate from wooden dishes made by some prisoners. One of the thirteen companies of prisoners in the mid-forties consisted entirely of blacks.[26]

Corporal punishment was used for all infractions. The lash, or cat-o'-nine-tails, was resorted to frequently. The lash had a short handle with four yard-long strings of cat-gut attached to it. The ends of the strings were tightly wrapped with waxed silk cord. Stories about the frequency and severity of the lash's use were circulated in town, which led to increased pub-

Inner courtyard of the Ohio Penitentiary. From Howe, *Historical Collections of Ohio*, vol. 1.

lic criticism. Others defended the discipline. Francis Lieber, for instance, wrote, "The whip is the physical means to enforce the principle of silence, and, besides, it is not as much the actual pain inflicted upon the convict, which induces him to keep silence, as the knowledge of an inevitable and immediate punishment for any contravention of the rule." Other forms of punishment included the ducking tub, the bullrings, solitary confinement, the sweat box, and later, an electric battery shock called the "humming bird" by those subjected to it. Discipline was harsh during the terms of the first three wardens: Nathaniel Medberry, W. B. Van Hook, and Richard Stadden.[27]

The new warden in 1843, John Patterson, made changes in the methods of punishment. He used the lash less frequently and substituted a cold shower bath. This involved tying a naked prisoner to an upright plank with a leather belt and fastening his feet to a platform so that his head and body couldn't move. Icy water was suddenly dumped on the prisoner, who may have regretted Patterson's determination to avoid unnecessary severity in his discipline. Apparently this type of punishment was first given in New York in April 1842. It was considered kinder than the lash, but critics still condemned it as "cruel, degrading, and potentially injurious." It was not until 1856 that a state law abolished corporal punishment in prisons.[28]

Before Patterson's arrival some Columbus citizens were recommending more humane discipline. In 1843 a long editorial in the *Ohio State Journal* focused public attention on the miserable conditions in the penitentiary: "If half we have heard on good authority is true, the walls of the Ohio penitentiary, could they speak would disclose 'prison house secrets' that would make the blood curdle. We are against flogging in the army, navy, madhouse or Penitentiary. . . . If the managers of that Institution could substitute such a persuasive as cold water for cats and other instruments of torture and blood-letting as heretofore employed, we are certain they would elicit an expression of universal commendation from the community."[29]

Prison conditions and the prisoners were frequently criticized by Columbus residents. The editorial comment in an issue of the *Ohio Statesman* was typical. The editor wrote, "[T]he discharged convicts from our Penitentiary are becoming a crying evil to the peace of our city, and it would be well for the city council to take early measures to rid community of the nuisance."[30]

The lives of the women prisoners were especially harsh. Because there were relatively few of them, prison directors generally neglected them. Although after 1837 they were housed in a separate, gloomy-looking building, they were exposed to the scrutiny, pressures, and sexual attacks of the male guards. An 1856 expose claimed, "The female prison is the Harem of a certain individual connected with the Penitentiary."[31] Supervision was inconsistent. Nicole Rafter used the word "pandemonium" to describe conditions in women's prisons. A representative of the Boston Prison Discipline Society visited Ohio in the 1840s and reported that the nine women there were more trouble than the five hundred men. He wrote, "The women fight, scratch, pull hair, curse, swear and yell, and to bring them to order a keeper has frequently to go among them with a horsewhip."[32]

There was no woman matron until 1846. When Dorothea Dix visited the penitentiary on August 19 and 20, 1844, she was particularly critical of the conditions in which the women convicts were forced to live. She supplied the *Ohio State Journal* with a long article detailing her criticisms: "The cells are decidedly too small, and are not ventilated," there was no chaplain, and "a State prison is not a proper place for women, except a matron is appointed to superintend, and to maintain order and some kind of regulation over their conduct and conversation." Later, in her book, she wrote about the women convicts in Columbus: "[T]hey were not slow to exercise their good and evil gifts on each other." On her tour Dix counted 167 women in prisons from Maine to Virginia.[33] According to one penitentiary chaplain, "To be a male convict in this prison, would be quite tolerable, but to be a female convict for any protracted term, would be worse than death." The most devastating criticism of the female department was made by Benjamin Dyer in his *History of the Ohio Penitentiary*. He called its architecture "antiquated" and its condition "dilapidated." He wrote about the "Screams, that were once heard to issue daily from the sombre pile, as some inmate was receiving punishment by the man-Matron."[34]

One of the ironies women faced at that time was that they were not expected by males to break laws. Women had their "separate sphere."

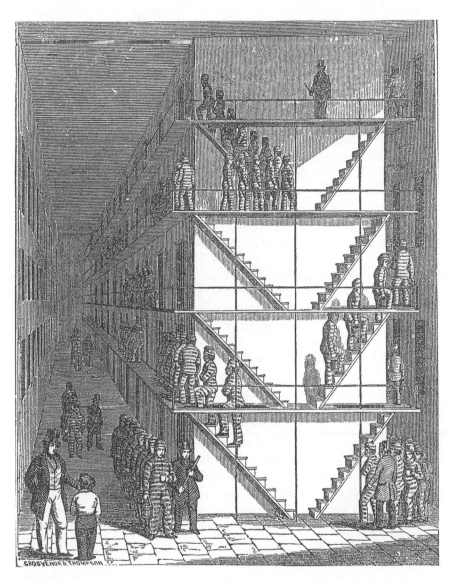

Prisoners returning to their cells at the Ohio Penitentiary. From Finley, *Memorials of Prison Life*.

They were supposed to be nobler, purer, more gentle than men. The domestic circles in which they were expected to live were not supposed to contain the temptations for lawbreaking that business and politics held. Because they presumably were not as hardened as men to the rough, raucous competition in life, they were supposedly more susceptible to temptation when it occurred. As W. David Lewis observed, man used his reason while woman relied upon her feeling. He may have based this generalization on Francis Lieber's assertion that "The two sexes have been destined by the Creator for different spheres of activity, and have received different powers to fulfill their destiny. The woman destined for domestic life, and that sphere in which attachment and affection are the most active agents, has been endowed with more lively feeling and acute sensibility: she feels, man reasons. Her morality has its roots more in her feelings than in her understanding or reasoning faculty."[35]

A "fallen" woman, then, supposedly fell much lower in everyone's esteem than did a man. Furthermore, many of the crimes that women did commit were not as easily detected, and they were more likely than men to be acquitted by judges and juries. There was a double standard in the courts as well as in society at large. According to Estelle Freedman, in 1840 the ratio of male to female prisoners in the United States was six to one. Ann Jones has concluded that favoritism toward women in the criminal law seemed to justify to men their denying civil rights to women. When women were found guilty, there were governors and others who favored light sentences or pardons. Every female convict in Ohio from 1815 to 1834 was pardoned by a governor.[36]

There is some evidence, however, that crimes committed by women increased considerably in the period before the Civil War. Some criminologists refer to this trend as a "masculinization" of female crime that resulted from some women assuming traditional male occupations, especially in the frontier and less populated regions of the country.[37]

The typical male attitude toward women and crime can be seen in the reports of the directors of the Ohio Penitentiary. In 1839 they wrote: "Since establishment of this institution, out of 751 convicts, only two white females have been sent to prison. At this time we have but one, and she is not a native of this state. The small number of native offenders, and none of them females, speaks volumes of praise in favor of our women, who occupy a more elevated station in this country than in any other, and that too, more deservedly."[38]

The directors praised women too quickly. By 1840 there were seven female convicts, and in 1842 there were nine. By 1846 the directors had to face up to their limitations. That year they wrote, "We had been impressed for some time with the fact, that sufficient provision had not been made for the female convicts. Though few in number, yet left so much to themselves, with no one of the pure and virtuous of their own sex to direct and modify their conduct, their condition, in a moral point of view, and so far as reformation was concerned, seemed deplorable enough. Discord, evil dispositions, excited temper and sharp contention, would frequently bear away, without control, among them."[39]

The prison population in 1840 included 481 males, of whom 50 were black and 2 were Native Americans. Two hundred fifty had never married. Only 10 had a college education, and 199 could read, write, and cipher. According to the chaplain, 126 were "grossly intemperate" and 115 were "addicted to gambling." Ninety-three had been "professors of religion" when arrested, and the same number were "hopefully converted in prison." However, 155 "have been accustomed to associate with lewd women."[40]

Grand larceny seemed to be the most prevalent crime at that time. However, after 1835 a theft of thirty-five dollars or more constituted that crime. Horse stealing and counterfeiting also were major offenses, as were robbery and burglary. Eighteen prisoners had been convicted of first- or second-degree murder, nine were in prison for manslaughter, and twenty-eight for assault with intent to murder. Nearly one-quarter of the convicts were younger than twenty-one, and two-thirds were under thirty years of age.[41]

Although convicted prisoners were sentenced for a certain number of years, they lived in constant hope that they would be pardoned. The haphazard way in which pardoning was done was, according to W. David Lewis, "an evil." There was no systematic way to make sentences or their commutation uniform. Abuse of the pardoning power was "demoralizing." Ohio seemed to abuse it more than other states. The pardon ratio in Ohio in the 1840s was one to eleven. The national average was one to nineteen.[42]

The most important, and most lucrative, part of the Auburn system was the requirement that prisoners worked. If a convict didn't know a particular skill, he soon learned one. The penitentiary used a contract labor system and advertised for bids for contractors that included brick making, carpentry, masonry, and stonecutting. When the building was under construction, the convicts even "forged the grates, doors, and locks."[43]

One of the first contracts was with Peter Hayden in 1835 to employ up to one hundred convicts for a five-year period in the manufacture of saddling and harness trimmings. A five-year contract was awarded in 1837 to Johnson and Burdell for twenty workers for tailoring. There was one for making corn brooms and another for the production of "sacks, shovels and men's silk hats." Although in 1840 20 percent of the inmates were farmers, there were also plenty of blacksmiths, carpenters, and other laborers. In 1842, there were fifty convicts working in iron smithing, a similar number weaving lace, and more than sixty in the shoe and tailor shops. That year the penitentiary boasted two steam engines that supplied power for the shops.[44]

Thanks to all the contracts, the Ohio Penitentiary earned a greater profit than any other state prison. The profit in 1841 was $21,897. In 1842 it was $28,794, which included $945 from visitors' admissions. Visitors could pay twenty-five cents to tour the prison, but it cost an extra ten cents to visit the women's building. The penitentiary was a tourist attraction for both men and women. Four days after Anson Buttles arrived in Columbus he visited the penitentiary and recorded in his diary that he was "well pleased." Even as late as the first decade of the twentieth century, elementary-school children were given tours of the penitentiary. The visitor charge was not dropped until 1930. Dorothea Dix thought the practice of charging admission was harmful to the reformation of the prisoners and favored dispensing with the income. Nevertheless, practically all government officials throughout the country insisted upon a self-supporting prison system.[45]

The contract labor system was criticized from its inception primarily because it undercut the income of free laborers. Some four hundred mechanics met in Heyl's Tavern in April 1835 to express concern about the "cheap labor" of the convicts. Later that summer the Columbus Mechanics Association agreed not to support candidates who would not pledge to abolish the prison labor system. They met again in October to publicize their cause. Workers held large protest meetings throughout Ohio to object to the state's farming out of prison labor, which they claimed was detrimental to their income. A long article complaining about convicts working appeared in the April 19, 1839, issue of the *Ohio Confederate and Old School Republican:* "The evil has grown to such an alarming extent, that business men, of all branches of trade, have felt, and are now feeling, all the bad effects of thwarting the operations of that productive class of our citizens." The writer feared that when convicts were released, the city's young men would be forced to be "shopmates of thieves and malefactors." More articles appeared in subsequent issues criticizing the notion that convict employment had to be part of the penitentiary system. A meeting of mechanics was held in Columbus on July 16, 1839, to pass resolutions on the subject.[46]

Gov. Wilson Shannon commented on the increased number of complaints and called for an investigation. There was also concern about fraud. One of the resolutions passed by the state Whig convention that met at Broad and High on February 22, 1840, stated, "That our Penitentiary system, as carried out in practice, operates injuriously on the interests of a numerous and respectable class of our citizens, and should be so modified as not to come in competition with the free labor of the honest mechanic, so far as the same can be done without making that institution a burthen upon the State Treasury."[47]

The *Ohio State Journal* followed up with an editorial on August 11 of that year criticizing the state prison's monopoly and asserting that convict employment in shoemaking, cabinetwork, and joiners work "depresses and distresses the mechanical interests." [48]

The penitentiary directors were put on the defensive. They were charged by the legislature with running the place at a profit and were condemned for competing unfairly with the poor laborers and businesses in town. In their 1841 report they tried to defend their policy: "Our great object has been to avoid, so far as possible, engaging in business that would do so, and to employ the men at such business as was not carried on in the country; but it is found to be a very difficult matter, if not impossible, to so employ the whole of them. The law for the regulation of the prison, requires that they be kept at labor, and consequently, must be employed at something." [49]

When the Senate convened on December 15, 1841, a resolution was introduced requiring the directors "to employ the convicts in such labor as will not conflict with the mechanics of Ohio, as fast as the present contracts expire." That winter mechanics from all over the state sent petitions to the General Assembly complaining about the contract labor system. Both Columbus newspapers supported the petitioners, although the Whig paper blamed the Democrats for continuing the policy. Samuel Medary, in response, claimed that he had objected to the practice from its beginning. [50]

In their 1843 report the directors announced that cabinetmaking had been abandoned entirely and that the shoemaking contract would not be renewed when it expired. Nevertheless, they continued to defend their actions and declared, "The contractors appear to be doing well, and are all anxious to increase their business, and a number wanting to enter into new contracts, as soon as there are convicts to dispose of." [51] Because some Columbus residents profited from the contract system, there was no unanimity in town on the subject.

The controversy continued into 1844. The January 3 issue of the *Ohio Statesman* contained a letter to the editor from "A Mechanic" complaining that the prison labor system undercut free labor in the state. He wrote, "[W]hen the State becomes a competitor with the mechanics of the State, and will hire their convicts out to contractors at thirty cents per day, it is impossible for mechanics to live and keep their families, pay their taxes or their rents." At a mechanics meeting in the city council chamber on February 12, a resolution was passed to urge "nothing short of a law to put an immediate stop to the system as at present pursued" in order to benefit the workers in the state. That meeting was followed by one on March 27 at which the Columbus Anti-Prison Monopoly Association was created. Its members signed a pledge "to use all honorable means to secure a repeal of the law regulating the convict labor in the Ohio Penitentiary, so that it will not come in competition with the mechanical or laboring interests of the

State." James Cherry was named the president. When the Mechanics' State Convention met in July, many motions were passed criticizing the Ohio Penitentiary labor contracts, which were called "oppressive."[52]

Perhaps because the wardens were political appointees, the Ohio Penitentiary had a rapid turnover. Both W. B. Van Hook and Richard Stadden were fired. Van Hook was dropped by the directors in June 1842. His sudden departure aroused some of the residents and led to a legislative investigation. Van Hook was accused of taking hogs and two bolts of muslin belonging to the penitentiary and of stealing money from the visitors' account. The two newspapers in town entertained their readers with accounts of the ex-warden's crimes. One editor wrote, "The massive walls of that institution were not designed to cover up the iniquities which its superintendent may be guilty of perpetrating." What irritated some people was that while Van Hook was fired for bad conduct, the directors gave him a certificate stating that he had been "industrious and had made money for the state." Inasmuch as more than twenty-eight hundred pounds of pork seemed to be involved in his transgressions, his firing attracted considerable attention. The affair became news again the following spring when the majority and minority reports of the legislative committees were released.[53]

Richard Stadden, Van Hook's replacement, had trouble from the first day of his appointment. Articles in the July 12, 1842, *Ohio State Journal* raised questions about his selection. One asked whether he was the person who had been reported as a defaulter when he served as superintendent on the National Road. Another asserted, "This Stadden has hardly sense enough to shoe a horse, and yet he is entrusted with the management of the affairs of the State!" During the February 1843 term of the Franklin County Court of Common Pleas Stadden had to spend time in court representing the penitentiary in a suit against Jacob Strickler, who had failed to pay a promissory note for $359.30. Stadden was suddenly fired and replaced by John Patterson on March 15, 1843.[54]

Many irate residents rushed to Stadden's defense. A public meeting, called "unusually large" by the *Ohio Confederate and Old School Republican,* was held on March 18. There were eloquent speeches praising Stadden as a faithful public servant. The crowd was told that he had been fired by directors Andrew McElvain and Robert Lee, who reported that he "was not removed for any want of attention, capacity or integrity, or for any official delinquency whatever" and that he had been "a faithful, honest and judicious public officer." The group passed resolutions expressing regret at his dismissal and registering support.[55]

Partly because of prison conditions and partly as a result of the religiously inspired humanitarian efforts in the early years of the nineteenth century, there were sporadic efforts at prison reform. Penal codes were revised, there was a reduction in the number of capital offenses, and the harshest types of discipline were curtailed. Beyond that, some reformers also sought to rehabilitate the criminals. The prison reform movement, however, did not receive the support that was given to the temperance and antislavery efforts. Reformers were opposed by prison administrators and politicians who put profit and punishment above the welfare of prisoners. The two groups had different attitudes toward criminals and the purpose of prisons.[56]

Not all of the descriptions of the Ohio Penitentiary were negative. Warren Jenkins, who wrote the annual *Ohio Gazetteer and Travellers Guide* in the 1840s, was impressed with the imposing structure. He wrote, "There is no possibility of any individual escaping from the cells. Nothing could be calculated for security, combined with cleanliness, healthy atmosphere and good order."[57] His boast was ill-advised, for there were several escapes from the building over the years.

In 1867 Enoch C. Wines and Theodore W. Dwight wrote their critical *Report on the Prisons and Reformatories of the United States and Canada* after visiting many institutions, including the Ohio Penitentiary. They discovered that the daily proportion of prisoners in the penitentiary's hospital was more than 15 percent, that discipline was enforced "with much strictness," and that the penitentiary was a "busy hive of industry." They were opposed to allowing visitors and quoted a warden in Wisconsin who had declared, "The influence upon convicts of admitting general visitors cannot be otherwise than injurious. This being gazed upon again and again, as criminals, tends to destroy all sense of shame, if there be any left. It further tends to harden their feelings, and make them indifferent to public opinion. These visits have, also, a very bad effect upon the discipline."[58]

One of the weaknesses in prison management in the 1840s was that little attention was given to preparing convicts for their return to the outside world. Even as late as 1851 discharged prisoners were given only five dollars as an allowance to make their way again in society.[59]

Affairs at the Ohio Penitentiary continued to attract the attention of the legislature and the public. It remained the main tourist attraction in town. Rumors and tales about the scandals, harsh discipline, and guards' brutality spread. The menacing, fortresslike walls were a constant, grim reminder of crime and terror to many residents. John Patterson, the warden, was subjected to increasing criticism in April 1845. Democrats accused him of showing favoritism to one of the Whig directors, John Greenwood, by buying his goods. Greenwood in turn was condemned for pressuring Dr. William Trevitt, the physician, to resign, the first time a physician was fired for political reasons.[60]

The legislature had stipulated that convicts should be employed in public works. The directors were ordered to purchase a nearby stone quarry in order to begin work on the new state capitol building. Several Columbus businessmen were able to persuade the directors to buy a quarry owned by William S. Sullivant, a Whig, instead of one owned by Samuel Medary. A letter in the April 16, 1845, issue of the *Ohio Statesman* claimed Sullivant had received $15,000 for his quarry and that Medary's could have been acquired for $4,000 less. Furthermore, Medary's quarry was on the east side of the river and closer to the city. Citizens from as far away as Perry County held a public meeting to protest the conduct of the warden and directors. The *Ohio Statesman* smugly observed, "The Penitentiary war still rages! The convicts out of the Penitentiary seem to be in a much worse condition, just now, than the convicts in!"[61]

The purchase of the quarry enabled the penitentiary to deliver stone at a much lower price than at market, thus delighting the politicians but enraging some merchants and laborers. Convicts built the railroad bridge and lines to the public square. Convicts were also used to construct an expansion of the insane asylum. Around 1845, some prisoners were used to repair roads and clean the city streets. According to Benjamin Dyer, "The idle and vulgar would insult these poor convicts and sometimes conflicts would occur to the scandal of order and decency."[62]

Lobbying against the competition of convict labor continued after 1845. Mechanics in Columbus held a meeting on November 20, 1845, and passed a series of resolutions criticizing the prison contract labor system. Lobbying against the penitentiary's contract labor, however, was ineffective partly because its use brought profits to the state. The politicians wanted a profitable prison. It was not until 1884 that the legislature passed a law providing that convicts should be employed only for state projects and that as current contracts expired, the convicts affected would be transferred to state work.[63]

Stung by criticism of penitentiary conditions by several visitors, the directors finally decided to make personnel changes. The annual report of the Prison Discipline Society of Boston singled out the Ohio Penitentiary one year for keeping prisoners in their cells on Sundays, and the next year for profiting so much from convict labor. Dorothea Dix's important volume *Remarks on Prisons and Prison Discipline* contained caustic comments about the institution and its living conditions and practices. Her most critical words were: "The Ohio State Penitentiary, at Columbus, is so totally deficient of the means of moral and mental culture directly imparted, that little remains to be said, after stating the fact."[64]

Whig victories in the fall 1845 election made it possible for the legislature to support replacing the warden and hiring a chaplain. Petitions calling for the appointment of a chaplain had been submitted for several years.

Lamin Dewey was appointed warden in 1846 to replace John Patterson. Dewey had been a sheriff in Portage County and editor of the *Ohio Star* and *Akron Beacon*, both Whig papers. Dewey was in favor of moderating prison discipline. He preferred what he called the "silent associated system."[65] James B. Finley, the well-known Methodist preacher who had been missionary to the Wyandots in the 1820s, was named chaplain. He commenced his duties on April 2, and Dewey arrived in June.[66]

Finley lost no time in trying to improve conditions and reform discipline. He described his first impressions in the May 21 issue of the *Ohio State Journal.* "I believe the government of the prison, at this time, is as mild as the nature of the case will admit," he wrote. He must have been aware of public criticisms of the guards for their conduct. He declared, "Showering with cold water is the most general mode of punishment for the ordinary violation of prison rule." His description of the inmates was favorable: "I have never preached to a more attentive congregation in my life. These men have souls, and have strong feelings of the need of a Savior." Finley ended his article with a plea for gifts of books for the prison library: "Here is the place for your benevolent enterprise." In three years he managed to solicit 7,000 books, 1,500 pamphlets, and 20,000 pages of tracts for the prison. The Columbus prisoners must have been the best-read convicts in the nation! Gaslights were installed in the penitentiary by 1849, and the *Ohio State Journal* commented that the inmates could "spend the long evenings in reading the books of the library, instead of as formerly, remaining in darkness and solitude."[67]

A matron for the women's wing was finally appointed in 1846. In addition to having charge of her department, her duties included making sure the cells were neat and orderly, teaching those who could not read, and administering "such moral and religious instruction and advice to them as shall be calculated to promote order, decorum, propriety of behavior and reformation." Prison reformers sought to improve conditions without much success. Although discipline was made less severe and meals more palatable, little else was done. In 1847 the Senate committee on the penitentiary sought to pass a resolution "enquiring into the expediency of abolishing . . . the lock step," but action was postponed.

On Saturday afternoon, May 8, 1847, fire destroyed all the workshops on the eastern side of the penitentiary yard. The loss of supplies and machinery to Peter Hayden's saddle operation was estimated at $20,000.[68] In the summer of 1849 a cholera epidemic swept the penitentiary. More than one-quarter of the inmates died, along with two of the attending doctors. Although the prisoners were forced to remain in their cells, discipline was relaxed. The penitentiary population dropped from 425 at the beginning of 1849 to 336 at the end of the year.[69]

By the 1850s, crimes against property, thefts, larcenies, and forgeries were the most common crimes for which inmates had been convicted. A foreign visitor, who found the penitentiary "more gloomy" than others, attributed this fact to "the respect of American society for the 'Almighty Dollar,'" a phrase she must have learned in her travels.[70]

In 1843 the General Assembly passed legislation relating to the regulation and improvement of county jails in the state. The one in Columbus was attached to the new courthouse at the corner of Mound and High. Dorothea Dix visited it and found that it fulfilled the legal requirements, unlike most others in the state. The average annual number of prisoners spending time in the jail ranged from thirty to fifty-four. The *Ohio State Journal* was proud to report on Thursday, August 17, 1848, that there were no prisoners in the jail that night.[71]

That may have been the only such night in the decade. More people in the city usually meant more crime. There were complaints of ruffians disturbing the peace, of garbage accumulating, and of obstructions to traffic. More serious crimes also occurred. One hundred thirty-nine persons in Franklin County went to jail in the twelve months ending October 31, 1846. Forty-two of them were foreign born, twenty-one were black, and thirteen were women. Fifteen were repeat offenders. Thirty-nine were arrested for breaking a city ordinance, twenty-one for assault and battery, twenty-one for petit larceny, and three for grand larceny. Six were arrested for robbing the mails, seven for counterfeiting, and five for kidnapping. Sixteen were in jail because of their debts. Two were charged with murder, one with burglary, and two were jailed for insanity. Only one was accused of rape. It was a crime that was probably not easily reported nor seriously prosecuted. Nine of those jailed were acquitted. The remainder either paid their fines, spent time in jail or the Ohio Penitentiary, or, as in the case of twenty culprits, were confined "to dungeon on bread and water."[72] An ordinance was passed in 1848 that required streets, alleys, and lanes to be cleared. In 1849 the city council created the "city watch," police who went on duty every night after sunset.[73]

10

Journalism and
Literature

Writing in 1850, George Brewster declared, "The Press is an engine of mighty power. That power is not physical, but intellectual and moral. Its extent for good or for evil is incalculable."[1]

The move of the *Western Intelligencer* from Worthington to Columbus on March 16, 1814, was an indication of how important the town was to become. Early nineteenth-century newspapers were generally four-page weekly sheets that included national, state, and local information. International events were sometimes included. The first page usually consisted of local advertisements. Newspaper articles and editorials often were characterized by exaggeration. Because papers were generally identified with a particular political party, the line between reporting and editorializing was often blurred. The press served to advocate civic pride through its articles. Editors were among the most optimistic boosters. As early as July 20, 1814, the *Western Intelligencer* boasted, "The town is rapidly improving and bids fair to become a place of consequence in a short time."[2]

The press primarily supplied information about current events. It encouraged business through its advertising, which commanded a large proportion of space, and through publishing current prices and articles about mercantile activity. In the early years, papers inserted many news items from other published sources. Newspapers published stagecoach timetables and lists of persons for whom the post office held mail. As the years passed, thanks to technological improvements that resulted in decreased printing costs, newspapers increased their readership and popularity. The press was one of the most influential institutions and continued to foster an increased sense of community. Newspapers provided helpful information to the newcomer. About thirty newspapers had been printed in Columbus by 1840, most of them small weekly papers that lasted a short time or that merged with others.[3]

The *Western Hemisphere,* a Democratic paper, was started in 1832 and was the first daily the following year. The Medary brothers bought it two years later, and under Samuel Medary's editorship the *Ohio Statesman* became the main Democratic voice in Columbus. Medary also edited the *Ohio Farmer and Western Horticulturist.*[4] The first issue of the *Ohio Statesman* was on July 5, 1837. Samuel Medary continued to edit it, except for a brief interlude, throughout the 1840s and until 1857, when he was appointed governor of the Minnesota Territory. He was named postmaster of Columbus in May 1858 and governor of Kansas in November of that year. He returned to Columbus in 1860 and died in 1864. He is probably most frequently remembered for his opposition to the Union effort in the Civil War when, as editor of the *Crisis,* he claimed that the South could not be defeated.[5]

The *Ohio Press* started in 1847 as a Democratic rival to the *Ohio Statesman* when Medary sold it temporarily, but despite Eli Y. Tappan's and Matthias Martin's efforts it died after a couple of years. Eli Tappan was Sen. Benjamin Tappan's son, and even his father's stinging editorials couldn't save the paper. The *Westbote,* a weekly German paper, was started October 2, 1843, by Jacob Reinhard and Friedrich Fieser. It supported the Democrats in the 1840s, much to the pleasure of the editor of the *Ohio Statesman,* who wrote, "The rapid increase of our German population makes such a paper highly necessary. . . . The *Westbote* will be purely democratic in principles, and firm in its course."[6] It continued printing until August 1918.

The *Ohio State Journal,* which originally had been the *Western Intelligencer,* became the leading Whig newspaper. John M. Gallagher, William Gallagher's youngest brother, became the manager. It absorbed other papers in the 1820s and 1830s.[7] Its first daily issue came out on Monday evening, December 3, 1839. Control of the *Ohio State Journal* passed to Charles Scott in 1840 and later to William B. Thrall. The *Ohio Confederate,* a states rights paper, was established in 1838. In 1841 its name was changed to *Old School Republican.* It stopped publication two years later.

The two major newspapers were the *Ohio State Journal* and the *Ohio Statesman.* Both devoted about one-half of their few pages to advertising. Both focused on state and national political news. They published daily when the General Assembly was in session and reported details of the debates and votes. At the end of the legislative sessions, which usually were in early March, the newspapers printed lists of all the laws that had been enacted. Information on congressional debates and legislation and on presidential policies was regularly included. Those residents who read a paper regularly were kept well informed about legislative actions and issues of the day, but the news they received was frequently politically slanted. The two papers produced special editions during political campaigns. They were supplemented by other brief political sheets that solicited votes. *Facts for the People,* for instance, was an 1844 Democratic paper that provided arguments for the support of James K. Polk.

Other papers in the mid-1840s included the *Palladium of Liberty,* edited by a capable, energetic black man, David Jenkins. It was first published in December 1843 but lasted only one year because of insufficient adver-tising and subscriptions. The selection of "palladium," a word meaning "protection" or "safeguard," revealed the editor's knowledge of ancient history and reflected the strong emphasis the black community placed on education.[8]

Some publications specialized. The *Ohio Mechanic* began in June 1844 as a weekly journal to focus on the rights of workers. Few, however, could afford the two-dollar annual subscription. The *Ohio Cultivator,* a semi-monthly agricultural paper, was started by M. B. Bateham in 1845. His wife, Jane, assisted him by heading up the ladies department and running articles on women's rights until she died of diabetes in 1848 at the age of twenty-seven. In 1848 a religious paper of the German Reformed Church in America, the *Western Missionary,* started publication.[9]

The *Land Seller and General Advertiser,* published monthly in 1848, was the city's first alternative paper. J. H. Purdy was its publisher, and it consisted entirely of advertisements. Purdy distributed three thousand free copies to county recorders, post offices, other agencies, hotels, and steam-boats. Although he charged for insertions, the four pages of advertisements were a service especially to new entrepreneurs in town. The paper con-tained ads for merchants, manufacturers, dentists, druggists, livery stables, hotels, bookstores, and attorneys. Real estate deals were listed. Investment attractions were described in glowing terms. C. C. Rose, boarding at the City House, announced, "A Splendid Opportunity to Make Money—sell-ing new articles." Some of the listings were in German. Purdy profited from the increased commercialism in the city.[10]

Newspapermen were held in high regard because what they wrote fre-quently touched upon political and economic themes, subjects of great in-terest to the people. Samuel Medary, the editor of the *Ohio Statesman* from 1837 to 1857, was one of the city's leading citizens and an effective Demo-cratic journalist. He was a strong supporter of President Andrew Jackson. Later, when the issue of the border between the Oregon Territory and Can-ada became critical, the chauvinistic slogan "Fifty-four forty, or fight" was attributed to him.[11]

Even newspaper editors had their problems. On July 8, 1839, a con-vention of twenty-two editors from Ohio and elsewhere met in the Senate chamber in Columbus to discuss the rising cost of printing. They passed resolutions and agreed to adopt a scale of prices, keep personal abuse out of editorials, and charge for advertisements of meetings. Little changed, however, and the papers remained biased in their political reporting.[12]

In 1849, reflecting the social ferment of the time, a more radical paper sought acceptance. The *People's Weekly Journal and Freeman's Standard* had a short career. According to its prospectus, civilization was about to abolish war and enter a new age of brotherhood. In order to accomplish this feat, people had to "pass through a preparatory or educational stage . . . to a higher sphere of individual and social life." The editor swore to "zealously plead the cause of the poor and enslaved" and insist upon "equal and exact justice for all men." The publication promised to work for the improvement of all classes and to advocate the prohibition of slavery's extension, the free grant of public lands to actual settlers, a cap on the total property owned by individuals and companies, cheap postage, a fairer system of taxation, direct vote of those elected to office, universal suffrage, shorter and less frequent meetings of legislatures, reform of justice, and more schools, libraries, and lectures "free and open to all."[13] Because it undertook too many reforms at the same time, it soon failed.

In its first forty years, Columbus did not attract large numbers of writers. Cincinnati and Cleveland contributed more to the flowering of Ohio fiction and nonfiction in the first half of the nineteenth century than did Columbus. Cincinnati was the publishing center of the West in the years before the Civil War, and the production of books in Columbus was meager in comparison. The earliest books published in the city were almanacs, lists of public officials, compilations of laws, brief histories, county registers, and geological surveys. Because Columbus was the state capital, however, the state printing was done in town. In addition to public documents and political tracts, several hundred pamphlets and educational, legal, medical, and religious titles had been published by 1850. Columbus had at least four printing companies by the 1830s.

The first literary periodical in town was the *Hesperian,* which was published in 1838 and priced at five dollars a year. It was started by William Davis Gallagher and Otway Curry and focused on western themes. Gallagher wrote many of the articles in the ninety-four-page journal and probably did more to advance western periodical literature than anyone else. In his prospectus he commented on such publications' low status: "In this country, especially in the newer section of it, the excitement of party, the turmoil of change, and the incentive to gain so engross the attention and employ the time of the mass of the people, that efforts to create an interest in the Belles-Lettres are often entirely overlooked, or regarded with the most discouraging indifference."[14] Six months later, Gallagher moved to Cincinnati, where the *Hesperian* survived for another half a year.

In 1844, the *Democratic Monthly Magazine and Western Review* began its brief career. B. B. Taylor, the editor and publisher, wrote eloquently in his prospectus about the contribution westerners would make to American culture and patriotism. He declared, "At no period of American history have those moral influences, which mould and fashion society . . . been in more active operation than at the present epoch. . . . There is among the people of this vast Region, a robust spirit and energy, not yet thoroughly nationalized, capable of being formed with a national character more elevated and grand than any the world has yet seen . . . in short, a character thoroughly American."[15] Taylor promised articles that would reflect a democratic principle. The *Western Literary Magazine, and Journal of Education, Science, Arts, and Morals* was another Columbus periodical. Its first volume was published in April 1850.

The public's interest in books was strong, for the early settlers in Columbus were eager to have much of the same culture they had left behind. The first book published in Columbus became a best-seller. John Kilbourn, nephew of Worthington's founder, opened a bookstore shortly after 1812. His *Ohio Gazetteer: or Topographical Dictionary, containing a Description of the Several Counties, Towns, Villages and Settlements in the State of Ohio,* published in 1816, went through many editions and served to attract settlers to the state. Kilbourn supplied helpful information about roads and travel routes. The book's tenth edition in 1826 was called *The Ohio Manual.* Fourteen thousand copies were sold in four years. Two years later Kilbourn published *Public Documents, concerning the Ohio Canals.* In 1830 he wrote *A Geography of the State of Ohio.* In 1837 Warren Jenkins expanded Kilbourn's book under the title *The Ohio Gazetteer and Travellers Guide.* It contained 546 pages and a map. Jenkins issued revised editions through 1841.[16]

Most of the writers living in Columbus were men, but the most prolific author was Margaret Coxe. In addition to her books on women, in 1840 she wrote *The Life of John Wycliffe,* whom she called "the father of the English Reformation." The 272-page book was more than a biography. In its first chapters Coxe gave a sweeping account of religious activity going back to the time of Gregory the Great. She was critical of Catholicism and credited Wycliffe with freeing the English people from "the shackles of a slavish superstition." She wrote that Wycliffe's "strong and discriminating mind, enlightened by the spirit of God, saw and deeply felt the evils under which his countrymen were suffering."[17] It was a remarkable book for its time. Her other books included *Botany of the Scriptures, Wonders of the Deep, The Infant Brother,* and *Woman: Her Station Providentially Appointed.* Coxe was director of the Cincinnati Female Seminary from 1849 to 1851.[18]

The year 1833 marked the publication in Columbus of Thomas Chalmers's book *On Political Economy.* Chalmers was professor of divinity at the University of Edinburgh and wrote about the moral aspects of economic issues. The first American edition of William Shepherd's *A History of the American Revolution* was published by Whiting in 1834. That same year William T. Martin wrote the *Franklin County Register*. It contained the names of all officials who had served the county since its organization. Martin contributed a short history to the 1843 business directory. He wrote the first *History of Franklin County* in 1858.[19]

Eleanor Campbell, widow of John Campbell, completed his *Biographical Sketches* in 1838. John Campbell was a lawyer who served in Congress for ten years and was a U.S. district judge. He came to Columbus in 1831 but died of cholera two years later. The book contained chapters on early Ohio leaders and miscellaneous papers and speeches by Campbell.[20]

Phineas B. Wilcox, a lawyer, came to Columbus about 1821. His first publication in 1836 was titled *A Few Thoughts by a Member of the Bar*. It was a defense of Christianity, and he addressed the question of why so few influential men were its avid supporters. His law library was one of the most extensive in the state. He was the author of several legal volumes, including *Tracts on Law Reform* in 1849.[21]

William W. Mather, the state geologist, wrote the *Annual Report on the Geological Survey of the State of Ohio* in 1838. In 1842, he produced the *Catalogue of the Geological Specimens, Collected on the Late Survey of the State of Ohio*. Interest in this book was indicative of the growing awareness townspeople had of many areas of science. Joseph Sullivant's *An alphabetical catalogue of shells, fossils, minerals and zoophytes* was also published in 1838. Joseph was the third son of Lucas Sullivant, founder of Franklinton. He became a successful businessman, community leader, and a trustee of The Ohio State University.[22]

The year 1840 marked an increase in the publication of scientific books. In February *A Catalogue of Plants, Native and Naturalized, in the Vicinity of Columbus, Ohio*, written by William S. Sullivant, the oldest son of Lucas, was in the bookstores. William Sullivant was a botanist who had graduated from Yale. The sixty-three-page book was published by Charles Scott. Sullivant received a microscope from Asa Gray in April 1840. Five years later, Sullivant produced a two-volume, illustrated work on plants. He was one of the first American scientists to use a microscope in his botanical research and was made a member of the American Academy of Arts and Sciences. He was one of the more prolific scientists in the city's history. His second wife, Eliza, helped him with his research and became an excellent botanist. Some of her drawings are at Harvard University.[23]

Several other books were published in Columbus in 1840, including John G. Miller's *The Great Convention: Description of the Convention of the People of Ohio, held at Columbus, on the 21st, and 22nd February 1840*. Miller's work was considered one of the best contemporary accounts

Mrs. William Sullivant. From White, ed., *We Too Built Columbus.*

of the huge Whig gathering at the corner of Broad and High and was more readable than most of the political campaign tracts. Miller established a Democratic paper, the *Ohio Confederate,* in 1836 but supported Harrison in 1840. He was named postmaster of Columbus from 1841 to 1845 and practiced law through 1857.[24]

The Harrison campaign generated income for Columbus publishers who brought out *A Sketch of the Life and Services of William Henry Harrison* (published by I. N. Whiting), *Harrison and Log Cabin Song Book* (a 108-page book of campaign songs that sold for twenty-five cents), and a book in Welsh on Harrison's life by H. R. Price.

Among the other books published in Columbus in the 1840s, Andrew

Coffinberry's account of the Wayne campaign, *The Forest Rangers: A Poetic Tale of the Western Wilderness in 1794,* published in 1842 but written in 1825, was instrumental in glorifying the winning of the area for white settlers.

Philo Olmsted sought to satisfy residents' demands for books in his store as quickly as possible. By 1817 he was offering for sale biographies of Napoleon, Alexander Hamilton, and Israel Putnam. A memoir of George Washington, the *Ohio Gazetteer,* an introduction to geography, and a spelling book were best-sellers. A German almanac was also available.[25]

By 1830, the bookstore run by Thomas Johnson was selling Waverley novels by Sir Walter Scott, Strickland's book on railroads and canals, a biography of Richelieu, a narrative of Johnson's captivity among the Indians, Thompson's medical theory of practice, and the ninth edition of Kilbourn's *Ohio Gazetteer.*[26]

The Bible continued to be a best-seller in the bookstores. Other popular books published elsewhere in 1840 included James Fenimore Cooper's *The Pathfinder,* Edgar Allen Poe's *Tales,* and Richard Henry Dana Jr.'s *Two Years Before the Mast.* Dickens was the favorite author in the Northern states. His *Barnaby Rudge* and *The Old Curiosity Shop* were published in 1841, as was Cooper's *The Deerslayer* and Ralph Waldo Emerson's *Essays.* Dickens's *American Notes* came out in November 1842. He finished *A Christmas Carol* and *Martin Chuzzlewit* two years later.

New books appeared in the bookstores as the decade progressed. Other best-sellers included Alexandre Dumas's *The Three Musketeers,* Edgar Allan Poe's *The Raven and Other Poems,* Hans Christian Andersen's *Fairy Tales,* and Charlotte Brontë's *Jane Eyre.* When Macaulay's *History of England* was published in 1849, cheap, pirated copies sold for fifteen cents a volume. The Methodist minister Uriah Heath was reading it as early as May of that year.[27]

The public also gained access to the State Library and its eight thousand volumes in March 1845. This action was one more example of society's increased democratization and the interest of many Columbus residents in self-improvement.[28]

Most of the books read in Columbus were written by eastern authors or by foreigners. By 1850, however, there was an increased desire to see works written by those in the West. An author in the first issue of the *Western Literary Magazine* wrote, "The West must have its own literature, and not rely wholly on foreign products for her necessary supply."[29]

Columbus residents shared with their western neighbors a feeling of inferiority when they compared their culture with that of eastern cities. During its first decades of existence the city could not offer what Boston, Philadelphia, or New York could provide in the variety of educational institutions, bookstores, and musical and dramatic events. Nevertheless, many thought that eventually the region would catch up with the East and even possibly surpass it in terms of its contributions to American progress. B. B. Taylor, the editor of the *Democratic Monthly Magazine and Western Review,* published in Columbus, represented this attitude in 1844 when he wrote, "We predict then, that, when the Western type of civilization shall be fully formed, and assume distinctiveness of feature, it will display humanity in a state of perfection and on a scale of moral grandeur, of which we now have no adequate conception." He believed that from the area comprising the Ohio and Mississippi valleys "is yet to go forth a spirit which shall rouse the nations, reform the civilization of the world, and reconstruct it upon an entirely new basis . . . that shall elevate the condition of mankind, and realize the high destiny of the human race."[30]

11

Education

Columbus residents were proud of the fact that the Land Ordinance of 1785 stipulated, "There shall be reserved the Lot No. 16, of every township, for the maintenance of public schools within said township," and that the Northwest Ordinance in 1787 contained the words, "Religion, morality, and knowledge being necessary to good government and the happiness of mankind, schools and the means of education shall forever be encouraged." The 1802 Ohio Constitutional Convention proposed, and Congress accepted, a requirement that the United States give one thirty-sixth of the land area in Ohio for school support and 3 percent of the proceeds from the sale of public lands in the state.

Schools became another force in fostering community loyalty, but in their early years they were private institutions and most of them closed within a few years. In the first winter after Columbus was established, some residents hired a teacher "by voluntary donation" to teach in a log cabin on the public square. A "Ladies Academy" opened in December 1814 and taught reading, writing, plain sewing, music, grammar, arithmetic, and geography. It was run by Mrs. Smith, newly arrived from Boston. Two years later, Mrs. Stebbins started a dancing school. William T. Martin, who later wrote a history of Franklin County, started a school in December 1816 that included a night school for those who worked during the day. Four more schools were started in the town's first decade. Parents wanted their children educated, and their determination was so strong they couldn't wait for the legislators to get around to their duties.[1]

In 1821 some Columbus residents agreed to create a "Columbus Seminary." The trustees were James Hoge, the Presbyterian minister; Ralph Osborn; and Gustavus Swan, who was one of the first lawyers in town. The trustees found a house, hired a teacher, and opened the school on Monday morning, June 4. Tuition ranged from ten dollars for reading, orthography, and writing to sixteen dollars for studying Greek and Latin. Publicity for the school promised that "Strict attention will be paid to the moral conduct and orderly deportment of all the scholars, both in and out of school." In 1827 two teachers started another "Female Academy" in Jarvis Pike's home. Tuition ranged from $2.50 to $4. Girls from out of town were promised boarding with private families. A teacher named Chute was equally concerned with pupil morals when he taught Latin and Greek in 1828. Philo Olmsted started a private high school in 1832 with tuition ranging from three to five dollars. It was not until later that public schools became a major factor in educating children.[2]

The legislature might not have acted on school legislation had Caleb Atwater not been elected to the House of Representatives. In Atwater's *History of the State of Ohio,* published in 1838, he recorded his role in discovering that in its early years, the legislature had neglected to honor the intention of the U.S. Congress in setting aside one thirty-sixth of the land granted the state for support of education. The main method of survey was a rectangular one that carved townships six miles square with thirty-six sections one mile square. Initially the legislature allowed temporary leases, but from 1817 to 1823 it authorized permanent ones. After 1827 the state sold the school lands. Some were occupied by squatters who made few improvements. Atwater wrote in his book, "Members of the legislature, not infrequently, got acts passed and leases granted, either to themselves, to their relations, to their warm partisans." He claimed that these actions cost the people $1 million that might have gone to the support of common schools.[3]

The first law enacted by the General Assembly in 1821 authorized school districts, the election of three resident householders to a school committee, and local taxes for the construction of schools. This law was inadequate, and little was done as a result.[4]

Atwater was on a 1821 committee that recommended that the governor appoint seven commissioners "to devise a system of law" for schools. The commission, with Atwater as chair, met in Columbus throughout 1822. Atwater wrote three pamphlets on the condition of school lands, a proposed bill, and the proposed school system. A majority of his colleagues, however, were opposed to a school system, and the proposed legislation failed. Those who favored public education campaigned in the 1824 state elections and helped elect majorities favorable to schools.

People were understandably concerned about the delay in making formal public education available to their children. Just before the legislature acted on the subject, the *Columbus Gazette* printed a long editorial expressing concern about the abortive efforts to educate the young: "Ignorance and stupidity form fit subjects for tyrants. . . . Free governments cannot exist without the people are enlightened. . . . The middling class cannot well afford the expense of educating their sons abroad. . . . The poor are without any opportunity."[5] The new editor of the *Ohio State Journal and Columbus Gazette,* after commenting on the rapid growth of the state and the amount of political harmony, expressed regret that the subject of common schools seemed to be treated with so much apathy and even prejudice. He concluded, "That it is education alone that places man above the brute; that it is the great and only source of happiness, and the sole foundation upon which the perpetuity of our government rests, are axioms admitted by the ignorant and the enlightened to be undeniable." He thought that one-half cent yearly out of every hundred dollars of appraised property was a minimal expense.[6]

The 1825 law was also inadequate, for it contained no centralized control of common schools. It did, however, provide for minimal taxation, a one-half mill on taxable property. The rate was increased in 1829 to three-quarters of a mill and in 1834 to one mill. Trustees of incorporated towns were instructed to establish school districts in terms of population and to make lists of householders. Meetings were authorized for householders and inhabitants to elect three school directors who would manage the districts and hire and pay teachers, who had to be approved by examiners appointed by courts of common pleas. Two years later, the legislature passed a supplementary act encouraging school districts to hold public meetings in order to get property owners to agree to be taxed for school construction. A three-fifths vote requirement was included.[7]

Columbus leaders acted promptly in 1826 to hold the first school meeting after the 1825 act. Orrin Parish was chair, and William McElvain, one of the first settlers, participated. They hired a Mr. Smith as teacher, but because of the shortage of funds the school ran for only three months. McElvain became one of the directors in 1830.[8]

The 1825 law was a small step in the direction of public education. Columbus residents had to wait until 1837 for the next significant legislation for education. In the meantime, small private schools opened and closed. The most successful one was the Columbus Female Seminary, which opened in December 1829.[9]

In terms of support for public education, the general population showed more leadership than the politicians. There was also a difference between theory and practice. As indicated earlier, the state legislature had established a common school system in 1825 and required taxes from property owners but provided for no centralized control, so it still took a while for schools to open. Most of the teaching was inadequate. Evan Edmiston may have been representative of most of the children. He quit school at age thirteen. Later he wrote, "I was not very studious. Plaid the truent a graid deal and many a time had my Back Paid for it." By the mid-1830s, public pressure was increasing for a better educational system. A convention of teachers was held in Columbus on January 13, 1836, to publicize the need for universal education.[10]

Alfred Kelley, the Columbus representative to the convention, was successful in getting a committee to consider creating an office of superintendent of common schools. The legislature created the position in 1837, and Samuel Lewis was appointed at a salary of five hundred dollars. He went about his duties as a one-man task force with diligence and perseverance, collecting information and publicizing the need for a better system. He also reminded his readers about the previous failures of the legislature to devote sufficient funds to public education. In his first annual report Lewis wrote, "[O]ur work is first to adopt a system of building school-houses and establishing schools; and when that is done we may advance the next step, and, as fast and far as possible, introduce proper systems of instruction."[11]

The legislature passed another act in March 1838 to authorize a comprehensive common school system. Although it provided for its supervision, there were defects. It covered only white children, lacked standards for the employment of supervisors, did not provide adequate salaries for teachers or for their training, and did not require children's attendance. As a result, fewer than half of all children were in school. William H. McGuffey was active with Lewis in promoting school reform. The author of *Eclectic Readers* for children, who was soon to become president of Ohio University, came to Columbus on December 31, 1838, to speak on common school education.[12]

Lewis kept traveling to collect information and from his office in Columbus became a champion for better education. In his third report he wrote, "Unless the Common Schools can be made to educate the whole people, the poor as well as the rich, they are not worthy the support of the patriot or philanthropist." He thought the lack of sufficient support for education of the poor was "a reproach to the state." He announced his intention to resign in this report. His letters frequently mentioned his illness, but he may also have felt frustrated at the failure of more people to accept his ideas. For example, in his 1838 report, he recommended a system of secondary schools. He also favored more schools for girls.[13]

The annual meetings of the friends of education held in Columbus served to give Lewis's views more publicity. Because of his exposure of legislative abuses in leasing and selling school lands, political leaders were extremely critical of him. The legislature abolished his position in 1839. Responsibilities for education were given to the secretary of state. Caleb Atwater continued his efforts to improve schooling. In his *Essay on Education* he wrote, "We live in an age of innovation and change, and the signs of the times are awful and portentous."[14]

In 1839 Columbus residents voted to purchase three schoolhouse lots and approved a tax of $3,500 to pay for them, but the free common schools opened in rented rooms costing $600. Four hundred students attended. According to the 1841 report of the directors of the common schools in Columbus, eight women were employed as teachers and they earned fifty dollars a quarter.[15] By 1843, even though schools were inadequate by most standards, educational opportunities were available in fifteen free common schools serving about seven hundred students. Some Columbus residents and recent immigrants criticized the schools' operation for a variety of reasons. In his 1839 annual message, Gov. Wilson Shannon commented on these complaints but noted that those made by recent German-speaking arrivals had decreased in fervor.[16]

The German immigrants wanted to keep their own culture and language. Catholic immigrants also believed that the common schools were anti-Catholic in their teaching. Because of these complaints, made mostly by German immigrants in Cincinnati, the Ohio legislature in 1838 voted to permit school subjects other than reading, writing, and arithmetic to be taught in a foreign language. The following year the legislature allowed all subjects to be taught in a foreign language. German settlers in Columbus during the 1840s had three such schools for their children, attended by 207 students who were taught by nineteen German teachers.[17] In addition, after 1838 one of the first kindergartens, directed by Caroline Frankenburg, opened. It was in the area now known as German Village.[18]

As early as January 1841, the directors of the common school opened an evening school three nights a week for the benefit of white male youth who could not attend a school during the day. Arithmetic, bookkeeping, geography, "and other useful branches" were taught. Instruction was free but pupils had to bring their own light. This innovation reflected a dedication to the concept of public support of education of young men regardless of their economic status.[19]

Public education was given a boost by a February 1845 law that authorized the election of six directors to a board to manage public schools in Columbus. In the spring of 1846 voters approved a tax totaling eight thousand dollars to erect three schoolhouses of six rooms each. The schools opened in mid-July of 1847. Three hundred pupils registered the first day. The grades were primary (ages four to six or seven), secondary (six or seven to eight or nine), grammar, and high school.[20] Asa D. Lord was appointed the first superintendent of schools in 1847. Lord was a leader in educational reform. He started teaching when he was twenty-one. In 1846 he founded the *Ohio School Journal,* a semimonthly, sixteen-page magazine that focused on educational topics. It was published in Columbus after its first year. As superintendent of schools Lord organized the first public high school in Columbus and helped create the Ohio State Teachers Association.[21]

Fifteen teachers were employed in 1848, and the average daily attendance of pupils was 798. By 1850 average daily attendance was more than one thousand, and twenty teachers were employed. Women taught in the primary and secondary schools, and men taught at the grammar-school level. Schools ran from late July until late December and January to late June, and were open five days a week from nine to noon and two to five in the warm season, one to four in the cold season. Singing was taught at all levels in addition to the traditional subjects. Residents and tourists were encouraged to visit the schools. However, even as late as 1850, the high school had no building of its own and was meeting in the basement of the Reformed Church on Town Street.[22]

An act passed in 1848 required the board of education to report annually in May on its financial needs to keep the schools in operation. The president of city council in turn notified voters of the amount of tax that had to be raised, and those qualified males voted for or against the levy. By the end of the decade tuition cost each student $1.44 per quarter, even though the schools were supposed to be free. Interest in education was generated by the publication in Columbus in 1847 of Calvin E. Stowe's *Report on Elementary Education in Europe*. Asa D. Lord probably wrote the idealistic bylaws that stated, "[B]eing free, these schools furnish ample opportunity to all children and youth . . . for acquiring an education that will fit them for almost any station in life." The board assumed that poor children were placed in "entire equality" with those "more favored."[23]

When the delegates to the 1850 Constitutional Convention met in Columbus that December, they debated the question of public support of education. They finally agreed to accept wording that stipulated: "The General Assembly shall make such provisions, by taxation, or otherwise, as, with the income arising from the school trust fund, will secure a thorough and efficient system of common schools throughout the state." Thus, another decision made at that time was decisive in mandating solid public and state support for education, a decision reaffirmed by the Ohio Supreme Court in 1997. That same section also stipulated that no religious sect was to have any exclusive right to the state's school funds.[24]

Subscription schools provided an elementary education for the children of families who could afford them. There were charity schools for others. Because black children were excluded from the public school system, black residents supported a school for their children in south Columbus in the 1830s. In 1839 an organization of black residents sought funds for a school. The trustees, David Jenkins, B. Roberts, and C. Lewis, wrote in their advertisement that they felt "compelled by our indigent circumstances to appeal to the white citizens" and emphasized the importance of education to improve their children's condition. They had $225 subscribed and needed an additional $415. With financial assistance from some whites, the trustees bought a lot and erected a school. This one was called the Alley School because it was at the intersection of Lafayette and Lazelle Alleys.

Before 1849 there was no state money for black schools. The high importance that black families placed on education served to persuade some white residents to support public education for black children as well.[25]

In 1840 a "Young Gentlemen's Select School" opened in the third story of a building on the corner of High and Town Streets for twenty students. The teacher was J. S. Brown. For eight dollars one could study reading, writing, arithmetic, geography, and grammar; for ten dollars, philosophy, chemistry, and "geography of the heavens"; and for twelve dollars, Greek and Latin, algebra, and surveying. Abiel Foster and his sister, Catherine, opened the Columbus Institute later that year. Their school was in a new building at the corner of Rich and Front Streets.[26]

In September 1840, a "Select School for Young Ladies" was started in the Exchange Building by the Reverend Timothy Steams, who had been principal of the Worthington Academy. The school was limited to twenty-five pupils, and tuition was eight dollars. Steams declared it his object "to aid his pupils to think and reason for themselves, and to induce them to feel that accurate comprehension is more important than rapid progress in study." Support at that time for educating all women, however, was not universal.[27]

A competing "Young Ladies Seminary" offered instruction by Miss Covert in her house at the corner of Friend and High Streets. Tuition ranged from three to seven dollars a quarter depending upon the subject to be taught. Principles of natural science were included. Pupils could also learn French and drawing, and they were admitted free to science lectures at the Columbus Academical and Collegiate Institute on Town Street. The institute was housed in a two-story brick building that contained some chemical instruments and a library of hundreds of books. Another "Female Seminary" was opened in June 1843 by the Shenks, a couple who had recently arrived in town. He was a graduate of West Point and she of Emma Willard's Seminary in Troy, New York, so they were able to charge a higher tuition: four dollars for the twenty-two-week introductory course, six dollars for the second class, and eight dollars for the highest class. In addition, they charged twenty-five dollars for boarding students and promised that their pupils would be "parentally watched over." They also gave assurance that they followed "a mild but firm discipline" and listed as their primary purpose "to teach the pupil to think for herself." Piano and guitar instruction required additional fees.[28]

By 1845 the Columbus Female Seminary had attracted eighty-five girls, many of whom were daughters of the city's leading families, including the Deshlers, Medarys, Ridgways, Stanberys, and Thralls. There were three Sullivant girls, plus three other girls who lived in Franklinton. The Columbus Female Seminary's popularity among the elite was evidence that they thought little of the common school. These prominent families started the tradition of favoring private over public education for their children.[29]

In addition to the Columbus Female Seminary, the Columbus Academical and Collegiate Institute had good enrollments. In 1844 the institute had 125 male students and 85 female students. Some of these schools sent home weekly reports grading recitations and deportment. Some distributed small "Reward of Merit" cards for diligence and good behavior that children collected and saved.[30]

At a higher level, the Literary and Botanical Medical College of Ohio was founded in 1837. Lectures were given in anatomy, obstetrics, physiology, and surgery. There was also strong interest in botanic medicine. Students were required to buy tickets, priced at fifteen dollars, for each professor at the medical college. Use of the library cost five dollars, the hospital ticket cost five dollars, and a dissecting ticket cost ten dollars. The graduation fee was twenty-five dollars, which made medical education an expensive proposition.

Among medical schools in the area, Columbus residents were familiar with the Ohio Reformed Medical College in Worthington, for it was frequently mentioned in Columbus newspapers. It was founded in 1830. The six men on the faculty in 1840 were considered highly qualified. Dr. Ichabod G. Jones, who had been assistant to Dr. Thomas V. Morrow, the college's president, moved to Columbus and lived at the northeast corner of Third and State Streets. He opened an office on Town Street because of his increased practice. In 1839, however, because cadavers were scarce, some persons from the college were suspected of stealing three bodies from the potter's field north of Columbus and from cemeteries near Delaware. A riot occurred in Worthington that December because some residents were incensed that bodies were being stolen from graves for college use. Because of the furor, the General Assembly withdrew the institution's authority to grant medical degrees in 1840. President Morrow and most of the faculty moved to Cincinnati and helped establish the Eclectic Medical Institute.[31]

Teachers and others interested in education met in Columbus in December 1842 and agreed to form a county association "for the improvement of schools, and the elevation of the teachers' profession." The week of activities began on Monday, December 26, with a lecture by Henry Barnard, who had gained national recognition as the former superintendent of common schools in Connecticut. Barnard was also an associate of Emma Willard and publisher of the *Journal of Education*. The association members met in the hall of the House of Representatives on Wednesday evening, December 28, and continued the next day at the Methodist church and on December 30 at the Presbyterian church. Papers were read, and the group approved a resolution to the legislature calling for improvements in the school system. There was also discussion of whether the Bible should be used as a class book in common schools, but no vote was taken on the question.[32]

Community leaders looked to the schools to do more than educate youth. Schools were expected to play a role in social reform. City dwellers were concerned about what they considered urban life's deleterious influences on youth and their sense of values. The schools, it was believed, could help acculturate the young and encourage them to become effective citizens.[33]

Although Ohioans had long maintained strong support for universal education at the elementary level, before 1850 secondary education was looked upon as a privilege to be paid for by those who could afford it. The legislature's involvement consisted of approving the incorporation of private secondary schools, most of which were supported by the selling of company shares and by tuitions. But education was given a low priority by most legislators, who were more concerned with banking issues, commercial development, canal and railroad construction, and reducing costs. Characteristic of this low priority was the abolition of the office of state superintendent of education.[34]

Interest in theological education also developed in this period. The Theological Seminary of the Evangelical Lutheran Synod of Ohio moved to Columbus from Canton in 1831. Two loyal Lutherans, Gustavus Swan and Christian Heyl, offered $2,500 to lure the seminary to the capital. Those in Canton could raise only $2,000. In addition to Swan and Heyl, John Leist and F. A. Schneider were the other lay members of the board of directors. William Schmidt, a minister in Canton, agreed to run the seminary without any income for the first two years. The seminary bought land near the canal from Lyne Starling and erected a small building. The cornerstone was laid July 15, 1832.[35]

In reference to the seminary, John W. Campbell read a paper at the Columbus Lyceum in 1833 and described the pupils as "peaceful, assuming and studious." He thought the principal was "assiduous in the discharge of his duties."[36] A literary department at the seminary was begun in 1840 because the founders eventually intended to expand it into a college. In 1843 the General Assembly authorized the Lutheran Theological Seminary to create Germania College, something that was never done. The seminary's collegiate department offered Greek, Latin, German, French, English, ancient and modern history, geography, and mathematics. Free music instruction was given once a week. There was student unrest in the 1840s and a controversy over the issue of whether German or English should be used in the courses. As a compromise, the institution was bilingual for a while. In the summer of 1845, tuition for the eighteen-week summer term at the seminary was $11.50. Room rent was $3, board was $22.50, and washing was $2.50. Students had to provide their own light and fuel. Costs were slightly higher in the longer winter term.[37]

The seminary moved in 1850 to a building called the Covert School on Town Street between Fifth and Sixth Streets. It managed to sell its old building near the canal to Peter Hayden at a 264 percent profit. The school was able to realize a considerable gain in its investment in an undesirable part of town in only twenty years.[38]

That year the institution received its charter as Capital University. Once Capital was started, the seminary became the university's theological department. William R. Reynolds, who was at Gettysburg College, was the first president. Lincoln Goodale gave four acres of land to the college, and the cornerstone of a building at a North High Street campus was laid in 1852. Thus Columbus residents at this time witnessed the beginnings in their city of the national effort by Protestant churches to found colleges in the old Northwest.[39]

Otterbein College, twelve miles away in Westerville, opened with eight students on September 1, 1847. The new coeducational college was named after one of the United Brethren Church's first bishops. A resident of Westerville, R. R. Arnold, had been in a Columbus clothing store in 1846 when he overheard two United Brethren ministers discussing their plans for establishing a college. He returned home, called a meeting, and persuaded the trustees of the Blendon Young Men's Seminary to sell it to the men. (The seminary, a Methodist institution, had been given a charter in 1839. Matthew and Peter Westervelt contributed land for the school, which thrived for a few years. The last classes were held in 1844.) The United Brethren Church paid thirteen hundred dollars for the seminary's eight acres of land and two buildings. Otterbein College had eighty-one students by the end of its first year and received a charter from the legislature in 1849.[40]

12

The Role of Religion

Religion in the early nineteenth century was more significant and more pervasive in the western reaches of the new republic. Regardless of denomination, belief in a Providence that somehow favored white Americans and a will for personal salvation characterized the frontier settlers. Families that faced personal and economic uncertainties, disease, and death needed steadfast faith. Religion provided a practical and emotional satisfaction that was given high priority. Independence for the country opened the door for a number of Protestant sects that sought to serve and save the new communities. Beginning with the Cane Ridge, Kentucky, revival in 1801, people living north and south of the Ohio River witnessed a strong resurgence of religious interest, later called the Second Great Awakening, that continued for several decades. One early settler observed in 1811, "[T]here are here a large congregation of very sober pious people and I think I have seen more of what I call real Religion in this country than I ever saw before."[1]

The first settlers in Columbus soon sought to form churches in town. The churches helped bind people together and were stabilizing forces in times of stress. Religion played an important role in the young town as, indeed, it had in the formative years of the state. Churches were constructed early in the city's history, and they supplied a social as well as a religious function. By giving people a common experience, they served as a way for newcomers to become integrated into the life of the community and brought those of diverse backgrounds together in a common cause, namely, the salvation of their souls. Those who arrived with letters from their former congregations were accepted immediately into a new community of believers.

Churches also were a force for morality in the community through sermons and rituals, and through their existence as permanent institutions in a place experiencing constant change. Ministers held a higher place in society than they do today and were more influential in the life of the city. Churches encouraged their members to provide charity to those less fortunate at a time when there was little or no aid for the unemployed and those in poverty. Church leaders were also concerned with creating and maintaining order. Evangelical Protestantism fostered stability by preaching self-discipline and providing a rationale for regulating members' private and social lives. Page Smith has credited Protestantism in the small towns both with supplying a justification for respecting and preserving values and with maintaining a social order. As Catholicism increased in influence in Columbus it too served as a stabilizing moral force.[2]

Churches played an educational role before the advent of common schools. Although their main focus was religious, moral, and ethical, Sunday schools provided one way for children to learn to read and write. An article in the *Sunday School Journal,* reprinted in a Columbus newspaper, asserted that Sunday schools "diffuse the wisest modes of instruction" and stimulated the intellectual powers of the pupil.[3] Columbus residents also reflected changing attitudes toward children by placing more emphasis on the importance of influencing their future conduct not only at home but also in Sunday school classes. These classes encouraged behavior patterns that would result in a more orderly, stable society.[4]

Political leaders recognized the vital role religious institutions played in developing a cohesive community. When Gov. Thomas Worthington implemented the action of the General Assembly in holding a day of thanksgiving and prayer on Saturday, May 23, 1818, he called on people to give thanks for "the very extraordinary blessings bestowed on them by Almighty God" and also "for free enjoyment of civil and religious liberty." He requested that "the good people of Ohio meet at their respective places of worship." He was continuing the encouragement of what Martin Marty has called "civil or public religion" favored by George Washington and other political leaders of his generation.[5]

Because most people accepted the custom of stopping work on Sundays, the churches were magnets for the populace on that day. Middle- and upper-class men and women dressed in their best clothes. Churches were used for both religious and secular meetings through the rest of the week. Because of the shortage of buildings for large assemblies, a number of city and statewide organizational meetings were held in them.

George McCormick, a Methodist layman and carpenter, was on the scene in Columbus as early as 1812 and invited circuit riders to visit. Two years later, Samuel West organized a Methodist class consisting of McCormick and his wife, George B. Harvey, Jane Armstrong, and Moses Freeman, a black man who later went to Liberia as a missionary. John Brickell cut the logs for the structure built in 1815 on Town Street between High and Third that became the Methodist Episcopal Church. It was replaced by a brick building in 1826.

The class was the smallest Methodist unit, and the leader was responsible for the spiritual welfare of his group between visits of the circuit rider. Because frontier areas lacked churches, the Methodist Episcopal Church created circuits and had its preachers travel daily from settlement to settlement to preach and meet with church members. One-third of the residents in Columbus at that time were Methodists. Methodism's success in attracting members resulted from the church's organization, its dedicated ministers, and its message of salvation for all.

Camp meetings were popular. One in June 1818 was held thirteen miles northeast of Columbus, along Alum Creek on the road leading to Sunbury. A newspaper notice promised, "Horse keeping provided for." In 1821 the popular site for Methodist camp meetings was near Big Walnut Creek. By this time the planners had to warn, "The sale of ardent spirits will be prevented at or near the camp ground." Camp meetings were frequently interrupted by rowdies, some of whom were drunk. The tradition of frequent revivals continued in later decades. In other groves across the country, devout Christians were singing the same hymns and hearing similar biblical messages as revivals spread across the land.[6]

Methodism continued to thrive in Columbus. The Clinton Methodist Chapel was built in 1839. Jason Bull, who lived on High Street across from the chapel, conducted services and hid escaping slaves in his basement. Charles H. Peters was assigned to the Columbus circuit in 1840. Joseph M. Trimble, who had been professor of mathematics at Augusta College since 1835, was a preacher from 1840 to 1842. State senator James Loudon, who heard Trimble preach in 1843, wrote that he had "a pretty good sermon." The Methodists experienced a revival during the winter of 1840 and again in March 1842 when more than one hundred people joined the church. Trimble was followed by David Whitcomb. A revival in January 1843 attracted mostly young people.[7]

The original Baptist church in Columbus was organized by George Jeffries, who was a carpenter, painter, and teacher as well as a preacher. He first held services in his log house on High Street. The church building first stood on Front Street south of Friend Street, and a later building was constructed on the northwest corner of Rich and Third Streets. Three of the church's first members in 1824 were blacks: Patsy Booker, Lydia Jones, and George Butcher. Some Welsh Baptists moved to Columbus in 1833 and formed a church led by the Reverend John Harris. When T. R. Cressy came in 1835, sent by the American Baptist Home Missionary Society, he persuaded the groups to unite and form the First Baptist Church. The church bought a lot at the corner of Rich and Third Streets from Lincoln Goodale for eight hundred dollars. A building was constructed and dedicated on November 1, 1840. Its tall spire became a familiar landmark.[8]

In 1834, black members decided to form what became the Second Baptist Church, which was initially recognized as the African Baptist Church. Its first pastor was Ezekiel Fields. Originally it met on Gay Street. The African Methodist Church was organized in 1823. Black church members felt the discrimination when they were required to sit in black pews or in the balcony. In 1849 a convention of blacks in Columbus protested against the "negro pew." Black churches provided more than religious services for their members. They served as social, economic, and political centers for the black community and were a major institution in cultural preservation.[9]

James Hoge, the Presbyterian minister, contributed a lot near Spring and Third Streets so that Presbyterians could build a cabin of hickory logs in 1814. Hoge later moved to Columbus from Franklinton, where he had lived and preached since 1805, and served as pastor of the First Presbyterian Church from 1816. Because membership increased, the congregation moved into a larger building at Front and Town Streets.[10]

The third move of the First Presbyterian Church was to a brick building with a steeple and bell near the southeast corner of State and Third. Hoge became moderator of the Presbyterian General Assembly in 1832 and was the first president of the Presbyterian Historical Society. He frequently lobbied the legislature to improve conditions for the handicapped. His home was on Broad Street where the Athletic Club now stands. Hoge was extremely active in the town. His appearance was dour and forbidding to many. Horace Wilson, however, claimed that "under the seeming cold exterior he had a great deal of tenderness and warmth." Hoge's conservative sermons were considered profound. He campaigned for temperance and favored colonization for free blacks.[11]

First Presbyterian was probably the most influential church in town because many of its members were business and political leaders, including Lyne Starling, Gustavus Swan, and Robert W. McCoy. By the 1840s some of the church's members rebelled against the custom in services of having an elder line off the hymns to help the congregation sing. Thanks to the efforts of women who did some fund raising, First Presbyterian soon had an organ. Joseph Sullivant later wrote, "Grave doubts and fears were expressed by some of the older members as to its effects upon the congregation. But the ladies were unanimous for it, and while the men doubted and discussed, they carried the day, and decided the matter by declaring that they would get it themselves and pay for it. They diligently labored for the purpose, and brought in the congregation to help them at last." [12]

In 1839, a group of First Presbyterian's newer members thought Hoge and the older members were too conservative. They were new arrivals in Columbus and did not feel completely welcomed by the older residents. They decided to form a Congregational church, but after Lyman Beecher, the famous Cincinnati evangelist, preached to them for ten days they agreed to call it the Second Presbyterian Church. Beecher gave high priority to this effort. He wrote his preacher son, William, asking for help: "No event at this moment can be more important to the church in Ohio than the formation in her capital of an efficient Presbyterian Church." To Beecher, the word "efficient" meant "in agreement with his views."[13]

Initially, the new church rented a room from Joel Buttles in which to meet. The first trustees were Warren Jenkins, Horatio N. Hubbell, and Abiel Foster. Hubbell, who was a teacher of the deaf, contributed $1,000 toward the $3,300 needed for the church building, which was constructed on the west side of Third between Rich and Main Streets. The pastor for two years beginning in 1839 was George S. Boardman. Henry L. Hitchcock, who later became president of Western Reserve College, served as pastor from 1841 to 1845. Hitchcock was twenty-seven when he came to Columbus; he had graduated from Yale at the age of nineteen and had studied theology at Lane Seminary in Cincinnati.[14]

Trinity Episcopal Church was organized in 1817. Bishop Philander Chase was its first rector. Services were held in a building until a stone church was built after 1832. It was constructed in the style of a Grecian Ionic temple with a handsome bell tower. Joel Buttles was the first secretary and a vestryman who generously supported the church financially over the years. The building was on Broad Street opposite the public square, and it contained an organ. Many of the wealthier families were the church's earliest members. Rev. William Preston was pastor until 1841 and returned from 1850 to 1854. St. Paul's Episcopal Church at Third and Mound was organized in 1841 as an offshoot from Trinity.[15]

An Independent Protestant Church was formed on Mound Street by German and Swiss immigrants in 1843. One of its noteworthy policies was that women members had equal rights in terms of the church property and had an equal voice in the business of the church.[16]

When the Germans came in large numbers, they quickly formed churches. Religious organizations were important to them in assisting in their adjustment to Ohio and in preserving their religious heritage. The first German Lutherans held services in 1818 in a room of Christian Heyl's Perry Inn, later called the Franklin House. Their church in 1820 was on Third Street between Town and Rich Streets. Lutheran churches changed names frequently. The German Evangelical Church changed its name to Evangelical Lutheran and later to the German Lutheran Church. The Reverend Charles F. Schaeffer started holding services in English. When the Reverend Conrad Mees arrived, he was instrumental in building St. Paul's Church at Mound and High. Controversy broke out, however, and in 1845, two new groups were formed, the Trinity German Evangelical Church and the First English Lutheran Church.[17]

Catholic settlers were relatively late arrivals. In 1815 there were only fifty Catholic families in all of Ohio. In May 1834, Bishop Flaget held a service at the home of John McCarty on Friend Street. By then Columbus was home to eighty Catholics, most of whom were laborers. A few of them contributed land in Samuel Crosby's addition at the northeast corner of Rich and Fifth Streets with the condition that a church be built there within five years. Bishop Purcell visited Columbus on Sunday, August 30, 1835, and spoke in the courthouse. Having earlier urged Catholics to raise funds and build a church, he lectured the audience on Catholic dogma and refuted some of the public criticisms that were expressed at that time.[18]

Subscriptions were collected, limestone was acquired, and St. Remegius Church, measuring thirty feet by fifty-five feet, was built. The building of pews, plastering, and painting were completed the summer of 1838. Father William Schonat was the first resident pastor. He organized a parochial school in 1843, and it enrolled fifty children. Soon the church was too small. There were seven hundred Catholics in town by then; one-half of them were German. Many were Irish immigrants. The congregation decided to build a larger church in December 1844, conducted another fund drive, and started construction on a lot bought from Matthew Gilbert for six hundred dollars. When their funds were exhausted the members sought help abroad and received major gifts from Munich and Vienna. The cornerstone for the new Catholic church was laid May 18, 1845, at Rich and Fifth Streets. It was to become the largest church building in town. Holy Cross Catholic Church was dedicated January 16, 1848. Bishop Purcell preached to a large congregation.[19]

By 1843 there were thirteen congregations of different denominations worshipping in eight buildings, with another under construction. The total membership was 3,162, which constituted at least 44 percent of the population. Actual church attendance was probably higher because membership requirements varied in the different sects.[20]

More churches were built as the city increased in size. The German Methodist Church was built in 1844 at the northwest corner of Third and South Public Lane, later named Beck Street. Granville Moody was assigned to the other Methodist church that year, and its membership increased to 644 members. He led the efforts to form another Methodist congregation. Thanks to William Neil's generosity, a lot was purchased for the Wesley Chapel. The new building on the west side of High Street was dedicated on August 29, 1847, at three services. St. Paul's Lutheran Church was built in 1844. The German Reformed Church was organized May 1, 1846. Trinity German Evangelical Lutheran Church began January 28, 1848, and met originally in Mechanics Hall. Universalists met beginning in 1837, and a church was incorporated in March 1845 and a building purchased on Third Street. Nelson Doolittle was the Universalist minister in 1850. The first Jewish congregation, Temple Israel, was organized in 1846 with about thirty members.[21]

In 1845 James Hoge and his First Presbyterian Church helped recent arrivals from Wales form a Union Welsh Church, but three years later some of the Calvinistic Methodists in that congregation withdrew for their own worship in a building at Long and Sixth Streets. Charles Lyell, when he visited Columbus, heard a minister preaching in Welsh to a congregation of three hundred. He characterized them as "poor settlers, Irish and German, ignorant of the American Laws and institutions, and wholly uneducated." It was an inaccurate, unfair description because the Welsh immigrants were some of the most pious and industrious workers.[22]

The Ohio Conference of the African Methodist Episcopal Church decided in 1844 to create a seminary to educate young men for the ministry. One hundred seventy-two acres of land on Darby Creek twelve miles west of Columbus were bought for ten dollars an acre. Major James Wilkerson, who had purchased his freedom in 1835, volunteered to raise money for the institution. He met with the planning committee in Columbus on October 20, 1844, and conceived the enterprise as consisting of a manual labor school, an orphans' home, and a retirement home for ministers, as well as a theological seminary. He spent the next eight years raising money throughout the nation. The ambitious project started slowly and eventually failed. By 1854 there were only thirteen students.[23]

Church fairs were frequent and popular events during this decade. The Ladies Sewing Society of the First Presbyterian Church held a sale after Christmas in December 1842. On December 21 and 22, 1843, the women of Trinity Episcopal Church sold both useful and expensive articles to raise money toward the cost of the building's expansion. Admission was twenty-five cents; children were admitted at half price.

Religious revivals were common in the 1840s in Columbus as well as in the rest of the nation. The *Ohio Statesman* editorialized favorably about the many revivals in the state and concluded that there was more profit in them than in the creation of new debts (a political criticism of the Whigs). The August 15, 1843, issue of the *Ohio State Journal* contained notice of a camp meeting scheduled to start in three days on a farm in Franklinton. The following July there was a camp meeting at Samuel M. White's land on Big Run. Peddling wagons were warned to stay at least two miles away from the camp. In June 1844, blacks in Columbus were invited to an August camp meeting near Cincinnati. A Methodist revival occurred in Columbus in November 1845. A union camp meeting was held at Hayden's Run, twelve miles outside of town, at the end of July 1846. Camp meetings occurred in subsequent summers.[24]

Church membership fluctuated during the 1840s as residents moved and as new churches were erected. The largest increases were at the African Methodist, Trinity Episcopal, Welsh Presbyterian, and St. Paul's Episcopal Churches. By 1850 twenty religious congregations were worshipping regularly.[25]

The religious documents that people saved and passed on to their children were evidence of how important religion was to them. Many families treasured Bibles that were kept from generation to generation. Elizabeth Bentz joined the Evangelical Lutheran Church on Sunday, December 5, 1840. Her certificate of confirmation still exists, stating that she, "having publicly professed her faith and confirmed and ratified the solemn vows and promises made to her by her sponsors at her baptism, renewing and assuming the same for herself and engaging evermore to observe them by the Grace of God, was received, after the administration of the Holy Rite of Confirmation, as a Communicant Member."[26]

13

The Arts

Although early settlers in Columbus were interested in the arts, they felt neglected in their isolation. Opportunities for programs were limited. One major art event that was well recorded was a visit from a traveling theatrical troupe that performed at the market house in July 1827. There probably were earlier plays, but this one was reviewed by a critic who disliked "the strolling company of players" because they "mouthed it so horribly." During the intermission a violinist played and a curly-haired black boy in the audience started dancing. When the actors returned, the audience hissed them and commanded the boy to continue his jig. In April 1828, Mr. Harper's Thespian Corps produced *She Stoops to Conquer*. A patron expressed his gratification at enjoying "the pleasure of this fascinating art, embosomed as we are in the backwoods." Plays were performed in the early 1830s at the Eagle Coffee House.[1]

The first theater building was erected in the fall of 1835 on the west side of High north of Broad Street. It opened December 21 and hosted productions in January and February. Initially there was considerable prejudice against plays because pious church members thought the theater was sinful. In 1837, however, an editorial defended them. The writer recognized the religious source of the criticism but asserted there were others who disagreed, who "feel no moral obstacle to moderate and timely amusement." The editor stated that no disturbance had interrupted performances and that they had been attended by "the most respectable class of society."[2]

Political leaders sought to limit the number of plays performed. In 1831 an earlier ordinance to regulate players and public exhibitions was amended to require a license for the first week at the rate of five dollars for every evening. The rate for subsequent weeks was lower, but the licensing had a chilling effect on enterprising actors and directors. In 1836 and 1837, however, a Mr. Marble, one of the more successful Yankee characters and fresh from popular reviews in New York and Philadelphia, performed several nights. "Yankee theater" was a popular genre written by American authors stereotyping the manners and attitudes of the poorer classes. Eighteen-year-old Evan Edmiston saw the "celebrated" Mrs. Davenport play in Shakespeare's *Richard III* on July 14, 1839. He called her "admirable."[3]

Columbus was considered by many traveling artists from the East to be too far away and too difficult to get to. By the 1840s, however, the city's growing population had access to an increased number of programs and events. At first, concerts and dramatic performances were primarily classical, and audiences were limited to the well-to-do. The arts became more diversified and the audiences represented a broader segment of the population over the years.[4]

The production of *Romeo and Juliet* on January 1, 1840, at the Columbus Theater must have been a shortened version because it was followed on the same program by *Therese, the Orphan of Geneva* by John Howard Payne. Tickets for the two tiers of boxes cost a dollar, and seats in the pit were fifty cents. "Colored" persons paid twenty-five cents. Other plays were performed weekly during January and occasionally through May.

The theater was a popular though rowdy attraction early in its life. Its schedule in 1841 included shows that one observer called "almost unequaled elsewhere." Mrs. Drake played Lady Macbeth, and Miss Honey "appeared in the hornpipe." Fanny Fitzwilliam was onstage with Mr. Buckstone, a well-known London comedian, and entertained crowds for two nights in August. The play on December 31 was *Richard III,* called one of the most popular dramas in America before the Civil War. The next night Joshua Silsbee provided drollery for an audience celebrating the New Year with some of his "Yankee theater." When "Yankee" Hill, the celebrated George Handel Hill, performed in February 1848, the editor of the *Ohio Press* observed that the "comic genius is drawing tears which follow excessive laughter from the eyes of the assembled crowds."[5]

A highlight of 1842 was a performance of the play *The Cataract of the Ganges,* in which six horses participated in a procession onstage. The Columbus Theater, however, faced continual criticism from ministers and other respectable townspeople for failing to control its more boisterous customers. A saloon at the rear of the wood structure was often crowded and noisy. Under the accusing gaze of the citizenry, according to one resident, it fell into "ill repute." John Carey, who was frequently in the legislature, once wrote his wife after visiting the theater that it was "A gorgeous display of nonsense and mockery set forth by a set of knaves for the amusement of fools." When the theater closed for financial reasons in 1843, some leading citizens persuaded Mr. Gilbert, the man who bought the building, to use it for public events instead of tearing it down. A public meeting was held on April 25 at which a large majority favored having a town hall that could be used for lectures, concerts, and exhibitions. Their action probably was the first preservation success in the city. Gilbert remodeled the theater and for some time it was known as the city hall.[6]

Those not interested in the traditional arts also found entertainment galore. Circuses were annual popular and profitable amusements in the 1830s and 1840s. Raymond and Ogden's Menagerie displayed "wild beasts and birds" in August 1834.[7] In 1835 a circus came from the Philadelphia Zoological Institute, and the Eagle Circus in 1836 featured nine men and one female equestrian. The Philadelphia Circus came to town for performances at two and seven on August 18 and 19, 1840. Boxes cost fifty cents and the pit cost twenty-five cents, with half price for children under twelve. The acrobats were all men. Reflecting the attitude of the time, the *Ohio Statesman* explained, "It never was ordained by Nature that woman should degrade the reputation of her sex by a display of Gymnastic Feats, which are not calculated for any other than the stalwart man."[8]

The circus that came to town on August 23, 1841, boasted two elephants, a band, and a parade that included an "extensive collection of beasts and birds." A keeper entered the dens of lions and tigers, much to the delight of the spectators, who had paid twenty-five cents each to see the spectacle. In 1842 a circus and caravan arrived in town for two days of performances by wild animals, equestrians, and four Hungarian acrobats. This circus supposedly had the only living giraffe in America.[9]

June's & Turner's Equestrian Troupe gave several performances in April 1845. The next year Raymond and Waring brought their "Grand Zoological Exhibition" to Broad Street. They claimed to have the finest and largest group of rare animals ever exhibited in the West. The "mammoth menagerie" marched into town on May 1 preceded by four elephants in harness. Thousands of people paid a quarter for a three-hour show that afternoon and applauded Herr Driesbach, who controlled six ferocious animals simultaneously. Other circuses that year included Stickney's New Orleans Circus; Welch, Mann, and Delevan's Great National Circus; and Rockwell and Stone's Mammoth Circus, which performed on Rich Street. In addition to the hundred men and clowns, the troupe contained Mrs. Gossin, described as a "magnificent female rider," who rode in the ring assisted by six other women. The prejudice against women as circus acrobats quickly died.[10]

Concerts were especially popular. The Franklin Harmonic Society was founded around 1837 and frequently gave concerts that elevated the local musical standards. By 1839 the Columbus City Band and the Columbus Brass Band were giving monthly concerts. Partly because it was the seat of government, the town offered a better than average number of cultural opportunities.[11]

The Hungarian Singers performed at the State House on July 29, 1840. Professor Bronson, assisted by a German vocalist, Mr. Christian, gave two concerts in July 1841 in the Neil House dining room. Later that month, the Shaw sisters from Philadelphia sang in the old courthouse on the public square. Another "Grand Concert" was held there on August 3, 1842. Baron Rudolph de Fleur, who was soliciting pupils for lessons, gave a musical program November 9. The Rainers, an Austrian family who popularized "Silent Night," also sang often that winter. In 1843, the editor of the *Ohio Statesman* praised the organ recital by the Collegiate Institute students at the First Presbyterian Church and the "brilliant oratorio" at the Trinity Episcopal Church. On June 3, 1843, a new arrival in town, Anson W. Buttles, heard "some fine singing" by two women at the Parlance. On March 14, 1848, the Columbus Glee Club sang and contributed their proceeds to the Female Benevolent Society. That summer residents enjoyed band concerts by the Columbus Amateur Band.[12]

When Mechanics Hall opened in June 1843 it was used for musical events. The Antonio family put on a display of "graceful positions in Turkish costumes" there in October 1845. S. B. Duffield, a violinist, played to rapt audiences from June to December of that year.[13]

The many German arrivals who settled in what was called South Columbus or "Little Germany" brought with them a love of music and added considerably to the cultural life of the city. The Liederkranz singing club was formed in 1843, and the Mannerchor, led by John P. Bruck, was created in 1848.[14]

Some performers and lecturers on the regular circuit were foreigners. Audiences understandably were attracted to exotic, celebrated artists from overseas. Some of the so-called foreigners, however, were enterprising Americans taking advantage of unsuspecting audiences. The magician and ventriloquist Signor Blitz, who performed frequently in Columbus throughout the 1840s, may have been born in Ohio despite his European-sounding stage name.[15]

Because the population was becoming more diverse, artistic performances changed in character. Programs of operatic airs and traditional songs remained popular, and the upper classes still flocked to see Shakespearean actors. But new entertainments that appealed to less sophisticated tastes were scheduled more frequently.

On February 13, 1844, for instance, Christy's Original Band of Virginia Minstrels came to town, a year after premiering in New York. Minstrels—played by white men in blackface makeup who used what were supposed to be Negro dialects, dances, songs, and humor—appealed to those who were not particularly attracted to high culture. Like Yankee theater, minstrel shows, which developed in the 1820s, reflected the culture of the common man more interested in American than European art forms. They had more variety than classical concerts and favored slapstick and folksy themes.[16]

Although it reflected the racism of the period, the Negro minstrel show was a genuine American form of musical theater, and it became as popular in Columbus as it was in the rest of the country. E. P. Christy's

Cover of "Christy's Minstrels" (private collection).

minstrels returned several times, as did other groups. Some of these black-face performers were called Ethiopian. The Ethiopian Serenaders, Nightingale Ethiopian Opera Troupe, and Ethiopian Warblers all played in town. The Ethiopian Serenaders advertised "more amusement for twenty-five cents than ever before given." They tried to attract more women by reserving front rows for them and instructed men to remove their hats and not stand on the seats.[17]

Most of the players in minstrel shows were white men from the North, most of whom had never seen a plantation and knew very little about black culture. Most of the audiences were white men from the working classes, some of whom were recent immigrants still learning about a society that they must have found alien and difficult to understand. The blackfaced performers who told jokes and expressed humorous statements about contemporary political and social events were trying to entertain. However, their stereotypical portrayals of blacks as happy, ignorant, and sometimes shiftless members of the lowest class in society indirectly represented the worst of Jacksonian politics and served to defend slavery. For most of the audiences it may have been simple-minded entertainment.[18]

One of the Christy's Minstrels songs was called "We Live On De Banks Ob De Ohio." It went:

> We live on de banks ob de Ohio,
> > Tra, la la, tra la la,
> Whar de mighty waters do rapidly flow,
> And de steamboat streak it along.
> > We live on de banks ob de Ohio,
> > Ohio, Ohio,
> > We live on de banks ob de Ohio,
> > Ohio, Ohio.

The last stanza contained the message, "Old Massa to us darkies am good, . . . For he gibs us our clothes and he gibs us our food. And we merrily work for him." [19]

The visual arts flourished as well as the performing arts. As early as 1818, some people expressed interest in seeing public art. A panorama of the city of Rome and a wax museum were displayed at the market house.[20] William Dunlap exhibited his paintings several times. In December 1834 a painter named Bambrough showed his paintings in the post office. A statue of Cleopatra attracted many admirers in 1838.[21]

Annual subscriptions to the Columbus chapter of the American Art Union cost five dollars. Joseph Sullivant, the honorary secretary, announced when subscribers could pick up the engraving to which their memberships entitled them. In 1847 the union distributed by lot some 150 oil paintings to its members.[22]

An exhibition of paintings by someone named Phillips was at the old courthouse in May 1845. A year later, a painting of Pan and Bacchus owned by Henry Stanbery was displayed in Riley's bookstore on the west side of High. Later that month five paintings priced at from fifty to five hundred dollars were exhibited for sale at the Neil House. Residents became more accustomed to seeing art on display in town. In December 1850, they flocked to admire a portrait of the late president William Henry Harrison in Walcutt's gallery on Town Street. "The Child's Passage to Paradise," the top painting distributed in 1851 by the American Art Union, was displayed at Riley's bookstore in May.[23]

Other artists found employment in the small city. In 1840, an English traveler, James S. Buckingham, met a popular artist on tour who painted portraits for fifty dollars for half-lengths and a hundred dollars for full renditions. The ornamental painter Edmund Leeds specialized in tavern signs. Mr. Teliga, who advertised himself as a "Daguerreotype Artist," attracted customers, while another, who charged two dollars for a picture, offered to give instruction in the art. Several others opened shops to take "likenesses" of those who wanted pictures of themselves. Those who preferred a portrait painter could visit George Freeman beginning in 1847.[24]

One of the most illustrious artists born in Columbus in the early nineteenth century was William Walcutt, the son of John Walcutt. William was born in 1819 and studied art in New York. He became a prolific painter and sculptor, and his paintings of Ohio governors were eventually displayed in the State House. He designed the Walcutt Monument in Green Lawn Cemetery and was commissioned by David Taylor to paint several family portraits. Taylor was successful in business and was one of the founders of the Franklin County Agricultural Society.[25]

Cultural life continued to expand in other ways, some of which probably would fail to charm a modern audience. In 1848, the Mechanics Hall hosted an exhibition for three nights of "Brewer's Panorama": paintings of Mammoth Cave, Niagara Falls, and the Ohio and Mississippi Rivers. A highlight of the winter of 1849 was a week-long exhibit at the First Baptist Church of line illustrations of Milton's *Paradise Lost* with accompanying readings by Mr. Gaylord.[26]

By the late 1840s, eastern impresarios finally began to include Columbus on their tours of artists and performers. P. T. Barnum, the noted showman and circus operator, more than once booked his Swiss Bell Ringers in the capital city. They were a group of musicians from Lancashire, England, whose nationality Barnum had changed to make them more attractive to American audiences.[27]

Public entertainment gradually became more commercialized. A concert at the Odeon on January 28, 1851, featured fifteen artists and was sponsored by the Boston Piano Company. At the concert's conclusion, fifteen prizes of musical instruments were drawn from the one-dollar tickets. Top prize was a $400 piano. Other prizes were less expensive musical instruments. The next month, another sponsor held what was called "the grandest musical entertainments ever gotten up in Columbus." Tickets cost two dollars, and a hundred prizes were given.[28]

The city enjoyed theater performances again in 1847 when the new Neil building went up south of the Neil House. On opening night, Monday, December 27, Mr. T. F. Lennox's actors performed *The Soldier's Daughter,* followed by *A Husband in Sight.* The manager of the theater said he wanted to produce new works as well as classics. In the January 14, 1848, *Ohio Press* he announced a reward of twenty-five dollars "for the best farce handed in." When fire destroyed the building in 1848, the plays were moved to the Concert Hall on State Street. Kneass's Opera Troupe played

Tom Thumb (private collection).

to large audiences in October of that year. A group from Cleveland performed plays in 1848, and another theatrical group began performances in November 1849. The following March, Miss H. Fanning Read gave readings from Shakespeare's *The Merchant of Venice*. It was billed as the first such event in town, and, according to the *Ohio State Journal*, it "excited some curiosity."[29]

Another popular amusement in 1849 was the five-day appearance of Gen. Tom Thumb, who performed songs and dances twice daily, even on Christmas. Tickets for adults were twenty-five cents. Tom Thumb was billed as being seventeen years old, weighing fifteen pounds, and standing twenty-eight inches high. His real name was Charles S. Stratton, and he actually was only eleven. When P. T. Barnum discovered him in 1842 in Bridgeport, Connecticut, and displayed him in his museum, he exaggerated the child's age and claimed he had "just arrived from England." It was a typical Barnum tactic with typically lucrative results. Barnum was one of the more successful of the business entrepreneurs who managed entertainers.[30]

By 1850, entertainments of all kinds occurred almost weekly. One popular vocal group was called the Buckeyes. The Empire Minstrels and Barnum's Swiss Bell Ringers drew crowds. The Minstrels, a group of ten who were called "the best in the world," came to town in July with new songs, dances, jokes, and burlesques. The program featured Cool White, "the great Shakespearean Negro Jester." The Gibson Quartette, who performed twice in town that November, added a third concert for the four hundred prisoners in the Ohio Penitentiary.[31]

That summer, audiences, many of whom never expected to travel outside of central Ohio, flocked to the Odeon to see Seigler's grand panorama of a voyage from New York to California in which the artist had created an optical illusion of moving images. The diorama, painted by Charles R. Leslie, contained views of cities, of gold-digging on the Sacramento River, and, oddly, of the grotto at Lourdes, France. Barnum's "Olio Entertainment," a variety-type pageant and exhibition, attracted crowds to a pavilion on a vacant lot at Broad and Third Streets in October. Audiences were entertained with a panorama of Napoleon's funeral and an impersonation of Yankee characters by Billy Whitlock.[32]

By the beginning of the 1850s, when the population had reached 17,872 and the first passenger train had arrived, Columbus was a more attractive venue for traveling troupes. It was no wonder then that residents hoped to scale the heights of entertainment by being a stop on the western tour of the great Swedish soprano Jenny Lind, the most famous singer in Europe. Copies of her songs were on sale in Machold's music store in September when her tour started. The *Ohio Statesman* asserted, "Every lady should have a copy on her music stand." Newspapers ran articles almost every day about Lind's arrival; her contract with her agent, P. T. Barnum, to give 150 concerts; and her life, career, and popularity.[33]

Readers were impressed to learn that Lind contributed part of her earnings to charity in the cities she visited and amused to read that she received 120 letters a day seeking contributions. The *Ohio Statesman* claimed that she "has set the whole tribe of beggars after her, great and small, high and low, young men and maidens, bond and free."[34]

Newspaper readers eagerly followed Lind's tour through accounts in the *Ohio Statesman*. They were relieved to learn that rumors of her drowning were false. When she reached St. Louis in March 1851, people started asking if she would visit Columbus. The *Ohio Statesman* editor promised Barnum a bigger profit than the six thousand dollars he made in Natchez.

By April word was spreading that Lind would sing in Columbus in July. Some residents journeyed to Cincinnati to hear her, and their published praises of her singing increased local anticipation. But hopes were dashed when Barnum indicated there was "no probability" of Lind's ever singing in Columbus. Instead, he took her up the Ohio River to Wheeling and Pittsburgh.[35]

Lind broke her contract with Barnum in June and announced her intention to go west again. The papers wrote that she might yet be heard in Columbus. Finally, the public learned that Jenny Lind would perform in Odeon Hall on November 4 and 5, 1851. When tickets for the concerts went on sale, for as much as two to four dollars, people rushed to buy them. One man fainted in the long line. Both nights quickly sold out. In addition, more than a thousand men and women filled the streets around the hall to catch a glimpse of her.

Lind's entourage included two male singers, Signor Salvi and the baritone Enrico Belletti; a violinist, Joseph Burke; and Otto Goldschmidt, a pianist and conductor whom she had married in Boston. The first night she sang "Come unto Him" from Handel's "Messiah"; an aria by Bellini; Meyerbeer's "Cavatina"; "The Bird Song" by Taubert; and two Scotch ballads, "John Anderson My Jo" and "Comin' Through the Rye." She sang different songs in the second concert. The audiences were enraptured.[36]

Lind contributed her income from the performances to establish a Scandinavian professorship at the Lutheran Seminary, which was then connected with Capital University, but the struggling institution never managed to create the position. One newspaper reporter observed, "She is the Queen of song. By her noble acts of kindness and charity, much of human suffering has been alleviated."[37]

With the visit of Jenny Lind, Columbus at last could brag of having the cultural advantages of larger, more sophisticated cities. Two brief evenings marked one of its crowning artistic moments.

14

Columbus

Looks Westward

As westward migration increased throughout the nation, more attention in Columbus was devoted to accounts of travels to new territories. As early as 1832, the Oregon Trail became the major route to the West Coast. James Hall's *Legends of the West* enticed easterners to consider travel. In 1841, the first large group of forty-eight wagons traveled over the Oregon Trail to reach Sacramento. Two years later, on May 22, 1843, one thousand easterners left Independence, Missouri, for Oregon. Columbus residents were well aware that some new arrivals in their city quickly moved on to seek better opportunities as new lands became available or as new states entered the Union.

Columbus residents first read about the Oregon Territory in October 1825 when a newspaper article described the area favorably and predicted that in the future it would "enter the Republican Confederacy as Oregon State" and that its cities "shall rival New York or Philadelphia in their wealth and population. Then the busy hum of commerce and the shouts of freemen, shall echo from the Atlantic to the Pacific Oceans."[1]

Politicians and others frequently expressed patriotism and optimism in the nation's growth and development. A speech given in 1842 by Thomas W. Bartley, a Democratic legislator who became acting governor in 1844, was typical in its praise of Americans. He declared:

> No one can look into our vast extent of country, survey its features, search its history, and contemplate its institutions, and fail to observe the unexampled inducements to intellectual exertion, the new springs of mental activity which are here developed, calculated to give a new and distinctive character to the literature of our country, to extend vastly the limits of human knowledge, and to leave an enduring and distinguishing impress upon the page of history. . . . Here everything is excited and buoyant with the spirit of youth, and of hope, and of enterprise. . . . The universal ardor seems to be contagious. No one is contented to remain stationary or dormant. The general impulse of society is hastening and crowding every man forward.[2]

Columbus residents at that time were vitally interested in current events and were caught up in the fervor and widespread interest in acquiring Oregon. Some left to join the caravans winding their way westward. There was some concern over the possibility of war with England over the Oregon question. The newspapers kept people informed as the issue developed.

Early in 1843 public meetings were held in Columbus to discuss the Oregon dispute with England. One of the resolutions passed at a meeting on February 23 stated that "the governmental domain of these United States of America, is one and indivisible; and that it rightfully extends over the Oregon Territory." A committee of seven, headed by Samuel Medary, was appointed to collect and publish information about the region and the history of the dispute.[3]

The twenty-one-page pamphlet, *Report on the territory of Oregon*, was widely circulated. It included a map showing the boundary of 1818 up to the Russian settlement above the fifty-fourth parallel. (An 1824 agreement signed by the United States and Russia established the parallel as the southern limit of Russia's West Coast claims.) The pamphlet, probably written by Medary, quoted from several reports to Congress and from settlers describing in glowing terms the area's geography, beauty, natural resources, soil, rivers, beneficial climate, absence of disease, and vast size—along with the friendliness of the Indians. Oregon was portrayed as "a country of magnificent heights and distances; of bold and novel scenery." Several pages were devoted to scathing criticism of England: "Since the last war the English have pushed their settlements, through the agency of the Hudson Bay Company, with great perseverance. They are occupying the most important points, claiming the best soil, and monopolizing the whole trade and commerce . . . and dotting its whole face over with forts." The report also criticized the American government for not being more aggressive in its diplomacy. The pamphlet's conclusion was that Americans had a right to the entire territory and that the settlers there should be protected by American laws. The most forceful words were, "Our right to the country is not disputed by Americans. The only discussion seems to be as to the time and mode of throwing around the scattered population of that country the protecting arm of our national laws."[4]

This publication provided Columbus residents, as well as others, with extensive information about Oregon and fanned the fires of expansionism. What is significant about the pamphlet is that it was written by a Columbus leader and was published well before James K. Polk campaigned to acquire Oregon. In calling for all of the Oregon territory, the author must have known that the convention of 1818 established the forty-ninth parallel only to the Continental Divide.

Two years later, the *Ohio Statesman* echoed popular sentiment in an editorial: "Oregon is demanded by the voice of the mighty west. Let not that voice be unheeded, or the lion strength of our people will send a roar of thunder to the Capitol that will awaken the stupid federal bigots and

British flatterers, to a speedy sensibility of their condition." Feelings of manifest destiny were as strong in Columbus as they were in Washington. (Charles L. O'Sullivan, editor of the *United States Magazine and Democratic Review*, used the term to justify territorial expansion when he wrote in July 1845 defending "our manifest destiny to overspread the continent allotted by Providence for the free development of our yearly multiplying millions.") However, Samuel Medary wrote as early as 1834, "There is no portion of the globe destined to so much greatness, in an agricultural point of view, as the great Mississippi Valley." [5]

Similar expansionist sentiments were expressed elsewhere, especially by Democrats as they contemplated the possibility of acquiring new territory. An article in the *Democratic Monthly Magazine and Western Review* in 1844 was about as possessive as could be in staking out a claim for the country's borders: "Free institutions are capable of an indefinite expansion. Our system is far better adapted to a large than a small territory. Let our Union extend from the Atlantic to the Pacific, and from the Isthmus of Darien to Behring's [*sic*] Straits, if the people be homogenous, speaking the same language, living under the same general laws, guaranteed their equal rights and endowed with the spirit of liberty, connected and associated by the ties of blood, relationship and family connection, constant business and social intercourse." [6]

Anti-British sentiment was strong in 1844, as well. According to the January 11 issue of the *Ohio Statesman*, "A large and enthusiastic meeting of citizens of different parts of Ohio in favor of a repeal of the Irish Union, convened in the hall of the House of Representatives." Residents became more aware of Ireland and its political and economic problems as more Irish immigrants moved to central Ohio.[7]

On April 28, 1845, Samuel Medary wrote a strong editorial in the *Ohio Statesman* criticizing England for threatening war over American demands for Oregon. "Our cause can never be more just," he wrote. On May 7 he stated, "The question presented is not so much for the extension of territory, though it be over the fairest and most fertile of lands, as it is of national honor—of national faith to our own citizens." The issues of May 14 and 16 contained articles on the debates in parliament over the Oregon question and a map of the area. "The territory belongs to the United States," Medary concluded.[8]

Gov. Mordecai Bartley's special message to the House of Representatives on January 2, 1846, reveals how seriously some talked about the possibility of war with England. Bartley's message contained statistics on the militia and their arms. He wrote, "If we are to be involved in a war with Great Britain, an additional number of the various classes will be indispensable; and that arrangements should be speedily made to station a sufficient number of troops at each port on the lake shore, to repel any invasion that may be attempted by an enemy." At about the same time, the U.S. House of Representatives passed a resolution ending the Anglo-American joint occupation of the Oregon area.[9]

Columbus residents were aware of some of the diplomatic negotiations over the Oregon question but had expected President Polk to insist on the 54–40 line. The final treaty, however, gave the United States and England each about one-half of the area and extended the forty-ninth parallel boundary westward. When the Senate ratified the Oregon Treaty on June 15, 1846, most people treated it as a victory, although some thought more territory should have been acquired. Some of the Democrats in Ohio felt that President Polk had betrayed them by not insisting on more land.[10]

In June 1845, the city mourned the death of Andrew Jackson. "The greatest man of our age is no more," the *Ohio Statesman* declared, its columns draped in black.[11] In death, Jackson joined George Washington and William Henry Harrison as a revered military leader whose memories helped to intensify patriotic fervor.

An increase in militarism was an inevitable byproduct of the patriotism of the 1840s. By this time, a variety of wars and violent struggles between settlers and displaced Indian tribes were part of the nation's heritage. The exploits of Daniel Boone, William Crawford, Anthony Wayne, and other heroes instilled a darker, more violent spirit in men's hearts. Recent immigrants, seeking to adapt to their new homeland, joined in the popular gun culture. Members of the first regiment of German cavalry, captained by Peter Ambos, the candy merchant, paraded on Broad Street on May 30, 1840, and the Columbus Guards did the same on December 21 that year. An area between Rich and Friend Streets called the Sheep Pasture was used by military groups for drilling and giving vent to their aggressive tendencies.[12]

A radical fringe of the population carried its nationalist fervor to the extreme of plotting filibusters—military adventures to other countries—to expand American borders and advance its own violent interests. On December 30, 1841, for instance, Secretary of State Daniel Webster wrote a confidential letter to Demas Adams in Columbus to warn him that there were secret societies "artfully arranged and systematically organized . . . on the northern frontier" who planned to invade Canada to incite a revolution there. Webster reported that they had cannon and other arms, two steamboats on Lake Erie, and a January 8 date for their expedition.[13] The selection of January 8, the anniversary of Andrew Jackson's victory at New Orleans and a Democratic Party holiday, indicated that presumably the subversives were Democrats.

The most discussed event in 1846 was the war with Mexico, approved by Congress on May 13. President Polk had strong interest in acquiring Mexican lands in Texas and California as part of his expansionist drive. Texas, which had declared its independence in 1836, was pushing to become a state. Mexico resented American pressures and broke off diplomatic relations in March 1845. Polk sent Gen. Zachary Taylor to the Texas border in May of that year. Taylor's army invaded Mexico on March 29, 1846, on the excuse that a Mexican force had attacked.[14]

The war was so popular that three thousand Ohioans rushed to volunteer, and the state's quota was quickly filled. In May 1846 women gathered in the basement of the First Presbyterian Church to prepare clothing for the soldiers.[15] Patriotic fervor was high. Capt. George E. Walcutt started parading his Montgomery Guards through the streets as early as April 6 that year, accompanied by Captain Beck's German artillery company. The parades were always crowd-pleasers. Articles about the course of the war appeared in almost every newspaper issue. Columbus residents were cheered to learn that Ohio troops participated in the victory at Monterey. Patriotism was fanned as stories were shared about the heroics of the citizen-soldiers. A group of young men made plans to form a company of cavalry and sent an exuberant statement to the *Ohio Statesman* under the heading "To the Independent Young Men of Franklin County":

> Ever awake to the patriotic call of our invaded country, a number of us are now in preparation for a March to the blood-stained soil of Texas! Our national domain, consecrated to liberty, has been polluted by the touch of the semi-barbarous foe! Our unparalleled indulgence towards the repeated wrongs of that imbecile and arrogant people of Spanish Mexico, has been treated with contempt, and our national honor and national power scoffed and derided! They have crossed the boundary line, and in our faces flung defiance! Let us rally in hundreds and thousands beneath that flag which yields no earthly homage but to its own proud land.[16]

The city contributed the Columbus Cadets and the Montgomery Guards. Two additional units, the Franklin Guards and a German company, went in 1847. A farewell "demonstration" on High Street raised the patriotic spirit to an intense level. The German company assembled at 7 A.M. on May 26 at High and Friend Streets. They marched to Franklinton, followed by some one thousand cheering people who accompanied them to their coaches. A detachment of German artillery fired a salute as they departed. The Franklin Guards left on May 31, cheered on in a similar fashion. Columbus volunteers were in the second and fourth regiments that left Camp Washington, near Cincinnati, for Mexico.[17]

The receptions on Monday, July 5, 1847, for the returning troops were even more spirited. Their return coincided with the usual Independence

Day celebrations, which began with a morning parade that included the Sunday school children. Samuel Medary marked the occasion with another eloquent speech, after which the immense crowd gave three cheers for the returning soldiers and three more for Medary. A long march around town was followed by a huge supper at the Franklin Fire Company. The evening ended with fireworks.[18]

A complimentary dinner was given the troops on December 10, 1847. The war finally ended with the signing of the Treaty of Guadalupe Hidalgo on February 2, 1848. The United States gained more than 500,000 square miles of land and agreed to pay Mexico $15 million. The last of the soldiers returned to Columbus in the summer of 1848.

Opposition was also expressed in Columbus to the annexation of Texas and to the war, especially by Whigs who realized that the result would be an increase in the South's political influence and an extension of slavery. As early as March 3, 1845, the *Ohio State Journal* editorialized, "The Constitution Trampled under Feet! The Slave Power Triumphant!"[19] The conservative Joel Buttles wrote in his diary for June 6, 1846, "I cannot regard this war as at all justifiable on our part. It is entirely aggressive, which we have no occasion to perpetrate on a nation weak in itself by numerous dissensions among themselves. Could we acquire territory thereby, we should be the worse as a nation for having it."[20]

The most talked-about criticism of the Mexican War was Sen. Thomas Corwin's speech on the U.S. Senate floor on February 11, 1847. During an eloquent, emotional, two-and-a-half-hour criticism of Polk before a crowded gallery, Corwin raised questions about the constitutionality and expediency of the war. Hal W. Bochin was probably correct in calling Corwin's speech one of the least understood in congressional history. Columbus residents either praised him or condemned Corwin depending on their political views. The editor of the *Ohio State Journal* called the speech "an earnest and impassioned advocacy of what he believed to be RIGHT against all odds and the face of all opposition."[21]

James B. Finley, then a chaplain at the Ohio Penitentiary, recorded caustic criticism of the soldiers in his published journal: "The city is filled with these recruits, who are drinking and swearing, and rioting in every lane and alley, as if they were just from Pandemonium. They are a fair sample of the majority of those engaged in this unholy crusade against a helpless nation." He anticipated the judgment of most twentieth-century historians who, like Carey McWilliams, have condemned U.S. action in Mexico and believe that the war intensified the hatred many Americans held toward other ethnic groups in less developed countries.[22]

While those in Columbus saw expansion of the nation as the main result of the Mexican War, an equally significant outcome was the intensification of the slavery controversy. On August 8, 1846, Rep. David Wilmot offered an amendment to a House of Representatives appropriation bill that would have prohibited slavery or involuntary servitude in any part of the territories acquired from Mexico. The Senate adjourned before acting on the Wilmot Proviso, but continued controversy over the issue aggravated sectional division. For some people in Columbus, publicity about Wilmot's efforts strengthened their opposition to slavery's spread. As Charles G. Sellers has indicated, expansionism south of the border led to more defiant sectionalism that ultimately became a threat to the union.[23]

The potato famine in Ireland was another event that concerned Columbusites, some of whom had families there. An Irish relief meeting was held at the First Presbyterian Church on several days in February 1847. The call to the meeting ended with the plea: "Let no one who has sympathy for human misery, or compassion for a brother's woes, or is grateful for the services which the warm-hearted and generous sons of the Emerald Isle rendered this country in the war of the revolution, be absent."[24] Resolutions were passed deploring the suffering from starvation, and a committee was appointed to solicit gifts. Fifteen hundred dollars was collected in the first week. In addition to being acts of charity, however, gifts to Irish immigrants were ways to fan anti-British sentiment and show patriotic and revolutionary fervor.

Increased nationalist sentiment was partly based on the conviction that white Americans were superior to other ethnic groups and races. Slurs against those south of the Rio Grande during the Mexican War had racist overtones. The cover of schoolboy John Nelson's 1847 "Writing Book" contained a picture of Christopher Columbus's landing with a message designed to shape attitudes: "On landing, Columbus threw himself upon his knees, kissed the earth, and returned thanks to God with tears of joy. Then rising, he drew his sword, displayed the royal standard, and took possession in the name of the Castilian sovereigns, giving the island the name of San Salvador. During the ceremony of taking possession, the natives remained gazing, in timid admiration, at the complexion, the beards, the shining armour, and splendid dress of the Spaniards."[25]

Pride in their country increased as residents learned about new states admitted into the Union. Florida and Texas were admitted in 1845, Iowa in 1846, Wisconsin in 1848, and California in 1850. Although expansion of the country westward contributed to stronger nationalistic sentiments, Northerners expressed increased concerns about the spread of slavery and the greater political influence of the South.

The July 4, 1848, celebration was especially festive in Columbus. Large crowds watched a parade led by a fire engine decorated with flags and flowers, followed by the Sons of Temperance in full regalia. Barnum's traveling museum attracted hundreds. McKinney's balloon was flown in the evening. The German residents enjoyed a grand ball to celebrate American independence and the revolutions in Europe. The newspapers kept readers informed about the revolutionary fervor sweeping that continent. The sentiments expressed in the April 26, 1848, *Ohio Statesman* probably were representative of public opinion: "The sun of liberty which has gradually risen to its zenith in America, and shed light and life and happiness over the spirit of man, and imparted energy and animation to his actions, has been reflected back upon the millions of Europe."[26] News of revolutions in Europe confirmed Americans' conviction of the superiority of their own government and culture.

While westward expansion increased in the 1840s once gold was found in California, the Far West had an additional allure. In February 1848 some who were interested in joining a tour to the "Gold Regions" of California met at the North Engine House. James Marshall had discovered gold at Sutter's Mill, California, in January, and almost ninety thousand people had journeyed there the following year. Some young men from Columbus quickly left. The Franklin California Mining Company was created by John Watson; Joseph Hunter formed the Columbus and California Industrial Company. People invested two hundred dollars in the enterprise, but neither company succeeded in finding gold.[27] John Krum was one who invested and went west. He borrowed the money from his brother in return for promising him one-half of his fortune. By December 1850 the discouraged miner, who had been sick for three months, wrote his brother, "I am getting tired of California . . . it is a horabil [sic] place. The Columbus boys are scattered all through the country." The company disbanded. Krum never acquired enough money to pay his way home and ended up farming in Washington.[28]

The many wagon trains heading for California over the National Road helped encourage some residents to join them. The reason others did not may have been the result of a book published in Columbus in 1850 by Samuel McNeil, a shoemaker. He joined a dozen men going west and described his hazardous journey and disillusionment in California. He found that more profit was gained by selling provisions than by panning for gold. He wrote, "The person who digs for gold lives like the wild men, deprived of every comfort of life and society," and concluded, "I would not advise any person to come to this country." James Williams echoed these views when he wrote his wife from Sacramento, "Many a time have I wished that I never started."[29]

15

Causes and

Crusades

Samuel Medary captured the sentiment of his era when he observed, "This is the age of reform."[1] People in Columbus participated in several of the antebellum reform movements. Numerous organizations designed to improve society and remove its evils had been formed throughout the country. The reform movements were inspired to a great degree by the success of the many revivals that occurred in the Protestant churches in the early nineteenth century. Although many of the reform organizations started in the East they were strengthened by their chapters west of the Alleghenies. The national organizations spawned by the evangelical benevolent fervor included societies for the Bible, Sunday schools, education, temperance, peace, missions, antislavery, and women's rights. To a certain extent, Protestant evangelism in the cities was an organized effort to transfer to urban areas the orderly and religious values that were followed in rural areas and villages. The Sunday school, for instance, sought to do more than inculcate children with the moral teachings of their churchgoing parents. They also sought to encourage acceptable patterns of behavior that would ensure a stable, law-abiding citizenry.

One movement supported by religious people was the effort to keep Sunday as free as possible from activity other than churchgoing. Religious persons were concerned as interest in acquiring wealth and material possessions seemed to detract from commitment to Christian values and ideals. The Sabbatarian movement began in the East as early as 1810 when religious people crusaded to change postal regulations permitting mail delivery on Sundays. It gained momentum when Lyman Beecher and others formed the General Union for Promoting the Observance of the Christian Sabbath in May 1828. Activists encouraged petition campaigns and pressure groups. They created auxiliary chapters to end Sunday mail delivery. Congress was not persuaded. Later the reformers tried to stop canal traffic on Sundays. Some wanted to close offices, stores, and taverns. An agent from the American Bethel Society spoke in Columbus in May 1841 and urged his listeners to form an organization.[2]

The reformers in Ohio especially wanted to restrict Sunday canal traffic. A Sabbath Convention was held in the First Presbyterian Church in Columbus on January 4, 1844, and was attended by clergymen from all denominations. Even the legislature adjourned to permit members to attend. Many delegates were in the city for the three day meeting. Some resolutions were passed demanding that the Sabbath be kept holy. One stated that "the interests of commerce and of all the channels through which it flows throughout our country, do not forbid but require the faithful and universal observance of the Sabbath." The delegates were impressed to learn that four-fifths of the boats on Pennsylvania canals did not move on Sundays. Lyman Beecher and James B. Finley, both of whom were active supporters of the movement, gave speeches. The latter blamed "the relaxed discipline of the churches" for contributing to Sabbath breaking. Some of those who favored breaking the Sabbath, however, felt that their incomes were adversely affected by being forced to remain idle on Sundays. They looked upon the movement as an effort at social and economic control for religious reasons. The campaign soon went out of favor, but reformers for other causes copied its tactics.[3]

The temperance crusade was more successful in attracting support. Indeed, temperance was probably the most popular reform effort in Columbus. The first meeting of the Ohio State Temperance Society was in 1821. Its annual meeting at the Methodist church on January 6, 1825, drew large crowds.[4] The first issue of the *Ohio Temperance Advocate* was published in Columbus in 1834. It contained articles reminding its readers of the "poison" in ardent spirits and how essential for the permanence of free institutions was their crusade. Some people were surprised to learn in 1835 that there were forty-three groceries and other public places in town where liquor could be sold. The April 1836 issue contained the news that four hundred men and five hundred women, all Columbus residents, had petitioned the legislature to repeal the city's charter permitting the city council to grant licenses. A bill passed the House but the Senate tabled it. On January 26, 1837, Joshua R. Giddings, who was elected to Congress the following year, wrote to his wife from Columbus to report that the subject of temperance "has certainly made progress in this place." Heavy drinking, however, was still popular, and the taverns near the State House were often filled. In 1841 Ohio had 272 distilleries that annually produced more than 466,000 gallons.[5]

A meeting was held at the Baptist church on February 1, 1841, to consider reorganizing a city temperance society. Gustavus Swan was named chairman. Those attending discussed seeking the repeal of the law authorizing the sale of intoxicating liquors. Lectures on temperance were given later that month. Residents were quick to reflect national sentiment. The

Washington Temperance Society was founded by former drunkards in Baltimore on April 2, 1840. The Washington Temperance Society of Columbus held a week-long series of meetings in October 1841 at which reformed drunkards spoke. According to one report, the meetings every night were crowded and "some evenings the church could not hold the audience. About six or seven hundred men, women and children, have signed the pledge, cider and all." Another person claimed that 816 had signed the pledge. Meetings were held in March and April of 1842. One of the popular books published that year was *Temperance Tales; or, Six Nights With the Washingtonians* by T. S. Arthur.[6]

The Washington Temperance Society continued to sponsor public lectures in 1843 and 1844. Later that year a traveling troupe performed the *Drama of the Reformed Drunkard* three times to raise funds for the society. There also were regular meetings in town of the Sons of Temperance organization. Members of the black community were active in the temperance movement, and their meetings were reported in the *Palladium of Liberty*. In 1843 the black temperance society had 220 members.[7]

The temperance agitation gained supporters after 1845. The Washington Temperance House opened in March. The Columbus Temperance Society held meetings almost weekly that year and the next. A series of well-attended temperance meetings occurred in December 1845 at which the Reverend Granville Moody and Secretary of State Samuel Galloway spoke. John J. Janney, who attended, thought they were the best speeches he had ever heard. Janney, a Quaker, was critical of his newly adopted city. "There are but few places though that need reformation more than Columbus," he wrote. "Taverns, grog-shops, oyster houses, bowling saloons and such to get the public mind thoroughly aroused." Because so many members of the House of Representatives were delegates to the temperance convention in December 1845, the House adjourned to permit them to attend.[8]

The temperance meeting on January 12, 1846, was called "one of the biggest ever held in the city." Three hundred members of the Sons of Temperance accompanied by two bands marched around town on June 19, 1846. Meetings with many speeches followed. The Sons of Temperance was a national organization formed in New York in 1842. National membership totaled 160,000 in 1848, and Ohio had the largest number of chapters. A third division of the Sons of Temperance was created in Columbus in 1847. There also were two chapters of the Cadets of Temperance. A weekly journal, *Ohio Temperance Standard*, was published by O. H. P. Gabriel beginning on July 16, 1846.[9]

By the middle of the decade temperance reformers realized that it was not enough to write, preach, and parade in order to effect change. They had to influence the political process. The Columbus leaders in the movement, T. W. Tyson, A. B. Buttles, Joseph Sullivant, A. A. Stewart, and Walter Thrall, energized their followers to submit petitions to the legisla ture asking for a popular vote on the question of whether licensing should be permitted in different localities. They cleverly developed form petitions to be used by people who were either "legal voters," "Ladies," or "Minors." They declared, "A momentous issue is before you, and demands your prompt and efficient action. Vascillating [*sic*] and timid legislators have heretofore declined taking any decided measure of temperance reform for fear of public opinion." [10] Temperance petitions flooded both houses of the legislature throughout the 1846–47 session.

On January 12, 1847, some women held a fund-raising dinner for the benefit of a state temperance society, probably the Ohio division of the Sons of Temperance, which met the following day to discuss petitioning the legislature on the issue of license laws. The society must have lobbied well, for later that year the legislature passed an act to allow certain counties to vote on the issue of granting licenses to sell liquor. Three hundred delegates of the Grand Division of the Sons of Temperance met in Columbus for several days in October 1848 and kept up the attention focused on this reform movement. That year Lauretta Buttles hosted a meeting in her house for the Daughters of Temperance, who held a supper to raise three hundred dollars for the cause. Gen. S. F. Carey, the popular temperance lecturer, spoke to the convicts at the penitentiary on February 28, 1849, and converted some of them. The Sons of Temperance held another convention in town at the end of the decade. [11]

Hopes were raised in 1850 when the Senate debated a bill to make the sale of spirituous liquors unlawful. However, it was recommitted to the temperance committee and the legislature went on to other business. Despite the temperance crusade's popularity, it failed to achieve its goals. Writing at the end of 1849 to Joshua W. Swayne, Jeff Barrett sadly declared, "Just step into the basement of the American [Hotel] in your city and see the liquid fire bottled up and exhibited in as tempting a manner as possible in order to induce men to drink." [12]

The phrenology fad was another movement that attracted some attention. Phrenologists claimed that skull shape revealed mental faculties and character traits. It was a popular topic in the press and in conversations. Some people even thought of it as a science. According to David Bakan, the term "phrenology" was coined by Thomas Foster in 1815 (although others claim it was 1805). Phrenology was a theory, originated by Franz Joseph Gale and Johann Christopher Spurzheim, about the human brain's structure and function. The theory rested on the assumption that certain aspects of anatomy and physiology influenced mental activity. It was thought that different mental strengths and characteristics were located in different parts of the brain and that the strength of these "faculties," as they were called, could be detected by examination of the skull's shape and contours.[13]

Spurzheim came to the United States in 1832. He spoke at Yale and Harvard commencements and impressed so many faculty members that a phrenological society was formed. He died before he was able to give additional lectures. Another popularizer was Professor Charles Caldwell of Louisville, Kentucky, who taught the first phrenology course in the country. He published a paper in 1829 titled "New Views of Penitentiary Discipline and Moral Reform."[14]

Phrenology was further publicized by the Britisher George Combe, who developed a theory that sought to explain the connection between the human and nature and society. Combe came to the United States in 1838 and gave many lectures in most of the large eastern cities. He impressed so many people that additional phrenological societies were organized.[15]

Others got on the bandwagon and went on the lecture circuit primarily for personal gain. Soon the emphasis was more on encouraging people to improve themselves by learning about their brain's characteristics than on the scientific aspects of the movement. By the 1840s the fad had two components, the original "science," and its application to character reading in order to be practical to people. In this respect, it became, according to David Turnbull, a minor reform movement that appealed to the middle class by legitimizing the social and economic hierarchy that existed in society.

The most visible popularizers in this country were the Fowlers, who, in addition to speaking extensively on the subject, founded the *American Phrenological Journal* in 1837. It was a thirty-two-page monthly whose circulation reached twenty thousand by 1847. According to John D. Davies, Ohio had the distinction of having a greater circulation per capita than any other state by 1848.[16] The journal catered increasingly to a practical approach. In one of its issues, its mission was described in these words: "[T]o PERFECT OUR REPUBLIC, to reform governmental abuses, and institute a higher and better state of private society and common usage throughout all our towns and villages, That is, it wishes to place mankind upon the true basis of our common nature, by teaching them that nature."[17]

Many people, including Henry Ward Beecher, Walt Whitman, Ralph Waldo Emerson, and Daniel Webster, had the "bumps" on their heads read. People in Columbus became acquainted with phrenology in several ways. James Teeters published a book on the subject in 1838. The January 29, 1841, issue of the *Ohio Statesman* contained a long advertisement under the heading "Phrenological": "George A. B. Lazell, Bookseller and

Phrenologist, between Broad Street and the Theatre, has opened a room immediately over his Bookstore, for the reception of visitors who may desire either a written or oral phrenological description of powers, talents and dispositions. . . . Important hints will be given to individuals, relative to their character and propensities conducing to self-knowledge and government,—also to partners in business, in marriage. . . . N. B. The science of Phrenology never fortels [*sic*] what a person will be, but what he should or may be; its discoveries reach no further than to declare the innate power." [18]

A Dr. Wooster gave a lecture on phrenology in the crowded courthouse on October 12, 1841. The next year, Dr. Parnell gave two presentations on the subject in the hall of the House of Representatives. Dr. James Kilbourne, youngest son of Worthington's founder, gave two free phrenological lectures in Columbus, one on February 9, 1843, on "The Social Propensities" and the other the next evening on "The Organ of Self Esteem." Dr. Parnell spoke twice in March and performed experiments in "phreno-magnetism." There was also interest in the black community. Dr. E. R. Lewis lectured on phrenology in Hannibal Hall on September 28, 1844, at "early candle light." The money collected that evening was given to the *Palladium of Liberty*.[19]

The subject was discussed on other occasions. The Whiting & Huntington bookstore featured six books on phrenology as late as 1849.[20] Phrenologists argued against capital punishment on the basis of what they considered scientific evidence. They believed that criminals lacked a certain moral responsibility. It was partly because of the interest in phrenology that a number of doctors in Columbus insisted on attending the autopsy on William Graham after he was hanged on February 9, 1844, for the murder of a prison guard, Cyrus Sells. Graham's defense had been insanity, and although he was defended by the incomparable Gustavus Swan, he was found guilty. The doctors disagreed on what his brain revealed and continued their argument in the newspapers.

Although phrenologists favored abolition of capital punishment, that reform movement was not as strong in Ohio as it was in other states before the Civil War.[21] The Ohio Senate voted in its favor in 1835 and 1837 but the House refused. When the House debated the question in 1838 and 1839 the issue was postponed. The Senate debated the question again in 1844, 1845, and 1850 but postponed action. Although capital punishment was not abolished, the movement to eliminate public hangings was successful in 1844. That action succeeded partly because of public reaction against them following a double hanging at the foot of Mound Street in

Columbus on February 9 of that year that was attended by a rowdy crowd of between ten and twenty thousand persons. Hester Foster, a young black woman who was a convict, allegedly killed a white woman convict in 1843 and was deemed guilty, although no record exists of her trial and the crime may have been committed by someone else. Sheriff William Domigan decided to save money and execute both Foster and William Graham, the convict mentioned above, at the same time. It was the coldest day of the year. Sullivan Sweet, a blacksmith from Franklinton, was trampled to death by a horse when he was pushed and knocked down by the crowd. Dr. Ichabod Jones and his assistant dug up Graham's body after he was buried, and Jones kept Graham's foot preserved in alcohol in his Town Street office.[22]

Petitions had been submitted to the legislature for several years calling for executions to be private, but political leaders ignored them. A House bill in December 1838 was quickly amended and died. One petition received in December 1843 contained 212 signatures. The *Ohio State Journal* carried a long editorial in its December 19, 1843, issue urging the elimination of public hangings. The editor wrote that they had a demoralizing influence: "Crime and vice stalk abroad and obtain a harvest almost invariably, under the gallows and within sight of the wretched culprit whose death-throes were once supposed to be capable of impressing a lesson and conveying a warning lasting as life." After the hangings of Graham and Foster, vocal members of the middle and upper classes in Columbus sufficiently made known their fears of mobs and disorderly behavior that the General Assembly had to act. The bill to limit hangings to within the walls of the penitentiary passed the House 48 to 10 and the Senate 24 to 6. It was one of the few bipartisan acts passed that year.[23] Although hangings were no longer public, some people still found ways to observe them by climbing walls and standing on roofs.

Efforts to expand women's rights was another cause that increased in intensity, especially as midcentury approached. It attracted much attention among Columbus residents. Early feminism was fueled by antislavery agitation. A motion made by Angelina Grimké at a New York antislavery convention in 1837 gave women something to recall. She declared, "That as certain rights and duties are common to all moral beings, the time has come for woman to move in that sphere which Providence has assigned her, and no longer remain satisfied in the circumscribed limits with which corrupt custom and a perverted application of Scripture had encircled her."[24]

One of the most active feminists in Ohio was Jane Elizabeth Hitchcock

Jones. She had been recruited to the antislavery movement by Abby Kelley, who persuaded her to go on the lecture circuit. Kelley called her "elo quent." Jones spoke at many antislavery meetings throughout the state and was active in the Western Anti-Slavery Society. Along with many of the women who worked for the abolition of slavery in the 1840s, she began to realize that they also had to lobby for their own emancipation. William Lloyd Garrison's *Liberator* praised Jones for her feminist forcefulness and asserted, "Her ideal of a woman was one who could not only make bread and darn stockings, but also be the equal of her companion in judgment and scholastic attainments, and in her ability to earn an independent living." [25]

Jane Elizabeth Hitchcock, along with Benjamin Smith Jones, whom she married the next year, edited the *Anti-Slavery Bugle* beginning in June 1845. The masthead contained the phrase, "No Union with Slave Hold ers." It was a four-page, six-column paper called "an organ of agitation and propaganda" that favored articles on temperance, the abolition of capital punishment, and women suffrage. In 1848 Jane Hitchcock Jones wrote *The Young Abolitionist,* a book for children describing the evils of slavery and the good being accomplished by abolitionists. However, she became increasingly concerned about the status of women and after 1848 devoted much of her time and attention to women's rights. In fact, shortly before the famous Seneca Falls, New York, meeting that year, Jones wrote, "The 'lordly sex' has enslaved women in a narrow sphere and condemned her as 'unsexed' if she revealed any intelligence or creativity." [26]

In 1850 Jones wanted to bring some of the eastern speakers to Ohio, and she invited Lucretia Mott and Lucy Stone to speak in Columbus. They refused because of the great distance and poor traveling conditions and suggested that Jones find other speakers in her state. She wrote in the *Anti-Slavery Bugle,* "If you know one woman qualified and willing to go to Columbus, speak up at once that others may know where to find her and give her blessing and God-speed." [27]

Elizabeth Coit, married to merchant Harvey Coit, frequently advo cated women's rights throughout her life. Another Ohioan, Frances Dana Gage, became active in speaking and writing on behalf of antislavery and women's rights after her eight children were grown. Gage contributed fre quently to the *Ladies Repository* and the *Ohio Cultivator,* which was pub lished in Columbus. Her articles in the latter were signed "Aunt Fanny." She traveled widely and even spoke on women's rights in New Orleans. Gage and her family moved to Columbus in 1860, and she became associ ate editor of the *Ohio Cultivator* and *Field Notes.* Both women lobbied the legislature on behalf of the Married Women's Property Act. [28]

Although improvements in their status occurred, many women were unhappy that there had not been more change. They became more active for their own benefit and rejected the notion that they should be passive and patient. Partly inspired by the success of the 1848 Seneca Falls meeting, women in Ohio called for a women's suffrage convention, which was held in Salem on April 19–20, 1850. The Women's Rights Convention, attended by more than four hundred women, passed several resolutions, one of which stated, "[I]n those laws which confer on man the power to control the property and person of woman, and to remove from her at will the children of her affection, we recognize only the modified code of the slave plantation."[29] Although much more has been written about the Seneca Falls meeting, the Salem Women's Rights Convention meant more to the people in Columbus in terms of their awareness of the women's suffrage movement.

Twenty-two resolutions were passed, the first of which called all laws contrary to the principles in the Declaration of Independence not binding. Another demanded that the same legal protection should be given to both sexes. The eighth resolution read, "That all distinctions between men and women, in regard to social, literary, pecuniary, religious or political customs and institutions, based on a distinction of sex, are contrary to the laws of Nature . . . and ought to be at once and forever abolished." The next resolution objected strenuously to the "pedestal" notion: "That the practice of holding women amenable to a different standard of propriety and morality from that to which men are held amenable, is unjust and unnatural, and highly detrimental to domestic and social virtue and happiness." The Women's Rights Convention submitted a message to the members of the Constitutional Convention recommending that full equality for women, including the vote, be approved. While this memorial was debated, there was not serious effort to include it in the revised state constitution.

The highlight of the conference was an impassioned speech by Jane Elizabeth Hitchcock Jones, who talked at length on "the wrongs of women." Her first point was that "the present relation between man and woman, so far as rights are concerned, is like that which some slaveholders maintain toward their slaves." She expressed sorrow that more women were not fully aware of their subjected condition: "I say the fact that woman does not know that she is robbed of her rights, shows the extent of her enslavement; it shows that a long train of abuses and usurpations has completed the work of degradation, has blinded her to a sense of justice and of equal rights."[30] Jones bewailed the fact that women had no political rights. Her speech was well received.

Although Jones was disappointed that the Constitutional Convention failed to be responsive to women's rights, it did not deter her from continuing her efforts. She became active in the lobbying for the Married Women's

Property Act in Ohio. She, Frances Dana Gage, and Hannah Tracy came to Columbus and testified at a hearing of a joint legislative committee considering the question, and Jones's *Address to the Woman's Rights Committee of the Ohio Legislature* was published in 1861 when the law was enacted.[31]

These reform movements were only partially successful. There was only so much time and energy to devote to changing society. The causes of temperance, capital punishment, and women's rights gave way as more people realized that the worst crime in their society, and one legalized by the Constitution, was slavery.

The drive to abolish slavery was the most controversial reform movement. Initially, only a small minority of people were abolitionists, although many in Columbus were critical of slaveholding as an institution. Residents were well aware that fugitive slaves from south of the Ohio River were passing through town. The black community was certainly aware of them and helped them. Southern slave owners placed advertisements in Columbus papers offering rewards for their capture. A June 1821 notice offered "500 Dollars Reward—runaway Negro owned by Robert Turner within 2 mi. of Louisville May 20. Isham, sometimes called Jack, 5' 10" pretty dark complexion, strong." Reward offers usually were in the $100 to $150 range.[32]

Most whites at that time held racist views. Shortly after statehood, repressive laws were enacted. Ohio's Black Laws, passed in 1804 and 1807, required blacks and mulattoes to have a court certificate stating they were free. Black residents in Ohio had to register and list the names of their children at a fee of twelve and one-half cents per name. Employers who hired blacks lacking a certificate could be fined up to $50. The same penalty applied to those hiding a fugitive. Those helping a fugitive leave the state could be fined as much as a $1,000. The 1807 law required free blacks entering the state to post a $500 bond. The fine for hiding a fugitive was increased to $100. No black was permitted to testify in a court case involving a white. The law to give bond, however, was not universally enforced.[33]

As more slaves escaped north either to settle or to travel toward Canada, some Northerners were concerned about the balance between their love of freedom and their desire for stability. People disliked what they did not know, and the strangers moving north were a different color. The January 25, 1821, issue of the *Columbus Gazette* contained a long letter from a person in Washington, D.C., complaining that the Southern states were trying to "throw their worthless black population into Ohio, Indiana, and Illinois." The editor commented, "We think there is an absolute necessity that there should be some regulation of the black population of this state, which is so rapidly increasing." The black population in Ohio in 1820 was less than 1 percent, and most of the blacks were in Cincinnati. By 1827, Columbus readers were warned that many mulattoes were entering Ohio and that there should be "legislative interference" to prevent them.[34] The Columbus black population increased after 1828.

In the 1820s, some people supported the American Colonization Society, which was founded in 1817, not only because they were critical of slavery but also because they wanted to be rid of free blacks. The corresponding secretary of the Ohio State Colonization Society lived in Columbus. As early as January 17, 1824, the General Assembly sent a resolution to other state legislatures supporting the idea of colonization and calling slavery an evil. Its message in part stated, "That the consideration of a system providing for the gradual emancipation of the people of color, held in servitude in the United States, be recommended. . . . That in the opinion of the General Assembly a system of foreign colonization, with correspondent measures might be adopted that would in due time affect the entire emancipation of the slaves in our country without any violation of the national compact . . . by the passage of a law . . . which should provide that all children now held in slavery, born after the passage of such law, should be free at the age of twenty-one years . . . providing they then consent to be transported."[35]

The message served to stir up controversy on the issue. Eight Northern states endorsed the resolution, but six Southern states rejected the suggestion. The South Carolina legislature received it "with regret" and indicated to Ohioans that its people intended to adhere to slavery "now inseparably connected with their social and political existence."[36]

The majority of whites had little sympathy for their black neighbors. In Columbus, as early as 1827, a committee of the House of Representatives reported that free blacks had become "a serious political and moral evil" because they undercut white labor and supplied a disproportionate number of convicts for the penitentiary.[37] An 1827 editorial in the *Ohio State Journal and Columbus Gazette* stated that "their residence is becoming daily an evil of increasing magnitude."[38]

Many of the city's leading citizens were active in the Ohio State Colonization Society, which held its annual meeting in Columbus on December 29, 1828. James Hoge gave the opening prayer. Nathaniel McLean was the corresponding secretary, and David Deshler was recording secretary. Managers included Lyne Starling, Otis Crosby, Samuel Parsons, Lincoln Goodale, and J. R. Swan. Columbus residents helped send some blacks to Liberia in 1827.[39]

Articles appeared in the Columbus papers praising colonization and claiming that Ohioans were "deeply interested in the success of the society." An agent from the American Colonization Society gave a series of lectures in town in 1834. One editor was particularly vicious in his condemnation of blacks. He wrote, "Their fecundity is proverbial—They are worse than drones to society, and they already swarm in our land like locusts. The state of things calls loudly for legislative interference." Another editorial called blacks "idle, intemperate, dissolute." Reality was different from its perception. In 1820 there were 132 blacks in Franklin County, and ten years later there were only 288.[40]

Most members of the free black community opposed the colonization movement. Some white supporters of colonization believed that its efforts might be the only way to correct the evil of having forced Africans into slavery. They assumed that because the Constitution permitted it, slavery was unlikely to be eliminated. Others later dropped their support when they realized that only thirty-six hundred blacks were relocated in the society's first forty years.[41]

James G. Birney, editor of the *Philanthropist*, who had been living in Cincinnati when he moved north, was one of the earliest abolitionists to lecture in Columbus. He spoke for an hour in the courthouse on April 29, 1836, to what he called "a large and highly intelligent audience." Writing to Lewis Tappan, Birney described "the rabble all the while at the door opposite, discharging at me small missiles, pebbles, apples, etc." Hecklers followed him to a friend's house after the meeting. Handbills were posted the following morning warning him not to speak that night. The marshal in charge of the courthouse was afraid to open the building for a meeting, and Birney was unable to find another place to speak in town.[42]

Abolitionists were a small minority, but as early as 1834 some started sending petitions to the legislature "praying an abolition of all political distinctions between the white and colored population of the State." They turned to political activity in earnest in 1840 when the Liberty Party was organized. Benjamin Tappan, lawyer, judge, and Democratic senator, probably reflected the views of a large majority of Ohioans when he wrote his brother, Lewis, on March 6, 1836, to assert, "Ohio is abolition in principle but she will not be moved by religious motives to act on the subject." Most people considered abolitionists dangerous radicals. What they were advocating was considered unconstitutional. Although slavery and involuntary servitude north of the Ohio River had been forbidden by the Northwest Ordinance, some citizens who had migrated from Kentucky and Virginia still held Southern sympathies. Democrats for the most part were unsympathetic to antislavery efforts and blamed the Whigs for encouraging them. Under the headline "People Of Ohio Beware! BEWARE!" the *Ohio Statesman* warned in one issue, "The Union of the Ohio Abolitionists and Ohio

Whiggery is complete—the black spirits of fanaticism are at work—abolitionism like antimasonry, has sunk itself into federal whiggery—workingmen of Ohio, and Democrats, look out!"[43]

One of the earliest negative reactions to the abolitionist cause was the impression that their agitation was increasing the migration of free blacks to the state. The *Ohio Statesman* in 1839 took the position that abolitionists were indirectly strengthening the slaveholders' hands. They could encourage those slaves they wanted to dispose of by sending them north: "The Southern people are taking strong ground in favor of sending all their FREE NEGROES into the free states forthwith . . . we shall be over run with blacks, and those of the most worthless kind. . . . Are the laboring people of Ohio prepared to have such a population forced upon them as this?"[44]

Typical of the racism prevalent at the time was another comment in the *Ohio Statesman* in 1839. After reporting on a journey of twenty-one freed blacks through Dayton to Mercer County, the editor wrote, "It becomes a very serious question, whether Ohio is to become the depot for all the liberated or runaway blacks in the South. Those that live in the neighborhood of those colored settlements can give some information to those that are soon to find themselves surrounded by this kind of population. This subject is of the utmost importance to the peace and well being of our State, and the sooner it is met and decided upon the better. We are in a most delicate position and we must guide the storm as well as we can."[45]

An English traveler, Harriet Martineau, observed, "The personal oppression of the negroes is the grossest vice which strikes a stranger in the country."[46] On the positive side, however, the Supreme Court of Ohio ruled in June 1841 that every slave voluntarily brought into the state was free.

One antislavery society existed in Ohio in 1832. The statewide Ohio Anti-Slavery Society was organized in 1835. A chapter was formed in Worthington on March 28, 1835, and had a membership of forty-two men and twenty-five women. In 1838, when there were 251 such organizations in the state, the Ohio Anti-Slavery Society approved a memorial praying "that all those statutes which discriminate between men, on account of color, be immediately repealed . . . color is no crime . . . these people are men—The same general principles obtain in reference to them as to other men." The society called such laws unjust, oppressive, and hostile to liberty.[47]

At the same time, escaped slaves were being helped through the Underground Railroad and more people were being educated about the evils of slavery. Black residents played key roles and were especially important in creating and working the escape support system. Shepherd Alexander and Lewis and Thomas Washington drove wagons to deliver escaped slaves to safe houses and the haylofts of barns. Other blacks in Columbus who participated included David Jenkins, John Booker, James Poindexter, and Leslie Washington Sr. John T. Ward, who had been janitor of the city hall and was active in the Underground Railroad, wrote many years later, "We had some very strong friends among the white people."[48]

White citizens in Columbus who helped included Joseph Sullivant, James E. Coulter, L. G. Van Slyke, and Samuel H. Smith. James M. Westwater, a merchant, arrived in Columbus on July 18, 1840, and shortly afterward was hiding escaped blacks in a smokehouse in an alley near Fourth Street. A partially hidden candle at a back window was a beacon to the escaping slaves. At night they would be driven north up High Street to Clintonville. Coulter, who lived on Third Street just north of Long, hid fugitives in his attic and barn. The Kelton House on Town Street was built in 1852 and still attracts visitors interested in the Underground Railroad. Merchant F. C. Kelton and his wife, Sophia, probably participated in the secret effort as early as 1840. William Hanby was active in Westerville in helping escaped slaves, as was the merchant Philip Doddridge. After 1842, Dr. Eli M. Pinney hid escaping slaves in his brick house in Dublin. Wilbur H. Siebert's estimate that more than one-third of the Ohio workers in the Underground Railroad lived in the Columbus area may be too high, but his assertion that some forty thousand fugitive slaves escaped through Ohio is probably accurate.[49]

Black residents in Columbus were undoubtedly more active in the movement than they have been given credit for and more effective than their white neighbors realized. Hiding and conveying escaping slaves was done as secretly as possible. Some slaves went through Columbus on their own, too fearful to risk getting caught. David Barrett slept in a barn south of the city, was chased for several hours, and escaped through a cornfield.[50]

An Anti-Slavery Baptist Association was established in 1841 and spread opposition to slavery among its churches. The Baptist and Methodist Episcopal Churches split in 1844 over the issue of slavery. In 1847 a black family who had formerly owned and sold slaves moved from Virginia and joined the Second Baptist Church. About forty members left in protest and formed the Anti-Slavery Baptist Church. They worshipped at Town and Sixth Streets. James Poindexter, who became a leader in the city, was their pastor, and the congregation grew to more than 140 members. Poindexter's ancestry was African-American, Caucasian, and Native American, which made him black in the opinion of his contemporaries. He was a barber as well as a preacher and served on the city council for four years. Black ministers in Columbus and elsewhere had to counter the prevailing opinion held in white churches that law-abiding, religious people had to wait for God to eliminate slavery.[51]

Anti-abolitionist and racist feelings in Ohio frequently spawned violence in the 1840s. In fact, there were more anti-abolitionist mobs in Ohio than in any other state. Most of the violence occurred in Cincinnati, where Southern sympathies were strong. Riots occurred there in 1829, 1831, 1836, 1841, and 1843. Many prominent citizens participated in them.[52]

Some Ohio citizens who were not abolitionists were unhappy with the fugitive slave laws and with those who sought to return escaped blacks to slavery. Petitions were submitted to the legislature calling for repeal of the black laws in the 1829–30 and 1833–34 sessions. Citizens from both races continued to submit petitions, but in 1839 some legislators objected to receiving them from blacks. The General Assembly decided that blacks and mulattoes had no constitutional right to submit petitions and any reception of them would be "a mere act of privilege."[53] In 1839, the Ohio House of Representatives voted against repealing the Black Laws. Most Columbus residents probably supported the legislature's action.[54] The House of Representatives voted 46 to 24 to repeal the Black Laws in December 1842, but the Senate refused. In an editorial in his paper, the *North Star*, in 1848, Frederick Douglass wrote, "In no State of the Union are to be found laws more cruel, unjust and atrocious, than those on the Statute Book of Ohio."[55]

From 1840 on, in response to these petitions, legislative committees almost every year recommended no action. One of the more interesting appeals submitted to the legislature was one signed by sixty-eight persons on December 26, 1844:

> The undersigned citizens of the state aforesaid petition your honorable Body to pass a law to Disfanchise every man in the State of Ohio for a term of five years who will aid in recapturing a fugitive slave in the State of Ohio, either by physical power or furnishing a house . . . or other means of confinement for the purpose of securing said fugitive or fugitives . . . & likewise to prohibit under a like penalty the use of any county or state prison or other public building in the state of Ohio for the purpose of securing said fugitive slave or slaves . . . also to repeal all laws now in force in the state of Ohio that make a distinction on account of color.[56]

The first state abolition convention held in Columbus was on January 20–23, 1841. It was called to improve harmony among the activist abolitionists. Three hundred delegates attended, including Samuel Lewis, and the meetings generated considerable interest. One of its resolutions called on Congress to prevent the extension of slavery by not admitting new slave states. According to the *Ohio Statesman*, the convention intended "to force the Federal members of the Legislature to redeem their promises, and repeal the Fugitive law of winter before last, as well as the law disqualifying negroes from testifying in courts against white men." In August of that year, some Columbus citizens in favor of the antislavery movement met at the Baptist church and registered approval of James G. Birney's nomination for president. Under the editorship of John Duffy, the *Freeman,* which had formerly been a Whig paper, sought to advance the cause.[57]

A second convention was held in Columbus in December 1841, but the Liberty Party, formed in Warsaw, New York, on November 13, 1839, was still small in numbers. The Liberty Party was against the admission of additional slave states, favored the abolition of slavery in the District of Columbia, and opposed discrimination against free blacks. It was considered radical by many persons. Because of some community opposition, the meeting had to be held in the basement of the Baptist church. What was significant about this meeting was that Salmon P. Chase had written the call to it, having decided to participate more effectively in Liberty Party activities. Although few Columbus residents were party members, many people were impressed that the meeting attracted two hundred delegates from thirty-six counties and that the businessman and political figure Leicester King convened the meeting.[58]

Abolitionists held another meeting in Columbus in early January 1842. Joel Buttles recorded that the city was "filled to overflowing." Another convention was held in August 1842. In 1845, Abby Kelley, the famous orator who married Stephen Foster that year, lectured in Columbus against slavery. She stayed for a week visiting her sister, Ruth Pollard, and Ruth's husband, Warren, a successful farmer. Abby Kelley was the most outstanding of the women making public speeches against slavery, and she undoubtedly influenced other women to speak out. Because attending lectures was so popular, the influence of Kelley and other abolitionist speakers was probably great. Frances Watkins was born in Baltimore and had free black parents. She worked in a bookstore and read about the efforts to free slaves. She moved to Ohio as a young woman and often spoke on abolition. She was the first woman who taught at the Union Seminary, founded by the African Methodist Episcopal Church west of Columbus.[59]

Although there were no huge celebrations on January 19, 1843, it was an auspicious day for the black families in Ohio and for those active in the Underground Railroad. On that day the Ohio Legislature repealed the state's Fugitive Slave Law of 1839. Early in 1839, Kentucky had sent a delegation to the State House to lobby for a law to punish those who were helping escaped slaves to evade capture. It took only a month of persuasion for the legislature to enact a law authorizing slave masters or their agents to get warrants directing sheriffs to arrest fugitives, who would be returned to slavery if their owners proved in court that they had a legal right to them.

The act also provided for a fine of up to five hundred dollars and imprisonment for up to sixty days for anyone trying to prevent the execution of an arrest warrant or aiding in the rescue of a slave or his removal from the state. The same penalty applied to anyone who helped a slave escape or gave him food or money. Repeal of the law, however, did not eliminate escaped slaves' vulnerability to being recaptured. The original federal Fugitive Slave Act in 1793 that allowed a slave owner to recover an escaped slave was still in effect.[60]

The abolition meeting on January 3, 1844, attracted more Whigs as the movement gathered momentum as a political force, but the Liberty Party failed to attract a broad group of voters at that time. James G. Birney, the Liberty Party candidate for president, arrived in Columbus on June 3, 1845. He met with Whig leaders and antislavery activists trying to increase his support. The Democrats used every opportunity to link the Whig Party with abolitionism, much to the discomfort of many of its members. Joshua Giddings tried to get Salmon Chase to attend a Whig-dominated antislavery conference in Columbus in 1846 but was not successful. As more people realized that lecturing and writing against slavery were not sufficiently productive, turning to political action was the next logical step. However, the Free Soil Party, which succeeded the Liberty Party, was not solely concerned with keeping slavery out of the newly acquired territory. It campaigned for reducing the size of the federal government, using the tariff solely for revenue purposes, issuing land grants to settlers, and reducing postage rates.[61]

Even among those who hated slavery, prejudice and racism were rampant. Many who were opposed to slavery did not think the black and white races could live together. Segregation was becoming more extensive. Most whites assumed the inferiority of other races. The free black population suffered from many injustices. Blacks were not allowed to serve on juries and could not testify in court cases involving whites. Blacks received longer sentences than whites for the same crimes. The English traveler William Sturge, writing in 1842, quoted Gustave de Beaumont: "The prejudice against colour haunts its victim wherever he goes,—in the hospitals where humanity suffers,—in the churches where it kneels to God,—in the prisons where it expiates its offenses,—in the graveyards where it sleeps the last sleep."[62]

A curious example of how racism permeated the thinking of even the best-educated persons can be seen in a long article in the January 14, 1844, issue of the *Ohio Statesman*. The horse artillery from Dayton participating in the January 8 parade was attended by six whites and two black drivers. The writer of the article, after describing the operation of the artillery in great technical detail, criticized the practice of having blacks as "the driving canoniers" on the grounds that only men who could be relied upon in the heat of battle should be used for that important assignment. A February 20,

1845, editorial in the *Ohio Statesman* reflected one of the popular antago-
nisms toward the black race: "The liberation of the slaves can only be
popular where there is territory set apart for them. They can no more mix
with the white population on an equal footing, as is now to be done by the
whigs of Ohio, than the Indians, nor half so much so, and yet it is the policy
of the government to colonize the Indians themselves." [63]

Racism hurt blacks even after death. In 1841 the city council purchased
land north of Livingston Road for a larger cemetery and stipulated that
"colored persons should be buried under the direction of the north sexton
and in the same manner that strangers are buried." [64] Of more concern to
the living, however, was proposed legislation submitted in the Ohio Senate
in December 1846 that would have required blacks to be registered. The
Whigs opposed it. [65]

Many blacks became disappointed with the meager results of the abolitionist movement. They thought that there was more oratory than action,
more pious posturing than political clout. They believed that most white
abolitionists seemed more concerned with the abstract idea of equality
than in working wholeheartedly on practical problems related to blacks'
living conditions, economic opportunities, and the discrimination against
them. The first black state convention in Ohio was held in Columbus on
August 10–12, 1843. A statement from the meeting took up the entire first
page of the first issue of the *Palladium of Liberty:*

> We would briefly call your attention to our condition among you; and to the
> unjust and impolitic course which is pursued toward us; a course which grants
> us the name of freemen, but robs us of their attributes. . . . The prejudice of
> which we are the objects, is the most vindictive, cruel, and unprecedented of the
> age, in an enlightened and christian country. . . . The divine nature living and
> burning within us, inspiring us with high hopes, and giving both to lofty aspi-
> rations, tells us that we too, are entitled to all the privileges of humanity. . . . We
> ask only for the rights God has given us. [66]

David Jenkins, who came to Columbus from Virginia in 1837, lacked
money or an education. He became a painter, glazier, and paper hanger.
One of his friends later wrote that the first meeting of Columbus blacks
was held in his Front Street house. Jenkins found his people's economic and
social condition in the city slightly better than it was in slavery. He determined to try to improve circumstances for his race and was influential in
emphasizing the importance of education.

In 1844 Jenkins became the editor of the *Palladium of Liberty.* He was
active in the Underground Railroad and held many meetings to oppose
slavery. He always carried blank handbills that could be filled in to publicize his next speaking engagement. He received lucrative contracts to

work on the Neil House and some of the public buildings in town. He also found time to attend meetings of the legislature, where he earned the nickname "the member at large." He was a property owner and ran a boardinghouse for a while. Those who worked with him were Anthony Barret, John Brooks, William McAfee, and A. M. and L. D. Taylor.[67]

Opposition to slavery increased through the 1840s. More moderates joined the antislavery tide after the secession of Southern ministers in the Methodist Episcopal Church in June 1844. A Female Colonization Society met in July 1846. The agent of the American Colonization Society spoke in town on November 27, 1846. But rabid abolitionists were in the minority. One of the resolutions passed at the 1848 Democratic state convention was probably more representative of the attitude of most Ohioans: "That the people of Ohio look upon the institution of slavery in any part of the Union, as evil . . . [but also] that to each state belongs the right to adopt and modify its own municipal laws, to regulate its own internal affairs; to hold and maintain an equal and independent sovereignty with each and every other State; and that upon these rights the National Legislature can neither legislate, nor encroach."[68]

In 1845 efforts to repeal the Black Laws continued. William L. Perkins, reporting for the select committee in recommending passage of Senate Bill 23, called the laws "obsolete": "They are so unreasonable, so fraught with tyranny, so oppressive, so mean . . . that the public mind revolts against them."[69] Perkins called the provision that disqualified blacks from testifying in court unconstitutional and unjust. Beginning on February 3, the senators engaged in bitter parliamentary maneuvering to prevent a vote on the measure. Several motions to table and to recess were defeated by close votes. A tie vote on the motion to engross the bill led to its failure. More close divisions occurred on February 6 and 12 when attempts were made to reconsider the bill. The weary senators finally adjourned without taking action.[70]

The editor of the *Ohio Statesman* was distressed with the attempt at repeal. On February 13 he wrote, "Thus after forty years of peace and prosperity, under our laws, things are now to be changed, and the olive branch held out to all the floating negroes in the Union to rush into our State. . . . By encouraging negro emigration and elevating them by law to the same conditions as the white working man, and thus bring them into competition, in labor and importance, the insolence of wealth and corporate privileges will accomplish most of their purposes."[71]

A similar attempt to repeal was made in the House in 1846, but action on the bill was postponed by a margin of four votes. The *Ohio State Journal* editor wrote, "We regret very much the defeat of the proposition; for it is known to all that the law in question is a mere nullity; never having been enforced, to our knowledge." The House acted again in 1847, initially passing a bill but later reconsidering it.[72] Public sentiment in favor of repeal continued to increase.

An ugly racial incident occurred in Columbus on July 26, 1845. A thirteen-year-old black boy hit and allegedly molested a five-year-old white girl and was arrested. After learning of the event, some white men chased a black man down High Street. According to the *Ohio State Journal*, they kept shouting, "Kill him, kill him." Thomas Moseley recorded in his diary, "So incited was the reckless populace that at the enquiry court it was with much difficulty that the boy was saved from lynch judgment. Every black who showed himself was assailed and many were seriously injured." The following night a gang of about a hundred men and boys chased and beat some blacks and stoned their houses.[73]

Moseley, an engineer and inventor, considered himself a friend of blacks and boasted to Henry Clay that "those in my neighborhood look upon *me* as their friend and I am persuaded that I can exercise great influence over them." Nevertheless, even Moseley held racist ideas. He wrote a long letter to Clay on August 13, 1845, complaining that the process of colonizing to Liberia was too slow. He declared, "The free blacks of our state are a great burden to our people, while they are forbidden (perhaps as they should be) most privileges of a free citizen." He proposed, "If one of the great islands west of our continent was secured & given them; by labor and energy they might all be persuaded to migrate to it." He asked Clay's help in implementing his plan.[74]

Many people in Columbus were agitated on March 27, 1846, when Jerry Finney, an escaped slave who had become a popular waiter at one of the hotels, was kidnapped after having been lured to Franklinton under the pretense of delivering a trunk to the office of William Henderson, justice of the peace there. A huge public meeting was held at the Methodist church at which Samuel Galloway, Granville Moody, and others spoke and at which resolutions were passed. Uriah Heath, the Methodist itinerant minister, happened to be in Columbus on his way to Worthington and attended the protest meeting. He wrote in his journal about what he called "the late outrage committed on the dignity of the law and on the liberty of a fellow being by two ruffians in kidnapping a colored man. . . . The feeling was intense. The indignation of the whole people arose. Money was subscribed."

Although Finney was carried to the Kentucky Penitentiary, prominent citizens raised five hundred dollars to purchase his freedom. Columbus residents were irate when they learned that the warden there had paid money to Finney's captors, who had offered to release him if he told them where escaped slaves were hiding. Gov. Mordecai Bartley also offered a five-hundred-dollar reward for the capture of the two kidnappers, Alexander C. Forbes and Jacob Armitage. Henderson and the others were arrested, and Henderson was in prison until the U.S. Supreme Court granted his appeal on a technicality. Finney finally returned to his wife and children in Columbus on September 17, 1846.[75] This incident, which dramatized the reality of slavery's horrors and the brutality of Southern slaveholders in implementing fugitive slave laws, probably spurred more antislavery support than abolitionist agitators. Antislavery sentiment also increased partly because of the pro-slavery stance of the *Ohio Statesman*.

Petitions calling for repeal of the Black Laws increased in number in 1846. Most of them came from northern counties in the state. Action was postponed in 1847, and bills to repeal were defeated in 1848. That year the majority report of the Select Committee on the Repeal of the Black Laws was made by A. H. Lewis and Brewster Randall, who wrote, "These laws . . . rest upon no higher or better principle than the prejudice before hinted at. They are more degrading and oppressive to the colored man than the laws of any other state or nation in Christendom, except those where he is absolutely enslaved. They are a stigma upon the character of our State."[76] The minority on the committee submitted a long statement in opposition, written by Andrew H. Byers. Public opinion was divided. Those who opposed repeal were more outrageous in their racial prejudice. An editorial in the *Ohio Press* for January 2, 1847, declared, "It is simply whether our people shall be lead [*sic*] away by a feeling of sympathy for those who have no right to be here, and ought never to have been permitted to enter the State. . . . The evils of a mixed population are becoming more and more apparent every day."[77]

Antislavery support among white residents was still limited to a minority in 1850, but there was increased awareness of the evil of slavery and greater concern about its expansion westward. The black population in the city was obviously in favor of abolition but could do little to end the institution except participate in the Underground Railroad. One thing blacks could do in the summer of 1849 was march in town to celebrate an anniversary of the end of slavery in the British West Indies. The *Ohio Statesman* commented favorably on the "orderly and gentlemanly conduct . . . of the colored male population, each dressed in his holiday's best."[78] After the parade the men held a dinner, listened to speeches, and made many toasts.

16

Antislavery's
Influence on Politics

Criticism of the Black Laws and irritation with the defense of slavery were part of the reason why the slavery issue came more to the fore in Ohio political campaigns. The Liberty Party, and later the Free Soil Party, enjoyed an increase in support thanks to a series of developments. These included a greater realization that the South would gain the most from the Mexican War, the failure of the Wilmot Proviso seeking to prevent the extension of slavery in the newly acquired territory, and the effective writings and speeches of abolitionists. Antislavery sentiment also increased in the two major parties. When it appeared likely that the United States would gain vast territories at the end of the Mexican War, the *Ohio State Journal* increased its criticism of President James K. Polk and called for restrictions on the expansion of slavery. The paper reflected Whig popular opinion in an 1847 editorial: "With slavery as it exists within the limits of particular states we say . . . let it alone. . . . We are not called upon by any consideration to stand quietly by, and see the power and influence of the federal government prostituted to the propagation and perpetuation of that institution."[1]

The two national parties gradually began to weaken from 1844 on, and by 1848 the weakness probably became irreversible. Antislavery sentiment increased every year. Those in Columbus who closely followed political developments were aware that significant changes were occurring before their eyes. The slavery issue led to sectionalism and a realignment of political forces. As Stephen E. Maizlish has indicated, from the mid-1840s on, politics disintegrated from a stable, two-party system to bitter sectional rivalries over deeply held doctrines. Ohio Democratic leaders had avoided public statements critical of slavery, but after 1844 they were aware of increased antislavery feeling among their members. For many of them, slavery was an unfortunate fact of life, but the prospect of its expansion westward greatly disturbed them. At their state convention on January 8, 1848, they passed a resolution "That the people of Ohio look upon slavery as an evil in any part of the Union, and feel it their duty to prevent its increase, to mitigate, and finally to eradicate the evil."[2]

The Whigs were affected first. Gen. Zachary Taylor was nominated for the presidency on June 9, 1848. Ohio Whigs were not the only ones who were exceedingly unhappy. Taylor was a Southerner whose military reputation was made in the Mexican War, and he lacked political experience. Salmon P. Chase wrote a call for a meeting of antislavery people from all political parties. Chase was one of the most consistent critics of slavery. However, even he expected that once slaves were free, they would prefer to emigrate instead of living in predominantly white communities.[3] Chase became better known to Columbus residents through his legal and political activities. After an 1836 riot in Cincinnati when James G. Birney's printing press was destroyed, Chase stopped a crowd looking for Birney and later defended Birney before the Supreme Court. He made enough visits to Columbus to have influence with politicians.[4]

When a people's convention met in Columbus on June 21, 1848, residents had a front-row seat to the unraveling of political parties. One thousand delegates, members of all three parties, poured into the city and passed resolutions at what became known as the Free Territory Convention. Out of it emerged a stronger Free Soil Party that would wreak havoc on the Whigs locally and on the Democrats nationally. Chase was the big winner in this convention because he was one of the leading speakers and was instrumental in increasing the strength of the antislavery forces. He wrote his Democratic friend in New Hampshire, John P. Hall, to declare, "Our convention was one of the largest, most intelligent and most enthusiastic and most resolved political assemblies I have ever attended in the state."[5]

The sweep of the several resolutions written by Chase was impressive. The delegates registered their opposition to the extension of slavery, their resistance to what they called "the aggressions of the Slave Power," their unwillingness to support either Lewis Cass or Taylor, their conviction that Congress had no power to authorize slavery in new territory, their support for grants of the public domain to actual settlers, "retrenchment of the expenses and patronage of the Federal Government," election of government civil employees, and support for a newspaper in Columbus "devoted to Freedom, Free Territory and Free Labor." With some political realism, they did not call for slavery's abolition. The Ohio leaders of the Liberty Party sought to broaden the base of support for antislavery by seeking a coalition of all those threatened by the Southern slave power and muting the views of extreme abolitionists favoring immediate emancipation. This approach struck a favorable chord in Columbus.[6]

The political campaign in 1848 was fiercely fought at the state and national level. Salmon Chase spoke at the market house in Columbus on July 24. He tried to prove that the Northern Whigs were not bound to support the actions of their party and suggested that many in both major parties supported the idea of territories free of slavery. He even attended the August Free Soil Party convention that nominated Martin Van Buren for president. Other men, however, went to the polls singing the refrain, "Huzza for Zach." Taylor was elected president because enough Democrats supported the third-party candidate. John W. Allen succinctly summarized the result in writing William H. Seward on November 13, "We are beaten by our friends, and not by our old enemies."[7]

The race for governor in 1848 was the closest in Ohio history, and the results were not known officially for some time. In the meantime, another crisis hit the legislature and Columbus observers were treated to some highly questionable procedures. Earlier in the year the Whig-controlled legislature sought to secure some Whig representation from Hamilton County by dividing the county into two districts, in one of which they would have an opportunity to elect members of their own party. The Democrats were opposed to this move and absented themselves so that there would be no quorum, a technique the Whigs had used earlier in the decade. The Whigs passed the measure anyway, and when the new legislature met in December, there were two disputed slates elected from Hamilton County.[8]

On December 4, the first day the legislature was scheduled to meet, the Democrats arrived early and persuaded Ohio Supreme Court judge Nathaniel C. Read, a loyal Democrat, to swear in their slate. When the Whigs arrived, they had their slate sworn in, and the issue had to be decided by the House of Representatives later. Members of the Free Soil Party who were elected, three in the Senate and eight in the House, held the balance of power. A Free Soiler, Norton S. Townshend, was appointed to the committee to decide which slate from Hamilton County would be seated. Judge Read was severely criticized for his action and forced to resign from the bench. His reputation was so tarnished by his action that he soon joined the gold rush west. He died in San Francisco.[9]

The legislature was at a standstill because of the even division between the two leading parties. Although the Free Soilers held the balance of power, they were not united in agreeing upon a way to solve the impasse. Anxiety increased among Columbus residents as no progress occurred in either house during December. The *Ohio State Journal* editorialized, "No events now transpiring in any part of the United States are exciting so large a share of public attention, as those now occurring in this city."[10]

Another Free Soil state convention met in Columbus on December 28, 1848, and residents were made more aware of that party's objectives. Black residents in Columbus did what they could to support repeal of the Black Laws. They held a public meeting on December 18, 1848, to discuss the statewide convention of their race scheduled for January. John Booker was named chairman, and David Jenkins was appointed secretary. Four resolutions were passed, the most important of which was to invite Frederick Douglass to attend. They agreed to pay all expenses for Douglass's visit and appointed James Poindexter, David Jenkins, L. D. Taylor, and John Booker to solicit donations. What was called the State Convention of Colored Citizens met on January 10–13, 1849, in the hall of the State House. Influential black leaders, including William Day and Charles and John Langston, became better known to Columbus residents. The large audience contained members of both races. The meeting's purpose was to consider ways to secure repeal of the Black Laws, to work for the abolition of slavery, and to discuss means for improving blacks' conditions. According to the *Ohio Standard*, the proceedings were conducted "with ability, order, and decorum." [11]

There was not unanimity on all subjects. John M. Langston from Cincinnati initially argued in favor of blacks migrating out of the United States because of the prejudice against his race. He recalled the racial hostility that had erupted in the four Cincinnati riots and stated that he wanted to go where he could really be free. He doubted that the United States would ever protect him and asserted that blacks had to have a nationality before they could amount to anything. He declared that "the very fact of us remaining in this country, is humiliating, virtually acknowledging our inferiority to the white man." He was in the minority, however, and after lengthy debate, the convention approved a resolution stating, "[W]e will never submit to the system of Colonization to any part of the world, in and out of the United States; and we say once and for all, to those soliciting us, that all of their appeals are in vain; our minds are made up to remain in the United States, and contend for our rights at all hazards." [12]

Although the main reason for their meeting was to press for immediate repeal of the Black Laws, other efforts were put in motion. They agreed to recommend the appointment of William Day as superintendent of the colored schools. The convention also created the Ohio Colored American League to speak out and lecture between meetings on behalf of the vote and to travel through Ohio to solicit public support. [13]

Racist opponents were also active. On January 19 David Christy, agent for the American Colonization Society, gave a lecture in favor of African colonization in the hall of the House of Representatives. He described the increase in the free black population and said that blacks' concentration was beyond control: "They are, therefore, shut up, imprisoned among us, and instead of any diminution we must prepare for an increase of their numbers." Christy believed that blacks' presence had a "baneful effect upon the industry of whites." He thought something more was needed than the repeal of the Black Laws and asserted that responsibility for the improvement of blacks did not rest on Northerners but "upon those who have them in charge." His main point was that "opposition to granting them equal social and political privileges in Ohio is a fixed fact," and he concluded that "separation from the whites is essential to the prosperity of the colored man, and that colonization at some point offers him the only hope of deliverance." [14]

Christy wrote a memorial to the Ohio General Assembly that became part of the society's annual report for 1849. In it he declared, "[T]he Ohio Valley is the focus toward which nearly the entire free colored population of the country is concentrating . . . the Ohio Valley is, therefore, to become the asylum for the victims of slave oppression, and has been selected by the colored man as the theater upon which the great battle for the achievement of his rights is to be fought." [15]

A large number of people met in the Second Baptist Church in Columbus on January 29, 1849, to criticize Christy's views and to assert that the American Colonization Society's purpose was the removal of free blacks from the United States so that slaves would not be harmed by them.

The issue came to a head in 1849. The 1848 state elections had resulted in the election of the Whig candidate for governor, Seabury Ford, because the Free Soil Party supported him. However, the decision wasn't officially known until January 22, 1849, when all the ballots were counted and confirmed in the General Assembly. It took so long because some Democrats upset the decorum of the legislature for a while. Ford received 148,756 votes, and John B. Weller received 148,445. Franklin County gave a slim margin to Weller and favored Taylor over Lewis Cass, contrary to the rest of the state. Although the Whigs won in Ohio, the margin of victory was dangerously low. Whigs and Democrats were evenly divided in the legislature, and there were contested seats in the House. The House contained thirty-two Democrats, thirty Whigs, and eight Free Soilers. The Senate had seventeen Democrats, fourteen Whigs, and three Free Soilers. It took ten ballots to elect Brewster Randall speaker of the Senate, and John G. Breslin wasn't elected speaker of the House of Representatives until January 3. Two of the Free Soil members in the House were independents, not committed to support the Whigs. [16] Senate Bill 4 to repeal the Black Laws was stalled in that branch of the General Assembly. On January 14, 1849, an amendment to the bill, "That all colored persons be prohibited from holding any real estate within the state of Ohio," was defeated by a vote of 19 to 16. On March 14 a Senate bill to prevent additional black migration into the state was indefinitely postponed by a vote of 18 to 14. [17]

Salmon P. Chase succeeded in breaking the stalemate, with cooperation coming from the Free Soilers, especially Norton S. Townshend. Chase had written the platform for the Free Soil Party's convention in Columbus in 1848 and had included several provisions that were similar to those supported by the Democrats. Although the Whigs were the ones more likely to push for repeal of the Black Laws, their candidate for U.S. senator was Joshua Giddings. Chase wanted the position. After long negotiations and frustrating delays, the Free Soilers, led by Townshend, joined with the Democrats in sending Chase to the Senate on the fourth ballot. They succeeded in getting the Democrats to repeal partially the Black Laws and support John F. Morse's bill to authorize schools for black children. The Democrats were able to elect two of their candidates for the Ohio Supreme Court, Rufus Spalding and William B. Caldwell. The rancorous session of the legislature lasted 113 days, until March 26, and was one of the longest at that time.[18]

The editors of the *Ohio State Journal* followed the turmoil in the legislature with growing dismay and kept readers well informed. An article on February 12, 1849, titled "Tyranny of Third Parties" criticized the "treason" of Townshend and Morse for their deal with the Democrats. One editorial called the legislature's action "unconstitutional." The editors later castigated Salmon P. Chase and concluded that his election was "destined to be more unhappy to the state—more injurious to her fame abroad— more destructive of her political morals at home" than any other action taken by the legislature.[19] Despite this criticism, Chase benefited politically from his efforts in Columbus.

Chase was so pleased to have been elected to the Senate that he gave a banquet at the American Hotel. Although the Whig paper, the *Ohio State Journal,* was unhappy at Chase's election, it supported repeal of the Black Laws. Actually, the term describing the action should be "modification," not "repeal," because the act excepted the 1831 acts relating to juries and to poor relief. The *Ohio State Journal* commented, "It was doubtless thought by many that the repeal of these laws would greatly meliorate the condition of the colored race in Ohio. We think differently. . . . It is a fancied gain." The editor was realistic about the effect of repeal on the population at large. On April 26, 1849, he wrote, "The law of our nature, and even the force of education are often found to be more potential in their bearings upon men, than any legislative enactment, and we are mistaken if that 'labor of love' which undertakes to abolish 'all distinctions on account of color,' does not prove in the sequel to be an Utopian enterprise."[20]

The law providing for the education of black children was long overdue. The law provided for similar taxation of the property of blacks, with the money to be used to support colored schools wherever they were opened. Money was added to the common school funds in those districts where black children were permitted to attend common schools. If there were fewer than twenty black children in a district, they could attend common schools "unless there was a written protest filed by some one having a child in school." In that event, they were not allowed to attend and the property of blacks in that district was not taxed. The legislature in 1849 changed the law to require cities and towns to create districts for black children if they were prohibited from entering the common schools. In such cases, the black citizens were authorized to organize such schools and support them by taxation on their own property.[21]

Slavery and antislavery continued to influence politics not only in Columbus but throughout the nation. Incidents of violence increased on both sides. The aging Henry Clay proposed a compromise in 1850 that included admission of California as a free state and a postponement of any decision about slavery in the other territory won from Mexico. Clay also proposed barring the slave trade in the District of Columbia and a more stringent fugitive slave law. The even division between Whigs and Democrats in Ohio continued in the next session. It took 301 ballots for the Senate to elect Harrison G. Blake of Medina County, a Free Soil Whig, as speaker.[22]

17

A Capital City
at Forty

Migration into Columbus during the 1840s produced an impressive 200 percent increase in the population. The growth in the number of whites in Columbus from 1840 to 1850 was 203 percent, and that of blacks was 123 percent. Americans kept moving west from the eastern states. Immigrants wrote family members and friends to urge them to make the trip. One letter to a brother at home ended, "You will know we are far better off here than we should have been in England. A family costs very little here." [1]

The migration of German-speaking settlers increased. Many of them were attracted to what they had heard about life in mid-Ohio. When Maria Ecker Wolff arrived in Columbus she wrote her sister in Germany to report, "There is much in Columbus that reminds me of home. The cottages built close together along narrow streets, surrounded by gardens and grape arbors, are not so different from those of our neighborhood in Mannheim. The shops are owned by German-speaking people, the newspaper is printed in German, and everywhere we go, we hear our language spoken. It is almost as if, after three months of traveling, we have come home again." [2]

Migration out of the city also occurred as many people continued their westward march. Some left at the time of the Mexican War, others after gold was discovered in California in 1848. Migration into Columbus, however, was at a heavy pace in the late 1840s. John Jay Janney moved his family to Columbus in 1848. Janney had been born in Virginia in 1812. He moved to Warren County, Ohio, where he taught school, in 1833. He also surveyed land and became a merchant. When Samuel Galloway was secretary of state he appointed Janney his chief clerk. Janney, who hated slavery, wrote an opinion stating that blacks should be admitted to the common schools. Janney was active in Whig Party affairs, a member of the Sons of Temperance, and in 1850 started teaching Sunday school at the Ohio Penitentiary. [3]

As the city's population increased there was more demand for additional taverns and hotels. P. H. Olmsted's United States Hotel opened in 1846 on the northwest corner of Town and High Streets. It was a four-story building with a central entrance and two side entrances. A saloon opened in the basement in 1848. [4] William Kelsey made extensive improvements to the American Hotel. Overshadowing the other establishments was the popular

Neil House, which continued to attract important visitors. When Charles Elliott, editor of the *Western Christian Advocate*, stayed there he called his accommodations "excellent" and described the hotel as "the mammoth house of the West."[5] Its five floors accommodated two hundred persons, each of whom paid one dollar per night. The Neil House was the scene for many parties. John Armstrong Smith, a Hillsboro legislator, wrote his wife in 1842 to describe one event "crowded with the youth & beauty of the City, its rooms furnished in splendid style."[6]

Because there were more people, there were more deaths. An observer noted in the June 22, 1848, *Ohio State Journal* that "the old burying ground" was filling up. So were the East Graveyard on Livingston Road and the Catholic cemetery. As a result, the Green Lawn Cemetery Association was started in August 1848 and selected an eighty-three-acre, tree-covered area removed from houses. A newspaper writer gave the reason: "It is only in modern times that society has become conscious that the health of the living is injured by remaining near the dead." The trustees were some of the city's leaders. The first burial in Green Lawn was in July the following year. The stockholders voted ninety-one to twenty to deny blacks the privilege of being buried there. In 1849 a group of blacks created their own graveyard.[7]

Columbus residents were concerned about the adequacy of their medical care. The city probably lacked sufficient hospital facilities during its first few decades. A Literary and Botanical Medical College had been founded in 1837, and the faculty gave lectures in several specializations. Anyone could take a course by buying a ticket. But the institution specialized in botanic medicine and failed to satisfy the public that care was adequate. People followed with interest details of the meetings of the Ohio Medical Convention in May 1847. One hundred doctors attended and papers were read. Doctors and other civic-minded citizens arranged for the Willoughby Medical College to move to Columbus in 1846. The college's board of trustees met on February 19, 1847, and elected Noah H. Swayne president. Other trustees included Robert Neil, Samuel Medary, and J. R. Swan. Six doctors were on the faculty, including R. L. Howard, who taught surgery, and Samuel M. Smith, who taught medical jurisprudence and insanity. Smith had been assistant physician at the Ohio Lunatic Asylum until 1843, when he resigned to open an office at the corner of High and Town. The spring session of lectures began March 10. Initially the fees were twenty dollars. Room and board, including light and fuel, cost up to two dollars a week. Lectures continued in the summer in the Clay Club building (where supporters of Henry Clay in 1844 had previously met), which was moved from State Street to the northwest corner of High and Gay Streets.[8]

Lyne Starling gave thirty thousand dollars for the purchase of land and construction of a hospital building at the southeast corner of State and Sixth Streets, and the Starling Medical College was incorporated in 1848. The building contained three large lecture rooms, a museum, a library, dispensary rooms, and a hospital for forty patients that took up the west wing and eight rooms in the center of the building. A grand celebratory dinner was held on December 27, 1848, and was attended by the newly elected governor, Seabury Ford, and three hundred "ladies, students, editors, judges, and distinguished strangers." Unfortunately, Lyne Starling died before that date, but not before he contributed another five thousand dollars to complete the construction of the college's building. Its first commencement was on February 19, 1849, when fifty young men received their medical degrees and honorary medical degrees were awarded to six physicians. The college had a faculty of eight and 173 students. Twelve of the students, including Starling Loving, were from Columbus. Fees were sixty-four dollars, with an additional graduation fee of twenty dollars.[9] Many years later this institution became the College of Medicine at The Ohio State University. Lyne Starling was one of Columbus's most generous philanthropists. According to the obituary written by Gustavus Swan, Starling contributed more than $100,000 to charitable organizations in town.[10]

The development of a greater common interest in charity was evident at this time. The Germans in Columbus held a meeting on April 28, 1845, to solicit contributions for the victims of a disastrous fire in Pittsburgh. The next year, an article appeared in the *Ohio Statesman* under the heading, "Columbus, its progress and prospects." The writer boasted, "Our city is small, in comparison with some others; but, in some respects, it will favorably compare with many larger and older towns. Many of our edifices, both public and private, evince good taste, while they show substantial workmanship. . . . Columbus is progressive."[11]

It was so progressive that in 1847, an editorial in the *Ohio Statesman* spoke in favor of the city's having a statue of Christopher Columbus "and a City Hall worthy of her."[12] The cost of an appropriate statue was estimated at twelve hundred dollars. There was insufficient interest at that time in spending that much for a statue. Throughout its first forty years, Columbus remained less significant than the Queen City, Cincinnati, and the fact of being so much smaller in size and importance may have influenced its residents' attitudes toward their city.

One of the biggest events in 1849 was a firemen's celebration on April 17 that marked the founding of the Columbus Engine Company. Despite the rain, a parade started on High Street that featured the six fire engines, including the hook and ladder. The firemen were cheered by many spectators. That night three hundred people enjoyed a grand supper, speeches, and toasts that lasted from nine until midnight in the Odeon Hall, adjoining the Neil House.[13]

As midcentury approached, there was increased interest in encouraging more manufacturing. The press reflected this concern on several occasions. William B. Thrall, the editor of the *Ohio State Journal,* wrote an editorial under the heading, "Columbus and its Prospects": "During the severe revulsions in business of the last ten years, Columbus has kept steadily onward. For the last two or three years the city has been growing with unusual rapidity, and seems this year to be stretching faster than ever." Thrall indicated that people had taken it for granted that there were poor prospects for manufacturing: "But improvements in machinery in connection with steam, are destined we hope to introduce among us as much manufacturing enterprise as is desirable." He also called the city prosperous and said the population reflected "competence, contentment, and thrift."[14]

In the fall of 1849 the *Ohio Statesman* devoted several editorials to endorsing the advances in manufacturing. Peter Hayden's building was praised for employing one hundred mechanics and laborers in the manufacture of saddlery and coach hardware. Howlett's soap and candle factory on Front Street and Ridgway's and Kimball's car factory also were singled out for their contributions to the economy. Columbus residents became more aware of the increased industry around them as they walked the streets. A stonemason, Joseph Strickler, sold pedestals and tombstones near Broad and High. J. and J. Lennox's iron railings and lightning rods were available at Broad and Third Streets. Stores, factories, and residences crowded around the unfinished new state capitol building.[15]

But more profits continued to be made in land speculation. One *Ohio Statesman* article observed that "the present rapid improvements, and the prospective increase of business and population—life and bustle, tend to make investments in real estate safe and profitable. . . . We believe we have yet the first person to hear of who ever lost money by the purchase of real estate in this city." One of the craftiest speculators was probably the laborer David Jones. Jones bought lots with cabins on them at tax sales and rented them to poor persons who, when they couldn't afford the rent, had to pay in clothes or furniture. When land values soared Jones sold his property at handsome prices. At times, however, there was a shortage of low-rent houses on the market. It was difficult for construction to keep up with the population increase. In 1848, A. C. Brown sought to meet the demand by putting up houses called "cottage row."[16]

A definite business ethic was evident among those Columbus residents who were merchants, bankers, or factory owners. Joel Buttles spoke for this group when he advised, "Never risk a hazardous speculation, be satisfied with small profits, but take care to make some and to take good care of them when they are made. Perhaps this last suggestion is the most difficult of all, but it is indispensible [*sic*]. Large gains would be little in the end if spent as fast as made."[17]

Anyone walking down the west side of High Street in 1848 would have seen a wide variety of shops and services in a short distance. The Neil House was south of Broad Street, and Peter Ambos's candy store stood between the Neil House and the American Hotel. Bain's dry goods and hardware store was in the Exchange Building at 63 High. Next door was the office of Humphrey and Langworthy, physicians and druggists. Farther down the street at 105, John Westwater and Son sold china and glassware. Joseph R. Scroggs's books and stationery store was at 109. J. W. Constans sold boots and shoes at 113. Whiting's book store was at 129, and the H. Cowles and Co. dry goods establishment was at 131. Dr. J. Fowler, the dentist, had his office on the second floor at $133\frac{1}{2}$. One could stop in the Clinton Bank at the corner of High and State and hope to see its president, William S. Sullivant, who was more famous for his scientific publications. Farther down the street at 195 one could visit G. W. Free's tailor shop, walk past the Union Hotel at 211, Wood and Foncannon's gun store at 215, and the residence of the black teamster R. Butcher at 269.

On the east side of High Street, the surgeon Dr. G. Miesse had his office at 226, south of the new courthouse. Walking north, one passed L. Baldwin & Company's tobacco and cigar store at 190, the residence of Horton Howard, a druggist, at 188, and Nathan Gundersheimer's clothing store and residence at 170. Mrs. Lathrop, a milliner, lived at 164. A few doors north of the Franklin Hotel, one could buy boots or shoes at J. B. Griffith's store, number 152, arrange a funeral with Azzur W. Reader at 148, or purchase groceries at Marquart & Eberly's at 144. Continuing on, one passed the Bennfield residence at 98 High Street, I. B. Coffroth & Company's hat store at 82, and the bakery of C. I. L. Butler at 80.

One would naturally stop to marvel at the recently resumed, noisy construction of the new capitol building. At the end of the day, the prisoners working on the building would be quick-stepping back to the Ohio Penitentiary accompanied by armed guards. Their chaplain, James B. Finley, might be with them, his arms filled with books collected for the prison library. Depending on the time of year, a couple of legislators might be seen heading toward their favorite tavern. Uriah Heath, down from Worthington, might ask for a "subscription," a contribution for the struggling Worthington Female Seminary. A peddler might stop some laborers walking home from their work or wait for the stage to arrive from Cincinnati.[18]

The area immediately around the public square was a mix of housing, commerce, and light industry. People could easily shop for most of their necessities. There was a growing sense of what it meant to be living in proximity to neighbors instead of in rural isolation. There was also an understanding of what it meant to be close to a new capitol building being constructed at the city's heart. But a change was also occurring as additions were made to the original town. The city's limits reached eastward and southward and then to the north as the population grew. The result was a move of the wealthier residents, especially from the Front Street part of town, to Broad Street and the fringes of the city. The riverfront was left to businesses, industry, and poorer classes. This movement, ever outward, became characteristic of many cities that now are relatively empty at the core and surrounded by suburbs that seem to produce a centrifugal force threatening healthy urban growth.

Economic advancement, however, was as uneven in Columbus as it was in the rest of the country. The decades before the Civil War saw significant increases in inequality.[19] The concentration of wealth intensified in this period. The cost of living for poor families rose more rapidly than for affluent ones. There were two distinct groups in Columbus, the few wealthy men and their families and the many poor, most of whom did not own property. One visitor described the aristocratic section of the city in glowing terms: "A great many of the houses stand off from the spacious streets, affording room for grass plats, which are most tastefully laid out. . . . This adds greatly to the beauty of the city, and promotes the health and cheerfulness of the inhabitants, affording them at once pure air, and refining, elevating scenery."[20]

Although a few residents were self-made men, for most persons that goal was only a mirage. A visitor wrote the *Ohio State Journal* on June 17, 1847, to give a much different assessment of the city:

> I have been a traveller twenty years and have travelled many thousands of miles through seventeen or eighteen states of this Union, and positively I have not witnessed in the whole period and distance, half the destitution which has been presented to my view in the city of Columbus. . . . Until I witnessed the destitution in two wards of this city, I thought my own poverty about as great as could well be borne. . . . In the first ward full one fourth the families have not a competency and in a majority of such cases I found disease accompanying want. . . . The greatest portion of pauperism I found amongst the blacks; with them two out of four were in almost destitute circumstances at least so poor as barely to live at all; disease I found much more too with them than the whites.[21]

The increased population and industrialization in Ohio led a number of persons to conclude that the time had come to revise the state constitution. The question was debated in the legislature in 1846 but there was insufficient support to pass a bill. The *Ohio Press* raised the question in its June 10, 1846, issue: "There is scarcely a state in the Union whose constitution is so defective as that of Ohio, and scarcely a state with so distant a prospect of amendment." The editor claimed that the original constitution had been written hastily in only four weeks, that it contained inconsistencies, and that it had never been submitted to the people for approval: "All things cry out for reform. The abuse of the legislature, the weakness of the executive, the delays of the judiciary, all alike need reform." Later the *Ohio Press* again called for changes and asserted, "Our Constitution is a mass of uncertainties, and men of all parties are calling loudly for reform." Gov. William Bebb was one of the leading politicians to favor constitutional revision.[22] Sen. William M. Wilson of Darke County introduced a bill on December 21, 1847, calling for a vote at the next election for or against a convention to amend the state constitution.

Samuel Medary was a strong supporter of the movement. In 1849 he founded a paper, the *New Constitution,* to rally public support for a revised document. The first issue of his sixteen-page newspaper was dated May 5. The last issue, consisting of eight pages, was printed November 17 of that year. The paper's motto was, "Power is always stealing from the many to the few." Medary favored reform of the judiciary, popular election of government officers, and a strong educational system. He reprinted federal and state constitutions and described constitutional reform in other states. He was probably the most influential leader in articulating the need for a constitutional convention. When the vote was taken in 1849, voters favored calling a constitutional convention by a three to one margin. Sixty-five percent of those voting in Columbus favored revision.[23]

By 1850 Columbus was more of an urban city than it had been before. The population by that year had reached 17,872, 47 percent of whom were children and teenagers. Of the total, 1,255, or 7 percent, were blacks. Although blacks continued to live in all five wards, 37 percent of them were in the First Ward, and the trend toward segregation of the races had accelerated. Persons born in Germany and their native-born families constituted about one-quarter of the city's residents (despite the popular impression that one-third of the city's population was German). Slightly more than 3,000 had been born in Germany.[24] Almost 1,000 were from Ireland; many of the Irish were in their twenties and were working on constructing railroad lines. John Mitchell was the first from Ireland in Franklin County to file for intent to become a citizen in 1850. Six others born in Ireland also did so that year.[25] More than 430 residents had been born in England and 375 in Wales. France, Scotland, Canada, and Switzerland also were well represented. Foreign-born residents totaled 4,897. More than 5,000 of those born in the United States had been born in states other than Ohio, the majority in the Middle Atlantic states. In contrast to a 5 percent illiteracy rate in Northern states, in Columbus fewer than 1 percent of the white adults over twenty years of age were illiterate. One-half of the illiterate adults were in prison, and most of the others were recent immigrants. Only 4 percent of the black adults, one-half of them in prison, could not read or write. The oldest resident was Anita Dixon, a black woman who had been born in Virginia in 1744.

More than 1,900 residents worked as mechanics, blacksmiths, carpenters, and shoemakers, while more than 1,700 were unskilled laborers. There were 434 merchants, clerks, and grocers, 62 physicians, and 53 lawyers. Thirty-one hundred children attended school in 1850. That year, 257 couples were married.

The gap between the richest and poorest had widened during the decade. Most families rented their homes, and some took in temporary boarders. The homes of some of the poorer residents were crowded together in the narrow alleys. The most indigent persons probably were the 134 in the poorhouse, of whom 25 were children. Nine hundred ninety-six white men and 66 white women, most of whom were widows or single parents, owned real estate. Only 20 percent of white males were property owners, a figure slightly lower than the 26 percent of non-farm property owners nationwide. Fifty-seven blacks, or 17 percent of black adult men, were real estate owners. Ninety-six Columbusites owned property worth ten thousand dollars or more. Census figures did not reveal wealth in stocks, bonds, and other investments.[26] The largest owners of real estate in the city were:

William Neil	$400,000	(Clinton Township)
Robert E. Neil	200,000	
Lincoln Goodale	160,000	
William S. Sullivant	112,000	
Samuel Medary	75,000	
David W. Deshler	70,000	
Alfred Kelley	60,000	
Rosanna Latham	60,000	
William A. Platt	55,000	
Demas Adams	51,000	
Amanda Benfield	50,000	
William B. Hubbard	50,000	
Noah H. Swayne	50,000[27]	

Economic conditions improved by the end of the decade. Columbus could boast of four banks scattered along High Street. That street, the engine house, and the market house were lighted by gas. Some individual consumers were using gas before the end of the year. Dr. Samuel H. Smith caught the spirit of the day in Columbus when he declared in an address, "It is certainly a time of promise; it is also a period of feverish excitement; every one is rushing on he knows not where, aiming at something he knows not what; every one is looking to the future with hope or fear, seeking to be master of his destiny." [28]

All the construction in town had caused a shortage of materials and skilled labor. The editor of the *Ohio State Journal* was pleased with all the progress. In 1849, he wrote, "We have never known a time when Columbus was improving with so much rapidity as at present. Not a street in which some improvement is not in progress. Old buildings are being removed to make room for new ones, and lots hitherto vacant are rapidly filling up. . . . A second bridge across the Scioto river, which will connect the city with the Harrisburg turnpike at a point opposite the foot of Mound Street, is under contract, to be finished during the summer." He concluded by asserting, "Columbus is increasing in population and wealth faster than ever." [29] The Canal Street bridge, as people called it, did indeed open that September. William B. Thrall and Henry Reed, editors of the *Ohio State Journal,* praised the city for its energetic qualities. They wrote, "Columbus is emphatically a busy place. It possesses advantages which do not and cannot belong to other places." One advantage was that some Columbus women were quick to follow fashion changes. In the winter of 1850–51, feminists decided to rebel against their constricting clothing and express their modernity and opposition to restraints by dressing in bloomers. Elizabeth Smith Miller appeared in the bloomer dress in Seneca Falls in the winter of 1850–51. In July 1851, the *Ohio Statesman* reported, "There was a Bloomer out yesterday, attracting considerable attention. The costume looked cool and comfortable this hot weather." [30]

The generosity of residents toward civic and charitable projects was started early in the city's history. Settlers risked $50,000 and gave ten acres of land for a future state capitol and ten acres for the first prison. They contributed $8,000 to make the first bridge over the Scioto a free one, $5,000 toward a new courthouse, and $1,500 for land for the Ohio Penitentiary, the Deaf and Dumb Asylum, and the Blind Asylum. Later they gave $10,000 for the German Seminary, $12,000 for school buildings, and $10,000 for a new market house. Their investments in railroad and turnpike construction were extensive. Merchants and property owners, for instance, contributed $10,000 to help the Columbus and Worthington Plank Road Company begin its corduroy road. Contributions to churches and charity to the poor have never been fully recorded. [31]

Although the rate of population growth slowed considerably in the 1850s, other changes in that decade brought industrialization and commercialization. Urbanization and the continued increase in population weakened the close-knit fabric of Columbus society. By midcentury Columbus was no longer a small town but was on the threshold of joining the other major urban centers in the nation.

One event that marked a significant change for Columbus and Ohio was the convening on May 6, 1850, of the second Ohio Constitutional Convention. Residents followed the debates closely through July 9, when the convention adjourned because of the cholera epidemic. It reconvened in Cincinnati on December 2 and continued to deliberate until March 10, 1851. Although the majority of delegates were Democrats, they were not united and debate was lengthy on many of the reform petitions submitted by citizens. Close to one hundred petitions were submitted calling for prohibition of the "traffic in intoxicating liquors." The delegates took no action other than calling for a popular vote on licensing when the constitution was submitted for ratification.

Other partisan issues stimulated impassioned debate. Many petitions were submitted urging extension of the suffrage to blacks and to women. Other petitions were against equal suffrage. Norton Townshend made an impassioned speech favoring the vote for women. He thought that "woman is man's equal in intelligence and virtue" and deserved an equal interest in governmental matters. He declared that if women could accompany their husbands, fathers, or brothers to church or elsewhere, "I do not see why they could not as safely accompany the same person to the ballot box." The motion to delete the word "male" from the suffrage qualification was defeated 72 to 7.[32] Although women failed to win the vote, the fact that the issue was even discussed was a milestone. Some delegates thought the question was improper for public debate.

Some petitions calling for a provision requiring the removal of the black population from the state resulted in prolonged discussion. That proposal was voted down, but not before William Sawyer had spoken frequently in favor of it as the only way to prevent future migration. His most sweeping assertion was that "the United States were designed by the God in Heaven to be governed and inherited by the Anglo-Saxon race and by them alone."[33] Sawyer also wanted to exclude black children from common schools in order to discourage black migration, but he was defeated in that effort as well. The race question was probably the most controversial issue before the convention.

The delegates also wrestled with a rewriting of the suffrage rules because of the concern over the infusion into the state of so many temporary or transient residents. Extensions of voting rights to blacks and to women were defeated by large majorities. Blacks were denied the right to vote 75 to 13. They were kept out of the militia by a vote of 62 to 22, and their children were excluded from white schools 61 to 26.[34]

The abolition of capital punishment was sought by some petitioners. While there was extensive debate, efforts to eliminate it in favor of life imprisonment were defeated.[35] Petitions "praying that the rights of married women may be protected" were discussed, but the jurisprudence committee recommended that the question of control of women's property be left to the General Assembly to decide without "jeopardizing the unity and mutuality of feeling, affection and interest, which should always be cherished in the relation of husband and wife."[36]

The constitution was modernized and some changes were approved, although the legislature continued to be the dominant branch of government. Legislators had to be elected every two years. The governor still had no veto power. Important executive officers and judges had to be elected by popular vote. New district courts were added. Special chartering of corporations was eliminated. The convention approved the revised draft 79 to 14, and the voters ratified the constitution by a safe margin. It took effect on September 1, 1851.[37]

Women were not the only minority to appeal to the members of the constitutional convention. The Ohio State Convention of the Colored Citizens of Ohio met in Columbus in 1850 and sent them a message asking for permission to speak. Although their main objective was the right to vote, the convention passed twenty-eight resolutions. Their concerns failed to move the majority of delegates.[38]

In September 1850, Millard Fillmore, who became president when Zachary Taylor died of cholera in July, signed the five bills that came to be called the Compromise of 1850. More Northerners, including Columbusites, registered their opposition to the new fugitive slave law that strengthened the 1793 act. When a slaveholder swore that a person was his slave, federal marshals had to seize the alleged fugitive. Officers could draft citizens to assist them in such captures, and those not cooperating were liable to arrest and heavy fines. On September 18, the annual Convention of Colored Citizens of Ohio condemned the law. In Columbus, as early as October 7, a large number of determined black residents, led by David Jenkins and L. D. Taylor, met at the Second Baptist Church and passed a resolution calling the new law unconstitutional. They vowed to oppose it "by all the means in our power." Later, the *Ohio State Journal* asserted that most citizens "are so thoroughly opposed to kidnapping and so sensitive on the subject that any attempt of the kind would hardly escape the vengeance of Lynch law." Opposition to the fugitive slave law led more persons to participate in the Underground Railroad. A Columbus paper reported in 1852 that "the express train is doing a good business now."[39]

Columbus's first forty years saw rapid change and significant decisions for the entire country as well as for the city. The nation's borders extended westward to the Pacific Ocean. Patriotism intensified as the nation expanded. The federal government recklessly fought a war against a weak neighbor and almost precipitated one against a stronger opponent. The frontier continued its movement as immigration increased. Railroad construction and the discovery of gold contributed to geographical mobility. The debate over the evils of slavery and its abolition intensified as more of the population became involved. Positions for and against slavery hardened in the Congress and in society at large. As religious groups and other institutions aligned themselves with the North or South, the likelihood of a civil war became more certain.

In 1850, the General Assembly granted the city of Columbus a new charter in recognition of its growth and increased importance. The city was poised to enter the second half of the century with new potential but also with continuing problems. The city's debt, a paltry $22,000 in 1840, had risen to $130,000. The debt was more of an investment in the future than a liability, for it represented commitments of $50,000 each to the Columbus and Xenia and the Cleveland, Columbus, and Cincinnati Railroads and $30,000 borrowed from individuals and companies.[40]

Another happening that marked the midcentury was the death in the summer of 1850 of Joel Buttles, whose life and career reflected so much of what Columbus was and stood for. As residents faced the second half of the nineteenth century, they could agree with *Ohio Statesman* editor Samuel Medary, who wrote enthusiastically about the city's rapid strides: "What forty years ago, was a dense wilderness . . . is now a beautiful and blooming city . . . and enlivened throughout, by the busy hum of industry and activity."[41] James Bates, however, encountered a different aspect of the changing city that year when he wrote his wife, "Almost every day I meet some man staggering along the street. As our town increases in population vice seems not only to increase but is more open."[42]

Famous people continued to visit the city. The last one in this forty-year period was Louis Kossuth, the Hungarian revolutionary leader, who had sought independence for his people but was routed by Russian troops. The U.S. Congress invited Kossuth to this country because many Americans linked him with George Washington and supported the nationalistic revolutions in Europe. The Ohio General Assembly invited him to speak in Columbus. Kossuth arrived seeking arms and money. His large party, supplemented by Cleveland officials and others, arrived by rail late the night of February 4, 1852. According to one of his entourage, it was a "festive entry, with horsemen and trumpets, and torchlights, and music."[43]

The next morning a large, noisy crowd assembled around a temporary platform in front of the courthouse to hear his speech. Kossuth, who was feeling sick, made a fervent plea for support. He was frequently cheered, but few heard all that he was saying. He returned to his rooms and received a small amount of money. That night he attended a meeting at which a Hungarian Association was formed. He visited with the governor, who promised to lend him arms and an army of young Ohioans. On Saturday morning, February 7, he spoke to the legislature in impassioned words: "The spirit of our age is democracy." He ended by saying that he was the same age as the state: "My heart has always heaved with interest at the name of Ohio." He was given $211 contributed by senators. He left for Cincinnati without the arms he wanted.[44]

Rapid movement within and out of Columbus in midcentury made it all the more challenging to develop a solid sense of community. Population turnover also meant that by the 1850s, there were two types of residents, although they were not clearly defined to themselves or to others: those who already had roots in the city and were committed to remaining, and those who were passing through or staying a few years, settling until it was worth selling and moving farther west. The main result was that power and influence gravitated to those who had stayed the longest or who had profited the most in their careers. By the end of forty years, foundations for a future elite had already been created near Broad and High Streets.

The story of Columbus from its founding to 1852 is one partly of constants and partly of change, of depression and prosperity. Columbus attracted transplanted Northerners and Southerners and welcomed immigrants from Europe. It was home to Whigs and Democrats, whites and blacks, affluent property owners and the poor. The area around Broad and High Streets was both residential and commercial. People migrated in and out of the city. Its development and destiny were suspended in uncertainty until the railroad and industrialization reached the capital.

In its first few decades Columbus witnessed many changes, some beneficial and some harmful. While it may have been easier for a town of a few hundred to view itself as a cohesive community with an interesting past and a bright future, it was difficult for a more diverse population of almost eighteen thousand to do so. Direct, friendly, personal experience was becoming more challenging between employer and employee, between the two races, between native born and immigrant. Rich and poor were more segregated as they moved to other parts of town and economic inequality intensified. The open spaces between the city and its surrounding townships were disappearing. Residents had to adjust to becoming an urban center with more clearly defined divisions between work and home, between government and the private sphere.

Decisions made in early years influenced the city's direction and development. Columbus was finally made the permanent capital of the state. Banking and tax laws were passed that affected economic growth. The economy diversified. Population mobility continued, which enabled some of the long-standing families to increase their political influence. A pattern was established of land annexations to the city as arrivals settled in new areas. The city was given a revised charter in recognition of its growth. Common schools were improved, and public commitment to their support was affirmed and written into the 1851 Ohio Constitution. Efforts at higher education were begun. The odious Black Laws were partially repealed. Public executions were eliminated. Changes occurred in cultural life. Railroad transportation finally reached close to Broad and High.

As people started reading Harriet Beecher Stowe's *Uncle Tom's Cabin*, first in 1851 as a serial in the *National Era* and the following year as a book, Columbus was about to become an urban metropolis, moving from fragile uncertainty to optimistic stability. City leaders were hopeful as the 1850s began. The 1850 city directory predicted that the population would reach 50,000 by 1860 because of the increase in manufacturing and additional railroads. Instead, the population in 1860 was 18,629, an increase of only 800 over the decade because of the lure of California and other places in the West. The future presented new problems for the city to confront, such as opposition to foreigners and economic distress. Through the 1850s, Columbus and the nation careened toward the Civil War.

NOTES

Unless otherwise indicated, all letters, diaries, documents, and newspapers are in the Ohio Historical Society.

CHAPTER 1

1. Joel Buttles Diary, February 1, 1835, transcription from Trinity Episcopal Church, Columbus, Ohio.

2. The best account of these events is in Knepper, *Ohio and Its People*, 99–102. The most recent detailed analysis of political animosities is in Ratcliffe, *Party Spirit in a Frontier Republic: Democratic Politics in Ohio, 1793–1821*, 136–60. Other accounts of early factional disputes are in Brown, *Frontier Politics: The Evolution of a Political Society in Ohio, 1788–1814*, 346–47, 380, and Brown and Cayton, eds., *The Pursuit of Public Power: Political Culture in Ohio, 1787–1861*, 6–11.

3. Ohio General Assembly, *Journal of the House of Representatives*, December 20, 1809.

4. McCormick and McCormick, *New Englanders on the Ohio Frontier: Migration and Settlement of Worthington, Ohio*, 102–3.

5. Lyne Starling to Jane Starling, July 12, 1809, in Sullivant, *A Genealogy and Family Memorial*, 60.

6. Kerr to Vance, January 10, 1810, Joseph Vance Letters.

7. Lee, *History of the City of Columbus*, vol. 1, 634–35.

8. Peters, *Ohio Lands and Their History*, 212–15, 254; Soltow, "Inequality Amidst Abundance: Land Ownership in Early Nineteenth Century Ohio," *Ohio History* 88 (Spring 1979): 133–51.

9. Ohio General Assembly, *Journal of the House of Representatives*, January 16, 1811.

10. Ibid., January 20, 1811.

11. Ibid., December 16, 1811.

12. Ibid., January 18, 20, 1812.

13. Starling to Sullivant, January 22, 1812, quoted in Rodgers, *"Noble Fellow" William Starling Sullivant*, 62.

14. Kerr to Sullivant, January 22, 1812, Sullivant-Starling Papers.

15. Ohio General Assembly, *Journal of the Senate*, February 11–21, 1812; *Journal of the House of Representatives*, February 13, 1812; Rodgers, *"Noble Fellow,"* 66.

16. "Proposal from James Johnston and Others to State of Ohio," James Johnston Proposal. For additional details, see Martin, *History of Franklin County*, 263–72.

17. Ohio General Assembly, *Journal of the House of Representatives*, February 19, 1812; January 4, 1817.

18. *Columbus Dispatch*, February 21, 1962; Maxwell, *Early German Village History*, 1.

19. Ohio General Assembly, *Journal of the House of Representatives*, February 21, 1812.

20. The best account of early Worthington history is McCormick and McCormick, *New Englanders on the Ohio Frontier*.

21. Rodgers, *"Noble Fellow,"* 56; Martin, *History of Franklin County*, 290, 301.

22. Hayes, *Columbus Mayors*, 5–7.

23. Bailey, "The Foos Family of Pennsylvania and Ohio," *Pennsylvania Genealogical Magazine* 18 (1951): 109–11.

24. Chillicothe *Supporter,* February 29, 1812; *Columbus Gazette,* April 16, 1818.

CHAPTER 2

1. Reps, *Cities of the American West: A History of Frontier Urban Planning,* x, 16.

2. Elazar, *Building Cities in America: Urbanization and Suburbanization in a Frontier Society,* xii; Russo, *Families and Communities: A New View of American History,* 40.

3. Wright, "Joel Wright, City Planner," *Ohio State Archaeological and Historical Quarterly* 56 (July 1947): 290–91.

4. Ohio General Assembly, *Journal of the Senate,* December 17, 1812; Ludlow to Worthington, October 9, 1815, William Ludlow Letter.

5. Lee, *History of the City of Columbus,* vol. 1, 212–13.

6. Martin, *History of Franklin County,* 277–78. See also Birkbeck, *Notes on a Journey in America,* 67–68.

7. Rippley, "The Columbus Germans," *The Report: A Journal of German-American History* 33 (1968): 2, 30; *Columbus Business Directory for 1843–4,* 16; *Ohio Statesman,* March 24, 1841.

8. Martin, *History of Franklin County,* 280.

9. Chaddock, *Ohio Before 1850: A Study of the Early Influence of Pennsylvania and Southern Populations in Ohio,* 29; Lee, *History of the City of Columbus,* vol. 1, 868; *Directory of the City of Columbus for the Years 1850–51,* 67–68.

10. R. W. McCoy to Alexander McCoy Sr., December 22, 1811, Robert Watts McCoy Papers.

11. Joel Buttles Diary, February 1, 1835.

12. Jacobs and Tucker, *The War of 1812,* 31–32, 87, 89, 110; *Western Intelligencer,* March 3, 1813; August 13, 1814.

13. *Western Intelligencer,* August 13, 1814.

14. Randall and Ryan, *History of Ohio: The Rise and Progress of an American State,* 427–28; *Columbus Business Directory for 1843–4,* 20; Lee, *History of the City of Columbus,* vol. 1, 255; Cox and Hoby, *The Baptists in America,* 307–8; Twiss, ed., "Journal of Cyrus P. Bradley," *Ohio Archaeological and Historical Publications* (1906): 238–39.

15. Cotton quoted in King, *Ohio: First Fruits of the Ordinance of 1787,* 339.

16. Martin, *History of Franklin County,* 347–49.

17. Ohio General Assembly, *Journal of the House of Representatives,* December 9, 1816; January 4, 1817.

18. Ibid., December 9, 1816.

19. Ohio General Assembly, *Laws of Ohio, Acts passed at the first session of the sixteenth General Assembly,* 57; Ohio Penitentiary, *Report of Directors and Warden of the Ohio Penitentiary, 1827,* 83.

20. Ohio General Assembly, *Laws of Ohio, Acts passed at the first session of the fifteenth General Assembly,* vol. 1, 218–19. According to one account, the proprietors received thirty-five thousand dollars. See Lee, *History of the City of Columbus,* vol. 1, 257.

21. *Western Intelligencer,* December 3, 1816.

22. Ohio General Assembly, *Laws of Ohio . . . fifteenth General Assembly,* vol. 1, 220.

23. Lee, *History of the City of Columbus,* vol. 1, 256.

24. *Western Intelligencer,* January 30, 1817; *Columbus Gazette,* March 10, 1818.

25. Lee, *History of the City of Columbus,* vol. 1, 215; Bender, *Community and So-*

cial Change in America, 5–8, 43, 86; Buber, *Paths in Utopia,* 135; Boyer, *Urban Masses and Moral Order in America, 1820–1920,* 1, 43–45, 69–75.

26. *Columbus Gazette,* July 9, 1818.

27. Ibid., April 29, August 5, 1819; *1802 Ohio Constitution,* Article V.

28. *Columbus Gazette,* July 28, 1819.

29. Ibid., June 4, July 2, 30, 1818; July 8, 1819; May 31, November 22, 1821; *Ohio State Journal and Columbus Gazette,* August 17, 1827; January 20, 1830.

30. A Citizen of Ohio, *The Township Officer's and Young Clek's* [sic] *Assistant: Comprising the Duties of Justices of the Peace,* 59–66.

31. Hayes, *Columbus Mayors,* 35–36.

32. *Ohio State Journal and Columbus Gazette,* January 30, April 22, July 1, 1830; June 30, 1832.

33. City of Columbus, *Record of Ordinances of the City of Columbus,* 35–36, 40.

34. *Columbus Gazette,* December 28, 1817; November 5, 19, 1818; January 19, 1819; March 28, July 11, 1822; Clifton, "Beginnings of Literary Culture in Columbus, Ohio, 1812–1840," 133.

35. Dana, *Geographical Sketches on the Western Country Designed for Emigrants and Settlers,* 74–75.

36. Bushman, *The Refinement of America,* 239.

37. *Ohio State Journal and Columbus Gazette,* March 2, 1826.

38. *Columbus Gazette,* August 29, 1822.

39. Ibid., March 21, 1822; Elizabeth Deshler to parents, September 1822, quoted in Lee, *History of the City of Columbus,* vol. 1, 265; Dunlop to Pain, October 26, 1823, Joseph Dunlop Letters; *Columbus Gazette,* July 15, 1824.

40. *Columbus Gazette,* July 29, 1824.

41. Lee, *History of the City of Columbus,* vol. 1, 304; *Ohio Statesman,* February 15, 1844; *Ohio State Journal and Columbus Gazette,* September 21, November 9, 1833.

42. James Louden to Elizabeth Louden, January 10, 1844, DeWitt Clinton Louden Papers.

43. Hooper, *History of Columbus Ohio,* 42, 270; Forman, "The First Year of the Second Epidemic of the Asiatic Cholera in Columbus, Ohio-1849," *Ohio Archaeological and Historical Publications* 53 (1944): 303–12; *Ohio Statesman,* July 13, September 17, 1849.

44. Rodgers, *"Noble Fellow" William Starling Sullivant,* 207; Sullivant, "Reminiscences of Joseph Sullivant," Joseph Sullivant Papers; Uriah Heath, Journal, July 26, August 1, 1850; Lord to Hall, July 31, 1850, Asa D. Lord Letter; Mooder to Severance, August 8, 1850, Thomas Mooder Letter.

45. *Ohio State Journal,* January 2, 4, 1847; Joel Buttles Diary, January 1, 1847.

46. *Ohio State Journal and Columbus Gazette,* March 22, 1834; March 28, 1835; City of Columbus, "Record of Ordinances."

CHAPTER 3

1. Rodgers, *"Noble Fellow" William Starling Sullivant,* 57.

2. "Extracts from the Diary of Joel Buttles," 4–22; *Western Intelligencer,* March 26, 1814; *Western Intelligencer and Columbus Gazette,* September 4, 1817; *Columbus Gazette,* March 12, 1818. Buttles sought assistance in being appointed postmaster from his future father-in-law, who was in Congress: "I shall say now as I have often before, that I will not solicit appointments. Business is, however, greatly increasing, and the Post Office in a couple of years would be of use to a man, and on that account I should like to have it." Buttles to Kilbourne, April 15, 1814, in Jones, ed., *Correspondence of the late James Kilbourne,* 20.

3. Deshler, *Early History of Columbus,* 3–6.

4. *Columbus Gazette,* June 4, 1818; January 16, 1830. See also McCabe, *Don't You Remember?,* 62; Dodds, *Central Market House,* 1; Garrett with Lentz, *Columbus, America's Crossroads,* 45; *Directory of the City of Columbus for the Year 1848.*

5. *Ohio State Journal and Columbus Gazette,* January 23, 1828.

6. *Western Intelligencer,* July 30, May 18, 1814; June 15, 1816; December 11, April 24, 1817; *Columbus Gazette,* May 28, June 4, October 1, 1818; March 18, 1819; January 22, 1823.

7. *Ohio State Journal and Columbus Gazette,* January 5, 1826.

8. *Western Intelligencer,* January 30, 1817; *Columbus Gazette,* June 11, 1818.

9. Lee, *History of the City of Columbus,* vol. 1, 634.

10. Sakolski, *Land Tenure and Land Taxation in America,* 255, 104.

11. Birkbeck, *Notes on a Journey in America,* 66.

12. Tocqueville, *Journey to America,* 276.

13. *Western Intelligencer,* August 13, 1814; *Columbus Gazette,* May 28, 1818.

14. Deshler, *Early History of Columbus,* 53; *Columbus Gazette,* February 20, 1817.

15. C. C. Huntington, "A History of Banking and Currency in Ohio before the Civil War," *Ohio Archaeological and Historical Publications* 24 (1915): 270.

16. P. W. Huntington, "A History of Banking in Ohio," *Ohio Archaeological and Historical Publications* 23 (1914): 315, 319; Williams Brothers, *History of Franklin and Pickaway Counties, Ohio,* 64; Sells, "Reminiscences."

17. Hooper, *History of Columbus Ohio,* 33; Vesey, *Franklin County at the Beginning of the Twentieth Century,* 130; James McCoy to R. W. McCoy, August 28, 1817, Robert Watts McCoy Papers.

18. Barrett, "Some Reminiscences of Dr. Starling Loving," *Columbus & Central Ohio Historian* 1 (1984): 69; Lee, *History of the City of Columbus,* vol. 1, 656.

19. Hunker, *Industrial Evolution of Columbus, Ohio,* 27, 29–34, 36.

20. *Columbus Business Directory for 1843–4,* 39.

21. *Ohio State Journal and Columbus Gazette,* August 30, 1844.

22. Ibid., January 20, 1830.

23. Clifton, "Beginnings of Literary Culture in Columbus, Ohio, 1812–1840," 16, 18.

24. Dunlop to Pain, June 3, 1820, Joseph Dunlop Letters.

25. Huntington, "History of Banking and Currency," 317–33.

26. *Columbus Gazette,* January 28, July 8, 1819; July 4, August 29, October 17, November 21, 1822; January 30, May 29, September 11, 1823; Howe, *Historical Collections of Ohio,* vol. 1, 620.

27. *Columbus Gazette,* December 14, 1820; March 15, 1831.

28. Ohio General Assembly, *Laws of Ohio,* January 29, 1818; February 8, 1819; February 2, 1821; February 2, 1822; February 25, 1824; February 1, 1825.

29. *Columbus Gazette,* March 28, 1822.

30. Ibid., December 31, 1818; March 14, 1822.

31. Ibid., July 10, 1823; February 4, 1824; August 22, 1830; *Ohio State Journal and Register,* January 3, May 22, 1839.

32. *Ohio State Journal and Register,* February 13, 16, March 13, 30, May 30, October 25, 1843; February 3, 7, 12, 15, 21, 27, March 2, 7, 1844.

33. Columbus Insurance Company, *Instructions . . . for the use and direction of their agents,* 3, 12.

34. *Columbus Gazette,* January 2, 9, April 17, August 7, October 9, November 6, 13, 1823; January 15, June 3, September 2, December 18, 1824.

35. *Ohio State Journal and Columbus Gazette,* March 22, April 12, May 10, June 20, September 13, December 19, 1827.

36. Ibid., July 12, 1827.

37. Rodabaugh, "From England to Ohio, 1830–1832, the Journal of Thomas K. Wharton," *Ohio Historical Quarterly* 65 (1956): 1–27; *Western Hemisphere,* June 10, 1833.

38. *Ohio Statesman,* May 10, 1835.

39. Lee, *History of the City of Columbus,* vol. 1, 316–21.

40. Huntington, "History of Banking and Currency," 352–68; *Ohio State Journal and Columbus Gazette,* May 18, 1837.

41. Branch, *The Sentimental Years, 1836–1860,* 83.

42. Swayne to Kelley, December 10, 1841, in Bates, *Alfred Kelley, His Life and Work,* 116.

43. Swan to Kelley, January 13, 1842, in ibid., 117; Scheiber, *Ohio Canal Era: A Case Study of Government and the Economy, 1820–1861,* 143.

44. Bates, *Alfred Kelley,* 208.

45. Quoted in Scheiber, *Ohio Canal Era,* 124–25.

46. Studer, *Columbus, Ohio: Its History, Resources, and Progress,* 166; *Ohio Statesman,* December 14, 1841.

47. *Ohio Statesman,* June 14, December 13, 1842.

48. *Columbus Business Directory for 1843–4;* Burnham, *Bad Habits,* 8, 11; Bartlett, *Dictionary of Americanisms,* 143.

49. *Columbus Business Directory for 1843–4;* McEwen, *The mysteries, miseries, and rascalities of the Ohio Penitentiary,* 16.

50. *Columbus Gazette,* July 16, 1818; January 7, 1819.

51. Ohio Anti-Slavery Society, *Memorial of the Ohio Anti-Slavery Society,* 4.

52. Schob, *Hired Hands and Ploughboys: Farm Labor in the Midwest, 1815–1860,* 259. Price indexes prior to 1913 must be considered estimates. See U.S. Department of Commerce, Bureau of the Census, *Historical Statistics of the United States* (1975), vol. 1, 191.

53. Alfred Kelley to Mary Kelley, August 14, 1841, Alfred Kelley Papers; *Ohio State Journal,* May 28, 1844.

54. Columbus Board of Trade, *Memorial on the Death of James M. Westwater,* 4–11; *Kinney's Directory for Columbus 1845–6.*

55. *Ohio State Journal,* June 26, 1845; March 3, 1846; Jones, *History of Agriculture in Ohio to 1880,* 152.

56. *Ohio Statesman,* January 7, 1849; Brown to parents, August 11, 14, 1849, Amos H. Brown Papers; Noe to Condit, December 9, 1849, Aaron M. Condit Papers.

57. *Directory of the City of Columbus for the Year 1848,* 82; Martin, *History of Franklin County,* 409.

58. Joel Buttles Diary, November 29, 1841.

59. Jones, *History of Agriculture in Ohio to 1880,* 49.

60. *Kinney's Directory for Columbus 1845–6;* Ohio Anti-Slavery Society, *Memorial,* 4.

61. *Columbus Business Directory for 1843–4,* 39.

62. Hooper, *History of Columbus Ohio,* 220; Lee, *History of the City of Columbus,* vol. 2, 320–21; *Directory of the City of Columbus for the Years 1850–51;* Hunker, *Industrial Evolution of Columbus,* 37; *Directory of the City of Columbus for the Year 1848.*

63. *Ohio State Journal,* November 7, 1843; September 1, 1848; Columbus Gas Light and Coke Company, *Act of Incorporation and By-laws.*

64. Ohio General Assembly, *Journal of the Senate,* December 5, 1845; *Ohio Statesman,* August 11, 1847; Hooper, *History of Columbus Ohio,* 121, 123; *Ohio Statesman,* November 14, 1849.

65. One hundred forty-five occupations were listed by the white males in the 1848

directory. The most frequently mentioned categories were laborer (176), clerk (157), carpenter (147), merchant (90), shoemaker (72), and tailor (53). The remaining leading occupations were grocer, blacksmith, saddler, physician, attorney, teamster, cooper, printer, cabinetmaker, prison guard, mason, baker, teacher, and farmer. *Directory of the City of Columbus for the Year 1848.*

66. *Columbus Business Directory for 1843–4; Directory of the City of Columbus for the Year 1848.*

67. Cochran and Miller, *The Age of Enterprise: A Social History of Industrial America,* 41.

68. Marty to Condit, July 25, 1846, Aaron M. Condit Papers.

69. Thernstrom and Knights, "Men in Motion: Some Data and Speculations about Urban Population Mobility in Nineteenth Century America," *Journal of Interdisciplinary History* 1 (1970): 7–35; Blumin, "Residential Mobility within the Nineteenth-Century City," in Davis and Haller, eds., *The Peoples of Philadelphia,* 37, 49.

70. Graf, ed., "The Journal of a Vermont Man in Ohio, 1836–1842," *Ohio State Archaeological and Historical Quarterly* 60 (1951): 187.

71. Peck, *A New Guide for Emigrants to the West,* 111.

72. Joel Buttles Diary, September 24, 1844; July 31, 1850.

73. *Kinney's Directory for Columbus 1845–6; Directory of the City of Columbus for the Year 1848.*

74. Obetz, *The First Regular Baptist Church and Other Baptist Churches of Columbus and Central Ohio 1825–1884.*

CHAPTER 4

1. Taylor, *Centennial History of Columbus and Franklin County, Ohio,* vol. 1, 510–15.

2. Hulbert, "The Old National Road—The Historic Highway of America," *Ohio Archaeological and Historical Publications* 9 (1901): 433n.

3. Ibid., 46, 437; Martin, *History of Franklin County,* 132; Weisenberger, *The Passing of the Frontier 1825–1850,* 110; Peattie, ed., *Columbus, Ohio: An Analysis of a City's Development,* 34.

4. "The National Road," *Historical Bulletin* (Franklin County Historical Society) 1 (1949): 74; Hulbert, "The Old National Road—The Historic Highway of America," *Ohio Archaeological and Historical Publications* 9 (1901): 449.

5. White, ed., *We Too Built Columbus,* 87; Taylor, *Centennial History,* vol. 1, 510–15; Rodgers, *"Noble Fellow" William Starling Sullivant,* 93. See also Holmes and Rohrbach, *Stagecoach Days in the East from the Colonial Period to the Civil War.*

6. Dickens, *American Notes for General Circulation,* vol. 2, 150; Sullivant, "Recollections," Joseph Sullivant Papers. See also Williams Brothers, *History of Franklin and Pickaway Counties, Ohio,* 49, 233; Holmes and Rohrbach, *Stagecoach Days in the East,* 47; Reed and Matheson, *A Narrative of the Visit to the American Churches,* vol. 1, 101; Buckingham, *The Eastern and Western States of America,* vol. 2, 282–83.

7. The best brief account is George Knepper's introduction in Gieck, *A Photo Album of Ohio's Canal Era, 1825–1913.*

8. Williams Brothers, *History of Franklin and Pickaway Counties,* 51; Martin, *History of Franklin County,* 126.

9. *Ohio State Journal and Columbus Gazette,* December 29, 1825; October 7, 1824; Scheiber, *Ohio Canal Era: A Case Study of Government and the Economy, 1820–1861,* 275, 307.

10. Hooper, *History of Columbus Ohio,* 225; Bates, *Alfred Kelley, His Life and Work,* 176–77.

11. Benham, "The Mercantile Interest of Columbus," *Ohio Magazine* 3 (December 1907): 470.

12. *Ohio State Journal,* August 15, 1848.

13. Steiner, "A Story of Columbus Railroads," (typewritten), 65–78; *Ohio Statesman,* April 1, 1844.

14. *Ohio Statesman,* February 25, 27, 1850; Hooper, *History of Columbus Ohio,* 226.

15. Steiner, "Story of Columbus Railroads," 6; *Ohio State Journal,* February 25, 1851.

16. Steiner, "Story of Columbus Railroads," 7.

CHAPTER 5

1. Smith to wife, December 27, 1842, John Armstrong Smith Papers. A useful reference book for political information is Curtin, *Ohio Politics Almanac.*

2. Twiss, ed., "Journal of Cyrus P. Bradley," *Ohio Archaeological and Historical Publications* 15 (1906): 242. The most recent comprehensive account of the Whig Party is Holt, *The Rise and Fall of the American Whig Party.*

3. *Ohio State Journal and Columbus Gazette,* July 7, 1837; *Ohio Statesman,* July 5, 1837; City of Columbus, "Record of Ordinances," April 15, 1830.

4. *Ohio Confederate and Old School Republican,* February 18, 1840; Holt, *Party Politics in Ohio, 1840–1850,* 47–48.

5. Miller, *The Great Convention,* 1–3. Harrison's military career is summarized in Brock, *Parties and Political Conscience: American Dilemmas 1840–1850,* 2; McCormick, *The Presidential Game: The Origins of American Presidential Politics,* 175, 192.

6. Norton, *The Great Revolution of 1840: Reminiscences of the Log Cabin and Hard Cider Campaign,* 17–37.

7. Quoted in Bates, *Alfred Kelley, His Life and Work,* 98.

8. *Ohio State Journal,* February 26, 1840; Miller, *Great Convention,* 5.

9. Quoted in Gunderson, *The Log Cabin Campaign,* 74; Peterson, *The Presidencies of William Henry Harrison & John Tyler,* 29.

10. Miller, *Great Convention,* 4–6, 10, 37.

11. *Ohio State Journal,* February 22, 24, 25, 26, 29, 1840; Gunderson, *Log Cabin Campaign,* 116–17; Norton, *Great Revolution of 1840,* 48. The words written to be sung to the "Marseillaise" are in Norton, *Tippecanoe Songs of the Log Cabin Boys and Girls of 1840,* 1.

12. Woodbridge to uncle, February 22, 1840, "Letters of John M. Woodbridge," *Ohio State Archaeological and Historical Quarterly* 50 (1941): 135–36.

13. Schlesinger, ed., *History of American Presidential Elections, 1789–1968,* vol. 1, 679. An extremely high estimate of fifty thousand is given in Norton, *Great Revolution of 1840,* 374.

14. Quoted in Norton, *Great Revolution of 1840,* 53; Miller, *Great Convention,* 5.

15. *Ohio State Journal,* February 24, 1840; *Ohio Statesman,* February 22, 1840. The Whig meeting was called a "federal convention of abolitionists, bankers, office holders, merchants, lawyers, and doctors."

16. "The Campaign of 1840," *Historical Bulletin* 1 (1949): 47; Hayes, *Columbus Mayors,* 32–34; "the Harrison Whirlwind" quoted in Green, *William Henry Harrison: His Life and Times,* 344; "triumph of demagogy" quoted in Lacour-Gayet, *Everyday Life in the United States before the Civil War 1830–1860,* 254.

17. Graf, ed., "The Journal of a Vermont Man in Ohio, 1836–1842," *Ohio State Archaeological and Historical Quarterly* 60 (1951): 197.

18. *Ohio Statesman,* May 15, July 3, 1840.

19. Davis to Moseley, March 29, 1840, Thomas W. H. Moseley Papers.

20. Buckingham, *The Eastern and Western States of America,* vol. 2, 296.

21. *Ohio State Journal,* June 9, 16, 1840; Gunderson, *Log Cabin Campaign,* 164–65, 151.

22. *Ohio State Journal,* October 6, 1840; Holt, "Party Politics in Ohio," 484–85; *Ohio State Journal,* September 25, 1840; Gunderson, *Log Cabin Campaign,* 197.

23. Norton, *Tippecanoe Songs,* 37, 21; *Ohio Statesman,* June 9, 1840.

24. *Ohio Statesman,* June 9, 1840.

25. Silbey, *The American Political Nation, 1838–1893,* 8–9.

26. Medary to Van Buren quoted in Weisenberger, *The Passing of the Frontier 1825–1850,* 395.

27. Williams, ed., *Diary and Letters of Rutherford Birchard Hayes,* vol. 1, 40–44.

28. Carwardine, *Evangelicals and Politics in Antebellum America,* x, 52–55; Howe, *The Political Culture of the American Whigs,* 9.

29. Joel Buttles Diary, March 6, 1844.

30. Watson, *Liberty and Power: The Politics of Jacksonian America,* 122; Ryan, *Women in Public: Between Banners and Ballots, 1825–1880,* 136; *Daily Political Tornado* quoted in Gunderson, *Log Cabin Campaign,* 134.

31. Gunderson, *Log Cabin Campaign,* 136–37.

32. See Taylor, *Ohio Indians and Other Writings,* 20–21. The text of Harrison's speech is contained in Dawson, *A historical narrative of the civil and military services of Major-General William H. Harrison,* 396.

33. Norton, *Tippecanoe Songs,* 40.

34. *Ohio State Journal,* April 7, 1841.

35. Stanton to Tappan, March 7, 1841, Benjamin Tappan Papers.

36. Buckingham, *Eastern and Western States,* vol. 2, 409.

37. Williams, ed., *Diary and Letters,* vol. 1, 68.

38. *Ohio State Journal,* September 6, 1841. The meeting in the market house, organized by William Neil, passed resolutions supportive of President Tyler. Immediately after its adjournment, two hundred other Whigs passed resolutions critical of Tyler for vetoing the bank bill.

39. Reeves to McLean quoted in Holt, *Party Politics in Ohio,* 160, 178.

40. *Columbus Business Directory for 1843–4,* 43. See also Ryan, *A History of Ohio with Biographical Sketches of Her Governors and the Ordinance of 1787,* 130.

41. James Emmitt's *Chillicothe Leader* clipping, June 1, 1886, Joseph Sullivant Papers.

42. *Ohio State Journal and Columbus Gazette,* August 18, 1837.

43. Lee, *History of the City of Columbus,* vol. 2, 8–14.

44. Ford to Hitchcock, February 20, 1840, Charles E. Rice Papers.

45. Ohio General Assembly, *Journal of the Senate,* vol. 38, 1838–1840, appendix, 17, 4.

46. Ibid., vol. 44, January 22, 1846; *Ohio Statesman,* January 23, 1846.

47. Barkin to Brown, December 6, 1844, Ezekiel Brown Papers.

48. 1851 Ohio Constitution, Article XV, Section 1.

49. Hooper, *History of Columbus Ohio,* 148; *Ohio State Journal,* August 10, 1847.

50. *Ohio Statesman,* July 6, 1841.

51. Holt, "Party Politics in Ohio," 452–559; Shade, *Banks or No Banks: The Money Issue in Western Politics, 1832–1865,* 11, 18, 102–3; Gilbert, "Thomas Ewing, Sr.: Ohio's Advocate for a National Bank," *Ohio History* 82 (Winter-Spring 1973): 5–7.

52. Clark Guernsey Journal, February 23, 1837; Buckingham, *Eastern and Western States,* vol. 2, 312–13.

53. Holt, "Party Politics in Ohio," 527. The *Ohio State Journal* reported "tremen-

dous" support for the Whig legislators who absented themselves and resigned in order to fight the Democrats' plans for revising congressional districts.

54. *Ohio Statesman*, June 7, 1842.

55. Stanton to Tappan, July 17, 1842, Benjamin Tappan Papers.

56. Bartlett, *Dictionary of Americanisms,* 251.

57. Stanton to Tappan, December 27, 1842, Benjamin Tappan Papers.

58. Flinn, "Continuity and Change in Ohio Politics," *Journal of Politics* 24 (1962): 524; Volpe, *Forlorn Hope of Freedom: The Liberty Party in the Old Northwest, 1828– 1838,* 53–54; *Ohio State Journal,* December 31, 1841.

59. *Ohio Statesman,* August 16, 1837.

60. Shade, *Banks or No Banks,* 104.

61. Whig Party (Ohio) Central Committee, "1844 Broadside."

62. Joel Buttles Diary, September 23, 1844.

63. Bates, *Alfred Kelley,* 107–8, 137; Cox to Sloane, January 25, 1845, John Sloane Papers; *Ohio Statesman,* January 10, 1845.

64. Brooks, "The Financial Interests of Columbus," *Ohio Magazine* 3 (1907): 504; Scheiber, *Ohio Canal Era: A Case Study of Government and the Economy, 1820– 1861,* 143.

65. Studer, *Columbus, Ohio: Its History, Resources, and Progress,* 125.

66. Bates, *Alfred Kelley,* 148, 170–72.

67. *Ohio Statesman,* March 2, 1846; *Ohio Eagle,* March 31, 1846.

68. Sullivant, *To The Liberty Party in Ohio,* 7.

69. *Ohio Statesman,* April 7, 1845. A useful account of this issue is in Winkle, *The Politics of Community: Migration and Politics in Antebellum Ohio,* 30–31, 419.

70. Gladden, "Samuel Galloway," *Ohio Archaeological and Historical Publications* 4 (1895): 263, 275–76.

71. The Democrat quoted in Maizlish, *The Triumph of Sectionalism: The Transformation of Ohio Politics, 1844–1856,* 3; *Ohio Statesman,* September 17, 24, 1845.

72. Fox, *The Group Bases of Ohio Political Behavior, 1803–1848,* xii.

73. Joel Buttles Diary, October 14, 1842.

74. White, ed., *We Too Built Columbus,* 117; McCabe, *Don't You Remember?,* 141, 145.

75. *Ohio Statesman,* January 9, 10, 1843.

76. Ibid., December 27, 1843; Vance to friend, December 16, 1843, Charles E. Rice Papers.

CHAPTER 6

1. *Columbus Gazette,* May 17, 1821.

2. Rosabaugh, *The Craft Apprentice,* 121–22.

3. *Columbus Gazette,* January 15, 29, July 8, 1824.

4. Atwater, *A History of the State of Ohio,* 268.

5. Martin, *History of Franklin County,* 290; *Ohio State Journal and Columbus Gazette,* July 29, 1830; June 15, 1833.

6. Dickens, *American Notes for General Circulation,* vol. 1, 205.

7. Dickens to Foster, April 24, 26, 1842, House, Storey, and Tillotson, eds., *The Letters of Charles Dickens,* vol. 3, 205; Putnam, "Four Months with Charles Dickens During His First Visit To America," *Atlantic Monthly* 26 (November 1870): 595; Dickens, *American Notes,* vol. 1, 159.

8. "Distinguished Visitor," *Historical Bulletin* 7 (1849): 69–70.

9. Adams, ed., *Memoirs of John Quincy Adams, Comprising Portions of His Diary from 1795 to 1848,* vol. 11, 422–23.

10. *Ohio State Journal and Columbus Gazette,* July 28, 1832.

11. Lee, *History of the City of Columbus*, vol. 1, 915–16; Sittler, "The German Element in Columbus before the Civil War," 45.

12. Studer, *Columbus, Ohio: Its History, Resources, and Progress*, 335; Clifton, "Beginnings of Literary Culture in Columbus, Ohio, 1812–1840," 144.

13. "Regular Toasts," James Kilbourne Family Papers.

14. Venable, *Beginnings of Literary Culture in the Ohio Valley: Historical and Biographical Sketches*, 147–46; Clifton, "Beginnings of Literary Culture," 110; Ratcliffe, "The Autobiography of Benjamin Tappan," *Ohio History* 85 (Winter 1976): 110–11; Walker, *Annual Discourse Delivered before the Ohio Historical and Philosophical Society at Columbus on the 23rd of December, 1837*, 16.

15. *American Pioneer* 1 (1842): 1.

16. *Palladium of Liberty*, December 27, 1843; *Columbus Business Directory for 1843–4*, 72; *Ohio State Journal*, November 1, 1845; Parham and Brown, *An Official History of the Most Worshipful Grand Lodge Free and Accepted Masons for the State of Ohio*, 16.

17. *Ohio State Journal and Columbus Gazette*, December 20, 1836; *Ohio Statesman*, March 3, May 3, 1842; McCormick and McCormick, *Probing Worthington's Heritage*, vol. 1, 102–4; *Old School Republican and Ohio State Gazette*, January 2, 1843.

18. James Kilbourne Family Papers; *Ohio Statesman*, April 4, 1845.

19. *Directory of the City of Columbus for the Year 1848*, 82; Joel Buttles Diary, March 22, 1843. Public opinion about the comet was divided. William Miller and his followers believed the world would end in 1843 and saw the comet as proof. The comet is currently identified as the Kreutz sungrazer. See *Course of Lectures on Astronomy by Dionysius Lardner*, 3d ed., 92–96, and Yeomans, *Comets*, 178–79, 349.

20. Brown, *Knowledge Is Power*, 244; Larkin, *Art and Life in America*, 49; Scott, "The Popular Lecture and the Creation of a Public in Mid-Nineteenth Century America," *Journal of American History* 66 (March 1980): 791–809; John Campbell read a paper at the lyceum, "On Imprisonment for Debt," on February 14, 1832, Campbell, *Biographical Sketches*, 103–18; Clifton, "Beginnings of Literary Culture," 106, 107, 120; *Ohio State Journal and Columbus Gazette*, January 14, 1832.

21. Buckingham, *The Eastern and Western States of America*, vol. 2, 315; *Ohio Statesman*, November 12, 1842; June 23, August 11, November 24, 1843. Additional information about the popularity of lectures is in Scott, "The Popular Lecture."

22. *Ohio Statesman*, December 4, 13, 1843; Bode, ed., *American Life in the 1840s*, 92; Larkin, *Art and Life in America*, 150.

23. *Ohio Statesman*, January 9, 1847; *Directory of the City of Columbus for the Years 1850–51*, 82.

24. *Ohio State Journal*, December 1, 1846; Franklin, *The Autobiography of Benjamin Franklin*, 74.

25. *Ohio Statesman*, December 23, 1831; Venable, *Beginnings of Literary Culture*, 236; *Palladium of Liberty*, July 3, 1844; *Ohio State Journal*, May 14, September 3, December 28, 1844; January 13, 27, 1845; *Ohio Statesman*, October 28, December 15, 1846.

26. *Ohio State Journal and Columbus Gazette*, January 9, 1833.

27. Twiss, ed., "Journal of Cyrus P. Bradley," 243.

28. Gladden, "Francis Charles Sessions," *Ohio Archaeological and Historical Publications* 4 (1895): 300.

29. Evan Edmiston Diary, December 30, 1839; January 1, 1840; Clifton, "Beginnings of Literary Culture," 423; Smith to wife, January 2, 1843, John Armstrong Smith Papers.

30. Buckingham, *Eastern and Western States*, vol. 2, 288. See also Winkle, *The Politics of Community: Migration and Politics in Antebellum Ohio*, 10–11, 93.

31. *United States Population Census for 1840*, Manuscript Census Schedules.

32. *United States Population Census for 1850*, Manuscript Census Schedules.

33. Lee, *History of the City of Columbus*, vol. 1, 876.

34. Gutman in Thernstrom and Sennett, eds., *Nineteenth-Century Cities*, 98. See also Pessen, "The Egalitarian Myth and the American Social Reality: Wealth, Mobility, and Equality in the 'Era of the Common Man,'" *American Historical Review* 70 (1971): 989–1034.

35. Martineau, *Society in America*, vol. 1, 202.

36. Cole, "Uriah Heath: Scholarly Circuit Rider, Successful Fund-Raiser," *Methodist History* 36 (1998): 251–52.

37. Joel Buttles Diary, April 28, 1843.

38. McCabe, *Don't You Remember?*, 89, 96; Weisenberger, *The Passing of the Frontier 1825–1850*, 126; Evan Edmiston Diary, August 25, 1838; *Ohio Statesman*, January 21, 1846; September 12, 1855.

39. McCabe, *Don't You Remember?*, 73; *Directory of the City of Columbus for the Years 1850–51*, 12; Reed and Matheson, *A Narrative of the Visit to the American Churches*, vol. 1, 101; Knittle, *Early Ohio Taverns*, 29.

40. Bartlett, *Dictionary of Americanisms*, 33, 61, 233.

41. Barrett, "Some Reminiscences of Dr. Starling Loving," *Columbus & Central Ohio Historian*, 1 (1984): 67–68; *Ohio Statesman*, April 10, 1840; *Columbus Business Directory for 1843–4*; Uriah Heath Journal, September 12, 1851; Niven, *Salmon P. Chase: A Biography*, 122.

42. *Ohio State Journal*, July 21, 1841; Moseley Diary, Thomas W. H. Moseley Papers.

43. Williams, ed., *Diary and Letters of Rutherford Birchard Hayes*, vol. 1, 28–30, 110.

44. Platt Family Papers.

45. *Ohio State Journal*, July 5, 1842. For details on balloon flights from Cincinnati, see Crouch, "Up, Up, and—Sometimes—Away," *Cincinnati Historical Bulletin* 28 (1970): 109–29.

46. *Ohio State Journal*, April 20, July 13, 1843.

47. Anson W. Buttles Diary, June 1, 1843.

48. *Ohio Statesman*, July 4, 1843. For the role of special events in defusing class resentment, see Waldstreicher, "Rites of Rebellion, Rites of Assent: Celebrations, Print Culture, and the Origins of American Nationalism," *Journal of American History* 82 (1995): 37–61. See also Marty, *Righteous Empire: The Protestant Experience in America*, for his perspectives on public religion.

49. *Ohio Statesman*, July 18, 28, 1843.

50. Ibid., August 1, 2, 29, October 17, 1843; June 23, 1845.

51. *Ohio State Journal*, December 15, 1843.

52. *Columbus Business Directory for 1843–4*.

53. Hahn and Prude, eds., *The Countryside in the Age of Capitalist Transformation: Essays in the Social History of Rural America*, 333; Swan to Livingston, July 20, 1843, Thomas W. H. Moseley Papers; Joel Buttles Diary, September 21, 1844.

54. Bender, *Community and Social Change in America*, 92; Cummings, "The Alfred Kelley House," (typewritten); Scheiber, "Alfred Kelley and the Ohio Business Elite, 1822–1859," *Ohio History* 87 (Autumn 1978): 381–87; Hansen, *Westward the Winds, Being Some of the Main Currents of Life in Ohio, 1788–1873*, 81; *Franklin County, Ohio, Wills, 1803–1864*.

55. Wittke, "Ohio's Germans, 1840–1875," *Ohio Historical Quarterly* 66 (October 1957): 340; Martin, *History of Franklin County,* 43; Williams Brothers, *History of Franklin and Pickaway Counties, Ohio,* 561, 88; Raphael, *Jews and Judaism in a Midwestern Community: Columbus, Ohio, 1840–1875,* 6; Rippley, "The Columbus Germans," *The Report: A Journal of German-American History* 33 (1968): 35; *Directory of the City of Columbus for the Years 1850–51,* 85.

56. Joel Buttles Diary, January 11, 1846; January 22, 1847. Foreign-born people constituted 43 percent of the Fifth Ward, *United States Population Census for 1850,* Manuscript Census Schedules.

57. Conzen, "Mainstream and Side Channels: The Localization of Immigrant Cultures," *Journal of American Ethnic History* 11 (1991): 16.

58. Joel Buttles Diary, January 11, 1846; January 22, 1847; *Ohio Statesman,* March 18, 1848; *Ohio Confederate and Old School Republican,* August 23, 1839; Briggs to Goodale, March 16, 1849, Lincoln Goodale Papers.

59. *United States Population Census for 1850,* Manuscript Census Schedules; Pessen, "Egalitarian Myth"; Joel Buttles Diary, January 26, 1846.

60. Prugh, ed., *Goodale Park Centennial 1851–1951,* 2–19; Swearington to Goodale, March 23, 1849; Goodale to Casey, December 10, 1849; Briggs to Goodale, July 20, 1851, Lincoln Goodale Papers.

61. See Thernstrom and Sennett, eds., *Nineteenth-Century Cities,* 168–88; Pessen, *Riches, Class, and Power before the Civil War,* 42.

CHAPTER 7

1. *Columbus Gazette,* November 11, 1824.

2. *Ohio State Journal and Columbus Gazette,* October 6, 1825.

3. Ibid., August 14, 1835. See also Welter, "The Cult of True Womanhood, 1820–1860," *American Quarterly* 18 (1966): 151–74.

4. Mansfield, *The Legal Rights, Liabilities and Duties of Women,* 13; Warbasse, *The Changing Legal Rights of Married Women, 1800–1861,* 265; Calhoun, *A Social History of the American Family from Colonial Times to the Present,* vol. 2, 129.

5. Stanton, reporter, *Report of Cases Argued and Determined in the Supreme Court of Ohio December Term, 1843, 1844,* vol. 12, 129.

6. Warbasse, *Changing Legal Rights,* 138–229, 124; Basch, *In the Eyes of the Law: Women, Marriage, and Property in Nineteenth-Century New York,* 16–17, 114; Salmon, *Women and the Law of Property in Early America,* 193; Rabkin, *Fathers to Daughters: The Legal Foundations of Female Emancipation,* 12.

7. *Ohio Observer,* April 13, 1837.

8. Alcott, *The Young Wife, or Duties of Woman in the Marriage Relation,* 22, 55, 351. See also Welter, "Cult of True Womanhood."

9. Garrett with Lentz, *Columbus, America's Crossroads,* 45; White, ed., *We Too Built Columbus,* 20; Williams Brothers, *History of Franklin and Pickaway Counties, Ohio* 64; Taylor, *Centennial History of Columbus and Franklin County, Ohio,* vol. 1, 510–15; McCabe, *Don't You Remember?,* 167.

10. Tuana, *The Less Noble Sex: Scientific, Religious, and Philosophical Conceptions of Woman's Nature,* 169.

11. An article in the *Ohio Statesman,* June 11, 1841, condemned the low wages paid to women and ended with the recommendation that those concerned with the welfare of slaves should worry first about alleviating suffering closer to home.

12. Joel Buttles to Julia Buttles, February 25, 1814, Julia Buttles Case Papers; Boydston, *Home and Work: Housework, Wages, and the Ideology of Labor in the Early Republic,* 74.

13. Sorin quoted in Bode, ed., *American Life in the 1840s,* 59; Palmer, *The Moral*

Instructor; or Culture Of The Heart, Affections, And Intellect While Learning To Read,
17. See Gorn, ed., *The McGuffey Readers,* 102–5.

14. Tappan quoted in Lerner, *The Female Experience,* 334–35.

15. Disney, *Address Delivered at the Celebration of Columbus Lodge No. 9, I.O.O.F.,* 10.

16. Coxe, *The Young Lady's Companion: In A Series of Letters,* iv, 197.

17. Coxe, *Claims of the Country on American Females,* vol. 1, 29.

18. Ibid., 32, 239. See also Degler, *At Odds: Woman and the Family in America from the Revolution to the Present,* 377–78.

19. Beecher, *An Essay on Slavery and Abolitionism with Reference to the Duty of American Females,* 100–101, 137.

20. Beecher, *A Treatise on Domestic Economy for the Use of Young Ladies at Home and at School,* 27.

21. Ibid., 52, 61. Valuable insight into her views is provided by Melder, *Beginnings of Sisterhood: The American Woman's Rights Movement, 1800–1850,* and Sklar, *Catharine Beecher: A Study in American Domesticity,* 151–53.

22. Beecher, *Treatise on Domestic Economy,* 166–67, 178.

23. Beecher, *Letters to Persons Who Are Engaged in Domestic Service,* 55, 75.

24. Beecher, *The Evils Suffered by American Women and American Children: The Causes and the Remedy,* 10; Bradley, *Men's Work, Women's Work,* 216.

25. Brown, *America: A Four Years' Residence in the United States and Canada,* 48.

26. Anon., "Woman as Wife," *Ladies Repository and Gatherings of the West* 3 (1843): 54. See also Welter, "Cult of True Womanhood."

27. *Palladium of Liberty,* March 27, 1844.

28. Brown, *America, A Four Years' Residence,* 46. For comments on men's resentment, see Epstein, *The Politics of Domesticity: Women, Evangelism, and Temperance in Nineteenth-Century America,* 63.

29. Hersey, *The Midwife's Practical Directory; or Woman's Confidential Friend,* 35.

30. Sigourney, *Letters to Mothers,* 9, 10. Sigourney, who was well educated, taught in Connecticut and wrote many books. See Weaver, *The Heart of the World,* 562.

31. Quoted in Hart, *The Popular Book,* 86.

32. Alfred Kelley to Mary Kelley, January 11, 1823, Alfred Kelley Papers.

33. Mary Kelley to Alfred Kelley, September 20, 1830, Alfred Kelley Papers.

34. Cummings, "The Alfred Kelley House," (typewritten).

35. Mary Kelley to Alfred Kelley, July 28, 1841; April 23, 1842; October 24, 1849; Alfred to Mary, August 8, 1849; Mary to Alfred, Thursday evening, n.d., Alfred Kelley Papers.

36. *Ohio State Journal,* January 19, 1846.

37. Maria Kelley Bates Journal, Alfred Kelley Papers.

38. Lee, *History of the City of Columbus,* vol. 1, 911; *Ohio State Journal and Columbus Gazette,* January 8, 11, 1834.

39. *Columbus Female Benevolent Society 1835 Constitution,* 5, 81. See also Garrett with Lentz, *Columbus, America's Crossroads,* 45.

40. *Ohio State Journal and Columbus Gazette,* November 26, 1836; *Ohio State Journal and Political Register,* December 1, 1837.

41. *Palladium of Liberty,* July 3, 1844.

42. Martineau, *Society in America,* vol. 2, 156.

43. Smith-Rosenberg, "The Female World of Love and Ritual: Relations between Women in Nineteenth-Century America," *Signs* 1 (Autumn 1975): 14.

44. *Columbus Gazette,* July 8, 1819; *Ohio Statesman,* January 6, 1845; January 9, 1846; January 9, 1847.

45. *Anti-Slavery Bugle,* May 21, 1847.

46. Foner and Walker, eds., *Proceedings of the Black State Conventions, 1840–1865*, vol. 1, 227.

47. *United States Population Census for 1850*, Manuscript Census Schedules; Columbus city directories for 1848, 1850–51, and 1852. See also Ryan, *Womanhood in America*, 12, 117, 119, 122, 147.

CHAPTER 8

1. Welling, *Information for the People: or The Asylums of Ohio*, 49.

2. *Directory of the City of Columbus for the Year 1848*, 65; Bender, *Community and Social Change in America*, 133.

3. State Centennial Education Committee, *Historical Sketches of the Higher Educational Institutions and also of Benevolent and Reformatory Institutions of the State of Ohio*. See also Jones, *Manual and History of the Ohio State School for the Deaf*, 24–25.

4. Ohio Institution for the Education of the Deaf and Dumb, *1827 Report*, 5; Jenkins, *The Ohio Gazetteer and Traveller's Guide*, 141; Jones, *Manual and History*, 10–17, 26–27, 48; *Ohio School Journal* 2 (1847): 116–17.

5. Ohio Institution for the Education of the Deaf and Dumb, *1845 Report*, *1840 Report*, 18.

6. Ohio Institution for the Education of the Deaf and Dumb, *1850 Report*, 8; *Directory of the City of Columbus for the Years 1850–51*, 58; Ohio Institution for the Education of the Deaf and Dumb, *1845 Report*, 12.

7. Pulszky, *White, Red, Black: Sketches of American Society*, vol. 1, 286.

8. *Western Monthly Magazine* 3 (1835): 150; Hoge et al., *Report of the Trustees Appointed by the Last General Assembly to collect information respecting the education of the blind*, 23.

9. Ohio Institution for the Instruction of the Blind, *Annual Report, 1839*, 3, 12; Best, *Blindness and the Blind in the United States*, 332.

10. Ohio Institution for the Instruction of the Blind, *General Information, 1838*, 7–8; *1843 Report*.

11. *Ohio Statesman*, December 31, 1841; January 9, 1842; January 20, 1847; Best, *Blindness and the Blind*, 312; Uriah Heath Journal, September 7, 1847.

12. Grob, *Mental Institutions in America: Social Policy to 1875*, 233; Ferguson, *Abandoned to Their Fate: Social Policy and Practice toward Severely Retarded People in America, 1820–1920*, xvii, 7; Gamwell and Tomes, *Madness in America: Cultural and Medical Perceptions of Mental Illness before 1914*, 9; Rothman, *The Discovery of the Asylum: Social Order and Disorder in the New Republic*, 129, 133, 154.

13. Deutsch, *The Mentally Ill in America: A History of Their Care and Treatment from Colonial Times*, 132, 162; Gamwell and Tomes, *Madness in America*, 90, 93; Rothman, *The Discovery of the Asylum*, 129, 133, 154.

14. Gollaher, *Voice for the Mad: The Life of Dorothea Dix*, 164, 236; Deutsch, *The Mentally Ill in America*, 109.

15. Ohio Lunatic Asylum, *Report of the Directors and Superintendent, 1839*.

16. Ibid., *1838*, 3.

17. Ibid., 5–6.

18. *Ohio State Journal and Columbus Gazette*, June 8, 1833; Browne, *What asylums were, are, and ought to be*, 181–83.

19. Weisenberger, *The Passing of the Frontier 1825–1850*, 141; Ohio Lunatic Asylum, *Report of the Directors and Superintendent, 1839*, 13, 29; Shannon, *Annual Message of the Governor of Ohio to the Thirty-Eighth General Assembly, December 3, 1839*, 26.

20. *Ohio Statesman*, November 12, 1839.

21. Ohio Lunatic Asylum, *Report of the Directors and Superintendent, 1840.* The supposed causes of insanity are listed in the 1839 report. See also Rothman, *The Discovery of the Asylum,* 137, 142.

22. Ohio Lunatic Asylum, *Report of the Directors and Superintendent, 1840,* 5; ibid., *1843,* 20. The recovery rate of the 473 patients admitted in five years was just under 43 percent, ibid., *1846,* 4; Dix, "Memorial Soliciting a State Hospital for the Insane," in Gollaher, *Voice for the Mad,* 192.

23. *Ohio Statesman,* January 25, 1843; Welling, *Information for the People,* 68.

24. Ohio Lunatic Asylum, *Report of the Directors and Superintendent, 1846,* 29.

25. *Directory of the City of Columbus for the Years 1850–51,* 64; Grob, *Mental Institutions in America,* 223.

26. Deutsch, *The Mentally Ill in America,* 154, 201–2.

27. Grob, *Mental Institutions in America,* 116; Dix, *Remarks on Prisons and Prison Discipline in the United States,* 43.

28. *Ohio State Journal,* October 31, 1851; Pulszky, *White, Red, Black,* vol. 1, 287.

29. Williams Brothers, *History of Franklin and Pickaway Counties, Ohio,* 41; Martin, *History of Franklin County,* 90.

30. Katz, *In the Shadow of the Poorhouse: A Social History of Welfare in America,* xi–xii, 30. See also Ginzberg, *Women and the Work of Benevolence: Morality, Politics, and Class in the Nineteenth-Century United States.*

CHAPTER 9

1. Hirsch, *The Rise of the Penitentiary: Prisons and Punishment in Early America,* xiii.

2. Rothman, *The Discovery of the Asylum: Social Order and Disorder in the New Republic,* xviii. For a critique of his views, see Hirsch, *Rise of the Penitentiary.*

3. Morgan, *Historical Lights and Shadows of the Ohio State Penitentiary,* 9.

4. Ohio General Assembly, *Report of the Joint Committee on . . . Ohio Penitentiary,* 4–6.

5. Ohio Penitentiary, *Annual Report of the Directors and Warden of the Ohio Penitentiary, 1827,* 23, 83; Dix, *Remarks on Prisons and Prison Discipline in the United States,* 19.

6. Trimble quoted in Marshall, ed., *A History of the Courts and Lawyers of Ohio,* vol. 2, 627.

7. Lewis, *The Development of American Prisons and Prison Customs, 1776–1845,* 260–61.

8. Ohio General Assembly, *Journal of the House of Representatives, Report on the Ohio Penitentiary, 1831,* 115; Chamberlain, "Journal of Ebenezer Mattoon Chamberlain 1832–5," *Indiana Magazine of History* 15 (September 1919): 238; Twiss, ed., "Journal of Cyrus P. Bradley," *Ohio Archaeological and Historical Publications* 15 (1906): 241.

9. *Columbus Gazette,* January 9, September 11, October 9, 1823; *Ohio State Journal and Columbus Gazette,* February 20, 1830; April 28, May 5, 1831.

10. Jenkins, *The Ohio Gazetteer and Traveller's Guide,* 140; Hicks, *The History of Penal Institutions in Ohio,* 379, 400.

11. Beaumont and Tocqueville, *On the Penitentiary System in the United States and Its Application in France,* 13.

12. Ohio Penitentiary, "Rules and Regulations."

13. Martineau, *Retrospect of Western Travel,* vol. 1, 200; Thomas quoted in Whitcomb, *The life and confessions of Henry Thomas,* 5; Matthews, *Historical Reminiscences of the Ohio Penitentiary 1835 to 1884,* 156.

14. Lewis, *Development of American Prisons*, 78; Lewis, *From Newgate to Dannemora: The Rise of the Penitentiary in New York, 1796–1848*, 134.

15. Ohio Penitentiary, "Rules and Regulations."

16. Ohio Penitentiary, *Annual Report . . . 1835*, 3; Studer, *Columbus, Ohio: Its History, Resources, and Progress*, 378; Howe, *Historical Collections of Ohio*, vol. 1, 645; Hicks, *History of Penal Institutions*, 380.

17. Clark Guernsey Journal, March 7, 1837, quoted in Dillon, ed., "A Visit to the Ohio State Prison," *Ohio Historical Quarterly* 69 (January 1960): 70.

18. Ibid., 70.

19. Ohio Penitentiary, *Annual Report . . . 1837*, 4; Dyer, *History of the Ohio Penitentiary, Annex and Prisoners*, 45; Hicks, *History of Penal Institutions*, 379–82; Studer, *Columbus, Ohio*, 378–80; *Ohio State Journal and Columbus Gazette*, December 6, 1834; Twiss, ed., "Journal of Cyrus P. Bradley," 240.

20. Ohio Penitentiary, *Annual Report . . . 1835*, 3.

21. Hicks, *History of Penal Institutions*, 397–99; Howe, *Historical Collections of Ohio*, vol. 1, 645; *Ohio Statesman*, February 8, 1842.

22. Hicks, *History of Penal Institutions*, 399; Love, "Russell Bigelow The Pioneer Pulpit Orator," *Ohio Archaeological and Historical Publications* 19 (1910): 303; *Ohio Press*, March 14, 1846.

23. See Nussbaum, "The Ohio Penitentiary," 10.

24. Wines and Dwight, *Report on the Prisons and Reformatories of the United States and Canada*, 138.

25. Dix, *Remarks on Prisons*, 43; Lewis, *From Newgate to Dannemora*, 118.

26. See Howe, *Historical Collections of Ohio*, vol. 1, 874–75.

27. Matthews, *Historical Reminiscences*, 74; McEwen, *The mysteries, miseries, and rascalities of the Ohio Penitentiary*, 27, 177; Lieber in Beaumont and Tocqueville, *On the Penitentiary System*, ix.

28. Ohio Penitentiary, *Annual Report . . . 1844*; Hicks, *History of Penal Institutions*, 405; Lewis, *From Newgate to Dannemora*, 269–70.

29. *Ohio State Journal* quoted in Lee, *History of the City of Columbus*, vol. 2, 582.

30. *Ohio Statesman*, June 14, 1842.

31. McEwen, *Mysteries, miseries, and rascalities*, 5.

32. Rafter, *Partial Justice: Women, Prisons, and Social Control*, 7; Barrett, *Prison Discipline Society of Boston Report*, quoted in Lewis, *Development of American Prisons*, 263.

33. *Ohio State Journal*, August 27, 1844; Dix, *Remarks on Prisons*, 48, statistics on women in prison, 107–8.

34. Quoted in Rafter, *Partial Justice*, 4; Dyer, *History of the Ohio Penitentiary*, 45.

35. Lewis, *From Newgate to Dannemora*, 158; Lieber quoted in Beaumont and Tocqueville, *On the Penitentiary System*, xv.

36. Freedman, *Their Sisters' Keepers: Women's Prison Reform in America, 1830–1930*, 12; A. Jones, *Women Who Kill*, 93; Marshall, ed., *History of the Courts and Lawyers*, vol. 2, 626.

37. De Rham, *How Could She Do That? A Study of the Female Criminal*, 6.

38. Ohio Penitentiary, *Annual Report . . . 1839*, 3.

39. Ibid., *1846*, 2.

40. Ibid., *1839, 1840*; Rafter, *Partial Justice*, 4.

41. Ohio Penitentiary, *Annual Report . . . 1835*; Matthews, *Historical Reminiscences*, 2, 6.

42. O. Lewis, *The Development of American Prisons*, 335.

43. Gildemeister, *Prison Labor and Convict Competition with Free Workers in Industrializing America, 1840–1890*, 12, 51, 84.

---

44. Ibid., 55n; Hicks, *History of Penal Institutions*, 406; Gildemeister, *Prison Labor*, 51, 84.

45. Lewis, *Development of American Prisons*, 263; Anson W. Buttles Diary, June 4, 1843; Arter, *Columbus Vignettes*, vol. 2, 20; Dix, *Remarks on Prisons*, 1. See also a warden's view quoted in Wines and Dwight, *Report on the Prisons and Reformatories*, 218.

46. *Ohio State Journal and Columbus Gazette*, April 11, August 21, October 30, 1835; *Ohio Confederate and Old School Republican*, April 19, 1839. Other meetings of mechanics are reported in *Ohio State Journal*, August 14, 1841; March 2, 1842; April 11, 1844; *Ohio Statesman*, January 3, 1844.

47. *Ohio State Journal*, February 22, 1840.

48. Ibid., August 11, 1840.

49. Ohio Penitentiary, *Annual Report . . . 1841*, 5.

50. *Ohio Statesman*, December 15, 1841, February 17, 26, 1842.

51. Ohio Penitentiary, *Annual Report . . . 1843*, 3–4.

52. *Ohio Statesman*, January 3, February 13, March 27, July 10, 1844; *Ohio State Journal*, April 4, 1844.

53. *Ohio State Journal*, July 7, 12, 29, August 4, September 23, 1842; April 13, 1843.

54. Ibid., July 12, September 29, 1842; March 21, 1843.

55. Ibid., March 21, 1843; *Ohio Statesman*, March 21, 1843; *Ohio Confederate and Old School Republican*, March 22, 1843.

56. Resch, "Ohio Adult Penal System, 1850–1900: A Study in the Failure of Institutional Reform," *Ohio History* 81 (Autumn 1972): 236.

57. Jenkins, *Ohio Gazetteer*, 140.

58. Wines and Dwight, *Report on the Prisons and Reformatories*, 218–19.

59. Dewey, *Special Report of the Warden of the Ohio Penitentiary on Prisons and Prison Discipline to the Forty-Ninth General Assembly of the State of Ohio*, 31.

60. *Ohio Statesman*, April 16, 1845.

61. Marvin, "Ohio's Unsung Penitentiary Railroad," *Ohio State Archaeological and Historical Quarterly* 63 (1954): 254–61; *Ohio Statesman*, April 16, 1845.

62. Dyer, *History of the Ohio Penitentiary*, 12.

63. *Ohio Statesman*, December 23, 1845.

64. Lewis, *Development of American Prisons*, 263; Dix, *Remarks on Prisons*, 59. Other criticisms are on 2, 22, 26, 29, 43, 48.

65. Dewey, *Special Report*, 128–29; Resch, "Ohio Adult Penal System," 239.

66. Cole, *Lion of the Forest: James B. Finley, Frontier Reformer*, 162.

67. *Ohio State Journal*, May 21, 1846; March 29, 1849.

68. Ibid., May 8, 1847.

69. *Ohio Statesman*, July 3, 13, 14, 17, August 5, 1849. A list of those who died was printed in each issue.

70. Pulszky, *White, Red, Black: Sketches of American Society*, 286.

71. Dix, *Remarks on Prisons*, 105; *Ohio State Journal*, August 17, 1848.

72. Ibid., December 1, 1846.

73. Hooper, *History of Columbus Ohio*, 107.

CHAPTER 10

1. *Western Literary Magazine* 1 (1850): 1.

2. *Western Intelligencer*, July 20, 1814.

3. Clifton, "Beginnings of Literary Culture in Columbus, Ohio, 1812–1840," 215.

4. Ibid., 219–23.

5. Martin, *History of Franklin County*, 66; Hooper, *History of Ohio Journalism*,

1793–1933, 107–8. See also Smith, *Samuel Medary and the* Crisis: *Testing the Limits of Press Freedom.*

6. *Ohio Statesman,* June 23, 1843.

7. Studer, *Columbus, Ohio: Its History, Resources, and Progress,* 243–50; Clifton, "Beginnings of Literary Culture in Columbus, Ohio, 1812–1840," 216.

8. Hollins, "A Black Voice of Antebellum Ohio: A Rhetorical Analysis of the *Palladium of Liberty,* 1843–1844," 13–14. The paper's prospectus, "Address to the citizens of Ohio," was in the first issue.

9. Hooper, *History of Ohio Journalism;* Martin, *History of Franklin County,* 66–67; *Ohio State Journal,* October 30, 1847.

10. *The Land Seller and General Advertiser,* June 1848.

11. Samuel Medary Papers.

12. Clifton, "Beginnings of Literary Culture," 241.

13. *People's Weekly Journal and Freeman's Standard,* November 8, 1849.

14. *Hesperian,* "Prospectus"; Venable, *Beginnings of Literary Culture in the Ohio Valley: Historical and Biographical Sketches,* 80–81; Clifton, "Beginnings of Literary Culture," 224–25, 258.

15. *Ohio Statesman,* February 15, 1844.

16. Coyle, ed., *Ohio's Authors and Their Books,* 97.

17. Coxe, *The Life of John Wycliffe,* 26, 166.

18. Coyle, ed., *Ohio's Authors,* 138.

19. Hayes, *Columbus Mayors,* 14–16.

20. Coyle, ed., *Ohio's Authors,* 97.

21. Sullivant, *A Genealogy and Family Memorial,* 255.

22. Ibid., 611.

23. Moore, *History of Franklin County,* vol. 1, 320–21; Neely, ed., *Women of Ohio,* vol. 1, 53.

24. Hayes, *Columbus Mayors,* 32–34.

25. *Western Intelligencer,* January 9, 1817.

26. *Ohio State Journal and Columbus Gazette,* January 2, 1830.

27. Mott, *Golden Multitudes: The Story of Best Sellers in the United States,* 306–9.

28. Studer, *Columbus, Ohio,* 289.

29. *Western Literary Magazine* 1 (1850): 48.

30. *Western Democratic Review and Monthly Magazine* 1 (1844): 195.

CHAPTER 11

1. Petro, *Ohio Lands: A Short History,* 36; Lee, *History of the City of Columbus,* vol. 1, 217; *Western Intelligencer,* December 10, 1814; December 5, 12, 1816; *Columbus Gazette,* June 8, 25, 1818; January 7, October 28, 1819; Buley, *The Old Northwest Pioneer Period 1815–1840,* vol. 1, 331.

2. *Columbus Gazette,* June 7, 1821; *Ohio State Journal and Columbus Gazette,* February 8, 1827; June 12, 1828.

3. Atwater, *A History of the State of Ohio,* 253–65. See also Miller, "History of the Educational Legislation in Ohio from 1803 to 1850," *Ohio Archaeological and Historical Publications* 27 (1919): 18, 44, 72–78.

4. Burns, *Educational History of Ohio,* 389.

5. *Columbus Gazette,* December 11, 1824.

6. *Ohio State Journal and Columbus Gazette,* September 25, 1825.

7. Ohio General Assembly, *Laws of Ohio* (1825), vol. 23, 37–39; *Ohio State Journal and Columbus Gazette,* February 15, 1827.

8. Martin, *History of Franklin County,* 402–3.

9. White, ed., *We Too Built Columbus,* 211.

10. *Ohio School Journal* 1 (1846): 3–5; Evan Edmiston Diary, July 23, 1838; *Ohio State Journal and Columbus Gazette,* January 1, 1836.

11. Quoted in Lewis, *Biography of Samuel Lewis,* 129.

12. *Ohio State Journal and Political Register,* January 3, 4, 1839.

13. Lewis, *Biography of Samuel Lewis,* 245–46; Miller, "History of the Educational Legislation in Ohio," 93.

14. Atwater, *An Essay on Education,* 99.

15. White, ed., *We Too Built Columbus,* 215.

16. Shannon, *Annual Message of the Governor of Ohio to the Thirty-Eighth General Assembly, December 3, 1839,* 5.

17. Kamphoefner et al., *News from the Land of Freedom: German Immigrants Write Home,* 20–21.

18. Conte, *German Village,* 22.

19. *Ohio Statesman,* January 18, 1841.

20. Martin, *History of Franklin County,* 403–5; *Old School Journal* 2 (1847): 131; *Ohio State Journal,* July 22, 1847.

21. Burns, *Educational History of Ohio,* 422.

22. *Directory of the City of Columbus for the Year 1848,* 43.

23. Board of Education, *By-Laws of the Board of Education,* 3.

24. *1851 Ohio Constitution,* Article 6, Section 2.

25. *Old School Republican,* November 15, 1839; James, *The American Addition: History of a Black Community,* 7; Minor, "The Negro in Columbus, Ohio," 145.

26. *Ohio Statesman,* March 31, May 11, 1840; White, ed., *We Too Built Columbus,* 21.

27. *Ohio Statesman,* September 25, 1840.

28. *Old School Republican,* August 25, 1841; *Columbus Business Directory for 1843–4,* 73; *Ohio Statesman,* September 25, 1840; Columbus Female Seminary, *Catalogue,* 1845, 5.

29. Columbus Female Seminary, *Catalogue,* 1845, 14–16.

30. *Ohio State Journal,* August 14, 1844. For examples of children's merit cards, see Sarah H. Brant School Papers.

31. Clifton, "Beginnings of Literary Culture in Columbus, Ohio, 1812–1840," 49; McCormick and McCormick, *New Englanders on the Ohio Frontier: Migration and Settlement of Worthington, Ohio,* 256–57.

32. *Ohio State Journal,* January 6, 1843.

33. Bender, *Community and Social Change in America,* 121.

34. Miller, "History of the Educational Legislation in Ohio," 35.

35. Sheatsley, *History of the First Lutheran Seminary of the West, 1830–1930,* 8, 19; Clifton, "Beginnings of Literary Culture," 47–48; Martin, *History of Franklin County,* 398–99; *Ohio State Journal,* June 28, 1845.

36. Campbell, *Biographical Sketches,* 259.

37. Sheatsley, *History of the First Lutheran Seminary,* 27–31.

38. Ibid., 42.

39. Buehring, *These Hundred Years: the Centennial History of Capital University,* 41–48; *Directory of the City of Columbus for the Years 1850–51,* 91.

40. Bartlett, *Education for Humanity: The Story of Otterbein College,* 21–25; Hancock, "The History of Westerville, Ohio," (typewritten), 36–37.

CHAPTER 12

1. R. W. McCoy to Alexander McCoy Sr., December 22, 1811, Robert Watts McCoy Papers

2. Smith, *As a City Upon a Hill: The Town in American History,* 76. See also Miya-

kaawa, *Protestants and Pioneers: Individualism and Conformity on the American Frontier*, 3.

3. The article was reprinted in the *Ohio State Journal and Columbus Gazette*, March 31, 1832. Anne M. Boylan has estimated that by 1832, Protestant Sunday schools enrolled almost 10 percent of American children. See Boylan, "The Role of Conversion in Nineteenth-Century Sunday Schools," *American Studies* 20 (1979): 35–48.

4. Boyer, *Urban Masses and Moral Order in America, 1820–1920*, p. 43.

5. *Columbus Gazette*, April 16, 1818; Marty, *Pilgrims in Their Own Land: 500 Years of Religion in America*, 58–59.

6. White, ed., *We Too Built Columbus*, 78; King, "Introduction of Methodism in Ohio," *Ohio Archaeological and Historical Publications* 10 (1902): 209; Hooper, *History of Columbus Ohio*, 187; *Western Intelligencer*, May 28, 1818; *Columbus Gazette*, June 21, 1821. Of the many books on revivals, see especially Smith, *Revivalism and Social Reform*, and Weisberger, *They Gathered at the River*.

7. King, "Introduction of Methodism in Ohio," 209; James Loudon to Elizabeth Loudon, February 12, 1843, DeWitt Clinton Louden Papers; White, ed., *We Too Built Columbus*, p. 78.

8. Weaver, *First Baptist Church, Columbus, Ohio, 1824–1874*; Cox and Hoby, *The Baptists in America*, 307–8.

9. Horton and Horton, *In Hope of Liberty: Culture, Community, and Protest among Northern Free Blacks, 1700–1860*, 129; Hickok, "The Negro in Ohio, 1802–1870."

10. Columbus First Presbyterian Church, *One Hundredth Anniversary*. See also Martin, *History of Franklin County*, 333–37.

11. Marsten, *After Eighty Years, 80th Anniversary of the First Presbyterian Church*, 31–32, 115.

12. Sullivant quoted in ibid., 32.

13. Lyman Beecher to William Beecher, February 1, 1839, in Beecher, ed., *Autobiography, Correspondence, Etc., of Lyman Beecher*, vol. 2, 436–37.

14. Moore, *History of the Second Presbyterian Church*, 2; Ingraham, *A History of Central Presbyterian Church*, 17, 129.

15. Martin, *History of Franklin County*, 379. Joel Buttles's diary contains several references to the Trinity Episcopal Church and its ministers.

16. White, ed., *We Too Built Columbus*, 151; Hooper, *History of Columbus Ohio*, 203.

17. Martin, *History of Franklin County*, 284–58.

18. O'Gorman, *A History of the Roman Catholic Church in the United States*, 325; Clarke, "Early Catholic Church in Columbus," *Catholic Columbian*, April 24, May 1, 1875; Kappes, "History of the First Catholics in Columbus, Ohio," (typewritten), 2–5.

19. Sittler, "The German Element in Columbus before the Civil War," 39. See also McNamara, "The Catholic Church in Ohio (1830–1840)," 10–22, 53.

20. *Columbus Business Directory for 1843–4*, 45, 48.

21. Moody, *A Life's Retrospect, Autobiography of Rev. Granville Moody*, 173–74; Moore, *History of the Second Presbyterian Church*, 340; Taylor, *Centennial History of Columbus and Franklin County, Ohio*, vol. 1, 208; Jewish Historical Society, *Family Portrait Album*, 6; Hooper, *History of Columbus Ohio*, 216.

22. Lyell, *A second visit to the United States of North America*, vol. 2, 67–68; Williams, *The Welsh of Columbus, Ohio: A Study in Adaptation and Assimilation*, 56.

23. Wilkerson, *Wilkerson's History of his Travels and Labors in the United States as a Missionary*, 5–40.

24. *Ohio Statesman*, July 13, 1844; *Ohio State Journal*, August 15, 1843; *Palladium*

of Liberty, June 26, 1844; Studer, *Columbus, Ohio: Its History, Resources, and Progress,* 183–84

25. *Directory of the City of Columbus for the Years 1850–51.*
26. Marjorie Johnston Papers.

CHAPTER 13

1. *Western Hemisphere,* October 14, 1833; *Ohio State Journal and Columbus Gazette,* April 10, 1828; July 8, 1830.

2. Clifton, "Beginnings of Literary Culture in Columbus, Ohio, 1812–1840," 170, with an appendix containing a list of productions; *Ohio State Journal and Columbus Gazette,* March 7, 1837.

3. *Ohio State Journal and Columbus Gazette,* December 14, 1831; *Ohio Statesman,* January 30, 1837; Hodge, *Yankee Theater: The Image of America on the Stage, 1825–1850,* 255, 263; Evan Edmiston Diary, July 15, 1839.

4. Saxton, *The Rise and Fall of the White Republic: Class Politics and Mass Culture in Nineteenth-Century America,* 109, 114, 116.

5. Clifton, "Beginnings of Literary Culture," 423; Sheridan, *Those Wonderful Old Downtown Theaters,* 5; *Ohio Statesman,* August 10, 1841; McCabe, *Don't You Remember?,* 172; Hodge, *Yankee Theater: The Image of America on the Stage, 1825–1850,* 7, 31–32, 41–42, 216; *Ohio Press,* February 4, 1848.

6. *Ohio Statesman,* February 3, 1842; White, ed., *We Too Built Columbus,* 229, 230; Carey quoted in Kinney, "John Carey, An Ohio Pioneer," *Ohio State Archaeological and Historical Quarterly* 46 (1937): 175; *Ohio Statesman,* April 14, 21, 1843; *Ohio State Journal,* April 29, 1843.

7. *Ohio State Journal and Columbus Gazette,* July 10, December 17, 1834.

8. *Ohio Statesman,* January 3, May 23, 1835; July 28, 1840.

9. Ibid., August 23, 1841; February 15, 16, 1842.

10. *Ohio State Journal,* April 30, July 23, 1846; *Ohio Statesman,* April 30, 1845; November 4, 1846; June 30, July 14, August 7, 1847.

11. *Ohio State Journal and Columbus Gazette,* May 17, 1831; March 21, 1837.

12. *Ohio Statesman,* July 28, 1840; February 25, 1843; March 14, 1848; *Ohio State Journal,* July 7, 20, 1841; August 3, November 7, 1842; January 3, 1843; August 15, 1848; Anson W. Buttles Diary, June 3, 1843.

13. *Ohio State Journal,* June 21, 1843; October 31, 1845; *Ohio Statesman,* February 15, 1845; *Ohio State Journal,* December 15, 1845.

14. Teaford, *Cities of the Heartland: The Rise and Fall of the Industrial Midwest,* 89.

15. *Ohio State Journal,* February 29, 1844.

16. *Ohio Statesman,* February 12, 1844. A good description of minstrel performers is in Moody, ed., *Dramas from the American Theatre 1762–1909,* 475, 479.

17. *Ohio Statesman,* January 7, 1845; February 12, 14, 1851.

18. See Toll, *Blacking Up: The Minstrel Show in Nineteenth-Century America,* v, 3, 31, 33–34; Lott, *Love and Theft: Blackface Minstrelsy and the American Working Class;* Abrahams, *Singing the Master: The Emergence of African-American Culture in the Plantation South,* 131–32; Holt, "Marking: Race, Race-making, and the Writing of History," *American Historical Review* 100 (February 1995): 15; Saxton, *Rise and Fall of the White Republic,* 176–77.

19. *Christy's Panorama Songster,* 79.

20. *Columbus Gazette,* January 21, 1819; *Ohio State Journal and Columbus Gazette,* December 17, 1834.

21. Evan Edmiston Diary, November 28, 1838.

22. *Ohio State Journal,* August 24, 1847.

23. *Columbus Gazette,* May 4, 24, 1849; *Ohio Statesman,* May 16, 1845; December 19, 1850; May 16, 1851.

24. Buckingham, *The Eastern and Western States of America,* vol. 2, 316–17; *Ohio Statesman,* January 2, 1849; *Old Zak,* July 1, 1848.

25. Unsigned statement, Livingston/Taylor Papers.

26. *Ohio Statesman,* October 2, 1848; January 3, 1850.

27. Browne, ed., *Barnum's Own Story,* 245. One of the most recent biographies is Kunhardt et al., *P. T. Barnum: America's Greatest Showman.*

28. *Ohio Statesman,* January 9, February 1, 1851.

29. Ibid., December 2, 1847; Sheridan, *Those Wonderful Old Downtown Theaters,* 6; *Ohio Press,* January 14, 1848; *Ohio Statesman,* February 10, October 31, 1848; *Ohio State Journal,* March 8, 14, 1850.

30. *Ohio State Journal,* December 17, 19, 1849; Browne, ed., *Barnum's Own Story,* 133–34.

31. *Ohio State Journal,* December 17, 1849; *Ohio Statesman,* July 5, November 21, 1850.

32. *Ohio Statesman,* July 8, October 7, 1850.

33. Ibid., October 10, 1850. Details of Lind's contract and tour are in Browne, ed., *Barnum's Own Story,* 192, and Saxon, *P. T. Barnum: The Legend and the Man,* 163.

34. *Ohio Statesman,* September 25, 1850.

35. Ibid., March 17, April 14, 1851.

36. Ibid., November 3, 1851. Her marriage is mentioned in Browne, ed., *Barnum's Own Story,* 239.

37. *Ohio Statesman,* November 10, 1851; *Ohio State Journal,* November 3, 1851.

CHAPTER 14

1. *Ohio State Journal and Columbus Gazette,* October 27, 1825.

2. Bartley, *Address of the Hon. Thomas W. Bartley Delivered Before the Athenian Literary Society of Norwalk Seminary,* 4.

3. *Ohio Statesman,* February 23, 1843; May 7, 1845.

4. Columbus, Ohio Citizens, *Report on the territory of Oregon, by a committee, appointed at a meeting of the citizens of Columbus, to collect information in relation thereto,* 5, 13, 17, 18.

5. *Ohio Statesman,* April 28, May 7, 14, 16, 1845; O'Sullivan quoted in *United States Magazine and Democratic Review,* July 1845; Smith, *Samuel Medary and the Crisis: Testing the Limits of Press Freedom,* 40; *Ohio Farmer and Western Horticulturist* 6 (February 1, 1834): 21.

6. Taylor, "The West and the Western People," *Democratic Monthly Magazine and Western Review* 3 (1844): 21.

7. *Ohio Statesman,* January 11, 1844.

8. Ibid., April 28, May 7, 14, 16, 1845.

9. Bartley, *Special Message from the Governor to the House of Representatives, January 2, 1846,* Thomas W. H. Moseley Papers.

10. Bergeron, *The Presidency of James K. Polk,* 113.

11. *Ohio Statesman,* June 13, 1845.

12. Ibid., May 5, December 23, 1840.

13. Webster to Adams, December 30, 1841, Daniel Webster Letters.

14. Hooper, *History of Columbus Ohio,* 41. The most recent interpretations of the war are in Haynes, *James K. Polk and the Expansionist Impulse.*

15. *Ohio State Journal,* May 28, 1846.

16. *Ohio Statesman,* May 18, 1846.

17. Ibid., May 26, 31, 1846. See also Fisher, *A Short History of the Columbus Ca-*

dets, and Ryan, "Ohio in the Mexican War," *Ohio Archaeological and Historical Society Publications* 21 (1912): 277–95.

18. Hooper, *History of Columbus Ohio,* 41.

19. *Ohio State Journal,* March 3, 1845.

20. Joel Buttles Diary, June 6, 1846.

21. Bochin, "Tom Corwin's Speech Against the Mexican War: Courageous but Misunderstood," *Ohio History* 90 (1981): 33–54.

22. Finley, *Memorials of Prison Life,* 110. See also McWilliams, *North from Mexico: The Spanish Speaking People of the United States,* 16, 26, 309.

23. Pletcher, *The Diplomacy of Annexation: Texas, Oregon, and the Mexican War,* 475; Sellers, *James K. Polk, Continentalist, 1843–1846,* 287.

24. *Ohio Statesman,* February 15, 1847.

25. David and John Nelson Ledgers.

26. *Ohio Statesman,* April 26, 1848.

27. Hooper, *History of Columbus Ohio,* 41–42. For a typical agreement form between investors and "adventurers" going to California, see the one written by H. Martin Ramsey.

28. John Krum to Martin Krum, December 1, 1850, John Krum Letters.

29. McNeil, *McNeil's Travels in 1849, To, Through, And From The Gold Regions In California,* 28–29; James Williams to Sarah Williams, August 20, 1850, James Williams Papers.

CHAPTER 15

1. *Ohio Statesman,* December 27, 1841.

2. Wyatt-Brown, "Prelude to Abolitionism: Sabbatarian Politics and the Rise of the Second Party System," *Journal of American History* 58 (1971): 316–41; *Ohio State Journal,* May 25, 1841.

3. *Ohio Statesman,* January 4, 5, 6, 1844.

4. Clifton, "Beginnings of Literary Culture in Columbus, Ohio, 1812–1840," 124; *Ohio State Journal and Columbus Gazette,* December 24, 1834; Goldfield and Brownell, *Urban America,* 181.

5. *Ohio Temperance Advocate,* April 1836; Giddings to wife quoted in Weisenberger, *The Passing of the Frontier 1825–1850,* 128; *Ohio State Journal,* June 16, 1841.

6. *Ohio Statesman,* February 6, 12, October 29, November 5, 1841; March 22, 1842; Hitchcock to Jr., November 4, 1841, Charles E. Rice Papers.

7. *Ohio Statesman,* March 22, 1842; May 28, 1844; *Ohio State Journal,* January 10, 1843; January 18, May 28, 1844; *Palladium of Liberty,* October 2, 1844; Hollins, "A Black Voice of Antebellum Ohio: A Rhetorical Analysis of the *Palladium of Liberty,* 1843–1844," 36.

8. *Ohio State Journal,* March 10, 1845; *Ohio Statesman,* December 17, 1845; Janney to President, December 10, 1845, Janney Family Papers.

9. *Ohio State Journal,* January 15, June 20, 1846; January 25, October 20, 1848; Cole, *Lion of the Forest: James B. Finley, Frontier Reformer,* 121–24.

10. *Ohio State Journal,* December 10, 1846.

11. Ibid., January 12, 1847; February 3, 1848; *Ohio Standard,* February 28, 1849; *Ohio Statesman,* October 31, 1949.

12. *Ohio Statesman,* March 7, 1850; Barrett to Swayne, December 17, 1849, Joshua Swayne Papers.

13. Bakan, "The Influence of Phrenology on American Psychology," *Journal of the History of the Behavioural Sciences* 2 (July 1966): 201; Davies, *Phrenology: Fad and Science,* 8, 20; Haskins, *History and Progress of Phrenology,* 61; Adams and Hutter, *The Mad Forties,* 58.

14. Haskins, *History and Progress,* 105–10; Curti, *Human Nature in American Thought,* 164; Riegel, "The Introduction of Phrenology to the United States," *American Historical Review* 39 (October 1933): 73–78.

15. Turnbull, *Phrenology, the First Science of Man,* 2, 43, 13. A recent book on phrenology examines its influence on art. See Colbert, *A Measure of Perfection: Phrenology and the Fine Arts in America.*

16. Davies, *Phrenology,* 61.

17. *American Phrenological Journal* 11 (1849): 12. See also Stern, *Heads and Headlines: The Phrenological Fowlers,* 34, 39, 71.

18. *Ohio Statesman,* January 29, 1841.

19. *The Freeman,* October 13, 1841; January 4, 1842; *Ohio State Journal,* February 9, March 13, 1843; *Palladium of Liberty,* September 25, 1844.

20. *Ohio State Journal,* April 19, 1849.

21. Masur, *Rites of Execution: Capital Punishment and the Transformation of American Culture, 1776–1865,* 100.

22. Cole, "The Last Public Hanging," *Columbus Monthly* 19 (December 1993): 91–94. For Joel Buttles's comments on the hanging, see his diary, February 8, 10, 1844.

23. *Ohio State Journal,* December 19, 1843; Ohio General Assembly, *Journal of the Senate, 1843–1844,* 751, 777, 831, 836; *Ohio Statesman,* March 22, 1844.

24. Anti-Slavery Convention of American Women, *Proceedings of the Anti-Slavery Convention of American Women, Held in the City of New York,* 9.

25. Ibid., 45; Melder, *Beginnings of Sisterhood: The American Woman's Rights Movement, 1800–1850,* 123; *Notable American Women, 1607–1950,* vol. 2, 285, 263.

26. Galbreath, "Anti-Slavery Movement in Columbiana County," *Ohio Archaeological and Historical Publications* 30 (1921): 371–73; Jones quoted in Hersh, *The Slavery of Sex: Feminist Abolitionists in America,* 189.

27. *Anti-Slavery Bugle,* July 14, 1850.

28. Whitlock, ed., *Women in Ohio History,* 4–8; O'Connor, *Pioneer Women Orators,* 91–93; *The National Cyclopaedia of American Biography* (New York: James T. White & Co., 1893), vol. 2, 321.

29. Ohio Women's Convention, *Proceedings of the Women's Rights Convention held at Salem, April 19th and 20th, 1850,* 6–8.

30. Ibid., 34.

31. *Notable American Women,* vol. 2, 285; *National Cyclopaedia of American Biography,* vol. 2, 321.

32. *Columbus Gazette,* June 7, 1821. See other advertisements in January 7, 1819, and March 14, 28, April 1, 1824, issues.

33. Hickok, *The Negro in Ohio, 1802–1870,* 41–43.

34. *Columbus Gazette,* January 25, 1821; *Ohio State Journal,* July 27, 1827.

35. Ames, ed., *State Documents on Federal Relations: The States and the United States,* 203–4.

36. Ibid., 207–8.

37. Ohio General Assembly, *Journal of the House of Representatives, Committee Report, 1827.*

38. *Ohio State Journal and Columbus Gazette,* December 19, 1827.

39. *Ohio State Journal and Columbus Gazette,* January 10, 1829; October 18, 1827.

40. Ibid., January 11, 1834; July 12, October 18, December 22, 1827; Mark, "Negroes in Columbus."

41. Goodman, *Of One Blood: Abolitionism and the Origins of Racial Equality,* 18.

42. Birney to Tappan, May 2, 1836, in Dumond, ed., *Letters of James Gillespie Birney 1831–1857,* vol. 1, 234.

43. Benjamin Tappan to Lewis Tappan, March 6, 1836, Benjamin Tappan Papers;

Ohio State Journal and Columbus Gazette, January 22, 1834; *Ohio Statesman*, September 20, 1843

44. *Ohio Statesman*, September 10, 1839.

45. *Ohio Statesman* quoted in *Cincinnati Advertiser and Journal*, July 13, 1839.

46. Martineau, *Society in America*, vol. 2, 77.

47. "Minutes of the Anti-Slavery Society of Worthington," Wilbur H. Siebert Collection; Ohio Anti-Slavery Society, *Memorial of the Ohio Anti-Slavery Society to the General Assembly of the State of Ohio*, 3. For statistics on the growth of antislavery societies, see American Anti-Slavery Society, *Annual Reports*.

48. Horton and Horton, *In Hope of Liberty: Culture, Community, and Protest among Northern Free Blacks, 1700–1860*, 229. Additional information on the Underground Railroad in Columbus is in Siebert, *The Mysteries of Ohio's Underground Railroads*, 160; Minor, "The Negro in Columbus, Ohio," 267; Gara, *The Liberty Line, The Legend of the Underground Railroad*; interviews with Siebert, Wilbur H. Siebert Collection.

49. Siebert, *Mysteries of Ohio's Underground Railroads*, 162–65; Minor, "The Negro in Columbus," 272, Horton and Horton, *In Hope of Liberty*, 229.

50. Blassingame, ed., *Slave Testimony*, 195.

51. Second Baptist Church, *One Hundredth Anniversary of the Second Baptist Church*; Minor, "The Negro in Columbus," 267–69; Blockson, *The Underground Railroad*, 4.

52. *The Daily Cincinnati Republican and Commercial Register*, April 12, 1836; Richards, *"Gentlemen of Property and Standing," Anti-Abolition Mobs in Jacksonian America*.

53. Quoted in Quillin, *The Color Line in Ohio: A History of Race Prejudice in a Typically Northern State*, 52, 36.

54. Chaddock, *Ohio Before 1850: A Study of the Early Influence of Pennsylvania and Southern Populations in Ohio*, 85.

55. Quoted in Foner and Walker, *Proceedings of the Black State Conventions, 1840–1865*, vol. 1, 239.

56. "Petition signed by 68 persons," Ezekiel Brown Papers.

57. Lewis, *Biography of Samuel Lewis*, 286; *Ohio State Journal*, December 31, 1841; *Ohio Statesman*, August 13, 1841.

58. *Ohio State Journal*, December 9, 1841.

59. Joel Buttles Diary, January 7, 1842; *Ohio Statesman*, January 20, 1842; White, ed., *We Too Built Columbus*, 379; O'Connor, *Pioneer Women Orators*, 93–94.

60. *Ohio Statesman*, December 8, 1842; Hickok, "The Negro in Ohio," 170.

61. *Ohio Statesman*, June 13, 1845; Niven, *Salmon P. Chase, A Biography*, 95.

62. Beaumont quoted in Sturge, *A Visit to the United States in 1841*, 130.

63. *Ohio Statesman*, January 14, 1844; February 20, 1845.

64. Quoted in Schlegel, *The Columbus City Graveyards*, 46.

65. Holt, *Party Politics in Ohio, 1840–1850*, 240.

66. Bell, *Minutes of the Proceedings of the National Negro Conventions, 1830–1864*, 10; *Palladium of Liberty*, December 27, 1843.

67. Delany, *The Condition, Elevation, Emigration and Destiny of the Colored People of the United States*, 99; Hollins, "A Black Voice of Antebellum Ohio," 14–20; Parham and Brown, *An Official History of the Most Worshipful Grand Lodge Free and Accepted Masons for the State of Ohio*, 267.

68. *Ohio State Journal*, July 18, 1846; *Ohio Statesman*, January 10, 1848.

69. Ohio General Assembly, *Journal of the Senate, 1844–45*, appendix, 26–28.

70. Ibid., 411–16, 450–52, 504.

71. *Ohio Statesman*, February 13, 1845.

72. Ibid., December 3, 1845; February 10, 26, 1846; *Ohio State Journal,* February 10, 1846.

73. *Ohio State Journal,* July 26, 1845; Moseley, Diary, Thomas W. H. Moseley Papers.

74. Moseley to Clay, August 13, 1845, Thomas W. H. Moseley Papers.

75. *Ohio State Journal,* March 31, April 2, 4, September 12, 1846; *Ohio Press,* May 9, 1846; Galbreath, *History of Ohio,* vol. 2, 237–38; McCabe, *Don't You Remember?,* 93; Uriah Heath Journal, March 31, 1846.

76. Ohio General Assembly, *Journal of the Senate, 1847–48,* "The Report of the Select Committee on the Repeal of the Black Laws," 126.

77. *Ohio Press,* January 2, 1847.

78. *Ohio Statesman,* August 1, 1849.

CHAPTER 16

1. *Ohio State Journal,* March 13, 1847.

2. Maizlish, *The Triumph of Sectionalism: The Transformation of Ohio Politics, 1844–1856,* 27, 40; *Ohio Statesman,* January 10, 1848.

3. See Gara, *The Liberty Line, The Legend of the Underground Railroad,* 63.

4. Niven, *Salmon P. Chase: A Biography.*

5. Chase to Hall in ibid., 67–68.

6. Ibid., 107; Smith, *The Liberty and Free Soil Parties in the Northwest,* 129, 167.

7. *Ohio State Journal,* July 25, 1848; Price, "The Election of 1848 in Ohio," *Ohio State Archaeological and Historical Quarterly* 36 (1927): 285; Allen to Seward, November 13, 1848, quoted in Brock, *Parties and Political Conscience: American Dilemmas 1840–1850,* 228.

8. Maizlish, *Triumph of Sectionalism,* 147.

9. Article on Nathaniel C. Read in Charles E. Rice Papers; Marshall, ed., *A History of the Courts and Lawyers of Ohio,* vol. 1, 244; Brown and Cayton, eds., *The Pursuit of Public Power: Political Culture in Ohio, 1787–1861,* 147; Townshend, "The Forty-Seventh General Assembly of Ohio—Comments Upon Mr. Riddle's Paper," *Magazine of Western History* 6 (1887): 623–28. Townshend offered corrections to Riddle, "Recollections of the Forty-Seventh General Assembly," ibid., 341–51.

10. *Ohio State Journal,* December 16, 1848.

11. *Ohio Standard,* December 19, 28, 1848; January 13, 1849.

12. Foner and Walker, eds., *Proceedings of the Black State Conventions, 1840–1865,* vol. 1, 223, 229.

13. Ibid., vol. 1, 214.

14. Christy, *A Lecture on African Colonization,* 25, 26, 27, 29. See also Berwanger, *The Frontier Against Slavery: Western Anti-Negro Prejudice and the Slavery Extension Controversy,* 54–55.

15. Christy, "Memorial to the Senate and Representatives of Ohio," in the *Annual Report and Proceedings of the American Colonization Society, 1849,* quoted in Stebbins, *Facts and Opinions Touching the Real Origin, Character, and Influence of the American Colonization Society,* 109.

16. Maizlish, *Triumph of Sectionalism,* 241.

17. Ohio General Assembly, *Journal of the House of Representatives,* January 3, 14, 1849; *Journal of the Senate,* December 5, 1848; January 14, 1849.

18. Ohio General Assembly, *Journal of the House of Representatives,* February 22, 1849. Michael Holt asserts that control of the state legislature and local issues were more important than abolition and that the deal between the Democrats and Free Soilers "set a pattern for other northern states." See Holt, *The Rise and Fall of the American Whig Party,* 398, 402.

19. *Ohio State Journal,* February 12, 16, 22, 1849.

20. Blue, *Salmon P. Chase: A Life in Politics,* 70; *Ohio State Journal,* February 21, April 26, 1849.

21. Quillin, *The Color Line in Ohio: A History of Race Prejudice in a Typically Northern State,* 36; Riddle, "Recollections of the Forty-Seventh General Assembly," *Magazine of Western History* 6 (1887): 341–51; Hickok, "The Negro in Ohio 1802–1870," 90, 92; Miller, "History of the Educational Legislation in Ohio from 1803 to 1850," *Ohio Archaeological and Historical Publications* 25 (1919): 57.

22. *Ohio Statesman,* December 28, 1849.

CHAPTER 17

1. George and Orange Slade to Hunkin, June 6, 1841, Samuel Hunkin Letter.
2. Wolff in Walley, *Six Generations: The Story of German Village,* 12.
3. "Autobiographical Sketch of John Jay Janney," Charles A. Jones Papers.
4. Hayes, *Columbus Mayors,* 23–25; Hooper, *History of Columbus Ohio,* 136.
5. Quoted in Moody, *A Life's Retrospect, Autobiography of Rev. Granville Moody* 174.
6. Smith to wife, January 5, 1842, John Armstrong Smith Papers.
7. *Ohio State Journal,* June 22, 1848; Schlegel, *The Columbus City Graveyards,* 16–17, 37, 46; *Ohio Statesman,* July 10, 1841; Lee, *History of the City of Columbus,* vol. 2, 725.
8. *Ohio Press,* March 6, 1847; *Directory of the City of Columbus for the Year 1848,* 46–48; Loving, "History of Starling Medical College," *"Old Northwest" Genealogical Quarterly* 8 (1905): 108; Pinta, *A History of Psychiatry at The Ohio State University 1847–1993,* 3–7.
9. *Ohio State Journal,* October 4, 1848; Loving, "Some Reminiscences—General and Medical," *"Old Northwest" Genealogical Quarterly* 7 (1904): 217–19; *Ohio Statesman,* December 29, 1848; *Ohio Standard,* February 20, 1849; Barrett, "Some Reminiscences of Dr. Starling Loving," *Columbus & Central Ohio Historian* 1 (1984): 67–72.
10. Sullivant, *A Genealogy and Family Memorial,* 65.
11. *Ohio Statesman,* April 30, 1845; January 26, 1846.
12. Ibid., August 24, 1847.
13. *Ohio State Journal,* April 19, 1849.
14. Ibid., June 10, 1847.
15. *Ohio Statesman,* September 10, 14, 1849.
16. Ibid., June 2, 1848; *Directory of the City of Columbus for the Years 1850–51,* 47–48. For a consideration of a business ethic, see Atherton, "The Pioneer Merchant in mid-America," *University of Missouri Studies* 14 (1939): 5–15.
17. Joel Buttles Diary, n.d. (last entry).
18. High Street description based on details in the *Directory of the City of Columbus for the Year 1848.*
19. Williamson and Lindert, *American Inequality: A Macroeconomic History,* 5, 46, 103.
20. Welling, *Information for the People: or The Asylums of Ohio,* 26.
21. *Ohio State Journal,* June 17, 1847.
22. *Ohio Press,* June 10, December 10, 1846; biographical note in William Bebb Papers.
23. Dorn, "Samuel Medary: Politician, Statesman, and Journalist," preface; *Ohio Statesman,* October 12, 16, December 10, 1849.
24. *United States Population Census for 1850,* Manuscript Census Schedules. Ad-

ditional statistics are from *Columbus Directory for the Year 1852*, 65–66. Seventeen percent of the names in the business directories in the 1840s were German.

25. *United States Population Census for 1850*, Manuscript Census Schedules; Wolf, "Irish Immigrants in Ohio," (typewritten), 1–28. For a useful examination of an ideology of literacy, see Soltow and Stevens, *The Rise of Literacy and the Common School in the United States*, 58–88.

26. Soltow, *Men and Wealth in the United States, 1850–1870*, 41, table 2.4; *United States Population Census for 1850*, Manuscript Census Schedules.

27. *United States Population Census for 1850*, Manuscript Census Schedules. Although Joel Buttles died on August 14, 1850, and the census taker visited the house on September 29, Buttles was still listed. The real estate he owned totaled $110,000.

28. Smith, *A Discourse Pronounced before the Class of Starling Medical College at the Opening of the Winter Session of 1850–51*, 18.

29. *Ohio State Journal*, May 6, 1849.

30. Ibid., August 21, 1848; Hoffert, *When Hens Crow: The Women's Rights Movement in Antebellum America*, 23; *Ohio Statesman*, July 11, 1851.

31. *Ohio Statesman*, January 30, February 8, 1850.

32. Quoted in Isenberg, *Sex and Citizenship in Antebellum America*, 17.

33. Sawyer quoted in Berwanger, *The Frontier Against Slavery: Western Anti-Negro Prejudice and the Slavery Extension Controversy* 38, 39.

34. Quillin, *The Color Line in Ohio: A History of Race Prejudice in a Typically Northern State*, 75.

35. Smith, *Report of the Debates and Proceedings of the Convention for the Revision of the Constitution of the State of Ohio, 1850–1851* vol. 1, 1, 70, 167, 338, 340, 538, 714, 734; vol. 2, 2, 20, 26, 167, 328, 538.

36. Ibid., "Committee on Jurisprudence," vol. 1, 338.

37. Ibid., vol. 2, 870.

38. Sheeler, "The Struggle of the Negro in Ohio for Freedom," *Journal of Negro History* 31 (April 1946): 222. Ohio State Convention of the Colored Citizens of Ohio, *Minutes of the State Convention . . . and An Address to the Constitutional Convention of Ohio*, 19–23.

39. Foner and Walker, ed., *Proceedings of the Black State Conventions, 1840–1865*, vol. 1, 215; Hollins, "A Black Voice of Antebellum Ohio: A Rhetorical Analysis of the *Palladium of Liberty*, 1843–1844," 24; *Ohio State Journal*, October 16, 1850; Columbus, *True Wesleyan*, quoted in *Liberator*, October 29, 1852, and in Gara, *The Liberty Line, The Legend of the Underground Railroad*, 145.

40. *Directory of the City of Columbus for the Years 1850–51*, 81.

41. *Ohio Statesman*, December 18, 1850.

42. James Bates to wife, June 16, 1850, James Bates Correspondence.

43. Pulszky, *White, Red, Black: Sketches of American Society*, vol. 1, 285.

44. Huth, "Louis Kossuth in Ohio," *Northwest Ohio Quarterly* 40 (1968): 113–14; Lee, *History of the City of Columbus*, vol. 2, 41–43; *Ohio State Journal*, February 6, 1852; Randall, "Kossuth Before Ohio Legislature," *Ohio Archaeological and Historical Publications* 12 (1903): 114.

BIBLIOGRAPHY

PRIMARY SOURCES

Unless otherwise indicated, all letters, diaries, documents, newspapers, and unpublished materials are in the Ohio Historical Society Library/Archives, Columbus.

James Bates Correspondence, William Bebb Papers, Sarah H. Brant School Papers, Amos H. Brown Papers, Ezekiel Brown Papers, Anson W. Buttles Diary, Joel Buttles Diary, Letters of the Case and Buttles Families, Aaron M. Condit Letters, Letters of Appleton Downer, Joseph Dunlop Letters, Evan Edmiston Diary, First Baptist Church of Columbus Papers, Samuel Galloway Papers, Lincoln Goodale Papers, Clark Guernsey Journal, Uriah Heath Journal, Samuel Hunkin Letter, Janney Family Papers, James Johnston Proposal, Marjorie Johnston Papers, Charles A. Jones Papers, Dr. Ichabod G. Jones Miscellaneous Papers, Alfred Kelley Papers, James Kilbourne Family Papers, John Krum Letters, Samuel Lewis Letters, Livingston/Taylor Papers, Asa D. Lord Letter, DeWitt Clinton Louden Papers, William Ludlow Letter, Robert Watts McCoy Papers, Samuel Medary Papers, Thomas Mooder Letter, Thomas W. H. Moseley Papers, Robert Neil Family Papers, David and John Nelson Ledgers, Platt Family Papers, H. Martin Ramsey Agreement, Charles E. Rice Papers, William H. Sells "Reminiscences," Wilbur H. Siebert Collection, John Sloane Papers, John Armstrong Smith Papers, Isaac Strohm Papers, Sullivant-Starling Papers, Joseph Sullivant Genealogy and Family Memorial, Joseph Sullivant Papers, Joshua Swayne Papers, Benjamin Tappan Papers, Joseph Vance Letters, Daniel Webster Letters, James Williams Papers.

Official Records

Ames, Herman V., ed., *State Documents on Federal Relations: The States and the United States*, vol. 1 (New York: Da Capo Press, 1970).
City of Columbus, City Clerk, "Journal of Council Proceedings," vol. 1, 1834–42.
———, "Record of Ordinances."
Ohio General Assembly, *Journal of the House of Representatives*. vols. 42–49 (Zanesville, Chillicothe, Columbus, 1809–50).
———, *Journal of the Senate of the State of Ohio*, vols. 42–49 (Zanesville, Chillicothe, Columbus, 1809–50).
United States Population Census for 1830, 1840, and 1850 for Franklin County, Manuscript Census Schedules.

Newspapers

Chillicothe: *Chillicothe Supporter*
Cincinnati: *Advertiser and Journal, Daily Cincinnati Republican and Commercial Register, Daily Gazette*
Columbus: *Catholic Columbian, Columbus Gazette, Crisis, Daily Advertiser, Freeman, Land Seller and General Advertiser, New Constitution, Ohio Confederate, Ohio Confederate and Old School Republican, Ohio Eagle, Ohio Observer, Ohio Press, Ohio Standard, Ohio State Journal, Ohio State Journal and Columbus Gazette, Ohio State Journal and Political Register, Ohio State Tribune and Western Laborer, Ohio Statesman, Old School Republican, Old School Republican and Ohio Gazette,*

Old Zak, Palladium of Liberty, People's Weekly Journal and Freeman's Standard, Straight-Out Harrisonian, Westbote, Western Hemisphere, Western Intelligencer, Western Intelligencer and Columbus Gazette
Hamilton: *Intelligencer*
Salem: *Anti-Slavery Bugle*

Columbus Directories

Columbus Business Directory for 1843–4 (Columbus: J. R. Armstrong, 1843–44).

Kinney's Directory of Columbus for 1845–6 (Columbus: Chas. Scott and Co., 1845–46).

Directory of the City of Columbus for the Year 1848 (Columbus: John Siebert, 1848).

Directory of the City of Columbus for the Years 1850–51 (Columbus: E. Glover and Wm. Henderson, 1850).

Columbus Directory for the Year 1852 (Columbus: E. Glover, 1852).

SECONDARY WORKS

Books about Columbus and Ohio

Abbott, John S. C., *The History of the State of Ohio* (Detroit: Northwestern, 1875).

Allbeck, Willard D., *A Century of Lutherans in Ohio* (Yellow Springs, Ohio: Antioch Press, 1966).

Arter, Bill, *Columbus Vignettes,* 4 vols. (Columbus: Nida-Eckstein, 1966, 1967, 1969, 1971).

Atwater, Caleb, *An Essay on Education* (Cincinnati: Kendall & Henry, 1841).

———, *The General Character, Present and Future Prospects of the People of Ohio* (Columbus: P. H. Olmsted & Co., 1827).

———, *A History of the State of Ohio* (Cincinnati: Glazen & Shepard, 1838).

Barber, John M., *History of Ohio Methodism* (Cincinnati: Curts & Jennings, 1898).

Bartlett, Willard W., *Education for Humanity: The Story of Otterbein College* (Westerville: Otterbein College, 1934).

Bartley, Thomas W., *Address of the Hon. Thomas W. Bartley Delivered Before the Athenian Literary Society of Norwalk Seminary* (Norwalk: Hatch and Farr, 1842).

Bates, James L., *Alfred Kelley, His Life and Work* (Columbus: Clarke & Co., 1888).

Berquist, Goodwin, and Paul C. Bowers Jr., *The New Eden: James Kilbourne and the Development of Ohio* (Lanham, Md.: University Press of America, 1983).

Blue, Frederick J., *Salmon P. Chase: A Life in Politics* (Kent: Kent State University Press, 1987).

Board of Education, *By-Laws of the Board of Education* (Columbus: Thrall & Reed, 1848).

Bradford, David H., "The Background and Foundation of the Republican Party in Ohio 1844–1861." Ph.D. diss. (University of Chicago, 1947).

Brown, Samuel R., *The Western Gazetteer: or Emigrants' Directory* (Auburn, N.Y.: H. C. Southwick, 1817).

Buehring, Paul H., *These Hundred Years: the Centennial History of Capital University* (Columbus: Capital University, 1950).

Buley, Roscoe C., *The Old Northwest Pioneer Period 1815–1840,* 2 vols. (Indianapolis: Indiana Historical Society, 1950).

Burns, James J., *Educational History of Ohio* (Columbus: Historical Publishing Co., 1905).

Campbell, John W., *Biographical Sketches* (Columbus: Scott & Gallagher, 1838).

Carrington, Henry B., "First, Second & Third Presbyterian Churches" (bound manuscript, 1856).

Chaddock, Robert E., *Ohio Before 1850: A Study of the Early Influence of Pennsylvania and Southern Populations in Ohio* (New York: Columbia University Press, 1908).

Chase, Salmon P. ed., *The Statutes of Ohio . . . ,* 3 vols. (Cincinnati: Covey & Fairbank, 1833, 1835).

A Citizen of Ohio, *The Township Officer's and Young Clek's [sic] Assistant; Comprising the Duties of Justices of the Peace* (Columbus: T. Johnson, 1826).

Clifton, Lucille, "Beginnings of Literary Culture in Columbus, Ohio, 1812–1840." Ph.D. diss. (Ohio State University, 1948).

Clossman, Richard H., "A History of the Organization and Development of the Baptist Churches in Ohio from 1789 to 1907." Ph.D. diss. (Ohio State University, 1971).

Columbus Board of Trade, *Memorial on the Death of James M. Westwater* (Columbus: Board of Trade, 1894).

Columbus Female Seminary, *Catalogue* (Columbus: Hazewell, 1845, 1846).

Columbus First Presbyterian Church, *One Hundredth Anniversary* (Columbus: n.p., 1905).

Columbus Gas Light and Coke Company, *Act of Incorporation and By-laws* (Columbus: Osgood, Blake and Knapp, 1854).

Columbus Insurance Company, *Instructions . . . for the use and direction of their agents* (Columbus: C. Scott & Co., 1845).

Columbus Jewish Historical Society, *1992 Family Portrait Album* (Columbus: The Society, 1992).

Conte, Jeanne, *German Village* (Woodland Park, Colo.: Mountain Automation Corp., 1994).

Coyle, William, ed., *Ohio Authors and Their Books* (Cleveland: World Publishing, 1962).

Cummings, Abbott L., "The Alfred Kelley House" (typewritten, 1948).

Deshler, John G., *Early History of Columbus* (Columbus: Wm. P. Zinn, 1919).

Disney, David T., *Address Delivered at the Celebration of Columbus Lodge No. 9, I.O.O.F.* (Columbus: C. Scott, 1841).

Dodds, Gilbert F., *Central Market House* (Columbus: Franklin County Historical Society, 1967).

Dorn, Helen P., "Samuel Medary: Politician, Statesman, and Journalist." Master's thesis (Miami University, 1927).

Felter, Harvey W., Jr., *History of the Eclectic Medical Institute* (Cincinnati: Alumni Association, 1902).

Fess, Simeon D., *Ohio, A Four-Volume Reference Library on The History Of A Great State* (Chicago: Lewis Publishing, 1937).

Fisher, Dudley T., *A Short History of the Columbus Cadets* (Columbus: n.p., 1924).

Flood, Charles B., and E. Burke Fisher, *The Convention and Its Men* (Columbus: Medary, 1850).

Fox, Stephen C., *The Group Bases of Ohio Political Behavior, 1803–1848* (New York: Garland Publishing, 1989).

Franklin County Historical Society, *Historic Landmarks of Columbus and Franklin County* (Columbus: n.p., 1953).

Free Soil Party, Ohio, *Address and Proceedings of the State Independent Free Territory Convention* (Cincinnati: Herald Office, 1848).

Frontiers of America, Columbus Chapter, *Advancement: Negroes' Contribution in Franklin County, 1803–1953* (Columbus: Columbus Chapter of the Frontiers of America, 1953).

Galbreath, Charles B., *History of Ohio,* 5 vols. (Chicago: American Historical Society, 1925).

Garrett, Betty with Edward R. Lentz, *Columbus, America's Crossroads* (Tulsa: Continental Heritage Press, 1980).

Gieck, Jack, *A Photo Album of Ohio's Canal Era, 1825–1913* (Kent: Kent State University Press, 1988).

Gilkey, Elliot H., *The Hundred Year Book: A Hand-Book of the Public Men and Public Institutions of Ohio, 1787–1901* (Columbus: Fred J. Heer, 1901).

Green Lawn Cemetery, *Report of the Trustees* (Columbus: Ohio State Journal Print., 1849).

Hancock, Harold, "The History of Westerville, Ohio" (typewritten, 1973).

Hansen, Ann Natalie, *Westward the Winds, Being Some of the Main Currents of Life in Ohio, 1788–1873* (Columbus: Sign of the Cock, 1974).

Hayes, Ben, *Columbus Mayors* (Columbus: Columbus Citizen-Journal, 1975).

Hickok, Charles T., "The Negro in Ohio, 1802–1870." Ph.D. diss. (Western Reserve University, 1896).

Hollins, Dennis C., "A Black Voice of Antebellum Ohio: A Rhetorical Analysis of the *Palladium of Liberty,* 1843–1844." Ph.D. diss. (Ohio State University, 1978).

Holt, Edgar A., *Party Politics in Ohio, 1840–1850* (Columbus: F. J. Heer Printing Co., 1930).

Hooper, Osman C., *History of Columbus Ohio* (Columbus: Memorial Publishing, n.d.).

———, *History of Ohio Journalism, 1793–1933* (Columbus: Spahr & Glenn Co., 1933).

Hoster, Jay, and Christine Hayes, compilers, *The Ben Hayes Scrapbook* (Columbus: Ravine Books, 1991).

Howe, Henry, *Historical Collections of Ohio,* 2 vols. (Cincinnati: Derby, Bradley & Co., 1847).

Howells, William Cooper, *Recollections of Life in Ohio, From 1813 to 1840* (Cincinnati: Robert Clarke, 1895).

Hunker, Henry L., *Industrial Evolution of Columbus, Ohio* (Columbus: College of Commerce and Administration, Ohio State University, 1958).

Ingraham, James L., *A History of Central Presbyterian Church* (Columbus: n.p., 1991).

James, Felix, *The American Addition: History of a Black Community* (Washington, D.C.: University Press of America, 1979).

Jenkins, Warren, *The Ohio Gazetteer and Traveller's Guide* (Columbus: Whiting, 1841).

Jones, Emma, ed., *Correspondence of the late James Kilbourne* (Columbus: Tibbetts, 1913).

Jones, John W., *Manual and History of the Ohio State School for the Deaf* (Columbus: School Printing Department, 1911).

Jones, Robert L., *History of Agriculture in Ohio to 1880* (Kent: Kent State University Press, 1983).

Jordan, Philip D., *The National Road* (Indianapolis: Bobbs-Merrill Co., 1948).

Kappes, Rev. William E., "History of the First Catholics in Columbus, Ohio" (typewritten, 1975).

King, Rufus, *Ohio: First Fruits of the Ordinance of 1787* (Boston: Houghton Mifflin Co., 1888).

Klauprecht, Emil, *German Chronicle in the History of the Ohio Valley* (Bowie, Md.: Heritage Books, 1992).

Knepper, George W., *Ohio and Its People* (Kent: Kent State University Press, 1989).

Knittle, Rhea Mansfield, *Early Ohio Taverns* (Ashland, Ohio: Privately published, 1937).

Knopf, Richard C., *History of the Ohio State School for the Blind, 1837–1997* (Columbus: n.p., 1997).

Kohl, Susanne A., *Wilhelm Schmidt* (Bowie, Md.: Heritage Books, 1995).

Lee, Alfred E., *History of the City of Columbus,* 2 vols. (New York: Munsell, 1892).

Lentz, Ed, *As It Were: Stories of Old Columbus* (Delaware, Ohio: Red Mountain Press, 1998).

Lewis, William G. W., *Biography of Samuel Lewis* (Cincinnati: Methodist Book Concern, 1857).

Lossing, B. J., *A Pictorial Description of Ohio* (New York: Ensigns & Thayer, 1849).

Mark, Mary Louise, "Negroes in Columbus." Master's thesis (Ohio State University Press, 1928).

Marshall, Carrington T., ed., *A History of the Courts and Lawyers of Ohio*, 4 vols. (New York: American Historical Society, 1934).

Marsten, Francis E., *After Eighty Years, 80th Anniversary of the First Presbyterian Church* (Columbus: A. H. Smythe, 1886).

Martin, William T., *History of Franklin County* (Columbus: Follett, Foster, 1858).

Maxwell, Fay, *Early German Village History* (Columbus: Ohio Genealogy Center, 1971).

———, *History of German Village* (Worthington: Ohio Genealogy Center, 1971).

———, *Irish Refugee Tract Abstract Data* (Columbus: Ohio Genealogy Center, 1974).

McCabe, Lida Rose, *Don't You Remember?* (Columbus: A. H. Smythe, 1884).

McCormick, Robert, and Jennie McCormick, *Probing Worthington's Heritage,* vol. 1 (Worthington: Cottonwood Publications, 1990).

McCormick, Virginia E., *Scioto Company Descendants* (Worthington: Cottonwood Publications, 1995).

McCormick, Virginia E., and Robert W. McCormick, *New Englanders on the Ohio Frontier: Migration and Settlement of Worthington, Ohio* (Kent: Kent State University Press, 1998).

McNamara, Anna Marie, "The Catholic Church in Ohio (1830–1840)." Master's thesis (Ohio State University, 1935).

Minor, Richard C., "The Negro in Columbus, Ohio." Ph.D. diss. (Ohio State University, 1936).

Monkkonen, Eric H., *The Dangerous Class: Crime and Poverty in Columbus, Ohio, 1860–1885* (Cambridge: Harvard University Press, 1975).

Moore, Opha, *History of Franklin County,* 3 vols. (Topeka: Historical Publishing, 1930).

Moore, William E., *History of the Second Presbyterian Church* (Columbus: n.p., 1889).

Neely, Ruth, ed., *Women of Ohio,* 3 vols. (Cincinnati: S. J. Clarke Publishing, 1939).

Niven, John, *Salmon P. Chase: A Biography* (New York: Oxford University Press, 1995).

Niven, John, et al., *The Salmon P. Chase Papers,* vol. 1 (Kent: Kent State University Press, 1993).

Obetz, Genevieve M., *The First Regular Baptist Church and Other Baptist Churches of Columbus and Central Ohio 1825–1884* (Columbus: Franklin County Genealogical Society, 1984).

Ohio Anti-Slavery Society, *Memorial of the Ohio Anti-Slavery Society to the General Assembly of the State of Ohio* (Cincinnati: Pugh & Dodd, 1838).

Ohio State Convention of the Colored Citizens of Ohio, *Minutes and Addresses of the State Convention of the Colored Citizens of Ohio, January 10 to 13, 1849* (Oberlin: J. M. Fitch, 1849).

———, *Minutes of the State Convention . . . and An Address to the Constitutional Convention of Ohio* (Columbus: E. Glover, 1851).

Ohio Women's Convention, *Proceedings of the Ohio Women's Convention held at Salem, April 19th and 20th, 1850* (Cleveland: Snead & Cowles' Press, 1850).

Okey, George B., and John H. Morton, *The Constitutions of Ohio of 1802 and 1851* (Columbus: Nevins and Myers, 1873).

Parham, William H., and Jeremiah A. Brown, *An Official History of the Most Worshipful Grand Lodge Free and Accepted Masons for the State of Ohio* (n.p.: 1906).

Pearson, F. B., and J. D. Harlor, eds., *Ohio History Sketches* (Columbus: Fred J. Heer, 1903).

Peattie, Roderick, ed., *Columbus, Ohio: An Analysis of a City's Development* (Columbus: Chamber of Commerce, 1930).

Peters, William E., *Ohio Lands and Their History*, 3d ed. (Athens, Ohio: W. E. Peters, 1930).

Pinta, Emil R., *A History of Psychiatry at The Ohio State University 1847–1993* (Columbus: Ohio State University, 1994).

Prugh, Daniel F., ed., *Goodale Park Centennial 1851–1951* (Columbus: Stoneman Press, 1951).

Quillin, Frank U., *The Color Line in Ohio: A History of Race Prejudice in a Typically Northern State* (Ann Arbor: George Wahr, 1913).

Randall, Emilius, and Daniel J. Ryan, *History of Ohio: The Rise and Progress of an American State*, vol. 3 (New York: Century History Co., 1912).

Raphael, Marc Lee, *Jews and Judaism in a Midwestern Community: Columbus, Ohio, 1840–1875* (Columbus: Ohio Historical Society, 1979).

Ratcliffe, Donald J., *Party Spirit in a Frontier Republic: Democratic Politics in Ohio 1793–1821* (Columbus: Ohio State University Press, 1998).

Rings, Blanche, comp., *Franklin County, Ohio, Wills, 1803–1864* (Columbus: n.p., n.d.).

Rodgers, Andrew D., III, *"Noble Fellow" William Starling Sullivant* (New York: G. P. Putnam's Sons, 1940).

Ryan, Daniel J., *A History of Ohio with Biographical Sketches of Her Governors and the Ordinance of 1787* (Columbus: A. H. Smythe, 1888).

Scheiber, Harry N., *Ohio Canal Era: A Case Study of Government and the Economy, 1820–1861* (Athens: Ohio University Press, 1968).

Schlegel, Donald M., *The Columbus City Graveyards* (Columbus: Columbus History Service, 1985).

———, *Lager and Liberty: German Brewers of Nineteenth Century Columbus* (Columbus: Schlegel, 1982).

Scott, Margaret Hiles, ed., *The First Regular Baptist Church* (Columbus: Franklin County Genealogical Society, 1984).

Shannon, Wilson, *Annual Message of the Governor of Ohio to the Thirty-Eighth General Assembly, December 3, 1839* (Columbus: Samuel Medary, 1839).

Sheatsley, Clarence V., *History of the First Lutheran Seminary of the West, 1830–1930* (Columbus: Lutheran Book Concern, 1930).

Shedd, Carlos, *Tales of Old Columbus* (Columbus: n.p., 1951).

Sheridan, Phil, *Those Wonderful Old Downtown Theaters* (Columbus: Phil Sheridan, 1978).

Siebert, Wilbur H., *The Mysteries of Ohio's Underground Railroads* (Columbus: Long's College Book Co., 1951).

Sittler, Margaret L., "The German Element in Columbus before the Civil War." Master's thesis (Ohio State University, 1932).

Smith, J. Victor, *Report of the Debates and Proceedings of the Convention for the Revision of the Constitution of the State of Ohio, 1850–1851*, 2 vols. (Columbus: Medary, 1851).

Smith, Reed W., *Samuel Medary and the* Crisis: *Testing the Limits of Press Freedom* (Columbus: Ohio State University Press, 1995).

Smith, Samuel H., *A Discourse Pronounced before the Class of Starling Medical College at the Opening of the Winter Session of 1850–51* (Columbus: Medary, 1850).

Sons of Swayne, *Mr. Justice Swayne* (Columbus: n.p., 1881).

Stanton, Edwin M., reporter, *Reports of Cases Argued and Determined in the Supreme*

Court of Ohio December Term, 1843, 1844, vols. 12 and 13 (Cincinnati: Robert Clarke, 1983).

Starling Medical College, *Catalogue of the Officers and Students of the Starling Medical College for the Session of 1848–9* (Columbus: Thrall & Reed, 1849).

State Centennial Education Committee, *Historical Sketches of the Higher Educational Institutions and also of Benevolent and Reformatory Institutions of the State of Ohio* (Columbus: n.p., 1876).

Steiner, Rowlee, "A Story of Columbus Railroads" (typewritten, 1956).

Stuart, M., *Matthew Birchard* (Columbus: Ohio Law Publishing Co., 1884).

Stuckey, Ronald L., *First Botanists of Columbus: A Sullivant Family Scrapbook* (Columbus: Zip Services, 1987).

Studer, Jacob H., *Columbus, Ohio: Its History, Resources, and Progress* (Columbus: n.p., 1873).

Sullivant, Joseph, *A Genealogy and Family Memorial* (Columbus: Ohio State Journal, 1874).

———, *To The Liberty Party in Ohio* (Columbus: n.p., 1844).

Tappan, Benjamin, *A Discourse delivered before the Historical and Philosophical Society of Ohio* (Columbus: J. R. Emrie, 1833).

Taylor, Edward Livingston, *Ohio Indians and Other Writings* (Columbus: F. J. Heer Printing Co., 1909)

Taylor, William A., *Centennial History of Columbus and Franklin County, Ohio,* 2 vols. (Chicago: S. J. Clarke Publishing, 1909).

———, *Ohio Statesmen and Hundred Year Book, From 1788 to 1892, Inclusive* (Columbus: Westbote Co., 1892).

Thomas, Robert D., ed., *Columbus Unforgettables,* 3 vols. (Columbus: Robert D. Thomas, 1983, 1986, 1991).

Trimble, Joseph M., *Semi-Centennial Address* (Columbus: Gazette Steam Printing House, 1878).

Venable, William H., *Beginnings of Literary Culture in the Ohio Valley: Historical and Biographical Sketches* (Cincinnati: Robert Clarke, 1891).

Vesey, S. A., *Franklin County at the Beginning of the Twentieth Century* (Columbus: Historical Publishing Co., 1901).

Walcutt, Charles C., Jr., "The Walcutt Family of Franklin County" (typewritten, 1929).

Walker, Timothy, *Annual Discourse Delivered before the Ohio Historical and Philosophical Society at Columbus on the 23rd of December, 1837* (Cincinnati: A. Flash, 1838).

Walley, Constance, *Six Generations: The Story of German Village* (Columbus: German Village Stories, 1991).

Weaver, Don E., *First Baptist Church, Columbus, Ohio, 1824–1974* (Columbus: n.p., n.d.).

Weber, Scott T., *The Faces of Old Dublin* (Dublin, Ohio: Schanachie Publications, 1993).

Weisenberger, Francis P., *The Passing Of the Frontier 1825–1850,* vol. 3 of Carl Wittke, ed., *The History of the State of Ohio* (Columbus: Ohio State Archaeological and Historical Society, 1941).

Wheeler, Henry F., *A Brief History and Description of Franklin County, to Accompany Wheeler's Map* (Columbus: Wright & Legg, 1842?).

White, Ruth Young, ed., *We Too Built Columbus* (Columbus: Stoneman Press, 1936).

Wilcox, James A., *An historical sketch of Trinity Church, Columbus, Ohio, from 1817 to 1876* (Columbus: Nevins & Myers, 1976).

Wilhelm, Hubert G. H., *The Origin and Distribution of Settlement Groups: Ohio 1850* (Athens, Ohio: n.p., 1982).

Wilkerson, Major James, *Wilkerson's History of his Travels and Labors in the United States as a Missionary* (Columbus: n.p., 1861).

Williams, Charles R., ed., *Diary and Letters of Rutherford Birchard Hayes,* vol. 1 (Columbus: Ohio State Archaeological and Historical Society, 1922).

Williams, Daniel J., *The Welsh of Columbus, Ohio: A Study in Adaptation and Assimilation* (Oshkosh, Wis.: Privately published, 1913).

Williams, Samuel W., *Pictures of Early Methodism in Ohio* (Cincinnati: Jennings and Graham, 1909).

Williams Brothers, *History of Franklin and Pickaway Counties, Ohio* (n.p.: Williams Bros., 1880).

Wilson, Joseph M., "History of the First Presbyterian Church, Columbus," *Presbyterian Historical Almanac and Annual Remembrances,* vol. 5 (Philadelphia: Joseph M. Wilson, 1863).

Wolf, Donna M., "Irish Immigrants in Ohio" (typewritten, 1996).

Politics

Blight, David W., and Brooks D. Simpson, *Union and Emancipation: Essays on Politics and Race in the Civil War Era* (Kent: Kent State University Press, 1997).

Brock, William, *Parties and Political Conscience: American Dilemmas 1840–1850* (Millwood, N.Y.: KTO Press, 1979).

Brown, Jeffrey P., "Frontier Politics: The Evolution of a Political Society in Ohio, 1788–1814." Ph.D. diss. (University of Illinois at Urbana-Champaign, 1979).

Brown, Jeffrey P., and Andrew R. L. Cayton, eds., *The Pursuit of Public Power: Political Culture in Ohio, 1787–1861* (Kent: Kent State University Press, 1994).

Cleaves, Freeman, *Old Tippecanoe: William Henry Harrison and His Time* (New York: Charles Scribner's Sons, 1939).

Curtin, Michael F., *Ohio Politics Almanac* (Kent: Kent State University Press, 1996).

Dawson, Moses, *A historical narrative of the civil and military services of Major-General William H. Harrison* (Cincinnati: M. Dawson, 1824).

Dawson, Moses, *A historical narrative of the civil and military services of Major-General William H. Harrison* (Cincinnati: M. Dawson, 1824).

Fischer, Roger A., *Tippecanoe and Trinkets Too: The Material Culture of American Campaigns, 1828–1984* (Urbana: University of Illinois Press, 1988).

Goebel, Dorothy Burne, *William Henry Harrison: A Political Biography* (Indianapolis: Historical Bureau of the Indiana Library and Historical Department, 1926).

Green, James A., *William Henry Harrison: His Life and Times* (Richmond, Va.: Garrett and Massie, 1941).

Gunderson, Robert G., *The Log Cabin Campaign* (Lexington: University of Kentucky Press, 1957).

Hammond, John L., *The Politics of Benevolence: Revival Religion and American Voting Behavior* (Norwood, N.J.: Ablex Publishing Corp., 1979).

Hildreth, Richard, *The People's Presidential Candidate; or The Life of William Henry Harrison of Ohio* (Boston: Weeks, Jordan and Co., 1840).

Holt, Michael F., *The Rise and Fall of the American Whig Party,* (New York: Oxford University Press, 1999).

Howe, Daniel W., *The Political Culture of the American Whigs* (Chicago: University of Chicago Press, 1979).

Maizlish, Stephen E., *The Triumph of Sectionalism: The Transformation of Ohio Politics, 1844–1856* (Kent: Kent State University Press, 1983).

McCormick, Richard P., *The Presidential Game: The Origins of American Presidential Politics* (New York: Oxford University Press, 1982).

Miller, John G., *The Great Convention: Description of the Convention of the People of*

Ohio, held at Columbus, on the 21st, and 22nd February 1840 (Columbus: Cutler & Wright, 1840).

Norton, Anthony B., *The Great Revolution of 1840: Reminiscences of the Log Cabin and Hard Cider Campaign* (Mount Vernon, Ohio: A. B. Norton, 1888).

———, ed., *Tippecanoe Songs of the Log Cabin Boys and Girls of 1840* (Mount Vernon, Ohio: A. B. Norton, 1888).

Peterson, Norma Lois, *The Presidencies of William Henry Harrison & John Tyler* (Lawrence: University Press of Kansas, 1989).

Pletcher, David M., *The Diplomacy of Annexation: Texas, Oregon, and the Mexican War* (Columbia: University of Missouri Press, 1973).

Reichley, A. James, *The Life of the Parties: A History of American Political Parties* (New York: Free Press, 1992).

Saxton, Alexander P., *The Rise and Fall of the White Republic: Class Politics and Mass Culture in Nineteenth-Century America* (London and New York: Verso, 1990).

Schlesinger, Arthur M., Jr., ed., *History of American Presidential Elections, 1789–1968*, vol. 1 (New York: Chelsea House, 1971).

Sharp, James R., *The Jacksonians Versus the Banks: Politics in the States After 1837* (New York: Columbia University Press, 1970).

Silbey, Joel H., *The American Political Nation, 1838–1893* (Stanford: Stanford University Press, 1991).

Smith, Theodore C., *The Liberty and Free Soil Parties in the Northwest* (New York: Longmans, Green, 1897; rep. New York: Arno Press, 1969).

Whig Party (Ohio) Central Committee, "1844 Broadside."

Winkle, Kenneth J., *The Politics of Community: Migration and Politics in Antebellum Ohio* (New York: Cambridge University Press, 1988).

Women On and Off the Pedestal

Alcott, William A., *The Young Wife, or Duties of Woman in the Marriage Relation*, 2d ed. (Boston: George W. Light, 1837).

Basch, Norma, *In the Eyes of the Law: Women, Marriage, and Property in Nineteenth-Century New York* (Ithaca: Cornell University Press, 1982).

Baym, Nina, *American Women Writers and the Work of History. 1790–1860* (New Brunswick: Rutgers University Press, 1995).

———, *Woman's Fiction: A Guide to Novels by and about Women in America, 1820–1870* (Ithaca: Cornell University Press, 1978).

Beecher, Catharine E., *An Essay on Slavery and Abolitionism with Reference to the Duty of American Females* (Philadelphia: Henry Perkins, 1837).

———, *The Evils Suffered by American Women and American Children: The Causes and the Remedy* (New York: Harper & Brothers, 1846).

———, *Letters to Persons Who Are Engaged in Domestic Service* (New York: Leavett & Trow, 1842).

———, *A Treatise on Domestic Economy for the Use of Young Ladies at Home and at School* (Boston: Thomas H. Webb & Co., 1842).

Berg, Barbara J., *The Remembered Gate: Origins of American Feminism: The Woman and the City, 1800–1860* (New York: Oxford University Press, 1978).

Boydston, Jeanne, *Home and Work: Housework, Wages, and the Ideology of Labor in the Early Republic* (New York: Oxford University Press, 1990).

Bradley, Harriet, *Men's Work, Women's Work* (Cambridge, England: Polity Press, 1989).

Calhoun, Arthur W., *A Social History of the American Family from Colonial Times to the Present*, vol. 2 (Cleveland: Arthur H. Clarke Co., 1918).

Coxe, Margaret, *Claims of the Country on American Females*, 2 vols. (Columbus: I. N. Whiting, 1842).

————, *The Life of John Wycliffe* (Columbus: Isaac N. Whiting, 1840).

————, *Woman: Her Station Providentially Appointed* (Columbus: I. N. Whiting, 1848).

————, *The Young Lady's Companion: In A Series of Letters* (Columbus: I. N. Whiting, 1839).

Degler, Carl, *At Odds: Woman and the Family in America from the Revolution to the Present* (New York: Oxford University Press, 1980).

De Rham, E., *How Could She Do That? A Study of the Female Convict* (New York: Clarkson, Potter, 1969).

Donnelly, Mabel Collins, *The American Victorian Woman: The Myth And the Reality* (New York: Greenwood Press, 1986).

Epstein, Barbara Leslie, *The Politics of Domesticity: Women, Evangelism, and Temperance in Nineteenth-Century America* (Middletown: Wesleyan University Press, 1981).

Ginzberg, Lori D., *Women and the Work of Benevolence: Morality, Politics, and Class in the Nineteenth-Century United States.* (New Haven: Yale University Press, 1990).

Hanaford, Phoebe A., *The Daughters of America, or Women of the Century* (Augusta, Maine: True and Co., 1883).

Hersey, Thomas, *The Midwife's Practical Directory; or Woman's Confidential Friend* (Columbus: Clepp, Gillett, 1834).

Hersh, Blanche Glassman, *The Slavery of Sex: Feminist Abolitionists in America* (Urbana: University of Illinois Press, 1978).

Hoffert, Sylvia D., *When Hens Crow: The Women's Rights Movement in Antebellum America* (Bloomington: Indiana University Press, 1995).

Hymowitz, Carol, and Michaele Weissman, *A History of Women in America* (Toronto: Bantam Books, 1978).

Isenberg, Nancy G., *Sex and Citizenship in Antebellum America* (Chapel Hill: University of North Carolina Press, 1998).

James, Edward T., ed., *Notable American Women, 1607–1950,* vol. 2 (Cambridge: Belknap Press of Harvard University Press, 1971).

Jones, Ann, *Women Who Kill* (New York: Holt, Rinehart, and Winston, 1980).

Kessler-Harris, Alice, *Out to Work: A History of Wage-Earning Women in the United States* (Oxford: Oxford University Press, 1982).

Lerner, Gerda, *The Female Experience* (Indianapolis: Bobbs-Merrill, 1977).

Mansfield, Edward D., *The Legal Rights, Liabilities and Duties of Women* (Cincinnati: William H. Moore & Co., 1845).

Melder, Keith E., *Beginnings of Sisterhood: The American Woman's Rights Movement, 1800–1850* (New York: Schocken Books, 1977).

Neely, Ruth, ed., *Women of Ohio,* 3 vols. (Columbus: S. J. Clarke Publishing Co., n.d.).

O'Connor, Lillian, *Pioneer Women Orators* (New York: Columbia University Press, 1954).

Palmer, Thomas H., *The Moral Instructor; or Culture Of The Heart, Affections, And Intellect While Learning To Read* (Boston: Ticknor, Reed, and Fields, 1851).

Rabkin, Peggy A., *Fathers to Daughters: The Legal Foundations of Female Emancipation* (Westport, Conn.: Greenwood Press, 1980).

Riley, Glenda Lou Gates, "From Chattel to Challenger, the Changing Image of the American Woman, 1828–1848." Ph.D. diss. (Ohio State University, 1967).

Ryan, Mary P., *Cradle of the Middle Class: The Family in Oneida County, New York, 1790–1865* (Cambridge: Cambridge University Press, 1981).

————, *Womanhood in America,* 3d ed. (New York: Franklin Watts, 1983).

————, *Women in Public: Between Banners and Ballots, 1825–1880* (Baltimore: Johns Hopkins University Press, 1990).

Salmon, Marylynn, *Women and the Law of Property in Early America* (Chapel Hill: University of North Carolina Press, 1986).

Sigourney, Lydia H., *Letters to Mothers,* 6th ed. (New York: Harper & Brothers, 1845).

Sklar, Kathryn Kish, *Catharine Beecher: A Study in American Domesticity* (New Haven: Yale University Press, 1973).

Smith-Rosenberg, Carroll, *Disorderly Conduct: Visions of Gender in Victorian America* (New York: Alfred A. Knopf, 1985).

Theriot, Nancy M., *The Biosocial Construction of Femininity: Mothers and Daughters in Nineteenth-Century America* (New York: Greenwood Press: 1988).

Tiffany, Francis, *Life of Dorothea Lynde Dix,* rep. of 1918 ed. (Ann Arbor: Plutarch Press, 1971).

Tuana, Nancy, *The Less Noble Sex: Scientific, Religious, and Philosophical Conceptions of Woman's Nature* (Bloomington: Indiana University Press, 1993).

Warbasse, Elizabeth Bowles, *The Changing Legal Rights of Married Women, 1800–1861* (New York: Garland Publishing, 1987).

Weaver, G. S., *The Heart of the World: or, Home and Its Wide Work* (Columbus: Potts, Leach & Co., 1883).

Wertheimer, Barbara Mayer, *We Were There: The Story of Working Women in America* (New York: Pantheon Books, 1977).

Whitlock, Marta, ed., *Women in Ohio History* (Columbus: Ohio Historical Society, 1976).

Yellin, Jean Fagan, *The Abolitionist Sisterhood: Women's Political Culture in Antebellum America* (Ithaca: Cornell University Press, 1994).

————, *Women & Sisters: The Antislavery Feminists in American Culture* (New Haven: Yale University Press, 1989).

Asylums and Poorhouses

Best, Harry, *Blindness and the Blind in the United States* (New York: Macmillan, 1934).

Browne, William A. F., *What asylums were, are, and ought to be,* rep. of 1837 ed. (London: Routledge, 1991).

Deutsch, Albert, *The Mentally Ill in America: A History of Their Care and Treatment from Colonial Times* (Garden City, N.Y.: Doubleday, Doran & Co., 1937).

Ferguson, Philip M., *Abandoned to Their Fate: Social Policy and Practice toward Severely Retarded People in America, 1820–1920* (Philadelphia: Temple University Press, 1994).

Gamwell, Lynn, and Nancy Tomes, *Madness in America: Cultural and Medical Perceptions of Mental Illness before 1914* (Ithaca: Cornell University Press, 1995).

Gollaher, David, *Voice for the Mad: The Life of Dorothea Dix* (New York: Free Press, 1995).

Grob, Gerald, *Mental Institutions in America: Social Policy to 1875* (New York: Free Press, 1973).

Hoge, James, Noah H. Swayne, and William M. Awl, *Report of the Trustees, appointed by the last General Assembly to collect information respecting the education of the blind* (Columbus: James B. Gardiner, 1836).

Katz, Michael B., *In the Shadow of the Poorhouse: A Social History of Welfare in America* (New York: Basic Books, 1986).

Knopf, Richard C., *History of the Ohio State School for the Blind, 1837–1997* (n.p.: 1997).

Ohio Institution for the Education of the Deaf and Dumb, *Annual Reports.* (Columbus, 1827–58).

Ohio Institution for the Instruction of the Blind, *Annual Report of the Trustees* (Columbus, 1839, 1843).

————, *General Information* (Columbus: Cutler and Pilsbury, 1838).

Ohio Lunatic Asylum, *Reports of the Directors and Superintendent of the Ohio Lunatic Asylum,* vols. 1–12 (Columbus: Medary, 1839–50).

Parsons, Samuel, William M. Awl, and Samuel F. MacCracken, *Report of The Directors To Whom Was Committed the Charge of Erecting A Lunatic Asylum For The State of Ohio* (Columbus: n.p., 1838).

Parsons, Samuel, Samuel Spangler, and Aden G. Hibbs, *Annual Report of the Directors of the Ohio Lunatic Asylum* (Columbus: Samuel Medary, 1839).

Rothman, David J., *The Discovery of the Asylum: Social Order and Disorder in the New Republic* (Boston: Little, Brown, 1971).

Scull, Andrew T., ed., *Madhouses, Mad-Doctors, and Madmen: The Social History of Psychiatry in the Victorian Era* (Philadelphia: University of Pennsylvania Press, 1981).

Trimble, Allen, James Hoge, and Gustavus Swan, *First Annual Report of the Board of Trustees of the Ohio Institution for the Education of the Deaf and Dumb* (Columbus: n.p., 1827).

Welling, Rev. D. S., *Information for the People: or The Asylums of Ohio* (Pittsburgh: George Parkin & Co., 1851).

The Ohio Penitentiary and the Penal System

Allen, Harry E., and Clifford E. Simonsen, *Corrections in America: An Introduction* (Beverly Hills: Glencoe Press, 1975).

Andrews, William, *Old-Time Punishments* (Williamstown, Mass.: Corner House Publishers, 1980).

Beaumont, Gustave de, and Alexis de Tocqueville, *On the Penitentiary System in the United States and Its Application in France.* Trans. Francis Lieber (Philadelphia: Carey, Lea & Blanchard, 1833).

Dewey, Laurin, *Special Report of the Warden of the Ohio Penitentiary on Prisons and Prison Discipline to the Forty-Ninth General Assembly of the State of Ohio* (Columbus: Charles Scott, 1851).

Dix, Dorothea, *Remarks on Prisons and Prison Discipline in the United States,* 2d ed. (Philadelphia: Joseph Kite & Co., 1845).

Dumm, Thomas L., *Democracy and Punishment: Disciplinary Origins of the United States* (Madison: University of Wisconsin Press, 1987).

Dwight, Louis, *First Report of the Board of Managers of the Prison Discipline Society* (Boston: T. R. Marvin, 1827).

Dyer, Benjamin F., *History of the Ohio Penitentiary, Annex and Prisoners* (Columbus: Ohio Penitentiary Print., 1891).

Finley, James B., *Memorials of Prison Life* (Cincinnati: L. Swormstedt & J. H. Power, 1850).

Fogle, H. M., *The Palace of Death or The Ohio Penitentiary Annex* (Columbus: H. M. Fogle, 1908).

Fornshell, Marvin E., *The Historical and Illustrated Ohio Penitentiary* (Columbus: Marvin E. Fornshell, 1903).

Freedman, Estelle B., *Their Sisters' Keepers: Women's Prison Reform in America, 1830–1930* (Ann Arbor: University of Michigan Press, 1981).

Friedman, Lawrence M., *Crime and Punishment in American History* (New York: Basic Books, 1993).

Giallobardo, Rose, *Society of Women; A Study of a Women's Prison* (New York: John Wiley & Sons, 1966).

Gildemeister, Glen A., *Prison Labor and Convict Competition with Free Workers in Industrializing America, 1840–1890* (New York: Garland Publishing, 1987).

Gray, Francis C., *Prison Discipline in America,* rep. of 1847 ed. (Montclair, N.J.: Patterson Smith, 1973).

Hicks, Clara Belle, *The History of Penal Institutions in Ohio* (Columbus: F. J. Heer, 1924).

Hirsch, Adam J., *The Rise of the Penitentiary: Prisons and Punishment in Early America* (New Haven: Yale University Press, 1992).

Lewis, Orlando F., *The Development of American Prisons and Prison Customs, 1776– 1845* (New York: Prison Association of New York, 1922).

Lewis, W. David, *From Newgate to Dannemora: The Rise of the Penitentiary in New York, 1796–1848* (Ithaca: Cornell University Press, 1965).

Matthews, J. H., *Historical Reminiscences of the Ohio Penitentiary 1835 to 1884* (Columbus: Chas. M. Cott, 1884).

McEwen, R. S., *The mysteries, miseries, and rascalities of the Ohio Penitentiary* (Columbus: J. P. Santmyer, 1856).

McKelvey, Blake, *American Prisons: A Study in American Social History Prior to 1915* (Chicago: University of Chicago Press, 1936).

Morgan, Dan, *Historical Lights and Shadows of the Ohio State Penitentiary* (Columbus: Ohio Penitentiary Print., 1893).

Morris, Norvel, and David J. Rothman, eds., *The Oxford History of the Prison* (New York: Oxford University Press, 1995).

Nussbaum, David P., "The Ohio Penitentiary." Master's thesis (Ohio State University, 1991).

Ohio General Assembly, *Report of the Joint Committee, Appointed to Examine into the State and Condition of the Penitentiary* (Columbus: Columbus Gazette, 1823).

Ohio Penitentiary, *Annual Report of the Directors and Warden of the Ohio Penitentiary, 1827–1846* (Columbus: Ohio Penitentiary Print., 1827–46).

————, *The Ohio Penitentiary and Prisoners* (Columbus: Ohio Penitentiary Print., 1888).

————, "Rules and Regulations" (Columbus, n.d.).

Philip, Cynthia Owen, *Imprisoned in America: Prison Communications, 1776 to Attica* (New York: Harper & Row, 1973).

Rafter, Nicole Hahn, *Partial Justice: Women, Prisons, and Social Control,* 2d ed. (New Brunswick, N.J.: Transaction, 1990).

Rusche, Georg, and Otto Kircheimer, *Punishment and Social Structure* (New York: Russell & Russell, 1939).

Simpson, H. G., *The Prisoners of the Ohio Penitentiary* (Columbus: Hann & Adair, 1883).

Whitcomb, David, *The life and confessions of Henry Thomas* (Columbus: C. C. & G. R. Hazewell, 1846).

Williams, Vergil L., *Dictionary of American Penology* (Westport, Conn.: Greenwood Press, 1979).

Wines, Enoch C., and Theodore W. Dwight, *Report on the Prisons and Reformatories of the United States and Canada* (Albany, N.Y.: Van Benthuysen & Sons, 1867).

Columbus Looks Westward

Bergeron, Paul H., *The Presidency of James K. Polk* (Lawrence: University Press of Kansas, 1987).

Columbus, Ohio Citizens, *Report on the territory of Oregon, by a committee, appointed at a meeting of the citizens of Columbus, to collect information in relation thereto* (Columbus: Ohio Statesman, 1843).

Haynes, Sam W., *James K. Polk and the Expansionist Impulse* (New York: Longman, 1997).

Hietala, Thomas R., *Manifest Destiny: Anxious Aggrandizement in Late Jacksonian America* (Ithaca: Cornell University Press, 1985).

Johannsen, Robert W., *To the Halls of the Montezumas: The Mexican War in the American Imagination* (New York: Oxford University Press, 1985).

———, et al., *Manifest Destiny and Empire: American Antebellum Expansionism* (College Station: Texas A&M University Press, 1997).

Leckie, Robert, *From Sea to Shining Sea: From the War of 1812 to the Mexican War: The Saga of America's Expansion* (New York: Harper Collins, 1993).

Merk, Frederick, *The Oregon Question: Essays in Anglo-American Diplomacy and Politics* (Cambridge: Harvard University Press, 1967).

Sellers, Charles G., *James K. Polk: Continentalist, 1843–1846* (Princeton: Princeton University Press, 1966).

Singletery, Otis A., *The Mexican War* (Chicago: University of Chicago Press, 1960).

Travelers' Accounts

Birkbeck, Morris, *Notes on a Journey in America,* 4th ed. (London: Severn & Co., 1818).

Brown, William, *America: A Four Years' Residence in the United States and Canada* (Leeds, England: Kemplay and Bolland, 1849).

Buckingham, James S., *The Eastern and Western States of America,* 3 vols. (London: Fisher, Son & Co., 1842).

Chevalier, Michael, *Society, Manners and Politics in the United States.* Trans. T. G. Bradford (Boston: Weeks, Jordan and Co., 1839).

Combe, George, *Notes on the United States of North America during a Phrenological Visit,* 2 vols. (Edinburgh: Carey & Hart, 1841).

Cox, F. A., and J. Hoby, *The Baptists in America* (New York: Leavitt, Lord & Co., 1836).

Dana, Edmund, *Geographical Sketches on the Western Country Designed for Emigrants and Settlers* (Cincinnati: Looker, Reynolds & Co., 1819).

Dickens, Charles, *American Notes for General Circulation,* 2 vols. (London: Chapman and Hall, 1842).

Eyre, John, *Travels: Comprising a Journey from England to Ohio* (New York: R. Craighead, 1851).

Flint, James, *Letters from America* (Edinburgh: Tait, 1822).

Hamilton, Thomas, *Men and Manners In America* (Philadelphia: Carey, Lea & Blanchard, 1833).

Lyell, Sir Charles, *A second visit to the United States of North America,* 2 vols. (New York: Harper & Brothers, 1849).

———, *Travels in North America in the Years 1841–2,* 2 vols. (New York: Wiley and Putnam, 1845).

Marryat, Capt. Frederick, *A Diary In America with Remarks on its Institutions,* 3 vols. (London: Longman, Brown, Green and Longmans, 1842).

Martineau, Harriet, *Retrospect of Western Travel,* 2 vols. (London: Saunders and Otley, 1838).

———, *Society in America,* 2 vols. (London: Saunders and Otley, 1837).

McNeil, Samuel, *McNeil's Travels in 1849, To, Through, And From The Gold Regions In California* (Columbus: Scott and Bascom, 1850).

Murray, Charles A., *Travels in North America,* 2 vols. (London: Richard Bentley, 1839).

Pulszky, Francis and Theresa, *White, Red, Black: Sketches of American Society,* 2 vols. (New York: Redfield, 1853).

Reed, Andrew, and James Matheson, *A Narrative of the Visit to the American Churches,* 2 vols. (New York: Harper & Brothers, 1835).

Scott, Rev. James L., *A Journal of A Missionary Tour* (Providence, R.I.: Privately published, 1843).

Sturge, Joseph, *A Visit to the United States in 1841* (London: Hamilton, Adams, 1842).

Tocqueville, Alexis de, *Journey to America*. Trans. George Lawrence (Garden City, N.Y.: Anchor Books, 1971).

Nineteenth-Century Books on Other Topics

Adams, Charles Francis, ed., *Memoirs of John Quincy Adams, Comprising Portions of His Diary from 1795 to 1848,* vol. 11 (Philadelphia: J. B. Lippincott, 1876).

American Anti-Slavery Society, *Annual Reports* (New York: Dorr & Butterfield, 1834–39).

Anti-Slavery Convention of American Women, *Proceedings . . . Held in the City of New York* (New York: William S. Dorr, 1837).

Bartlett, John R., *Dictionary of Americanisms* (New York: Bartlett and Welford, 1848).

Beecher, Charles, ed., *Autobiography, Correspondence, Etc., of Lyman Beecher,* 2 vols. (New York: Harper & Brothers, 1865).

Brown, Samuel R., *The Western Gazetteer* (Auburn, N.Y.: H. C. Southwick, Printers, 1817).

Chalmers, Thomas, *On Political Economy* (New York: Daniel Appleton, 1832).

Christy, David, *A Lecture on African Colonization* (Cincinnati: J. A. & V. P. James, 1849).

————, *Lectures on African Colonization, and Kindred Subjects* (Columbus: J. H. Riley & Co., 1853).

Christy's Panorama Songster (New York: William H. Murphy, n.d.)

Combe, George, *The Constitution of Man Considered in Relation to External Objects* (Boston: Allen and Ticknor, 1834).

Cooper, Anna Julia, *A Voice from the South by a Black Woman Of The South* (Xenia, Ohio: Aldine Printing House, 1892).

Dana, Edmund, *Geographical Sketches on the Western Country: designed for emigrants and settlers* (Cincinnati: Looker, Reynolds & Co., 1819).

Delany, Martin R., *The Condition, Elevation, Emigration and Destiny of the Colored People of the United States* (Philadelphia: Privately published, 1852).

Duncan, Mary Grey L., *America As I Found It* (New York: Robert Carter & Brothers, 1852).

Haskins, R. W., *History and Progress of Phrenology* (Buffalo: Steele & Peck, 1839).

Jones, J. Elizabeth, *The Young Abolitionists; or Conversations On Slavery* (Boston: Anti-Slavery Office, 1848).

Moody, Granville, *A Life's Retrospect, Autobiography of Rev. Granville Moody* (Cincinnati: Curts & Jennings, 1890).

O'Gorman, Thomas, *A History of the Roman Catholic Church in the United States* (New York: Christian Literature, 1895).

Payne, Daniel A., *History of the African Methodist Episcopal Church* (Nashville: A.M.E. Sunday-School Union, 1891; rep. Arno Press and New York Times, 1969).

Peck, John M., *A New Guide for Emigrants to the West* (Boston: Gould, Kendall & Lincoln, 1836).

Stebbins, G. B., *Facts and Opinions Touching the Real Origin, Character, and Influence of the American Colonization Society* (Boston: John P. Jewett & Co., 1853).

Twentieth-Century Books on Other Topics

Abrahams, Roger D., *Singing the Master: The Emergence of African-American Culture in the Plantation South* (New York: Penguin Books, 1992).

Abzug, Robert H., *Cosmos Crumbling: American Reform and the Religious Imagination* (New York: Oxford University Press, 1994).

Adams, Grace, and Edward Hutter, *The Mad Forties* (New York: Harper & Brothers, 1942).

Bell, Howard H., ed., *Minutes of the Proceedings of the National Negro Conventions, 1830–1864* (New York: Arno Press and New York Times, 1969).

———, "A Survey of the Negro Convention Movement, 1830–1861." Ph.D. diss. (Northwestern University, 1953).

Bender, Thomas, *Community and Social Change in America* (New Brunswick: Rutgers University Press, 1978).

Berwanger, E. H., *The Frontier Against Slavery: Western Anti-Negro Prejudice and the Slavery Extension Controversy* (Urbana: University of Illinois Press, 1967).

Blakely, William A., *American State Papers Bearing on Sunday Legislation* (New York: National Religious Liberty Association, 1911).

Blassingame, John, ed., *Slave Testimony* (Baton Rouge: Louisiana State University Press, 1977).

Blockson, Charles L., *The Underground Railroad* (New York: Prentice Hall, 1987).

Blumin, Stuart M., "Residential Mobility within the Nineteenth-Century City," in Allen F. Davis and Mark H. Haller, eds., *The Peoples of Philadelphia* (Philadelphia: Temple University Press, 1973).

———, *The Urban Threshold; growth and change in a nineteenth-century American community* (Chicago: University of Chicago Press, 1976).

Bode, Carl, ed., *American Life in the 1840s* (Garden City, N.Y.: Anchor Books, 1967).

———, *The American Lyceum: Town Meeting of the Mind* (New York: Oxford University Press, 1956).

Boyer, Paul S., *Urban Masses and Moral Order in America, 1820–1920* (Cambridge: Harvard University Press, 1978).

Branch, E. Douglas, *The Sentimental Years, 1836–1860* (New York: D. Appleton-Century, 1934).

Brown, Richard D., *Knowledge Is Power: The Diffusion of Information in Early America, 1700–1865*.

Browne, Waldo R., ed., *Barnum's Own Story* (New York: Viking Press, 1927).

Buber, Martin, *Paths in Utopia*. Trans. R. F. C. Hull (London: Routledge & Kegan Paul, 1949).

Burnham, John C., *Bad Habits* (New York: New York University Press, 1993).

Bushman, Richard L., *The Refinement of America* (New York: Alfred A. Knopf, 1992).

Carwardine, Richard J., *Evangelicals and Politics in Antebellum America* (New Haven: Yale University Press, 1993).

Cary, John H., and Julius Weinberg, eds., *The Social Fabric: American Life from 1607 to the Civil War* (Boston: Little, Brown, 1975).

Cayton, Andrew R. L., and Peter Onuf, *The Midwest and the Nation* (Bloomington: Indiana University Press, 1990).

Cochran, Thomas C., and William Miller, *The Age of Enterprise: A Social History of Industrial America* (New York: Macmillan, 1942).

Cole, Charles C., Jr., *Lion of the Forest: James B. Finley, Frontier Reformer* (Lexington: University Press of Kentucky, 1994).

Curry, Leonard P., *The Corporate City: The American City as a Political Entity, 1800–1850* (Westport, Conn.: Greenwood Press, 1997).

———, *The Free Black in Urban America in 1800–1850* (Chicago: University of Chicago Press, 1981).

Curti, Merle, *Human Nature in American Thought* (Madison: University of Wisconsin Press, 1980).

Davies, John D., *Phrenology: Fad and Science* (New Haven: Yale University Press, 1955).

D'Emilio, John, and Estelle B. Freedman, *Intimate Matters: A History of Sexuality in America* (New York: Harper & Row, 1988).

Dolan, Jay P., *Catholic Revivalism: The American Experience, 1830–1900* (Notre Dame: University of Notre Dame Press, 1978).

Doyle, Don H., *The Social Order of a Frontier Community, Jacksonville, Illinois, 1825–70* (Urbana: University of Illinois Press, 1978).

Dumond, Dwight L., ed., *Letters of James Gillespie Birney 1831–1857*, 2 vols. (New York: D. Appleton-Century Co., 1938).

Elazar, Daniel J., *Building Cities in America: Urbanization and Suburbanization in a Frontier Society* (Lanham, Md.: Hamilton Press, 1987).

Etcheson, Nicole, *The Emerging Midwest: Upland Southerners and the Political Culture of the Old Northwest, 1787–1861* (Bloomington: Indiana University Press, 1996).

Foner, Philip S., and George E. Walker, eds., *Proceedings of the Black State Conventions, 1840–1865*, 2 vols. (Philadelphia: Temple University Press, 1979–80).

Fox, Richard W., and T. Jackson Lears, eds., *The Power of Culture: Critical Essays in American History* (Chicago: University of Chicago Press, 1993).

Gara, Larry, *The Liberty Line, The Legend of the Underground Railroad* (Lexington: University of Kentucky Press, 1967).

Gilje, Paul A., ed., *Wages of Independence: Capitalism in the Early American Republic* (Madison, Wis.: Madison House, 1997).

Goldfield, David R., and Blaine A. Brownell, *Urban America* (Boston: Houghton Mifflin, 1979).

Goodman, Paul, *Of One Blood: Abolitionism and the Origins of Racial Equality* (Berkeley: University of California Press, 1998).

Gorn, Elliot J., ed., *The McGuffey Readers: Selections from the 1879 Edition* (Boston: Bedford Books, 1998).

Griffin, Clifford S., *Their Brothers' Keepers: Moral Stewardship in the United States, 1800–1865* (New Brunswick: Rutgers University Press, 1960).

Grimsted, David, *Melodrama Unveiled: American Theater and Culture, 1800–1850* (Chicago: University of Chicago Press, 1968).

———, ed., *Notions of the Americans 1820–1860* (New York: George Braziller, 1970).

Hahn, Steven, and Jonathan Prude, eds., *The Countryside in the Age of Capitalist Transformation: Essays in the Social History of Rural America* (Chapel Hill: University of North Carolina Press, 1985).

Hareven, Tamara K., ed., *Anonymous Americans: Explorations in Nineteenth-Century Social History* (Englewood Cliffs, N.J.: Prentice Hall, 1971).

Hart, James, *The Popular Book* (New York: Oxford University Press, 1950).

Heininger, Mary, et al., *A Century of Childhood, 1820–1920* (Rochester, N.Y.: Margaret Woodbury Strong Museum, 1984).

Hine, Robert V., *Community on the American Frontier* (Norman: University of Oklahoma Press, 1980).

Hiner, N. Ray, and Joseph M. Hawes, *Growing Up in America: Children in Historical Perspective* (Urbana: University of Illinois Press, 1985).

Hodge, Francis, *Yankee Theatre: The Image of America on the Stage, 1825–1850* (Austin: University of Texas Press, 1964).

Hofstadter, Richard, and Seymour M. Lipset, eds., *Turner and the Sociology of the Frontier* (New York: Basic Books, 1968).

Holmes, Oliver W., and Peter T. Rohrbach, *Stagecoach Days in the East from the Colonial Period to the Civil War* (Washington, D.C.: Smithsonian Institution Press, 1983).

Horton, James O., *Free People of Color: Inside the African American Community* (Washington, D.C.: Smithsonian Institution Press, 1993).

Horton, James O., and Lois E. Horton, *In Hope of Liberty: Culture, Community, and Protest among Northern Free Blacks, 1700–1860* (New York: Oxford University Press, 1997).

House, Madeline, Graham Storey, and Kathleen Tillotson, eds., *The Letters of Charles Dickens,* vol. 3 (Oxford: Clarendon Press, 1974).

Jacobs, James R., and Glenn Tucker, *The War of 1812* (New York: Hawthorn Books, 1969).

John, Richard R., *Spreading the News: The American Postal System from Franklin to Morse* (Cambridge: Harvard University Press, 1995).

Kammen, Michael, *Mystic Chords of Memory: The Transformation of Tradition in American Culture* (New York: Alfred A. Knopf, 1991).

Kamphoefner, Walter D., Wolfgang Helbich, and Ulrike Sommer, *News from the Land of Freedom: German Immigrants Write Home* (Ithaca: Cornell University Press, 1991).

Katz, Michael, Michael J. Doucet, and Mark J. Stern, *The Social Organization of Early Industrial Capitalism* (Cambridge: Harvard University Press, 1982).

Kunhardt, Philip B., Jr., Philip B. Kunhardt III, and Peter W. Kunhardt, *P. T. Barnum: America's Greatest Showman* (New York: Knopf, 1995).

Lacour-Gayet, *Everyday Life in the United States before the Civil War 1830–1860.* Trans. Mary Ilford (New York: Frederick Unger Publishing Co., 1969).

Larkin, Oliver, *Art and Life in America* (New York: Rinehart & Co., 1949).

Levine, Bruce, *Half Slave and Half Free: The Roots of Civil War* (New York: Hill and Wang, 1992).

Lott, Eric, *Love and Theft: Blackface Minstrelsy and the American Working Class* (New York: Oxford University Press, 1993).

Luedtke, Luther S., ed., *Making America: The Society and Culture of the United States* (Chapel Hill: University of North Carolina Press, 1992).

Marty, Martin E., *Pilgrims in Their Own Land: 500 Years of Religion in America* (Boston: Little, Brown and Co., 1984).

Masur, Louis P., *Rites of Execution: Capital Punishment and the Transformation of American Culture, 1776–1865* (New York: Oxford University Press, 1989).

Matthews, Jean V., *Toward a New Society: American Thought and Culture, 1800–1830* (Boston: Twayne Publishers, 1991).

McPhail, Clark, *The Myth of the Madding Crowd* (New York: Aldine De Gruyter, 1991).

McWilliams, Carey, *North from Mexico: The Spanish Speaking People of the United States* (Philadelphia: Lippincott, 1949).

Miller, William L., *Arguing About Slavery* (New York: Alfred A. Knopf, 1996).

Minnigerode, Meade, *The Fabulous Forties 1840–1850* (New York: G. P. Putnam's Sons, 1924).

Miyakaawa, T. Scott, *Protestants and Pioneers: Individualism and Conformity on the American Frontier* (Chicago: University of Chicago Press, 1964).

Moody, Richard, ed., *Dramas from the American Theatre 1762–1909* (Cleveland: World Publishing Co., 1966).

Mott, Frank Luther, *Golden Multitudes: The Story of Best Sellers in the United States* (New York: Macmillan, 1947).

Novak, William J., *The People's Welfare: Law and Regulation in Nineteenth-Century America* (Chapel Hill: University of North Carolina Press, 1996).

Park, Robert E., Ernest W. Burgess, and Roderick D. McKenzie, *The City* (Chicago: University of Chicago Press, 1925).

Perry, Lewis, *Boats Against the Current: American Culture Between Revolution and Modernity, 1820–1860* (New York: Oxford University Press, 1993).

Pessen, Edward, *Riches, Class, and Power before the Civil War* (Lexington, Mass: D. C. Heath, 1973).

Reiner, Jacqueline S., *From Virtue to Character: American Childhood, 1775–1850* (New York: Twayne Publishers, 1996).

Reps, John, *Cities of the American West: A History of Frontier Urban Planning* (Princeton: Princeton University Press, 1979).

Richards, Leonard L., *"Gentlemen of Property and Standing," Anti-Abolition Mobs in Jacksonian America* (New York: Oxford University Press, 1970).

Rosabaugh, W. J., *The Craft Apprentice* (New York: Oxford University Press, 1986).

Rose, Anne C., *Voices of the Marketplace: American Thought and Culture, 1830–1860* (New York: Twayne Publishers, 1995).

Rusk, Ralph L., *The Literature of the Middle Western Frontier* (New York: Columbia University Press, 1925).

Russo, David J., *Families and Communities: A New View of American History* (Nashville: American Association for State and Local History, 1974).

Sakolski, Aaron M., *Land Tenure and Land Taxation in America* (New York: Robert Schalkenbach Foundation, 1957).

Saum, Lewis O., *The Popular Mood of Pre-Civil War America* (Westport, Conn.: Greenwood Press, 1980).

Saxon, A. H., *P. T. Barnum: The Legend and the Man* (New York: Columbia University Press, 1989).

Schob, David E., *Hired Hands and Plowboys: Farm Labor in the Midwest, 1815–1860* (Urbana: University of Illinois Press, 1975).

Shade, William G., *Banks or No Banks: The Money Issue in Western Politics, 1832–1865* (Detroit: Wayne State University Press, 1972).

Singleton, George A., *The Romance of African Methodism: A Study of the African Methodist Episcopal Church* (New York: Exposition Press, 1952).

Smith, Page, *As a City Upon a Hill: The Town in American History* (New York: Alfred A. Knopf, 1966).

Smith, Timothy L., *Revivalism and Social Reform: American Protestantism on the Eve of the Civil War* (Gloucester, Mass.: Peter Smith, 1976).

Soltow, Lee, *Men and Wealth in the United States, 1850–1870* (New Haven: Yale University Press, 1975).

Soltow, Lee, and Edward Stevens, *The Rise of Literacy and the Common School in the United States* (Chicago: University of Chicago Press, 1981).

Sterling, Dorothy, *Ahead of Her Time: Abby Kelley and the Politics of Antislavery* (New York: W. W. Norton & Co., 1991).

Stern, Madeline B., *Heads and Headlines: The Phrenological Fowlers* (Norman: University of Oklahoma Press, 1971).

Stevenson, Louise, *Scholarly Means to Evangelical Ends: The New Haven Scholars and the Transformation of Higher Learning in America, 1830–1890* (Baltimore: Johns Hopkins University Press, 1986).

Stradenraus, Philip J., *The African Colonization Movement, 1816–1865* (New York: Columbia University Press, 1961).

Teaford, Jon C., *Cities of the Heartland: The Rise and Fall of the Industrial Midwest* (Bloomington: Indiana University Press, 1993).

Thernstrom, Stephan, and Richard Sennett, eds., *Nineteenth-Century Cities* (New Haven: Yale University Press, 1969).

Thomas, George M., *Revivalism and Cultural Change: Christianity, Nation Building, and the Market in the Nineteenth-Century United States* (Chicago: University of Chicago Press, 1997).

Toll, Robert C., *Blacking Up: The Minstrel Show in Nineteenth-Century America* (New York: Oxford University Press, 1974).

Turnbull, David, *Phrenology, the First Science of Man* (Victoria, Australia: Deakin University Press, 1982).

Turner, Ralph, and Lewis Killian, *Collective Behavior*, 3d ed. (Englewood Cliffs, N.J.: Prentice Hall, 1987).

Tyler, Alice Felt, *Freedom's Ferment: Phases of American Social History from the Colonial Period to the Outbreak of the Civil War* (New York: Harper, 1944).

U.S. Department of Commerce, Bureau of the Census, *Historical Statistics of the United States*, vol. 1 (Washington, D.C.: Government Printing Office, 1975).

Volpe, Vernon L., *Forlorn Hope of Freedom: The Liberty Party in the Old Northwest, 1838–1848* (Kent: Kent State University Press, 1990).

Watson, Harry L., *Liberty and Power: The Politics of Jacksonian America* (New York: Hill and Wang, 1990).

Weisberger, Bernard A., *They Gathered at the River: The Story of the Great Revivalists and Their Impact upon Religion in America* (Boston: Little, Brown, 1958).

Wiebe, Robert H., *The Opening of American Society* (New York: Vintage Books, 1985).

Williamson, Jeffrey G., and Peter H. Lindert, *American Inequality: A Macroeconomic History* (New York: Academic Press, 1980).

Wilson, Major L., *The Presidency of Martin Van Buren* (Lawrence: University Press of Kansas, 1984).

Wittke, Carl, *The Irish in America* (Baton Rouge: Louisiana State University Press, 1956).

Articles in Periodicals

Anon., "Woman as Wife," *Ladies Repository and Gatherings of the West* 3 (1843): 54.

Atherton, Lewis E., "The Pioneer Merchant in mid-America," *University of Missouri Studies* 14 (1939): 5–15.

Bailey, Rosalie Fellows, "The Foos Family of Pennsylvania and Ohio," *Pennsylvania Genealogical Magazine* 18 (1951): 87–117.

Bakan, David, "The Influence of Phrenology on American Psychology," *Journal of the History of the Behavioural Sciences* 2 (July 1966): 200–220.

Barrett, Richard E. "Some Reminiscences of Dr. Starling Loving," *Columbus & Central Ohio Historian* 1 (1984): 67–72.

Benham, William G., "The Mercantile Interest of Columbus," *Ohio Magazine* 3 (December 1907): 466–75.

Berkhofer, Robert F., Jr., "Space, Time, Culture, and the New Frontier," *Agricultural History* 38 (1964): 21–30.

Blue, Frederick J., "The Ohio Free Soilers and Problems of Factionalism," *Ohio History* 76 (1967): 17–32.

Bochin, Hal W., "Tom Corwin's Speech Against the Mexican War: Courageous but Misunderstood," *Ohio History* 90 (1981): 33–54.

Bowers, Paul C., Jr. and Goodwin F. Berquist Jr., "Worthington, Ohio: James Kilbourn's Episcopal Haven on the Western Frontier," *Ohio History* 83 (Summer 1976): 247–62.

Boylan, Anne M., "The Role of Conversion in Nineteenth-Century Sunday Schools," *American Studies* 20 (1979): 35–48.

———, "Sunday Schools and Changing Evangelical Views of Children in the 1820s," *Church History* 48 (1979): 320–33.

Brooks, Herbert, "The Financial Interests of Columbus," *Ohio Magazine* 3 (December 1907): 502–12.

Brown, Jeffrey P., "Chillicothe's Elite: Leadership in a Frontier Community," *Ohio History* 96 (1987): 140–56.

Caldwell, Frank C., "A Review—Essay 'Noble Fellow': William Starling Sullivant By Andrew Denny Rodgers III," *Ohio State Archaeological and Historical Quarterly* 54 (1945): 395–408.

Chamberlain, Ebenezer M., "Journal of Ebenezer Mattoon Chamberlain 1832–5," *Indiana Magazine of History* 15 (September 1919): 233–59.

Cole, Charles C., Jr., "The Last Public Hanging," *Columbus Monthly* 19 (December 1993): 91–94.

———, "Uriah Heath: Scholarly Circuit Rider, Successful Fund-Raiser," *Methodist History* 36 (1998): 250–59.

———, "When The Arts Took Hold," *Columbus Monthly* 21 (May 1995): 123–25.

Conzen, Kathleen Neils, "Mainstream and Side Channels: The Localization of Immigrant Cultures," *Journal of American Ethnic History* 11 (1991): 5–20.

Copeland, Eleanor F., "James Hoge, Man of God," *Journal of the Presbyterian Historical Society* 36 (June 1958): 67–88.

Crouch, Tom D., "Up, Up, and—Sometimes—Away," *Cincinnati Historical Bulletin* 28 (1970): 109–29.

Davis, David B., "The Movement to Abolish Capital Punishment in America, 1787–1861," *American Historical Review* 63 (October 1957): 23–46.

Dillon, Merton L., ed., "A Visit to the Ohio State Prison," *Ohio Historical Quarterly* 69 (January 1960): 69–72.

Downes, Randolph C., "Evolution of Ohio County Boundaries," *Ohio Archaeological and Historical Publications* 36 (1927): 340–477.

Edwards, Linden F., "Body Snatching in Ohio During the 19th Century," *Ohio State Archaeological and Historical Quarterly* 59 (October 1950): 329–51.

Erickson, Leonard, "Politics and Repeal of Ohio's Black Laws, 1837–1849," *Ohio History* 82 (Summer-Autumn 1973): 154–75.

Flinn, Thomas A., "Continuity and Change in Ohio Politics," *Journal of Politics* 24 (1962): 521–44.

Forman, Jonathan, "The First Year of the Second Epidemic of the Asiatic Cholera in Columbus, Ohio-1849," *Ohio State Archaeological and Historical Quarterly* 53 (1944): 303–12.

Galbreath, C. B., "Anti-Slavery Movement in Columbiana County," *Ohio Archaeological and Historical Publications* 30 (1921): 355–95.

Gilbert, Abby L., "Thomas Ewing, Sr.: Ohio's Advocate for a National Bank," *Ohio History* 82 (Winter-Spring 1973): 5–24.

Gladden, Washington, "Francis Charles Sessions," *Ohio Archaeological and Historical Publications* 4 (1895): 292–310.

———, "Samuel Galloway," *Ohio Archaeological and Historical Publications* 4 (1895): 263–78.

Graf, LeRoy P., ed., "The Journal of a Vermont Man in Ohio, 1836–1842," *Ohio State Archaeological and Historical Quarterly* 60 (1951): 175–99.

Gross, Bella, "The First National Negro Convention," *Journal of Negro History* 31 (October 1946): 435–43.

Hicks, Clara Belle, "The History of Penal Institutions In Ohio to 1850," *Ohio State Archaeological and Historical Quarterly* 33 (January 1924): 359–426.

Holt, Edgar A., "Party Politics in Ohio, 1840–1850," *Ohio State Archaeological and Historical Quarterly* 37 (1928): 439–591.

Holt, Thomas C., "Marking: Race, Race-making, and the Writing of History," *American Historical Review* 100 (February 1995): 1–20.

Hoster, Jay, and Allen Young, "How beer brewing in Columbus dwindled to one big fish," *Columbus Monthly* (November 1976): 63–74.

Howe, Daniel W., "The Evangelical Movement and Political Culture in the North during the Second Party System," *Journal of American History* 77 (March 1991): 1216–39.

Hulbert, Archer B., "The Old National Road—The Historic Highway of America," *Ohio Archaeological and Historical Publications* 9 (1901): 405–519.

Huntington, C. C., "A History of Banking and Currency in Ohio before the Civil War," *Ohio Archaeological and Historical Society Publications* 24 (1915): 235–539.

Huntington, Pelatiah W., "A History of Banking in Ohio," *Ohio Archaeological and Historical Society Publications* 23 (1914): 312–22.

Huth, Ronald K., "Louis Kossuth in Ohio," *Northwest Ohio Quarterly* 40 (1968): 111–17.

Kilbourne, James, "Autobiography of Col. James Kilbourne, of Worthington, Ohio," *"Old Northwest" Genealogical Quarterly* 6 (1903): 111–21.

King, I. F., "Introduction of Methodism in Ohio," *Ohio Archaeological and Historical Publications* 10 (1902): 165–219.

Kinney, Muriel, "John Carey, An Ohio Pioneer," *Ohio State Archaeological and Historical Quarterly* 46 (1937): 166–98.

Knights, Peter R., "City Directories as Aids to Ante-Bellum Urban Studies: A Research Note," *Historical Methods Newsletter* 2 (September 1969): 1–10.

Love, N. B. C., "Russell Bigelow The Pioneer Pulpit Orator," *Ohio Archaeological and Historical Publications* 19 (1910): 293–303.

Loving, Starling, "History of Starling Medical College," *"Old Northwest" Genealogical Quarterly* 8 (1905): 105–35.

———, "Some Reminiscences—General and Medical," *"Old Northwest" Genealogical Quarterly* 7 (1904): 217–27.

Mahr, August C., "Indian River and Place Names in Ohio," *Ohio Historical Quarterly* 66 (April 1957): 137–58.

Marvin, Walter R., "Ohio's Unsung Penitentiary Railroad," *Ohio State Archaeological and Historical Quarterly* 63 (1954): 254–69.

Miller, Edward A., "History of the Educational Legislation in Ohio from 1803 to 1850," *Ohio Archaeological and Historical Publications* 27 (1919): 1–271.

Minor, Richard C., "James Preston Poindexter, Elder Statesman of Columbus," *Ohio State Archaeological and Historical Quarterly* 56 (1947): 267–86.

Parsons, Mira Clarke, "Historic Worthington," *Ohio Archaeological and Historical Publications* 13 (1904): 71–82.

Peckham, Howard H., "Books and Reading on the Ohio Frontier," *Mississippi Valley Historical Review* 44 (1957): 649–63.

Pessen, Edward, "The Egalitarian Myth and the American Social Reality: Wealth, Mobility, and Equality in the 'Era of the Common Man,'" *American Historical Review* 70 (1971): 989–1034.

Phelps, H. Warren, "Some Historic Records from Franklin County Commissioner's Books," *"Old Northwest" Genealogical Quarterly* 7 (1904): 186–93.

Post, Albert, "The Anti-Gallows Movement in Ohio," *Ohio State Archaeological and Historical Quarterly* 54 (April-June 1945): 104–12.
——, "Early Efforts to Abolish Capital Punishment in Pennsylvania," *Pennsylvania Magazine of History and Biography* 48 (January 1944): 38–53.
Price, Erwin, "The Election of 1848 in Ohio," *Ohio Archaeological and Historical Publications* 36 (1927): 188–309.
Price, Robert, "The Ohio Anti-Slavery Convention of 1836," *Ohio State Archaeological and Historical Quarterly* 45 (April 1936): 173–88.
Putnam, George Washington, "Four Months with Charles Dickens During His First Visit To America," *Atlantic Monthly* 26 (November 1870): 591–99.
Randall, Emilius O., "The Beginnings of Columbus Primeval and Capital," *Ohio Magazine* 3 (December 1907): 439–53.
——, "Kossuth Before Ohio Legislature," *Ohio Archaeological and Historical Publications* 12 (1903): 114–19.
Ratcliffe, Donald, "The Autobiography of Benjamin Tappan," *Ohio History* 85 (Winter 1976): 109–57.
Rayback, Joseph G., "The Liberty Party Leaders of Ohio: Exponents of Antislavery Coalition," *Ohio State Archaeological and Historical Quarterly* 57 (April 1948): 165–78.
Resch, John P., "Ohio Adult Penal System, 1850–1900: A Study in the Failure of Institutional Reform," *Ohio History* 81 (Autumn 1972): 236–62.
Riddle, A. G., "Recollections of the Forty-Seventh General Assembly," *Magazine of Western History* 6 (1887): 341–51.
Riegel, Robert E., "The introduction of phrenology to the United States," *American Historical Review* 39 (October 1933): 73–78.
Rippley, La Vern J., "The Columbus Germans," *The Report: A Journal of German-American History* 33 (1968): 1–46.
Rodabaugh, James H., "The Negro in Ohio," *Journal of Negro History* 31 (January 1946): 9–29.
Rodabaugh, Thomas K., "From England to Ohio, 1830–1832, the Journal of Thomas K. Wharton," *Ohio Historical Quarterly* 65 (1956): 1–27.
Rodgers, Andrew W., "Lucas Sullivant and the Founding of Columbus," *Ohio Archaeological and Historical Society Publications* 37 (1928): 162–76.
Ryan, Daniel J., "Ohio in the Mexican War," *Ohio Archaeological and Historical Society Publications* 21 (1912): 277–95.
Scheiber, Harry N., "Alfred Kelley and the Ohio Business Elite, 1822–1859," *Ohio History* 87 (Autumn 1978): 365–92.
Scott, Donald M., "The Popular Lecture and the Creation of a Public in Mid-Nineteenth Century America," *Journal of American History* 66 (March 1980): 791–809.
Sheeler, J. Reuben, "The Struggle of the Negro in Ohio for Freedom," *Journal of Negro History* 31 (April 1946): 208–26.
Shilling, D. C., "Woman's Suffrage in the Constitutional Convention of Ohio," *Report of the Ninth Annual Meeting of the Ohio Valley Historical Association* (1916): 166–74.
Smith-Rosenberg, Carroll, "The Female World of Love and Ritual: Relations between Women in Nineteenth-Century America," *Signs* 1 (Autumn 1975): 1–30.
Soltow, Lee, "Inequality Amidst Abundance: Land Ownership in Early Nineteenth Century Ohio," *Ohio History* 88 (Spring 1979): 133–51.
Taylor, B. B., "The West and the Western People," *Democratic Monthly Magazine and Western Review* 1 (1844): 184–92.
Thernstrom, Stephan, and Peter Knights, "Men in Motion: Some Data and Speculations

about Urban Population Mobility in Nineteenth Century America," *Journal of Interdisciplinary History* 1 (1970): 7–35.

Townshend, N. S., "The Forty-Seventh General Assembly of Ohio—Comments Upon Mr. Riddle's Paper," *Magazine of Western History* 6 (1887): 623–28.

———, "Salmon P. Chase," *Ohio Archaeological and Historical Publications* 1 (September 1887): 109–24.

Trimble, Allen, "Autobiography of Allen Trimble," *"Old Northwest" Genealogical Quarterly* 10 (1907): 1–54.

Twiss, George H., ed., "Journal of Cyrus P. Bradley," *Ohio Archaeological and Historical Publications* 15 (1906): 207–70.

Waldstreicher, David, "Rites of Rebellion, Rites of Assent: Celebrations, Print Culture, and the Origins of American Nationalism," *Journal of American History* 82 (1995): 37–61.

Welter, Barbara, "The Cult of True Womanhood, 1820–1860," *American Quarterly* 18 (1966): 151–74.

Wigger, John H., "Taking Heaven by Storm: Enthusiasm and Early American Methodism, 1770–1820," *Journal of the Early Republic* 14 (1994): 167–94.

Williams, Samuel W., "The Tammany Society in Ohio," *Ohio Archaeological and Historical Publications* 22 (1913): 349–70.

Wittke, Carl, "Ohio's Germans, 1840–1875," *Ohio Historical Quarterly* 66 (October 1957): 339–54.

Woodbridge, John M., "Letters of John M. Woodbridge," *Ohio State Archaeological and Historical Quarterly* 50 (1941): 135–36.

Wright, Alfred J., "Joel Wright, City Planner," *Ohio State Archaeological and Historical Quarterly* 56 (July 1947): 290–91.

Wright, Louise Heath, "The Methodist Episcopal Church of Worthington, Ohio," *"Old Northwest" Genealogical Quarterly* 7 (1904): 28–32.

Wyatt-Brown, Bertram, "Prelude to Abolitionism: Sabbatarian Politics and the Rise of the Second Party System," *Journal of American History* 58 (1971): 316–41.

INDEX

Lehman, Frederick J., 29
Leist, John, 152
Lennox, James, 44
Lennox, T. F., 168
Leonard, Theodore, 84
Leslie, Charles R., 170
Less Noble Sex (Tuana), 95
Letters to Mothers (Sigourney), 100
Letters to Young Ladies (Sigourney), 100
Lewis, A. H., 200
Lewis, C. Lindert, 149
Lewis, Dr. E. R., 185
Lewis, Orlando, 120
Lewis, Samuel, 73, 146–47, 194
Lewis, W. David, 126–27
Liberator, 187
Liberia, 190
Liberty, love of, 15, 76–77
Liberty Party, 69, 191, 195–96, 201–2
Libraries, 23, 56, 76, 80–81, 133, 142
Licking County, Ohio, 66
Lieber, Francis, 123
Liederkranz (singing club), 165
Life of John Wycliffe (Coxe), 139
Lind, Jenny, 115, 170–71
Lindeman, Louis, 90
Literacy, 215
Literature, 138–43
Literary and Botanical Medical College of Ohio, 151, 209
"Little Germany," 90, 165
Livingston, Edward, 89
Lloyd, William B., 66
Lobbying, 9, 66, 187
Lockbourne, Ohio, 51
Logan Historical Society, 79
Long, Edward D., 31
Looker, Othniel, 4
Lord, Asa D., 26, 148
Loudon, James, 156
Louisiana Territory, 37
Louisville, Ky., 184, 189
Loving, Starling, 210
Ludlow, William, 10, 17
Lyceum, 81–82
Lyell, Charles, 160

Macaulay, Lord Thomas Babington, *History of England*, 142
MacCracken, Samuel F., 112
Machold's music store, 170
Mad River, 59
Madison, James, 48
Madison Township, Ohio, 24
Maine, 37, 124

Maizlish, Stephen E., 201
"Manifest destiny," 174
Mannerchor, 165
Mannheim, Germany, 208
Mansferd, J., 47
Mansfield, Edward D., *Legal Rights, Liabilities and Duties of Women*, 94
Manufacturing, 32, 44
Marble, Mr. (actor), 162
Marietta, Ohio, 92
Market house, 23, 29, 44, 162, 216
Marquart & Eberly, 212
Married Women's Property Act, 94, 187, 189
Marshall, James, 179
Martin Chuzzlewit (Dickens), 142
Martin, John, 30
Martin, Matthias, 136
Martin, William T., 14, 140, 144; *Franklin County Register*, 140; *History of Franklin County*, 140
Martin, Mrs. William T., 16
Martineau, Harriet, 84, 103, 119, 192
Marty, L. D., 45
Marty, Martin, 155
Masons, 23, 79
Massachusetts, 109, 111
Materialism, 89, 91–92
Mather, William W., *Annual Report on the Geological Survey*, 140; *Catalogue of the Geological Specimens*, 140
Matthews, F. J., 86
Matthews, J. H., 120
Maysville Road Bill, 48–49, 56
McAfee, William, 198
McArthur, Duncan, 6, 34
McBeth, Alexander, 4
McCabe, Lida Rose, 95
McCarty, John, 158
McCormick, George, 155
McCormick, Mrs. George, 16
McCoy, I. W., 29
McCoy, James, 31
McCoy, John, 14
McCoy Robert W., 14, 29–30, 33, 157
McCullough v. Maryland, 33
McElvain, Andrew, 121, 130
McElvain, John, 19, 26, 33, 62
McElvain, William, 11, 146
McFarland, William, 3
McGowen, John, 10–11, 32
McGuffey, William H., 82; *Eclectic Readers*, 96, 147
McIntire, John, 30
McKibben, J., 113

McKibben, T., 113
McLaughlin, Alexander, 2, 4–5, 8, 16, 34
McLean, John, 65
McLean, Nathaniel, 119, 190
McNeil, Samuel, 179
McWilliams, Carey, 177
Mechanics, 128–30, 132
Mechanics Beneficial Society, 37, 42, 80–82
Mechanics Hall, 42, 80, 159, 165, 168
Mechanics Savings Institute, 71
Mechanics State Convention, 130
Medary, Samuel, 40, 69, 80, 150, 177, 180
  appointed governor in west, 136
  bought *Western Hemisphere,* 135
  Civil War critic, 136
  Columbus Gas Co. director, 44
  editor of: *Crisis,* 136; *Columbus States-
    man,* 135–37; *New Constitution,*
    214; *Ohio Farmer,* 135
  expansionist views, 174, 177
  improved sanitation, 26
  lost bid to supply quarry, 132
  opposition to contract labor, 129
  political views of, 60, 63, 72, 74–75
  postmaster, 136
  Report on the Oregon Territory, 173
  rode on first railroad link, 53
  Starling Medical College trustee, 209
  support for Constitutional Convention,
    214
  wealth, 215
Medberry, Nathaniel, 120, 123
Medical care, 209–10
Medical convention, 37
Mees, Rev. Conrad, 158
Melder, Keith, 98
Mentally ill, 111
Mercer County, Ohio, 192
Merchants, 26, 28–29, 36, 41, 74, 212;
  business in New York, 41
Merion, William, 32
Merritt, Mrs. Jane P., 105
Methodism, 156
Methodist Episcopal Church, 85, 104,
  155, 193, 198–99
Mexican War, 175–78, 201, 208
Mexico, 175–78
Miami County, Ohio, 4, 14
Michigan, 56–57, 59
Middle Atlantic States, 74, 84, 215
Middletown, Mrs. E. J., 43
Middletown, William, 89
Midwife's Practical Directory (Hersey), 100
Miesse, Dr. G., 212

Mifflin Township, Ohio, 24
Miflin, Polly, 17
Migration, 45, 78, 83, 172, 208; of free
  blacks, 192
Miller, Elizabeth, 216
Miller, John G., 57, 66, 78, 140–41; *The
  Great Convention,* 140
Miller, Nathaniel M., 80
Mills, Rev. Samuel F., 122
Milwaukee, Wisconsin, 47
Miner, Isaac, 32
Miner, Jeremiah, 32
Miner, Mary, 95
Minnesota Territory, 136
Minstrels, 165–67, 170
Missions, 180
Mississippi, 94
Mississippi River, 88, 143, 168
Mississippi Valley, 143, 174
Missouri, 37, 88, 90
Missouri Compromise, 37
Missouri River, 88
Mitchell, John, 214
Mitchell, Mrs. Margaret, 95
Mobility, 45–46
Monroe, James, 20, 31, 55
Monterey, Mexico, 176
Montgomery Guards, 176
Montgomery County, Ohio, 4
Montgomery Township, Ohio, 24
Mooder, Thomas, 26
Moody, Rev. Granville, 159, 182, 199
Moral Instructor (Palmer), 96
Morrow, Jeremiah, 77–78, 108
Morrow, Dr. Thomas V., 151
Morse, John F., 206
Moseley, Thomas W. H., 60, 86, 89, 199
Mott, Lucretia, 187
Mount Pleasant, Ohio, 105
Mt. Vernon, Ohio, 151
Munich, Germany, 159

Napoleon, 142
Natchez, Mississippi, 170
National Era, 221
National Road, 26, 49, 179
Nationalism, 172–79
Native Americans, 10, 14, 32, 56, 62, 64,
  85, 88, 127, 133
"Negro pew," 157
Neil, Hannah Schwing, 88, 102, 104
Neil House, 43, 48, 61, 77, 86, 168, 209,
  212
Neil, Robert, 50, 59, 90, 209
Neil, Robert E., 89, 215

Neil, William, 48, 50–52, 78, 89–90, 159, 215
Nelson, John, 178
New Constitution (Medary), 214
New England, 74, 80, 84
New England Federalists, 55
New England Institution for the Blind, 110
New Guide for Emigrants to the West (Peck), 46
New Hampshire, 56
New Jersey, 30, 42, 84, 113
New Orleans, 28, 48
Newspapers, 74, 81, 135–38
New York (city), 41, 46, 80, 168, 186
New York (state), 18, 30, 38, 50, 52, 84, 94, 109, 123, 150, 182, 188, 195
New York Hospital, 111
Newark, Ohio, 48, 87, 151
Nightingale Ethiopian Opera Troupe, 165
Noe, Jonathan C., 42
North Carolina, 106
North Engine House, 179
Northwest Ordinance, 72, 144, 191
Northwest Territory, 1–2
Notre, John, 14
Nova Scotia, 2
Nusbaum, Judah, 90

O. & S. Crosby, 36
Occupations, 40, 43–45, 47, 215, 227n65
Odeon Hall, 168, 170–71
Ohio, 1–2, 14–15, 41, 137–38; antislavery, 192–94; Black Laws, 189, 206, 217–18; economic depression, 38–39; lyceum, 81; migration to, 83; phrenology, interest in, 184; voting records, 74; women's rights, 188
Ohio Anti-Slavery Society, 192
Ohio Colored American League, 204
Ohio Confederate, 136, 141
Ohio Confederate and Old School Republican, 57, 136
Ohio Conference of the African Methodist Episcopal Church, 160
Ohio Constitution: of 1802, 1; of 1851, 218; printed in German, 18, 90, 213–14
Ohio Constitutional Convention, 1802, 144
Ohio Cultivator, 137, 187
Ohio Democratic Convention, 74, 109
Ohio Enabling Act, 49
Ohio and Erie Canal, 38, 50–51
Ohio Farmer and Western Horticulturist, 135
Ohio Gazatteer and Travelers Guide (Jenkins), 131, 139

Ohio Gazetteer (Kilbourn), 139, 142
Ohio General Assembly, 1, 10, 44, 108, 114, 151–52, 155, 181, 205, 214
    abolished 1839 fugitive slave law, 195
    border dispute with Michigan, 56–57
    capitol construction repealed, 67
    Columbus: confirmed as selected capital, 67–68; created as borough 1, 7; charter to, 219; incorporated, 26; selected as permanent capital, 6–7
    Kossuth invited, 219–20
    legislation: on abolition of debt imprisonment, 34; on banks, 69–71; on blacks, 189, 194; on canal system, 50–51; on capital punishment, 185–86; on county jails, 134; on encouragement of agriculture, 42; on penitentiaries, 16–18, 117–19, 121; on schools, 145–49, 152; on schools for black children, 206; on taxes, 71–72; on women, 94
    moved to Columbus, 17
    partial repeal of black laws, 206
    petitions to, 105, 114, 129, 194
    printed laws in German language, 18, 90
    redistricting, 68
    resolution on emancipation, 190
    to Smithsonian Institution, 80
    tried to impeach justices, 1
Ohio House of Representatives, 6, 18, 20, 34, 73, 145, 174, 185, 207
    Hamilton County slates, 203
    Lloyd expulsion failed, 66
    petitions to, 194, 200
    public meetings in, 81, 151, 185
    resolution on Oregon, 175, 204
    votes: on blacks, 190, 194, 198–99; on capital punishment, 185–86; on moving capital, 67; on selection of capital, 2, 4–7; on temperance, 181–82
Ohio Institution for the Education of the Blind, 110, 114, 216
Ohio Institution for the Instruction of the Blind, 110
Ohio Law Society, 23
Ohio Lunatic Asylum, 106, 111–15, 209
Ohio Manual (Kilbourn), 139
Ohio Mechanic, 137
Ohio Medical Convention, 209
Ohio Penitentiary, 10, 16, 106, 117–34, 170, 208, 216; Auburn system, 119–20, 127; chaplains, 118, 121–22, 133; cholera epidemic, 25, 133; conditions, 122; contract labor, 127–29, 132; contributed to economy, 117; criticism of, 118–

19, 123–24, 128–30, 132; discipline, 122–23; fire, 133; first building, 17; gas lights, 133; guards, 119, 122; library, 133; matron, 133; population of, 118, 121, 127, 133; praise of, 131; profits of, 128; quarry purchased, 132; role in society, 117; second building, 17–18; third building, 117–18, 120; tourist attraction, 118, 124, 128, 130–31; wardens, 123, 130, 133; women convicts, 121, 124–27; workshops, 120–21
Ohio Press, 136
Ohio Reformed Medical College, 85, 151
Ohio River, 50, 84, 88, 143, 154, 168, 189, 191
Ohio School Journal, 148
Ohio School Republican and Ohio State Gazette, 136
Ohio Senate, 129, 181, 183, 185, 203; permanent capital selected, 4, 6–7, and confirmed, 67–68; votes on repeal of black laws, 194, 198, 205
Ohio Stage Company, 50
Ohio Star, 133
Ohio State Colonization Society, 190
Ohio State Convention of the Colored Citizens of Ohio, 218
Ohio State Importing Co., 42
Ohio State Journal, 136
Ohio State Teachers Association, 148
Ohio State Temperance Society, 181
Ohio State University, The, 48 140, 210; College of Medicine, 210
Ohio Statesman, 135–36
Ohio Supreme Court, 1, 94, 149, 192, 202
Ohio Tavern, 11
Ohio Temperance Advocate, 181
Ohio Temperance Standard, 182
Ohio Tool Company, 86
Ohio University, 147
Ohio Valley, 143, 205
Ohio Whig Convention, 57–60, 63
Old Curiosity Shop (Dickens), 142
Olentangy River, 7–8, 115
Olmsted, Philo H., 24, 26, 142, 144, 208
On the Penitentiary System in the United States and its Application to France (Beaumont and Tocqueville), 119
On Political Economy (Chalmers), 139
Oregon, 172–75; Territory, 172–73; Trail, 172; treaty, 137, 175
"Orrery," 80
Osborn, Ralph, 19, 144
O'Sullivan, Charles L., 174

Otstot, John, 14
Otterbein College, 153
Oyler, Jacob, 87

Palladium of Liberty, 136–37
Palmer, Thomas, *Moral Instructor,* 96
Panic of 1837, 38
Parish, Orrin, 146
Parks, Mary, 106
Parliament, 174
Parnell, Dr. (phrenologist), 185
Parsons, Dr. Samuel, 32, 71, 112, 190
Pathfinder (Cooper), 142
Patriotism, 172–79
Patterson, John, 123, 131, 133
Patterson, Mrs. John, 102
Patton, Michael, 11, 30
Payne, John Howard, 163
Payne, Volney, 11
Peace movement, 180
Peck, John M., *New Guide for Emigrants to the West,* 46
Peddlers, 30
Penniman, A. W., 110
Pennsylvania, 14, 28, 33, 57, 74, 84, 94, 109, 120, 181
People's Convention, 202
People's Weekly Journal and Freeman's Standard, 137–38
Perkins, Simon, 39
Perkins, William L., 198
Perry, David, 89
Perry County, Ohio, 132
Perry Inn, 86, 158
Perry Township, Ohio, 24
Peters, Charles H., 156
Petitions, 78, 96, 107, 129, 132, 181, 183, 186, 191, 194, 200, 217–18
Philadelphia, 10, 50, 87, 95, 120
Philadelphia Circus, 164
Philadelphia Zoological Institute, 164
Philanthropist, 191
Phillips (painter), 167
Phrenology, 183–85
Pickaway County, Ohio, 6, 67
Pickaway Plain, 5
Pike, Jarvis W., 11, 15, 19, 144
Pinney, A. H., 43
Pinney, Dr. Eli M., 193
Pinney & Lampson's Co., 44
Pinney, O.P., 43
"Pipe-laying," 69
Pittsburgh, 46, 53, 171, 210
Platt, Benjamin, 79
Platt, Fanny Hayes, 86

Stickney's New Orleans Circus, 164
Stockholm, Sweden, 115
Stone, Eli, 33
Stone, Lucy, 187
Stowe, Calvin E., *Report on Elementary Education in Europe,* 149
Stowe, Harriet Beecher, *Uncle Tom's Cabin,* 221
Stratton, Charles S. *See* Tom Thumb
Street lighting, 44
Strickler, Jacob, 130
Strickler, Joseph, 211
Sturge, William, 196
Sullivant, Eliza Wheeler, 25, 140
Sullivant, Joseph, 49, 79, 140, 157, 167; *Alphabetical catalogue,* 140; antislavery advocate, 72; OSU trustee, 140; temperance advocate, 183; *To the Liberty Party,* 72; in Underground Railroad, 193
Sullivant, Lucas, 3, 72; assisted capital proposers, 4–7; bought lot in Columbus, 11; Franklin Bank president, 31; founded Franklinton, 2; largest land holder, 4; owned bridge over Scioto River, 48
Sullivant, Michael, 42, 90
Sullivant, William S., 25, 89–90, 132, 212; American Academy of Arts and Sciences member, 140; *Catalogue of Plants,* 140; wealth, 215
Sunbury, Ohio, 41
Sunday School Journal, 155
Sunday schools, 95, 155, 180, 208
Superintendent of Common Schools, 146–47
Sutter's Mill, California, 179
Swan, Amelia Aldrich, 95
Swan, Gustavus, 38, 40, 70, 79, 144, 147, 210; asylum trustee, 108; authored biography of Alfred Kelley, 39; canal commissioner, 39; Columbus Seminary trustee, 144; defended Graham, 185; examiner of state banks, 71; greeted Monroe, 31; invested in Ohio bonds, 39; loan repaid by City Council, 26; moved from Franklinton, 31; Presbyterian Church member, 157; speech at canal opening, 51; temperance society member, 181; Theological Seminary contributor, 152
Swan, Joseph R., 114, 190, 209
Swayne, Joshua, 183
Swayne, Noah H., 38–39, 109, 114, 209, 215
"Sweeping resolution," 1
Sweet, Sullivan, 186

Swiss Bell Ringers, 168, 170
Swiss immigrants, 158
Switzerland, 107, 214

Tales (Poe), 142
Tallmadge, Darius, 50
Tammany, 1
Tappan, Benjamin, 65, 69, 79, 96, 136; on abolition, 191
Tappan, Eli T., 136
Tappan, Lewis, 191
Tariff, 55–56, 62, 196
Taverns, 5, 23, 40, 46, 49, 83, 85–86, 167, 181
Taylor, A. M., 198
Taylor, B. B., 138–39, 143
Taylor, David, 168
Taylor, Isaac, 30, 57
Taylor, L. D., 198, 204, 218
Taylor, Zachery, 176, 201–3, 218
Teesdale, John, 41
Teeters, James, 184
Telegraph, 44
Teliga, Mr. (daguerreotypist), 168
Temperance, 180–83
Temperance Convention, 182
Temperance Tales (Arthur), 182
Temple Israel, 159
Texas, 176–78
Thanksgiving Day, 88, 155
Theater, 162–63
Theological Seminary of the Evangelical Lutheran Synod, 152, 171, 216
Thernstrom, Stephan, 46
Thomas, E., 36
Thomas, Henry, 120
Thompkins, Daniel, 20
Thompson, Benjamin, 3
Thompson, Fanny, 18
Thrall, Walter, 183
Thrall, William B., 136, 150, 211, 216
Three Musketeers (Dumas), 142
Thumb, Tom, 169
Tiffin, Edward, 1
To The Liberty Party in Ohio (Sullivant), 72
Tocqueville, Alexis de, 31, 119; *On the Penitentiary System,* 119
Tod, David, 73
Tod, George, 1
Tolls, 49
Tompkins, Daniel D., 20
Tontine, The (building), 85
Town-jobbing, 30
Townshend, Norton S., 203, 205–6, 217
Tract societies, 79

Westervelt, Peter, 153
Westerville, Ohio, 153
Westwater, James M., 41, 193
Westwater, John, 41
Westwater, William, 41
Wethersfield Prison, 119
Wharfing Fund, 33
Wharton, Henry, 95
Wharton, Thomas K., 37
What asylums were, (Browne), 112–13
Wheeling, Virginia, 49–50, 171
Whetstone River. *See* Olentangy
Whig national convention, 57
Whig Party, 56, 69, 74, 201–3, 205
Whig state convention, 57–59
Whitcomb, Rev. David, 156
White, Cool, 170
White, James, 35
White, Samuel M., 160
Whiting & Huntington bookstore, 185, 212
Whiting, Isaac N., 140–41
Whitlock, Billy, 170
Whitman, Walt, 184
Whittlesey, Charles, 82
Wilcox, Phineas B.: *A Few Thoughts,* 140; *Tracts on Law Reform,* 140
Wiley, Oren, 46, 60
Wilkerson, Major J., 160
Willard, Emma, 150–51
Williams, James, 179
Williams, Silas, 30
Willoughby Medical College, 209
Wilmot, David, 178
Wilmot Proviso, 178, 201
Wilson, Horace, 157
Wilson, William M., 214
Winchester, James, 14
Wines, Enoch C., *Report on Prisons,* 131
Winkle, Kenneth, 83
Wisconsin, 131, 178
Witlock, Billy, 170
Wolf Ridge, Ohio, 11
Wolff, Maria Ecker, 208
Woman Her Station Providentially Appointed (Coxe), 139
Women, 16, 93–107, 158, 176; in antislavery movement, 189–200; benevolence of, 102–3, 157, 183; Constitutional Convention, action on, 217–18; education of, 144–51, 105; inequality of, 93–95; in insane asylum, 114; in labor force,

40–41, 43, 95–96, 100, 105–6, 148; men's attitude toward, 93–94, 96, 100, 104, 126; in meetings, 81, 102; in prison, 121, 124–27, 133; in politics, 61, 64, 105; in poorhouse, 115; in public performances, 162–64, 170–71; in religion, 157–58; their "separate sphere," 94, 100, 105, 124; toasts to, 104; wealthiest, 215; as writers, 99, 139–40
Women's rights, 186–89
Women's Rights Convention, Salem, Ohio, 188
Wonders of the Deep (Coxe), 139
Wood and Foncannon, 212
Wood, William, 76
Woodbridge, John M., 59
Wooster, Ohio, 39
Wooster, Dr., 185
Worcester, Mass., 111–12
Worcester State Lunatic Hospital, 111–12
Worthington Academy, 150
Worthington Anti-Slavery Society, 192
Worthington Female Seminary, 85, 212
Worthington, Ohio, 1, 85, 121; advantages of, 8; bodies stolen from graves in, 151; Ohio Anti-Slavery Society chapter in, 192; population of, 85; residents offered town as capital, 2, 4; road linked to Columbus, 48; settled in 1803, 2
Worthington, Thomas, 1, 11, 16–18, 49, 155
Wright, Joel, 10
Wyandots, 10, 32, 64, 85, 88, 133

Xenia, Ohio, 39, 52–53

Yale University, 140, 158, 184
Yankee Tavern, 11, 19
"Yankee theater," 162–63, 165
Young Abolitionist (Jones), 187
Young & Brodrick, 36
Young Gentlemen's Select School, 150
Young, Jacob, 85
Young, John, 36–37, 85
Young Ladies Companion (Coxe), 96
Young Ladies Seminary, 150
Young Men's Prison Society, 121
Young Wife (Alcott), 94

Zanesville, Ohio, 1–3, 5–6, 34, 53, 67, 83
Zinn, Peter, 48
Zircle, Dr. Otto, 78